Evening Standard

Where to Live
in London

SARA McCONNELL

SIMON & SCHUSTER
A VIACOM COMPANY

First published in Great Britain by Simon & Schuster UK Ltd, 1999
A Viacom Company

Copyright© Sara McConnell, 1999

1 3 5 7 9 10 8 6 4 2

Simon & Schuster UK Ltd
Africa House
64-78 Kingsway
London WC2B 6SX

Simon & Schuster Australia
Sydney

Text design: Rachel Hardman Carter
Typeset by: Stylize Digital Artwork
Printed and bound in Italy

A CIP catalogue record for this book is available from the British Library

ISBN 0 671 0 3333 6

Also published in this series:
The London Pub & Bar Guide
Children's London
Where to Get the Look: Shopping for the home in London

All information was checked and correct at press time. London is a
constantly changing city however so some of the information may
change over time.

Barclays Bank PLC accepts no responsibility for the content of this book.

CONTENTS

FOREWORD

Choosing where to live is one of the most crucial decisions we have to make, not only in respect of the long-term investment if we are buying a home, or the cost if renting, but for more pragmatic reasons such as how it affects our journey to work, how well it is served by shops and schools, or what the area has to offer when we have leisure time to spare.

Of all places in this country in which to live, London surely offers the most diversity – which is a huge bonus, but also makes the task of deciding where to live even more onerous. Having lived in London myself, I can appreciate just what an invaluable guide this book will be to anyone considering moving to the capital – whether from other parts of the country, or from overseas. Even those who already live in London will no doubt find the book a rich source of information when planning a move of home. In fact, it makes fascinating reading for people like myself who just want to know more about different parts of London.

We always try to impress on our customers how important it is to find out as much as they can about an area before setting their heart on a particular property. For example, they should check out local amenities and transport, visit the area at different times of day to gauge its liveliness or privacy, talk to local people about the place to find out whether it's on the way up or down. This book does a great deal of the legwork for you, giving an insider's view of a unique collection of very different localities.

The guide prices both for buying and renting property are also extremely useful. Again, it can be heartbreaking to fall in love with an area or a property only to find out that it's way beyond your price range. Armed with the information in this book, prospective buyers can talk to their mortgage lender and work out what they can realistically afford, then start househunting in earnest.

At Barclays, we are always looking for new ways to help homebuyers, so we are delighted to sponsor this new book. Already a highly respected property and financial journalist,

Sara McConnell has shown incredible knowledge and resourcefulness in putting this book together. Not least, she has managed to assemble a highly informative and comprehensive guide, which also manages to hold your attention by being extremely readable.

I am sure that this book will be very helpful to anyone looking for a home in London. But perhaps best of all, you can discover the capital, or update yourself on parts you haven't visited for a while, without having to set foot outside your door.

Jim Chadwick

Sales and Marketing Director
Barclays Mortgages

don't mind
preferred

MAP 7

MAP OF LONDON BOROUGHS

INTRODUCTION

How do you make sense of London? It's one of the world's largest cities, teeming with 7 million people, stretching over more than 600 square miles of the south east of England. But it's incoherent, haphazard and almost totally unplanned. Most Londoners live in homes flung up by generations of speculative builders on any piece of spare land they could find. The capital's outward sprawl, unchecked for most of its history, has sucked up any settlement lying in its path and covered fields and woods with bricks and mortar. Expensive houses sit cheek by jowl with council blocks, respectable suburbs are just a couple of stops on the bus away from industrial estates, factories and warehouses. And to confuse things further, London's social landscape is constantly changing as new areas become fashionable and injections of government cash resuscitate areas left derelict by the disappearance of traditional industries.

All this makes the decision of where to live in London a daunting one. If you don't know London, where do you start? If you know your own bit of it but want or need to move elsewhere, what are your options?

This book will help you to answer these vital questions. It's not solely a property guide although it does of course contain information about the cost of buying and renting and the types of property in each area. Its main aim is to paint a physical, social and economic portrait of all the main areas of Greater London. What do places look like? Who lives there? Where's cheap and where's expensive? Are they fashionable, up-and-coming, rich, poor, suburban or cutting edge trendy? What are the shops and schools like? How quickly can you get to the centre of town? How much greenery is there and what is there to do in your spare time? How easy is it to park and how much does it cost? What are the crime levels? And how efficient (and expensive) is the council? It makes no apology for being opinionated but opinions are backed by a range of factual information and statistics.

HOW THE BOOK WORKS
The book is based on London's 32 boroughs plus the City of London, with a chapter devoted to each borough. The borough you live in can have a dramatic impact on the amount of council tax you pay as well as the standards of local schools and other amenities. But despite their importance to the daily lives of millions, the boroughs are seen as distant bureaucracies with arbitrarily drawn boundaries which slice through more familiar local areas. So each borough has been broken down into five or six main areas, which provide the main focus for the chapter. Consult the at-a-glance list of areas with their boroughs on pages 12 and13 to locate the places you're interested in. If an area straddles a borough boundary (Highgate and Blackheath for example both fall into more than one borough), it will be dealt with under the borough responsible for its largest part.

THE CHAPTERS

Each chapter starts with a general introduction to the borough. It tells you where it is, the areas contained within its boundaries, what sort of people live there, as well as information on the borough's ethnic makeup, unemployment rates, plans for regeneration and investment and local issues.

PROPERTY AND ARCHITECTURE

This isn't intended to be an exhaustive street by street guide (there are already guides which have done this job admirably) but rather a pen portrait of the main types of property, broken down into areas, along with prices for buying and renting. These are only meant to give you an idea: London prices change constantly and these are a snapshot of the market in the last months of 1998. Rentals are given monthly although some agents will quote weekly. The section shows which places are good for flats, which for houses, which places are favoured by families, which by first-time buyers or professional couples without children. If certain types of property (studios for example) aren't mentioned, this is because they either don't exist in the area or are very rare. Consult the at-a-glance guide on pages 14 and 15 to help you locate areas suitable for you. Remember that factors such as transport links have a big impact on prices. This section also lists conservation areas, which look attractive but which can be tricky if you want to alter your property.

POSTCODES

There's big postcode snobbery in some parts of London which can bump up or reduce prices by thousands of pounds. Each chapter has a pecking order of the best postcodes in the borough.

BOROUGH AMENITIES

Graded with a star system, with * being the lowest and ***** the highest and best. The grades are based on evidence which is both objective or semi-objective (performance statistics, league tables, extent of provision) and subjective (evidence of the author's own eyes, opinions of residents).

SCHOOLS

League tables may be controversial but they're all parents have to compare one school and one borough with another. The top three state primaries and the top three state secondaries in each borough in the latest (1998) league tables are listed. There is also an overall league table performance ranking for each borough's primary and secondary schools. This shows how each borough's schools have performed collectively compared to other local education authorities in England. There are 150 local education authorities. In the collective league tables, 1 is best and 150 worst. Private prep and secondary schools are also listed as are the numbers of state and private nurseries and playgroups in each borough and the proportion of under-fives in state nurseries. From September 1998 boroughs are working toward offering all four year-olds a nursery place, so figures for state nursery provision could change radically next year.

TRANSPORT

Includes details of public transport (trains and tubes) with cost, speed and frequency of direct journeys to central London from the main areas of each borough. Train journey times are measured to the nearest London terminus, while tube journey times are measured to the most central point possible without changing lines. Other parts of the section list main bus routes to town, traffic blackspots, and the cost and location of controlled parking zones where you have to buy a residents' parking permit. Other parking costs (car parks, meters) aren't included. Controlled parking zones are spreading like wildfire so you're likely to end up paying for the privilege of parking outside your own front door.

LEISURE FACILITIES

Lists theatres, concert halls, cinemas, museums, art galleries, local authority-run sports facilities and libraries. But this doesn't claim to be a listings book so clubs and some smaller theatres and temporary arts events (festivals or one-off performances) have been excluded as have private gyms and health clubs. Consult the excellent Time Out magazine for weekly listings.

GREEN SPACE

A run-down of the general state and nature of the parks, woods and greenery in each borough with personally tested recommendations for visits. But borough boundaries are strictly observed and nothing outside the greater London limit is included.

SHOPS & RESTAURANTS

A description of the main shopping centres and streets of each borough, including their physical appearance, the types of shops on offer and a (not exhaustive) list of the main superstores. As elsewhere, London's shopping is becoming depressingly uniform as major chains take over. The restaurant section indicates places where restaurants are plentiful or otherwise but doesn't list or test individual restaurants.

THE COUNCIL

Includes each borough's political affiliation and its plus and minus points (general efficiency at administration, rubbish collection, street-sweeping, recycling, turnaround and charges for property searches, collection of council tax), and a complete list of council tax charges for 1998-9.

SOME STATISTICAL EXPLANATIONS

See page 9 for explanations of school league tables. The average proportion of under-fives in state nurseries in London is 57%. The average number of library visits is 7.5 per head of population. Library-use league tables don't include the City of London because figures are distorted by the large daytime population. In the rankings, 1st is best and 32 worst. In the Metropolitan Police crime statistics tables, 1 is worst and 32 best. Again, the figures don't include the City of London because the City has its own police force and isn't under the jurisdiction of the Metropolitan Police.

This book is the result of six months of walking the streets of every London borough, from the grandest streets of Belgravia or Mayfair to the bleak Victorian terraces and tower blocks of Erith or Edmonton. It says a lot for the city that I only once felt fearful for my own safety. And London's public transport system may not be perfect but it got me there, to every corner.

SOURCES

Employment figures: *London Research Centre*

Deprivation index: *London Research Centre, Focus on London 1998, (The Stationery Office)*

Ethnic minorities: *Census figures 1991, London Research Centre*

Performance statistics: Proportion of under-fives in state nursery education, library use, turnaround of property searches, standard search fees, council tax collected: *Audit Commission: local authorities' performance indicators 1996-97 (latest available at time of going to press)*

Pre-school provision: *individual London boroughs* and *What School 1998-1999, On Course Publications*

School League Tables: *Secondary Schools, Department for Education and Science Listings 1998, Primary Schools DfEE listings 1998*

Private Prep and Secondary Schools: *The Independent Schools Information Service (ISIS); individual London boroughs.*

Train and Tube information: *National Rail Enquiries, London Underground Information*

Residents' parking costs, council tax rates, regeneration initiatives: *individual London boroughs*

Crime figures: *Metropolitan Police, Evening Standard, 1998*

Maps: *Nicholson, Greater London 5 sheet series, 1995*

ACKNOWLEDGEMENTS

I would like to thank the many people who have given up their time to answer questions and share their knowledge of London, including hundreds of estate agents, the staff of all the London Boroughs and the City, and individual residents, especially Dee Mitchell. Special thanks go to Peter Haler, Jenny Bloom, John Nicholson and Suresh Karthigesu who gave up valuable time to drive me round their home boroughs, and to Emily who has put up with months of maps, notebooks and walking boots, kept me company in several boroughs and provided constant support and encouragement.

FURTHER READING

The London Museums Guide, London Museums Service (1995) £4.95
What School? 1998–1999, On Course Publications £3.95
Guide to Ethnic London, Ian McAuley (1993) £12.95

LONDON AREAS AT A GLANCE

AREA	BOROUGH
Abbey Wood	Greenwich
Acton	Ealing
Addiscombe	Croydon
Anerley	Bromley
Balham	Wandsworth
Barbican	City of London
Barking	Barking & Dagenham
Barnes	Richmond upon Thames
Barnet	Barnet
Barons Court	Hammersmith & Fulham
Battersea	Wandsworth
Bayswater	Westminster
Beckenham	Bromley
Beckton	Newham
Becontree	Barking & Dagenham
Beddington	Sutton
Bedford Park	Hounslow, Ealing
Belgravia	Westminster
Belsize Park	Camden
Belvedere	Bexley
Bermondsey	Southwark
Bethnal Green	Tower Hamlets
Bexley	Bexley
Bexleyheath	Bexley
Blackfen	Bexley
Blackheath	Lewisham, Greenwich
Bloomsbury	Camden
Borough	Southwark
Bow	Tower Hamlets
Brentford	Hounslow
Brixton	Lambeth
Brockley	Lewisham
Bromley	Bromley
Brondesbury	Brent
Camberwell	Southwark
Camden Town	Camden
Carshalton Beeches	Sutton
Carshalton Village	Sutton
Catford	Lewisham
Chadwell Heath	Barking & Dagenham
Charlton	Greenwich
Cheam	Sutton
Chelsea	Kensington & Chelsea
Chelsea Harbour	Hammersmith & Fulham
Chessington	Kingston
Chingford	Waltham Forest
Chislehurst	Bromley
Chiswick	Hounslow
Clapham	Lambeth
Clapton	Hackney
Clayhall	Redbridge
Clerkenwell	Islington
Colliers Wood	Merton
Coombe	Kingston
Coulsdon	Croydon
Covent Garden	Westminster
Cricklewood	Brent
Crouch End	Haringey
Dagenham	Barking & Dagenham
Dalston	Hackney
Dartmouth Park	Camden
De Beauvoir Town	Hackney
Deptford	Lewisham
Dollis Hill	Brent
Dulwich	Southwark

AREA	BOROUGH
Ealing	Ealing
Earls Court	Kensington & Chelsea
Earlsfield	Wandsworth
Eastcote	Hillingdon
East Croydon	Croydon
East Dulwich	Southwark
East Greenwich	Greenwich
East Ham	Newham
East Sheen	Richmond upon Thames
Edgware	Barnet
Edmonton	Enfield
Elephant & Castle	Southwark
Eltham	Greenwich
Enfield Town	Enfield
Erith	Bexley
Farnborough	Bromley
Feltham	Hounslow
Finchley	Barnet
Finsbury	Islington
Finsbury Park	Haringey, Camden, Islington
Fleet Street	City of London
Forest Gate	Newham
Forest Hill	Lewisham
Fulham	Hammersmith & Fulham
Gants Hill	Redbridge
Gidea Park	Havering
Gipsy Hill	Lambeth
Golders Green	Barnet
Goodmayes	Redbridge
Greenford	Ealing
Grove Park	Lewisham
Gunnersbury	Hounslow
Hackney	Hackney
Hadley Wood	Enfield
Hainault	Redbridge
Ham	Richmond upon Thames
Hammersmith	Hammersmith & Fulham
Hampstead	Camden
Hampstead Garden Suburb	Barnet
Hanwell	Ealing
Hanworth	Hounslow
Harold Hill	Havering
Harrow	Harrow
Harrow-on-the Hill	Harrow
Hatch End	Harrow
Havering atte Bower	Havering
Hayes (Kent)	Bromley
Hayes (Middlesex)	Hillingdon
Hendon	Barnet
Highams Park	Waltham Forest
Highbury	Islington
Highgate	Haringey, Camden
Hillingdon	Hillingdon
Hither Green	Lewisham
Holborn	Camden
Holland Park	Kensington & Chelsea
Hornchurch	Havering
Hornsey	Haringey
Hounslow	Hounslow
Hoxton	Hackney
Ickenham	Hillingdon
Ilford	Redbridge
Isle of Dogs	Tower Hamlets

AREA	BOROUGH	AREA	BOROUGH
Isleworth	Hounslow	St Paul's	City of London
Islington	Islington	St Paul's Cray	Bromley
		Selsdon	Croydon
Kennington	Lambeth	Seven Kings	Redbridge
Kensington	Kensington & Chelsea	Shepherds Bush	Hammersmith & Fulham
Kentish Town	Camden, Islington	Shirley	Croydon
Kenton	Brent	Shoreditch	Hackney
Keston	Bromley	Sidcup	Bexley
Kew	Richmond upon Thames	Silvertown	Newham
Kidbrooke	Greenwich	Soho	Westminster
Kilburn	Brent	Southall	Ealing
Kingsbury	Brent	South Croydon	Croydon
Kings Cross	Camden	Southfields	Wandsworth
Kingston	Kingston	Southgate	Enfield
Knightsbridge	Westminster	South Kensington	Kensington & Chelsea
		South Norwood	Croydon
Lee	Lewisham	South Wimbledon	Merton
Lewisham	Lewisham	South Woodford	Redbridge
Leyton	Waltham Forest	Spitalfields	Tower Hamlets
Leytonstone	Waltham Forest	Stamford Hill	Hackney
Limehouse	Tower Hamlets	Stanmore	Harrow
London Fields	Hackney	Stockwell	Lambeth
		Stoke Newington	Hackney
Maida Vale	Westminster	Stratford	Newham
Manor Park	Newham	Strawberry Hill	Richmond upon Thames
Marylebone	Westminster	Streatham	Lambeth
Mayfair	Westminster	Surbiton	Kingston
Mill Hill	Barnet	Sutton	Sutton
Mitcham	Merton	Sydenham	Lewisham
Morden	Merton		
Mortlake	Richmond upon Thames	Teddington	Richmond upon Thames
Muswell Hill	Haringey	The Hamptons	Richmond upon Thames
		Thamesmead	Bexley, Greenwich
Neasden	Brent	Thornton Heath	Croydon
New Cross	Lewisham	Tolworth	Kingston
New Eltham	Greenwich	Tooting	Wandsworth
New Malden	Kingston	Tottenham	Haringey
Norbury	Croydon	Totteridge	Barnet
Northolt	Ealing	Tufnell Park	Islington
North Ealing	Ealing	Twickenham	Richmond upon Thames
North Cheam	Sutton		
North Kensington	Kensington & Chelsea	Upminster	Havering
Northwood	Hillingdon	Upper Holloway	Islington
Notting Hill	Kensington & Chelsea	Upper Norwood	Croydon
Nunhead	Southwark	Upton	Newham
		Uxbridge	Hillingdon
Orpington	Bromley		
Osterley	Hounslow	Victoria Park	Hackney
Paddington	Westminster	Wallington	Sutton
Palmers Green	Enfield	Walthamstow	Waltham Forest
Parsons Green	Hammersmith & Fulham	Wandsworth	Wandsworth
Peckham	Southwark	Wanstead	Redbridge
Penge	Bromley	Wapping	Tower Hamlets
Petersham	Richmond upon Thames	Waterloo	Lambeth
Petts Wood	Bromley	Wealdstone	Harrow
Pimlico	Westminster	Welling	Bexley
Pinner	Harrow	Wembley	Brent
Plaistow	Newham	West Chelsea	Kensington & Chelsea
Plumstead	Greenwich	West Ealing	Ealing
Ponders End	Enfield	West Greenwich	Greenwich
Primrose Hill	Camden	West Ham	Newham
Purley	Croydon	West Hampstead	Camden
Putney	Wandsworth	West Kensington	Hammersmith & Fulham
		West Kilburn	Westminster
Queens Park	Brent	West Norwood	Lambeth
		West Wickham	Bromley
Ravenscourt Park	Hammersmith & Fulham	Whitechapel	Tower Hamlets
Raynes Park	Merton	Whitton	Richmond upon Thames
Richmond	Richmond upon Thames	Willesden	Brent
Roehampton	Wandsworth	Willesden Grove	Brent
Romford	Havering	Wimbledon	Merton
Rotherhithe	Southwark	Wimbledon Village	Merton
Ruislip	Hillingdon	Winchmore Hill	Enfield
		Woodford	Redbridge
St Helier	Sutton	Wood Green	Haringey
St John's Wood	Westminster	Woodside	Croydon
St Margarets	Richmond upon Thames	Woolwich	Greenwich

WHERE TO LIVE AT A GLANCE

FIRST-TIME BUYERS & RENTERS

Anerley
Bermondsey
Brockley
Camberwell
Catford
Charlton
Cricklewood
Deptford
East Dulwich
East Greenwich
East Ham
Elephant & Castle
Forest Gate
Forest Hill
Grove Park
Ham
Hayes (Middlesex)
Hither Green
Kidbrooke
Kilburn
Kingston
Leyton & Leytonstone
Lewisham
Manor Park
New Cross
Peckham
Penge
Plumstead
Queens Park
Shepherds Bush
Stratford
South Norwood
South Wimbledon
Upton
Upper Holloway
Upper Norwood
Walthamstow
West Ealing
West Hampstead
West Kilburn
Willesden
Woolwich

YOUNG PROFESSIONALS

Acton
Battersea
Bayswater
Barbican
Beckenham
Belsize Park
Bermondsey
Bethnal Green
Blackheath
Bloomsbury
Brentford
Brixton
Bromley
Brondesbury
Bow
Camberwell
Camden Town
Chelsea Harbour
Chiswick
Clapham
Clerkenwell
Covent Garden
Crouch End
Dalston
De Beauvoir Town
Earls Court

East Dulwich
East Greenwich
Fleet Street
Finchley
Finsbury Park
Fulham
Grove Park
Hackney
Hammersmith
Harrow on the Hill
Highbury
Holborn
Hornsey
Kennington
Kensington
Isleworth
Isle of Dogs
Islington
Kew
Kilburn
Kings Cross
Lee
Limehouse
London Fields
Maida Vale
Muswell Hill
North Kensington
Notting Hill
Paddington
Pimlico
Queens Park
Richmond
Rotherhithe
St Pauls
Shepherds Bush
Soho
South Kensington
Stockwell
Stoke Newington
Stratford
Strawberry Hill
Streatham
Twickenham
Walthamstow
Wapping
Waterloo
West Greenwich
West Kensington
West Kilburn
Willesden Green
Wimbledon

OVERSEAS RESIDENTS

Acton (Japanese)
Barnes (Swedish)
Finchley (Japanese)
Holland Park
    (international)
Kensington (international)
Knightsbridge (Europeans)
Maida Vale (international)
Mayfair (Americans,
    Greeks, Asians, Arabs)
New Malden (Koreans)
Richmond (Germans)
Soho (Europeans)
St John's Wood
    (Americans)
South Kensington
    (Europeans, particularly
    French)
Wimbledon (Norwegians)

FAMILIES

Balham
Barnes
Barnet
Beckenham
Bexley
Blackheath
Bromley
Brondesbury
De Beauvoir Town
Carshalton
Chingford
Chiswick
Clapham
Coulsdon
Dulwich
East Sheen
Ealing
Earlsfield
Eltham
Enfield
Forest Hill
Fulham
Gidea Park
Hammersmith
Hampstead
Hanwell
Harrow
Havering Atte Bower
Hendon
Highams Park
Highgate
Holland Park
Hornchurch
Ilford
Kentish Town
Kingsbury
Kingston
Kensington
Kew
Lee
Mill Hill
Mortlake
Muswell Hill
New Eltham
New Malden
North Ealing
North Kensington
Palmers Green
Petersham
Primrose Hill
Purley
Putney
Richmond
St John's Wood
St Margarets
Sidcup
Southfields
Southgate
South Kensington
South Woodford
Stamford Hill
Stanmore
Stoke Newington
Strawberry Hill
Sutton
Sydenham
Teddington
The Hamptons
Tooting
Tufnell Park
Twickenham
Teddington
Upminster

Victoria Park
Wallington
Wandsworth
Wanstead
Wembley
West Greenwich
West Hampstead
Wimbledon
Winchmore Hill
Woodford

GLITTERATI & NEW MONEY

Chislehurst
East Sheen
Hadley Wood
Knightsbridge
Petersham
Totteridge
Winchmore Hill

ARTY, MEDIA, INTELLECTUAL TYPES

Barnes
Bermondsey
Blackheath
Borough
Brixton
Camberwell
Camden Town
Chelsea
Clerkenwell
Covent Garden
Greenwich
Hackney
Highbury
Hampstead
Hoxton
Islington
Kew
Notting Hill
Rotherhithe
Shoreditch
Soho
Spitalfields
Whitechapel

STOCKBROKERS, BANKERS & CAPTAINS OF INDUSTRY

Belgravia
Carshalton Beeches
Chelsea
Hampstead
Holland Park
Kensington
Knightsbridge
Marylebone
Mayfair
Northwood
St John's Wood

COMMUTER BELT

Beckenham
Bexley
Bromley
Carshalton Beeches
Cheam & North Cheam
Chislehurst
Eastcote
East Croydon & South Croydon
Eltham
Gidea Park

Hayes (Kent)
Ickenham
New Eltham
Petts Wood
Pinner
Purley
Ruislip
Shirley
Sidcup
Surbiton
Orpington
Wallington

JEWISH

Clapton
Edgware
Gants Hill
Golders Green
Hampstead
Hampstead Garden Suburb
Hendon
Kingsbury
Mill Hill
St John's Wood
Stamford Hill
Stanmore
West Hampstead

ASIAN

East Ham
Forest Gate
Kenton
Ilford
Manor Park
Neasden
St John's Wood
Seven Kings
Southall
Stanmore
Upton
Wealdstone
Wembley

AFRO-CARIBBEAN

Brixton
Brockley
Camberwell
Catford
Deptford
Hither Green
Kilburn
Lewisham
New Cross
Plaistow
Tottenham
West Ham
West Kilburn

TURKISH & GREEK

Hornsey
Lewisham
Wood Green

PIEDS-A-TERRE

Chelsea
Covent Garden
Knightsbridge
Marylebone
Soho
South Kensington
Stratford

BARGAIN BASEMENT

Becontree
Belvedere
Dagenham
Deptford
Edmonton
Erith
Feltham
Goodmayes
Hainault
Hanworth
Harold Hill
Hayes (Middlesex)
Mitcham
Plumstead
Ponders End
St Helier
Selsdon
Seven Kings
Southall
Thamesmead
Thornton Heath
Whitechapel
Woolwich

AFFORDABLE HOUSES
(4-bedroom house under £150,000)

Abbey Wood
Anerley
Barking
Bexleyheath
Catford
Chadwell Heath
Colliers Wood
East Ham
Forest Gate
Greenford
Harrow
Hither Green
Ilford
Lewisham
Leyton
Leytonstone
Morden
New Cross
Norbury
Northolt
Nunhead
Peckham
Penge
Romford
South Norwood
Stratford
Streatham
Uxbridge
Welling
Wembley
West Norwood
Whitton

EXPENSIVE

Barnes
Belgravia
Chelsea
Chislehurst
Hampstead
Hampstead Garden Suburb
Holland Park
Kensington
Knightsbridge
Islington
Notting Hill
Petersham
Richmond
South Kensington

CHOOSING YOUR NEW HOME

Most people have some idea of their perfect home. It may be a city flat, a mews property, or a detached house further from the centre. The golden rule is to be open minded – never decide on a home on your first visit.

Gather as much information as possible. Register with local estate agents and ask them to send you details on all properties within your price range. As a potential buyer, this service is free as it's the seller who pays their commission. And remember to buy the local papers whenever they feature a property section.

LOCATION

Location is crucial. No matter how beautiful a home, if you're not happy with the area it's in, then the chances are you won't feel settled. This book will help you to familiarise yourself with different parts of London, so you can narrow down your choice. You will no doubt then want to visit areas of interest yourself, to get more of a feel for them.

QUESTIONS YOU SHOULD ASK THE SELLER

Obviously the features of a property will be the main factor in your decision to buy. But it's also worth asking the current owners the questions below. Make a note of their answers. Then ask their estate agent the same questions and compare the responses. Beware of any discrepancies!

'Have you somewhere to move to?' A very important question that should be asked straight away and certainly before you go to the expense of a survey. Every year, hundreds of sales fall through because the seller can't find somewhere to move to.

'How long have you lived here?' If they've only been in the property a short time, it could point to problems.

'Why are you moving?' Their answer could give some clues about a potential problem with the property or area.

'How long has your house been on the market?' If it's been a while, they may be prepared to lower the price.

'Have there been any other offers?' Find out if a surveyor has looked at the property for someone else. If there have been other offers, why have they fallen through?

'What fixtures and fittings will be left?' These can include curtains, carpets, light fittings and kitchen appliances. If things are in good order and to your taste, negotiate a fair price and you could save hundreds of pounds on refitting the property.

EXTRA EXPENSE

Monthly outgoings can vary considerably, so ask to see the water and fuel bills for the last 12 months. And don't forget to find out how much the council tax is.

An older property is also likely to need running repairs. If you're not into DIY, then these could prove to be expensive.

If you buy a freehold property then you will own the land too. Most houses in Britain are usually sold freehold. On the other hand, flats are generally sold on a leasehold basis. In these cases the freeholder (owner) may own the building and the land and you become a lessee. In essence you buy the right to use the property for a number of years. Alternatively, the freehold may be shared by all the lessees. In either case, you may find yourself with extra charges and responsibilities. It's your solicitor's job to make sure that you are informed of the responsibilities required by the lease so that there are no nasty surprises once you've moved in.

MAKING AN OFFER

Even if you've found the home of your dreams, don't fall in love with it too soon. Remember to stay level-headed and visit it another two or three times. If you still like it, go ahead and arrange a valuation and mortgage.

Make your offer through the seller's estate agent, if they have one. But whatever you do, think carefully before offering the advertised price. There's virtually always room for negotiation.

On some occasions, sellers will be more open to lowering the price; for example, if the property market is slow, during the winter months, or if their house has been on the market a long time. Your offer should be below the seller's asking price, but not so low that it offends. They will then normally come back with a slightly reduced asking price and so on. Eventually a compromise will be reached and you could well have saved yourself thousands of pounds.

INFORMATION PROVIDED BY BARCLAYS MORTGAGES

SELLING YOUR HOUSE AND HOW TO HANDLE IT

Even if you've sold a house before, it can still be a daunting prospect. Right away, there's a tricky decision to make – should you try to sell your present home before or after you find a new one?

You may have already started looking at some properties in the area you want to move to. However, it is normally recommended that you put your property up for sale before you start house-hunting in earnest. This is to avoid the frustrating situation where you've found your perfect house but cannot sell your old one.

It's much better to have an acceptable offer before you start looking. That way you know how much you can afford to pay for your new home, and you'll also be in a much stronger negotiating position.

THE BEST TIME TO SELL

It may sound like an old wives' tale, but the time of year that you put your house on the market really does affect its chances of selling. Spring is generally thought to be the best time of year, but any point during the first six months could increase the likelihood of a sale. Another consideration is the state of the housing market. Sometimes it favours the buyer, other times the seller. So keep an eye on what the television and newspapers are saying. Choosing the right time could mean your house sells more quickly, or for a better price.

WHO SHOULD SELL YOUR HOUSE?

You may be tempted to try to sell your house yourself. Certainly some people have been lucky in the past and saved themselves hundreds of pounds in estate agents' fees. It can be hard work however, and if the market is slow moving, you could end up losing more on the final asking price than you manage to save. By far the most popular way is to sell through an estate agent, but be sure to shop around before your choose one. A good estate agent can often get you a better price, or sell your home faster.

CHOOSING AN ESTATE AGENT

To begin with, look at the property adverts in your local paper. Which estate agents are selling properties similar to yours? Then compare their method of presentation. If their advertisement doesn't catch your eye, the chances are it won't attract buyers either. The next step is to drive around your neighbourhood looking for 'SOLD' signs. This will give you a good idea of who is the best at selling properties in your local area.

INFORMATION PROVIDED BY BARCLAYS MORTGAGES

Now draw up a shortlist of possible estate agents, do some 'window-shopping' at their offices and finally, go inside and talk to their staff. Are they enthusiastic and helpful? Do they seem to be good at negotiating? Find out what their approach to selling your house would be, what their opening hours are and, of course, how much they charge. Ask them to give an approximate value for your property. However, be aware that some may quote a very high price just to get your business, with the result that your house becomes impossible to sell.

ESTATE AGENT'S FEES

Estate agent's fees are either fixed, or vary according to the value of the house. Both types have their merits. A fixed fee is normally cheaper than a variable one, whilst a variable sum can motivate the estate agent into pushing for a better deal. It's also worth noting that you can normally negotiate a discount on both types of fee.

HOW MUCH SHOULD YOU SELL YOUR HOUSE FOR?

Once you've chosen an estate agent, they will help you decide on an asking price. This will usually be based on what similar properties in your area are fetching, and how quickly you want to sell.

WHO MAKES THE BEST BUYERS?

It's most likely that you'll sell your house to the person who makes the highest offer. However, the most generous offer isn't necessarily the best one. That's because some people will be part of a long house-buying chain. This can be both frustrating and time-consuming. It's always preferable to sell your house to a first-time buyer, a cash-buyer or a person who has already exchanged contracts on their house. Your estate agent should be able to tell you if a would-be buyer has already sold their home and arranged a new mortgage.

ACCEPTING AN OFFER

If you're lucky, you'll sell your house at the price you want. But more commonly, you'll have to enter into a negotiation process. Your estate agent will advise you as much as possible, but there are a number of unwritten rules you should be aware of. Firstly, a buyer's initial offer is usually just an opening gambit, and they can normally be persuaded to raise their bids.

Secondly, always be aware of your own position. What state is the housing market in? How much can you realistically expect?

And finally, unless you're selling the house yourself, always avoid direct negotiation with a buyer – ask them to speak to your estate agent instead. They are the professionals after all.

INFORMATION PROVIDED BY BARCLAYS MORTGAGES

MONEY MATTERS

Buying a home is a very exciting time. But there's such a huge choice of properties on the market, it can be hard to know where to begin. So start by figuring out just what you can afford to pay for your new home. Once you know your price range, you can save time and heartache by ruling out the properties which fall outside it.

If you are selling as well as buying a home, it's vital that you are aware of all the costs involved in both aspects from the outset. Knowing about these costs, and being realistic about the amount you're likely to get from the sale of your existing property, will help you figure out what new properties you can afford.

DON'T BE TEMPTED TO OVERSTRETCH

It can be very tempting to borrow just that little bit too much to clinch that perfect home. But overstretching on a mortgage can leave you with precious little spending money. Remember that interest rates can rise overnight, and you could easily find that your monthly mortgage payment is a good deal more than you bargained for.

HOW MUCH COULD YOU BORROW?

With so much at stake, it's important to talk to your mortgage lender as early as possible in the process. They will be able to help you work out just how much you could comfortably borrow.

 There's no magic formula for working out what you could afford. As a rule of thumb, though, single people can normally borrow up to three times their annual income, and couples up to three times the main annual income plus one times the second annual income.

Usually, lenders can offer you up to 95 per cent of the purchase price of your new home, or the mortgage valuation, whichever is lower. Add to this the amount you can afford to put down as a deposit (usually a minimum of five per cent), and you'll have a clearer picture of the maximum you could afford to pay for your new home.

For your free copy of
**THE BARCLAYS
FIRST TIME BUYERS GUIDE**
or **HOMEMOVERS GUIDE**
call 0800 400121
quoting reference S9ES1

 **BARCLAYS**

INFORMATION PROVIDED BY BARCLAYS MORTGAGES

BARKING AND DAGENHAM

Most of Barking and Dagenham is a vast sprawling council estate. Not 1960s concrete tower blocks and deck-access flats but miles of low, functional red brick terraces built by the London County Council on its Becontree estate between 1920 and 1938 to house workers, many from slums in the East End. Even on a sunny day, the estate, which covers a large part of the borough's central area, is bleak, despite the hedged small gardens and curving streets. With more recent council estates spreading up to the borough's northern tip and only a smattering of privately built property, the borough can boast no salubrious suburbs. It's mostly flat (this was marshland), its parks are municipal, its shops unexciting.

But if you want a cheap house on a fairly reliable tube or train line, Barking and Dagenham's a contender as one of the cheapest areas of London. Many of the houses were sold to their tenants under the Right-to-Buy scheme (the clues are in the new double-glazed windows, elaborate front doors and porches installed to proclaim their separateness from their council tenant neighbours). From Barking, the borough's main shopping and adminstrative centre in the west, the Becontree estate stretches in a rough square as far east as Dagenham and nearly as far north as the 1930s semis of Chadwell Heath. As a glance at the A-Z will tell you, this doesn't leave much else.

There are plans for 350 new homes at Barking Reach by the river to add to the 450 already built as part of riverside regeneration plans, but they'll be earmarked for social housing. Over the next 20 years there are plans for 4,000 new homes on what is now a stretch of mostly derelict marshland.

Barking and Dagenham is mostly working class and mostly white, (although its current mayor is a Sikh). Only 7% of its population is from an ethnic minority, with Indians the largest single group. Unemployment is high compared with neighbouring outer London boroughs at 5.6% (although half that of Newham to the west) and the borough is the 18th most deprived in the country. Here people tuck into pie and mash not because it's trendy but because it's cheap, nourishing and filling. But although many residents originally came from the East End, they like to stress that Barking is Essex, nearly the country.

Like other eastern riverside boroughs, Barking's riverfront and tributaries were left decimated and contaminated by the death of London's traditional riverside industries. But more than £2.5 million of government money is being poured into creating walks along the River Roding (see also Redbridge), new employment opportunities and a "cultural industries quarter" providing studio space for artists just south of Barking town centre. As a further spur to artistic endeavour, a further £7 million is being invested in the Artscape Project, an ambitious public art and landscaping project for the main A13 trunk road running through the borough.

PROPERTY AND ARCHITECTURE

BARKING

A mixture of small Victorian terraces near the centre and larger Edwardian and interwar houses in roads between the town centre and Mayesbrook Park. Some of the houses still have their original decorative iron porches and front doors but others have suffered from pebble-dashing, double-glazing, louvred windows and other unsightly alterations. The best roads are in the series of crescents west of Mayesbrook Park, on the Leftley estate, with slightly cheaper houses in the grids off Longbridge Road. Despite being main roads, Longbridge Road and Upney Lane are both popular for their large houses. New property built on Barking Reach is starting to come back on to the market and there's lots of ex-council property alongside the privately built. Property at the lower end of the price ranges given is mostly ex-council.

ATTRACTS *First-time buyers; loyal locals; investors* • **CONSERVATION AREAS** *Barking Abbey and Town Centre; Abbey Road riverside* • **AVERAGE PRICES** *Flats: studio: £30,000-£35,000; 1-bed: £32,000-£50,000; 2-bed: £40,000-£60,000; 3-bed: £40,000-£45,000 Houses: 1-bed: £40,000-£45,000; 2-bed: £70,000; 3-bed: £75,000-£90,000; 4-bed: £65,000-£180,000* • **AVERAGE RENTS (MONTHLY)** *Flats: 1-bed: £400; 2-bed: £520-£560 Houses: 2-bed: £540-£585; 3-bed: £650; 4-bed: £695-£860.*

BECONTREE & DAGENHAM

The long low red brick terraces of the Becontree estate, mostly two- and three-bedroom houses, predominate. The older ones towards Goodmayes and the border with Redbridge are built in a more cottagey style with deep eaves and small paned windows. The later ones towards the centre and east are more functional and brutal. Some are set back from the roads around small squares and cul-de-sacs and the uniformity is broken by brick front door arches and passages to back gardens but the overall effect is still dreary. Some modern blocks in Dagenham mixed with 1930s speculatively-built terraces and semis.

ATTRACTS *Loyal locals; bargain hunters; first-time buyers* • **CONSERVATION AREA** *Dagenham Village* • **AVERAGE PRICES** *Flats: 1-bed: £32,000-£35,000; 2-bed: £40,000 Houses: 2-bed: £55,000-£65,000; 3-bed: £55,000-£85,000* • **AVERAGE RENTS (MONTHLY)** *Flats: 1-bed: £400+; 2-bed: £520-£560 Houses: 2-bed: £540-£585; 3-bed: £600-£650.*

CHADWELL HEATH

"If you live in Dagenham, you think Chadwell Heath's posh," says one longstanding resident. Possibly. A fairly dreary collection of 1930s semis and terraces with some new blocks by the station. The main reason it's

more up-market than Dagenham is because it has a certain snob value as an area where many of the houses were originally privately built.
ATTRACTS *Loyal locals; local first-time buyers* • **CONSERVATION AREA** *Chadwell Heath anti-aircraft gun site* • **AVERAGE PRICES** *Flats: studio: £35,000-£40,000; 1-bed: £45,000-£50,000; 2-bed: £50,000-£60,000 Houses: 2-bed: £75,000; 3-bed: £80,000-£110,000; 4-bed: £150,000-£200,000* • **AVERAGE RENTS (MONTHLY)** *Flats: studio: £390; 1-bed: £400-£470; 2-bed: £520+ Houses: 2-bed: £540+; 3-bed: £650; 4-bed: £690-£860.*

BEST POSTCODES
Irrelevant. Barking has Essex postcodes.

AMENITIES

SCHOOLS**

Not actually scraping the bottom of the overall league tables but generally undistiguished performance at both primary and secondary level. No single sex secondary schools. Poor performance here partly redeemed by the second most generous state provision for under-five year-olds in London. No private prep or secondary schools.
PRE-SCHOOL PROVISION *4 state day nurseries; 34 nursery classes in state primary and church schools; 41 private and community day nurseries and playgroups. Proportion of under-fives in state nurseries: 76%* • **STATE PRIMARY SCHOOLS** *Overall league table position: 106h out of 150. Top scorers: St Theresa RC (with nursery unit), Dagenham; William Ford C of E, Dagenham; St Joseph's RC (with nursery unit), Barks* • **STATE SECONDARY SCHOOLS** *Overall league table position: 131st out of 150. Top scorers: Barking Abbey (mixed); Barking; Warren (mixed), Chadwell Heath; All Saints Catholic School and Technology College (mixed) Dagenham.*

TRANSPORT***

Pretty good in most parts of the borough, with District line tubes and trains running west to east. Lines peter out a bit further up though, with only trains linking Chadwell Heath and central London.
TRAINS *Chadwell Heath: Zone 5. Cost of annual season ticket: £1280; No of trains per hour: to Liverpool Street 6; Fastest journey: 20 minutes* • **TUBES** *Barking: Zone 4. Cost of annual season ticket: £1068; Frequency: District to Embankment: every 4-6 minutes; Hammersmith and City to Liverpool Street: every 8 minutes (peak hours only); Fastest journey: to Embankment 30 minutes; to Liverpool Street 25 minutes. Dagenham Heathway: Zone 5. Frequency: District to Embankment: every 4-6 minutes; Fastest journey: 36 minutes* • **BUSES** *Vital if you want to travel north to south within the borough, as all trains and tubes run east to west. Generally efficient connections between Barking and Dagenham and other nearby shopping centres like Romford. Not many buses into town. Night bus services include: the N25 from Trafalgar Square to Chadwell Heath and the N15 from Trafalgar Square to Barking and Becontree Heath* • **TRAFFIC BLACKSPOTS** *The A13: Trafficky at the best of times since it's the main road into London from Essex and now even worse while being upgraded. Heathway: The main north/south drag to Dagenham shopping centre is*

cluttered with buses and delivery vans, especially in rush-hour. Barking: The pedestrianised centre of Barking around East Street pushes traffic out onto surrounding roads, causing traffic back-ups around the nearby north circular which marks the borough's western boundary • **PARKING** There are controlled parking zones in Barking Town Centre and around tube stations in Upney, Becontree, Dagenham Heathway, Dagenham East and Chadwell Heath to stop unofficial park and riding. Cost of annual resident's permit: £12.50.

LEISURE FACILITIES***

THEATRES & CONCERT HALLS The Broadway theatre in Barking has mostly local and family shows, golden oldie pop stars and amateur shows. Otherwise it's an out of borough trip to town or further out into Essex. Range of arts activities also at Eastbury Manor House, a National Trust-owned Elizabethan merchant's house in Barking • **CINEMAS** Well-endowed for a small borough although not a good bet if your idea of fun is a black and white French art movie. The six screen Odeon opposite the station is an impressive newly painted modernist building showing mainstream films. More of the same at the Warner Village multiplex on the A13 in Dagenham • **MUSEUMS & GALLERIES** Only one museum, Valence House, an attractive manor house dating in part from the 14th century with panelled rooms and a sweeping staircase. The local history museum is here although it's disappointingly small, particularly given the social interest of the development of the Becontree estate on its doorstep. A couple of moderately interesting mock-up rooms of typical Becontree estate homes of the 1930s. Collection of portraits and temporary exhibitions in the O'Leary Gallery. New gallery in Barking central library created as part of the A13 Artscape project • **SPORTS FACILITIES** Plentiful. Three leisure centres: one at Barking and two at Dagenham. Pools at Dagenham, gyms and fitness centres at all three venues. Boating lake at Mayesbrook Park. Fishing at Eastbrookend Country Park. Tennis, football and other sports in parks across the borough • **LIBRARIES** Handsome central library in Barking with helpful staff and reasonable opening hours in larger branch libraries throughout the borough. But some smaller branches are closed more than they're open, a classic sign of a borough strapped for cash. The borough failed to supply information to the Audit Commission on library use so there are no official figures. Unofficially, libraries looked well-patronised, even on a weekday morning.

OPEN SPACES**

On paper there's reasonable open space, but in practice most of it's flat and drab, its lack of natural interest not enhanced by litter, graffiti and uncared-for park furniture. Mayesbrook Park is particularly bad in this respect, with piles of old litter by the boating lake and burnt-out benches. Not recommended as a pleasant place to sit.

WIDE OPEN SPACE Eastbrookend Country Park. Created just three years ago from derelict land used first to provide gravel for the building of the Becontree estate after the estate was bombed during the blitz and then used as a dumping ground in the 60s and 70s. Now the borough's largest open space, with fishing lakes, wildlife and flat grasslands with big skies. The large Swedish-style building is the new Millennium Centre for environmental education. Good if you want to get away from it all but can be slightly intimidating if you're alone. The gypsy encampment doesn't help • **RIVER WALKS** Watch out for continuing improvements and access to the River Roding.

SHOPS* *

BARKING *A pleasant surprise. The borough's main shopping area has a recently built shopping centre, Vicarage Fields, in an elegant red brick building which, unusually for such buildings, looks as good from the back as it does from the front. Inside, it has distinctive shopfronts, not just plate glass and some interesting shops including jewellers, perfume shops and bookshops. Ilford, which always used to be smarter than Barking, looks in danger of being eclipsed. Indoor market on the ground floor complete with market traders with sales spiel. More down-market shops in the pedestrianised shopping streets around selling cheap clothes and "fancy goods" but the shops avoid being shabby. Somerfields in the shopping centre* • **CHADWELL HEATH** *The main 1930s shopping parade in the High Road could be quite distinguished if it was better maintained. Mostly local shops (cheap clothes, discount stores, furniture) mixed with the usual take-aways and banks. Big Sainsbury's* • **DAGENHAM** *Pretty much the pits. A dreary parade of discount shops, gift shops and sewing shops (often seen in poorer areas) around Heathway Station and a strictly functional shopping mall (low ceilings, harsh lighting, lots of stubbed out cigarette ends on the floor). Cheap chain stores with Poundstretcher and Poundstore dominating. Sainsbury's. Safeway at Beacontree Heath. A noticeable lack of ethnic stores.*

RESTAURANTS*

A culinary desert.

CRIME RATES* * *

113 crimes per 1,000 of population. Position in Metropolitan Police league table: 19th out of 32 (where 1 is worst and 32 best).

THE COUNCIL* * *

POLITICAL AFFILIATION *Labour* • **MINUS POINTS** *Litter collection and street-sweeping can be poor (dustmen left a large residue of litter from commercial rubbish bins by Barking Station in front of the author's very eyes). Park maintenance poor. Slow turnaround of property searches* • **PLUS POINTS** *Energetic participant in regeneration initiatives. High level of nursery provision. Door-to-door recycling being piloted in 22,000 homes, currently newspapers only but set to expand into other items* • **PROPERTY SEARCHES CARRIED OUT IN 10 WORKING DAYS** *83%* • **STANDARD SEARCH FEE** *£88* • **COUNCIL TAX COLLECTED** *94.9%* • **COUNCIL TAX 1998-99**

BAND	PROPERTY VALUE	CHARGE	BAND	PROPERTY VALUE	CHARGE
A	up to £40,000	£465.00	E	£88,001-£120,000	£852.50
B	£40,001-£52,000	£542.50	F	£120,001-£160,000	£1,007.50
C	£52,001-£68,000	£620.00	G	£160,001-£320,000	£1,162.50
D	£68,001-£88,000	£697.50	H	over £320,000	£1,395.00

BARNET

Barnet is sleek and prosperous. Its schools are good, its green spaces plentiful, its crime low and many of its residents wealthy. The inner city stops well to the south of its borders, contained on the other side of the railway tracks in Brent and the other side of Hampstead Heath in Camden. Its northern boundaries merge smoothly into Hertfordshire. All safely middle class. But it manages to have more bite than the average commuter suburb, thanks mainly to its many distinctive ethnic and religious communities. Nearly a quarter of the population is from an ethnic minority. Barnet has one of the largest and most established Jewish communities in London as well as the largest Gujerati population, bringing a satisfyingly cosmopolitan feel to its suburban streets.

The borough is large. At its narrowest point in the south is the seriously wealthy Hampstead Garden Suburb and the slightly (but only slightly) more restrained areas of Hendon, Mill Hill and Golders Green, full of large detached 1930s houses with neat gardens. East of Mill Hill is the popular, mostly Victorian suburb of Finchley. Further north, a large tract of fields and green space separates the council estates of Burnt Oak and the middling 1930s semis of Edgware from the expensive detached houses of Totteridge and the Georgian survivors of the suburban onslaught in Barnet and Hadley.

Most of Barnet grew up around the Northern line tube which stretched out into Edgware and High Barnet in the early years of this century, turning fields and villages into roads and houses. It has little of the post-industrial legacy of unemployment that has devastated some parts of inner London, with unemployment standing at just 4.3%. This is the home of managers and middle managers, a solid family area, increasingly leavened by young professionals who favour the large Victorian properties of Finchley, and growing numbers of entrepreneurs. (Barnet claims to have more self-employed people within its borders than any other part of Greater London).

The borough has the doubtful privilege of being home to the start of the M1 motorway, the first and still one of the busiest, and like other outer London boroughs, parts of Barnet are carved up by dual carriageways carrying fast traffic. But this doesn't put residents off car ownership – rather the opposite, as most households have at least one car and use it frequently, if the traffic's anything to go by.

Walking as a means of getting from A to B comes into its own on the Jewish Sabbath when Orthodox Jews are forbidden to drive their cars and Golders Green Road is a flurry of furs, high heels and black Homberg hats after the end of synagogue services. But the Jewish community has met with fierce opposition in its attempts to create an *eruv*, an area in which Sabbath laws can be relaxed.

The sticking point has been that the area's boundaries would be designated by tall poles linked with thin wire high above street level, which opponents say would be unsightly and dangerous. The council has approved the *eruv* and now it's up to the Highways Agency to give it the green light.

PROPERTY AND ARCHITECTURE

HAMPSTEAD GARDEN SUBURB

This area just north of Hampstead Heath proper was created as a social experiment in the early years of the century by energetic social reformer Henrietta Barnett. The original idea was to have rich and poor living and working side by side in healthy and morally uplifting (no pubs) surroundings. But nowadays even the more modest cottagey properties around Denman Drive north of Big Wood are way beyond the reach of the poor and the large, gloomy houses round the Central Square are seriously expensive. The Suburb (as it's known locally) also contains London's "millionaire" row, Bishops Avenue, home to princes, film stars and others with more money than taste. Lots of Dallas-style iron gates and porticoed, colonnaded porches but the overall effect is soulless. Few flats, mostly houses. A slightly self-conscious community, which was furious when it was portrayed on television recently as obsessed with making sure no one was allowed to make any changes to their properties.

ATTRACTS *The wealthy and aristocratic; the Jewish community; families* • **CONSERVATION AREA** *Hampstead Garden Suburb: Hampstead Village (Spaniards End); Hampstead Village (Heath Passage)* • **AVERAGE PRICES** *Flats: 1-bed: £80,000; 2-bed: £90,000-£100,000; 3-bed: £120,000+ Houses: 2-bed: £180,000+; 3-bed: £240,000-£300,000; 4-bed: £350,000+; 5-bed: £500,000+* • **AVERAGE RENTS (MONTHLY)** *Flats: 1-bed: £780; 2-bed: £1010; 3-bed: £1400 Houses: 2-bed: £1080; 3-bed: £1730; 4-bed: £2160; 5-bed: £3460.*

GOLDERS GREEN

Home to many of Barnet's Jewish community. Mostly large detached and semi-detached Edwardian and between-the-wars houses and less overwhelming than Hampstead Garden Suburb. A varying choice of styles from arts and crafts red brick with leaded windows to 1930s up-market surburban with half-timbered gables. Some of the houses have been converted into synagogues. A good choice of flats in modern blocks, many on wide main roads. The cheaper parts are near the Brent Cross shopping centre and prices rise sharply the nearer you are to Hampstead Garden Suburb.

ATTRACTS *Members of the Jewish community; families* • **CONSERVATION AREAS** *none* • **AVERAGE PRICES** *Flats: studio: £50,000-£70,000; 1-bed: £60,000-£100,000; 2-bed: £90,000-£150,000; 3-bed: £120,000-£175,000 Houses: 3-bed: £130,000-£220,000; 4-bed: £200,000-£225,000; 5-bed: £250,000-£300,000* • **AVERAGE RENTS (MONTHLY)** *Flats: studio: £540; 1-bed: £650-£750; 2-bed: £860-£1080; 3-bed: £1080+ Houses: 3-bed: £1080-£1300; 4-bed: £1300-£1730; 5-bed: £1950-£2160.*

HENDON & MILL HILL

Both areas are cruelly carved up by roads (Mill Hill has the M1 at the end of its main shopping street) and the semis on the main roads are generally uninspiring. But large and handsome detached houses in large gardens take over as soon as you turn off. The roads are quiet and tree-lined and the cars in the drives expensive. Good views from roads round Church Road and The Burroughs in Hendon, which still have a handful of cottages and old buildings as a reminder of Hendon's beginnings as farmland. Mostly houses, with flats in modern blocks. Hendon tends to be a bit more expensive than Mill Hill because the transport links are better.

ATTRACTS *Families; members of the Jewish community; young professionals (Hendon)* • **CONSERVATION AREAS** *Mill Hill; The Burroughs; Church End* • **AVERAGE PRICES** *Flats: studio: £50,000-£60,000; 1-bed: £60,000-£70,000; 2-bed: £75,000-£100,000 Houses: 3-bed: £120,000-£230,000; 4-bed: £200,000-£400,000; 5-bed: £300,000-£500,000* • **AVERAGE RENTS (MONTHLY)** *Flats: studio: £430; 1-bed: £560; 2-bed: £650+ Houses: 3-bed: £860-£1080; 4-bed: £1080-£1730; 5-bed: £1510-£1950.*

FINCHLEY

A sprawling area of Victorian and Edwardian terraces and villas, and the part of Barnet which feels most like London rather than suburbia or the Home Counties. A good place to look for conversions as many of the large red brick four-storey terraces have been divided up into flats. Central Finchley is the most consistently attractive part, with solid Victorian and Edwardian terraces. The nearer you go to Hampstead Garden Suburb in East Finchley, the more expensive it is. The cheaper parts, including council property are near the North Circular.

ATTRACTS *First-time buyers; young professionals; families; Japanese who established themselves here when there was a Japanese school* • **CONSERVATION AREAS** *Church End; Finchley Garden Village; Moss Hall* • **AVERAGE PRICES** *Flats: studio: £40,000-£60,000; 1-bed: £60,000-£100,000; 2-bed: £80,000+ Houses: 2-bed: £120,000+; 3-bed: £150,000-£250,000; 4-bed: £250,000-£300,000; 5-bed: £300,000+* • **AVERAGE RENTS (MONTHLY)** *Flats: studio: £430+; 1-bed: £520; 2-bed: £650+ Houses: 2-bed: £860+; 3-bed: £1080-£1500; 4-bed: £1500+; 5-bed: £2160.*

TOTTERIDGE

Totteridge's main road is called Totteridge Village but don't be misled. There's nothing villagey about it and no village centre, just a trafficky road lined with detached houses which get larger and grander as built-up areas give way to fields. The open space is the main attraction, tempting a fair smattering of pop stars, footballers and other celebrities to buy up houses here. Few flats or small houses.

ATTRACTS *Families; minor celebrities* • **CONSERVATION AREAS** *Totteridge* • **AVERAGE PRICES** *Flats: 2-bed: £220,000-£350,000; 3-bed: £300,000+ Houses: 4-bed: £400,000+; 5-bed: £700,000+* • **AVERAGE RENTS (MONTHLY)** *Flats: 2-bed: £1080 Houses 3-bed: £1516; 4-bed: £1950+; 5-bed: £3000.*

EDGWARE

A mixture of middling 1930s semis, larger detached redbrick houses in tree-lined roads and some newly built town houses and apartment blocks. Solid and unexciting. It never takes long to get to a major main road from almost anywhere in Edgware but the upside of this is that you can escape

fairly effortlessly to the countryside. One of the cheaper areas of Barnet and a good place to look for family homes. Some good value homes in Burnt Oak on the council estate built by the LCC at the beginning of the century – you can pick up a three-bedroom house here for around £85,000.
ATTRACTS *Families; members of the Jewish community; investors*
• **CONSERVATION AREAS** *none* • **AVERAGE PRICES** *Flats: studio: £50,000-£55,000; 1-bed: £65,000+; 2-bed: £80,000-£85,000; 3-bed: £100,000+ Houses: 1-bed: £60,000-£70,000; 2-bed: £100,000; 3-bed: £140,000+; 4-bed: £250,000; 5-bed: £300,000+* • **AVERAGE RENTS (MONTHLY)** *Flats: studio: £430; 1-bed: £560; 2-bed: £650; 3-bed: £860+ Houses: 3-bed: £860; 4-bed: £1120+; 5-bed: £1300.*

BARNET

Doesn't really feel like London at all but more like the market town it once was, with a curving main street of small shop buildings and a church looking out on to a green. Some large Victorian houses and smaller terraces off Wood Street near the centre of Barnet itself and a jumble of everything from large Victorian villas to modern blocks coming down the hill into the outlying roads of New Barnet. The grandest houses in Barnet (and some of the loveliest in the borough) are Georgian town houses facing onto Hadley Common on the way to Monken Hadley, which definitely feels villagey, with small white plastered and red brick cottages. High Barnet and New Barnet are more expensive than East Barnet.
ATTRACTS *Families; members of the Jewish community* • **CONSERVATION AREAS** *Monken Hadley; Wood Street* • **AVERAGE PRICES** *Flats: studio: £50,000-£60,000; 1-bed: £70,000-£90,000; 2-bed: £90,000; 3-bed: £130,000+ Houses: 2-bed: £130,000+; 3-bed: £150,000+; 4-bed: £300,000; 5-bed: £450,000* • **AVERAGE RENTS (MONTHLY)** *Flats: studio: £410+; 1-bed: £520; 2-bed: £560+; 3-bed: £730+ Houses: 2-bed: £780+; 3-bed: £860+; 4-bed: £1300+; 5-bed: £2160.*

BEST POSTCODES

The poshest postcode is Golders Green NW11 which includes Hampstead Garden Suburb. After this things get a bit more complicated because the postcode areas are mixed but Finchley N3, East Finchley N2, Hendon NW4 and Whetstone N20, which includes Totteridge, are all highly rated. Proximity to a tube line affects prices more than postcodes.

AMENITIES

SCHOOLS ★ ★ ★ ★

Excellent in most respects. Very good league table performance from both primary and secondary schools with some chart-topping (and oversubscribed) state schools. A good selection of private schools. A wide choice of private nurseries. The proportion of under-fives with state nursery places is only average but still better than that of several surrounding boroughs.
PRE-SCHOOL PROVISION *4 state nursery schools; 39 state, Church and Jewish primary schools with nursery units; 89 private day nurseries and playgroups. Proportion of under-fives in state nurseries: 57%* • **STATE PRIMARY SCHOOLS** *Overall league table position: 17th out of 150. Top Scorers: Menorah Foundation, Edgware; Menorah, Golders Green; St John's C of E,*

Whetstone • STATE SECONDARY SCHOOLS Overall league table position: 7th out of 150. Top Scorers: (all selective); Henrietta Barnett (girls), Hampstead Garden Suburb; St Michaels Catholic Grammar (girls), Finchley; Queen Elizabeth's School for Boys, Barnet • PRIVATE PREP SCHOOLS Hendon Prep (mixed from 3), Hendon; Belmont (Mill Hill Junior, mixed), Mill Hill • PRIVATE SECONDARY SCHOOLS Mill Hill (mixed), Mill Hill; Mount (girls), Mill Hill; St Martha's (girls), Barnet; King Alfred School (mixed from 4), Golders Green; Beth Jacob Grammar School (girls), Golders Green; Menorah Grammar (boys), Golders Green; Pardes House (Jewish, top scorer, boys), Finchley.

TRANSPORT***

People can be lulled into thinking that the furthest flung parts of the borough are nearer than they are because they're on the Northern line but the journey to High Barnet or Edgware is slow and tedious and tubes to Mill Hill East on the branch line almost as rare as hens' teeth. The Northern line is also plagued with delays and very overcrowded at rush hour. Some parts of the borough, notably Hampstead Garden Suburb, are a brisk walk from the tube (plans for a station here were scuppered by Henrietta Barnett who feared a rash of speculative building and bought up the land), but many of the wealthy residents probably don't feel the lack too deeply.
TRAINS Mill Hill Broadway: *Zone 4. Cost of annual season ticket: £1068. No of trains per hour: Thameslink to Kings Cross 4; Fastest journey: 20 minutes* • **TUBES** Golders Green: *Zone 3; Cost of annual season ticket £860; Frequency: Northern line to Charing Cross every 6-7 minutes; Fastest journey: 25 minutes.* Edgware: *Zone 5; Cost of annual season ticket £1280; Frequency: Northern line to Charing Cross every 6-7 minutes; Fastest journey: 35 minutes.* Finchley Central: *Zone 4; Frequency: Northern line to Charing Cross every 6-7 minutes; Fastest journey: 27 minutes.* High Barnet: *Zone 6; Cost of annual season ticket £1396; Frequency: Northern line to Charing Cross every 6-7 minutes; Fastest journey: 35 minutes* • **BUSES** *Bus journeys to town can be slow, travelling up trafficky main roads but unlike some outer London boroughs services do at least go all the way to the centre. The southern parts, particularly Finchley, Mill Hill and Golders Green are best served. Crossing from one side of the borough to another is a frustrating experience as few buses venture across the open space in the middle. Services to town include: the 113 from Edgware via Mill Hill and Hendon to Oxford Circus, the 82 from North Finchley via Golders Green to Victoria and the 43 from Friern Barnet to London Bridge* • **TRAFFIC BLACKSPOTS** Brent Cross: *A surreal tangle of concrete bridges, flyovers, underpasses, roundabouts, pedestrian bridges and subways separates Brent Cross shopping centre from the rest of civilisation. Getting there on foot is a challenge but it's worse by car, particularly in the Saturday afternoon shopping crowds.* Barnet: *An otherwise attractive shopping street is blighted by long queues of traffic coming from the north straight down Barnet High Street.* Hendon: *Sliced into pieces by a dual carriageway, which forces pedestrians into subways and long tail-backs particularly at the junction with the North Circular and the joining roads to the M1* • **PARKING** *Five controlled parking zones in the borough in Golders Green, High Barnet, around the Brent Cross shopping centre, and in Mill Hill and West Hendon. Residents in roads round the tube in East Finchley are pressing for controlled parking in their area. Cost of annual resident's permit: £20 per vehicle. Permits only valid in the zone for which they're issued.*

LEISURE FACILITIES * * *

THEATRES & CONCERT HALLS The Bull, housed in a small building with a recently revamped café in Barnet High Street has plays, dance, stand-up comedy, an art gallery and childrens' shows. Lots of new plays and one man shows. Live music and classical concerts also at The Bull. There are plans for a new £11.4 million arts centre at Tally Ho Corner, North Finchley, which should massively improve Barnet's relatively low theatre provision • **CINEMAS** The Phoenix Cinema in East Finchley has a mixture of mainstream West End hits and more rarefied repertory films on Sunday afternoons. Predictable programmes of blockbusters at Virgin, Staples Corner, Warner Village, Finchley and the Edgware Belle-vue • **MUSEUMS & GALLERIES** A small, fun, varied collection of specialist museums. The Museum of Jewish Life in Finchley has exhibitions of documents, photographs and oral history telling the social history of Jewish London. The Stephens Collection, the original house of Henry Stephens, of ink fame, has exhitibitons of writing materials. If you crave more excitement, try flying a Tornado at the Royal Airforce Museum in Hendon. Local history in Barnet and at Church Farmhouse in Hendon, a mellow seventeenth century reminder of Hendon's rural days. Mock-ups of nineteenth century rooms including kitchen with very realistic-looking food • **SPORTS FACILITIES** Five leisure centres in Hendon (two including youth sports centre), Barnet, Southgate (on Enfield borders, see Enfield) and Finchley. Finchley has a new Lido with saunas, jacuzzis and fitness classes. Tennis and other outdoor sports in open spaces throughout the borough. Sailing, canoeing and windsurfing on Welsh Harp Reservoir (see also Brent). Residents' discount scheme being piloted • **LIBRARIES** Well-visited and well-spaced throughout the borough. Opening hours are reasonable although there's some lunchtime closing in smaller branch libraries. Monday's not a good day. Sunday opening is now permanent at Golders Green. 9.5 library visits per head. Position in library-use league table: 8th out of 32 (where 1 is best and 32 worst).

OPEN SPACES * * * *

Excellent and well documented. Barnet council's an enthusiastic promoter of green walks and woodland trails and was one of the first to complete its section of the huge circular London Loop walk round the outskirts of London. **HEATHLAND** The Hampstead Heath extension. The less frequented part of the heath by Hampstead Garden Suburb, saved from development by Henrietta Barnet. More open and less wooded than other nearby parts of the heath • **TRAILS** You can walk all the way from Hampstead Heath to Woodside Park without walking on a main road (an amazing feat) by following the Dollis Valley Greenwalk along the Dollis and Mutton Brooks. Peaceful grassy banks and clear water within earshot of the roar of traffic • **WOODS** Monken Hadley Common, once part of the Royal hunting ground of Enfield Chase and now a fitting backdrop to the grand houses opposite.

SHOPS * * * *

GOLDERS GREEN Almost every other shop in Golders Green Road is Jewish, with kosher butchers and restaurants, bakeries and a bookshop with a window display of barmitzvah gifts. In vivid contrast to Brent Cross just a skip and a jump across a concrete bridge over the M1, the streets are deserted on Saturday morning while the owners and customers of the shops are at Synagogue. Brent Cross, which from the outside looks like a series of enlarged nuclear bunkers, was one of the first out-of-town shopping malls and now its size and choice of shops are nothing special as other places have caught up • **FINCHLEY** Ballards Lane has mostly chain stores, including a couple of interior design shops and junk shops by Finchley Central station. Estate agents abound, including a couple of Japanese operators to cater for the Japanese community near the Japanese school in Finchley. Tesco in Ballards Lane. More lively shops in East Finchley, with delis, brasseries, a fireplace shop and a real fishmonger • **HENDON & MILL HILL** Generally uninspiring local shops in Hendon around a series of dual carriageways crossed by litter-filled subways and lots of shops to let (the council's trying to reverse this trend). Mill Hill is much better, with long-established individual shops lining the Broadway, including childrens' clothes shops, antiques and furniture. Large M&S with carpark. Sainsbury's in West Hendon and London's only Eastern shopping mall, Oriental City, a cornucopia of Japanese, Vietnamese and Korean indoor market stalls, food court, bookshop and public massage service • **EDGWARE** Middle size, middle of the road but clean and pleasant shopping mall, The Broadwalk, in the main shopping street, a neo-Georgian 1930s red brick parade of tidy local shops and discount shops. A clutch of kosher bakeries and butchers' shops for the large Jewish population and travel agents advertising trips to Israel • **BARNET** Attractive looking, up-market shops particularly in the Spires shopping centre, cleverly converted from an old church. An eclectic collection of shops at the far end of the high street towards Hadley Common, including a tatooist and a cobbler.

RESTAURANTS * * *

GOLDERS GREEN & HENDON This is the place to come for Jewish food. Both places have a range of recommended bakeries and grander restaurants. A couple of Indian, Indonesian, Middle Eastern and Japanese restaurants also worth visiting • **ELSEWHERE** East Finchley rings the changes with a Hungarian brasserie. Otherwise mostly pizza and pasta chains, take-aways and local restaurants.

CRIME RATES * * * * *

The lowest crime rate in London. 75 crimes per 1000 of population. Position in Metropolitan Police crime table: 32nd out of 32 (where 1 is worst and 32 best).

THE COUNCIL * * * *

POLITICAL AFFILIATION No overall control • **MINUS POINTS** Has had the thumbs down from some residents over poor rubbish collections • **PLUS POINTS** Has pledged to clean up its rubbish collection act. Fortnightly door-to-door recycling collections (in nifty black boxes with lids). Generally praised by residents as efficient and effective. Excellent schools. Citizens' panel to give the council feedback. Good at sweeping the streets.
PROPERTY SEARCHES CARRIED OUT IN 10 WORKING DAYS 100% • **STANDARD SEARCH FEE** £100 • **COUNCIL TAX COLLECTED** 94.7%
• **COUNCIL TAX 1998-99**

BAND	PROPERTY VALUE	CHARGE	BAND	PROPERTY VALUE	CHARGE
A	up to £40,000	£485.38	E	£88,001-£120,000	£889.87
B	£40,001-£52,000	£566.27	F	£120,001-£160,000	£1,051.66
C	£52,001-£68,000	£647.18	G	£160,001-£320,000	£1,213.45
D	£68,001-£88,000	£728.07	H	over £320,000	£1,456.14

BEXLEY

For motorists on their way up from the Channel Ports, the eastern border of Bexley is where London starts (give or take a few yards through neighbouring Bromley). The dreary 1930s semis lining the main A20 Sidcup bypass manage to be both smug and down-at-heel, prompting people to put their foot down and escape as quickly as they can.

There's no getting away from it; Bexley is suburban, criss-crossed by main roads, with miles of streets of undistinguished semis flung up during the building booms of the 1920s and 1930s. But among the dross there are some beautiful properties, miles of rivers, meadows and woods, some excellent, sought-after state schools and as an antidote to the residential south, an industrial riverfront set for a face-lift.

Bexley stretches from the smart family homes of Sidcup, one of the best areas once you're off the main roads, to the Victorian village streets of Old Bexley with its river and mill (now a restaurant). Further north and west at Bexleyheath and Welling semi-detached suburbia takes over again, getting gradually shabbier towards Belvedere and the Victorian workmens' terraces of Erith on Bexley's northern shore. On the flat marshland of the northern-most tip are the new houses of Thamesmead North.

Riverside regeneration is on nowhere near the scale of that in next door Greenwich. But government grants and private sector investment totalling £48 million will be spent over the next two years on pedestrianisation and other improvements to Erith's town centre, (vandalised in the 1960s by a concrete shopping centre and multi-storey car park), a new infrastructure and employment initiatives in Erith and nearby Belvedere.

Like many of its outer London neighbours, however, Bexley generally has low unemployment at 3.5 % and low crime rates. It has its fair share of the affluent middle classes as well as upwardly mobile working classes. But life can be uncomfortable for non-whites in what is mostly a white area. Just 6% of the population is from an ethnic minority, mostly concentrated in the poorest, northern parts of the borough. The National Front bookshop in Welling has been a flashpoint for racial unrest.

PROPERTY AND ARCHITECTURE

SIDCUP & BLACKFEN

Sidcup is considered one of the best parts of the borough. Mostly houses with some purpose-built blocks of flats. Large Victorian and Edwardian detached and semi-detached family homes and smart semi-detached

houses with steep roofs and big gardens in roads off Main Road and the High Street. Smaller semi-detached mostly 1920s and 1930s houses in streets nearer the A20. Victorian cottages in Halfway Street. Mostly 1920s and 1930s in Blackfen with the best roads around Hollyoak Wood Park.
ATTRACTS *Affluent commuter families; people moving up from Welling or Bexleyheath* • **CONSERVATION AREAS** *The Hollies; Halfway Street; Old Forge Way; Christ Church; The Green; Longlands Road; North Cray Village; the Oval; Willersley Avenue and Braunton Avenue* • **AVERAGE PRICES** *Flats: studio: £40,000; 1-bed: £55,000; 2-bed: £60,000-£80,000; 3-bed: £60,000+ Houses: 2-bed: £65,000-£100,000; 3-bed: £85,000-£150,000; 4-bed: £130,000+; 5-bed: £250,000+* • **AVERAGE RENTS (MONTHLY)** *Flats: studio: £350-£400; 1-bed: £425-£475; 2-bed: £500-£600; 3-bed: £550-£600 Houses: 2-bed: £500-£550; 3-bed: £650-£800; 4-bed: £850-£1000; 5-bed: £900-£1000.*

BEXLEY

Bexley is pretty and villagey, with Victorian cottages and shop fronts in the High Street alongside larger Victorian and Edwardian terraces near the River Cray. Mostly houses rather than flats. A mixture of large modern and 1930s semis and detached houses in roads off Parkhill Road and Bexley High Street.
ATTRACTS *Families wanting green space, good schools; commuters; some first-time buyers* • **CONSERVATION AREAS** *Old Bexley; Parkhurst* • **AVERAGE PRICES** *Flats: 1-bed: £60,000; 2-bed: £90,000; 3-bed: £95,000 Houses: 2-bed: £85,000; 3-bed: £100,000-£180,000; 4-bed: £170,000-£190,000* • **AVERAGE RENTS (MONTHLY)** *Flats: studio: £400; 1-bed: £450; 2-bed: £500-£600; 3-bed: £600-£625 Houses: 2-bed: £550; 3-bed: £700-£850; 4-bed: £800-£1000.*

WELLING & BEXLEYHEATH

Welling is almost entirely a 1930s creation, with private housing development following council house building in the 1920s. Mostly fairly dull roads of two-, three- and four-bedroom suburban terraces and semis with the best near Danson Park. Some larger houses in slightly more up-market Bexleyheath but mostly interwar terraces and semis like Welling, with some flats above shops and in purpose-built blocks.
ATTRACTS *First-time buyers; people who can't afford Sidcup or Bexley; young couples; families wanting to be near good schools* • **CONSERVATION AREAS** *Red House, Bexleyheath* • **AVERAGE PRICES** *Flats: 1-bed: £50,000-£55,000; 2-bed: £55,000-£60,000; 3-bed: £65,000 Houses: 2-bed: £75,000-£80,000; 3-bed: £90,000-£120,000; 4-bed: £130,000-£150,000; 5-bed: £200,000+* • **AVERAGE RENTS (MONTHLY)** *Flats: studio: £350-£380; 1-bed: £425; 2-bed: £500-£550 Houses: 2-bed: £500-£550; 3-bed: £650-£700; 4-bed: £750-£1000.*

ERITH, BELVEDERE & THAMESMEAD

Roads of Victorian munition workers' terraces in industrial Erith, many "improved" with ugly new windows, doors or pebbledash. But this is a good hunting ground for cheap houses. A series of tower blocks dominates the town centre. Some modern blocks mixed with 1930s semis and bungalows in the anonymous areas of Northumberland Heath and Barnehurst just south of Erith. More messed-about Victorian terraces in Belvedere with some pleasant 1930s family houses in Upper Belvedere, the poshest bit of the area. Some attractive new warehouse-style developments by the river and new houses overlooking the marshes at Thamesmead North, popular partly because they're in Bexley rather than Greenwich which has higher council tax (see Greenwich for Thamesmead prices). **ATTRACTS** *First-time buyers; families wanting new or cheap houses; members of the Asian community (Belvedere)* • **CONSERVATION AREAS** *Erith Riverside; Woolwich Road, Belvedere; Crossness Pumping Station, Thamesmead* • **AVERAGE PRICES** *Flats: studio: £40,000; 1-bed: £40,000-£50,000; 2-bed: £50,000-£60,000 Houses: 1-bed: £45,000-£50,000; 2-bed: £50,000-£70,000; 3-bed: £55,000-£120,000; 4-bed: £110,000-£140,000* • **AVERAGE RENTS (MONTHLY)** *Flats: studio: £325; 1-bed: £350-£375; 2-bed: £400-£450 Houses: 1-bed: £375; 2-bed: £450-£500; 3-bed: £550; 4-bed: £600-£750.*

BEST POSTCODES

Only a small section of the north of the borough has London postcodes with Abbey Wood SE2 and Thamesmead SE28 ranking as among the least smart postcodes in the whole of London. Postcodes are almost irrelevant elsewhere as London codes give way to Kent.

AMENITIES

SCHOOLS★★★★

Several excellent, league-topping selective state secondary schools with hot competition for places, not least from middle class parents in the neighbouring inner London boroughs of Lewisham and Greenwich where state schools are poor. No private secondary schools. Both primary and secondary schools perform well overall in national league tables without being stunning. A good selection of pre-school provision, both state and private.

PRE-SCHOOL PROVISION *39 nursery classes attached to state and church primary and infant schools; 1 state nursery; 1 nursery class in a grant-maintained school; 73 private and voluntary day nurseries and playgroups. Proportion of under-fives in state nursery schools: 60%* • **STATE PRIMARY SCHOOLS** *Overall league table position: 65th out of 150. Top scorers: St Fidelis RC, Erith; Our Lady of the Rosary (with nursery unit) Sidcup; St Paulinus C of E, Crayford* • **STATE SECONDARY SCHOOLS** *Overall league table position: 42nd out of 150. Top scorers (all selective): Townley Grammar (girls), Bexleyheath; Chislehurst and Sidcup Grammar (mixed), Sidcup; Bexley Grammar (mixed), Welling* • **PRIVATE PREP SCHOOL** *Harenc School (boys), Sidcup.*

TRANSPORT★★

Only trains throughout the borough with provision particularly poor in Thamesmead where there's no station nearer than Abbey Wood. Stations fairly evenly spread throughout the borough but services slacken off outside rush hours and buses are a better bet for short journeys.

TRAINS *Sidcup: Zone 5. Cost of annual season ticket: £1280; No of trains per hour: to London Bridge 4; to Charing Cross 2; Fastest journey: 22 minutes. Bexley: Zone 6. Cost of annual season ticket: £1396; No of trains per hour: to London Bridge 3; to Charing Cross 1; Fastest journey:*

28 minutes. Welling: Zone 4. Cost of annual season ticket: £1068; No of trains per hour: to London Bridge 4; to Charing Cross 2; Fastest journey: 22 minutes. Erith: Zone 6. No of trains per hour: to London Bridge 6; to Charing Cross 4; Fastest journey: 35 minutes. Abbey Wood: See Greenwich ● **BUSES** *Strictly suburban services with only the daily 726 express service to Heathrow linking the area with the rest of London. Links to town improve radically at night with a choice of three night buses from Trafalgar Square – the N21 to Sidcup, the N53 to Thamesmead and the N81 to Welling and Bexleyheath* ● **TRAFFIC BLACKSPOTS** *Sidcup: Roads around the narrow, curved High Street can get jammed with cars, delivery lorries and buses. The busy A20 usually flows, if not freely then at least slowly, but traffic is constant. Bexley & Bexleyheath: Trafficky in the narrow streets of Old Bexley, particularly at the confluence of three roads at the roundabout at the top of the High Street. Bexleyheath is crossed by the main A2 to Dover which is too narrow for the pressure of traffic here* ● **PARKING** *Getting more difficult as the borough tries to discourage unofficial Park-and-Ride by commuters. There are eight controlled parking zones with residents' bays in the borough. Permits issued for one zone aren't valid in another. Bexleyheath: Around town centre. Cost of annual resident's permit: £50 a year; around the station: £20 a year; Hamilton Road and Stanhope Road (near the station): £40 a year. Elsewhere: Crayford Station; Falconwood Station; New Eltham Station; Sidcup Station; Welling Station: all £20 a year.*

LEISURE FACILITIES * * *

THEATRES & CONCERT HALLS *Well provided for. Four theatres including the Geoffrey Whitworth Theatre, Crayford; Playhouse Theatre, Erith; Edward Alderton Theatre, Bexleyheath; Old Barn Theatre and Theatre in the Road, Rose Bruford College, Sidcup with performances by students of the college. Concerts at Hall Place (see below)* ● **CINEMAS** *Currently two; the ABC at Sidcup and the new nine screen Cineworld in a 1930s wireless-style building at Bexleyheath* ● **MUSEUMS & GALLERIES** *Surprisingly interesting and varied choice including a number of gracious country houses saved from the building onslaughts of the 1920s and 1930s. The list includes Hall Place, a Tudor mansion set in formal gardens with rooms open to the public (although the grand effect from the front is slightly spoilt by its position on a busy main road); Lesnes Abbey, the remains of a 12th-century Abbey in quiet gardens framed by woods; the Red House built in 1860 for William Morris, the designer and writer, containing some of the original furnishings. Also local history musuem at Erith housed in listed library building* ● **SPORTS FACILITIES** *Good choice. Two sports centres, including fitness centres, at Erith and Bexleyheath, and three swimming pools at Bexleyheath, Erith and Sidcup. Discount card system in operation. Also watersports centre in the beautiful setting of Danson Park with sailing, canoeing and windsurfing, and tennis, golf, football and cricket at Danson Park and other parks throughout the borough* ● **LIBRARIES** *Well-used and helpful. Conveniently long opening hours at the central library in Bexleyheath but truncated hours in some smaller branch libraries including all day closing on Wednesday or Thursday. No Sunday opening yet. Local history centre at Hall Place. 9.5 library visits per head. Position in library-use league table: 13th out of 32 (where 1 is best and 32 worst):*

OPEN SPACES * * * *

Excellent variety of open space from formal parks to river walks, meadows and woods with the Thames in the north of the borough. Bexley is quite hilly, with good views over neighbouring wooded hills towards Kent from various vantage points and even from Bexleyheath shopping centre. Green spaces from Thamesmead to Lesnes Abbey and Lesnes Abbey Woods are part of the 40 mile green chain walk through South East London to Crystal Palace (see Bromley).

RIVER WALKS *The Cray Riverway Walk along the River Cray from Footscray Meadows to the Thames. A quiet walk through meadow and marshland except when brutally interrupted by the A2. Also worth checking out is the riverside at Erith. Crumbling piers, freight boats and the remains of a once-thriving industrial riverside* • **WIDE OPEN SPACE** *Footscray Meadows with mature trees and views over distant hills* • **FORMAL PARKS** *Danson Park landscaped by the eighteenth century landscaper "Capability" Brown with lake, mature trees and the Danson Mansion with stable block renovated as a restaurant* • **WOODS** *Lesnes Abbey Wood. Woods as deep as any in the remote countryside. As an added bonus, paths open out on to the ruined Lesnes Abbey.*

SHOPS * *

SIDCUP *Pleasant even if there is a trafficky high street with mainly chains and local shops. Feels more like the Kent town it really is than part of London. Somerfields in the High Street; Tesco by the A20* • **BEXLEY & BEXLEYHEATH** *Self-consciously villagey shops in Old Bexley including a choice of delis and bakeries, childrens' clothes and antique shops. The centre of Bexleyheath is dominated by a pleasant pedestrianised shopping street with a large Edwardian Clocktower and the Broadway indoor shopping centre. Good if predictable choice of clothes and other chains including a large M&S. But there are plans to expand the shopping centre still further to combat competition from the massive new Blue Water shopping centre near Dartford. Asda at Bexleyheath* • **WELLING** *Undistinguished High Street. Roads off the High Street are lined with chains and local shops – many are cheap or discount shops selling second-hand furniture or hardware. Co-op superstore* • **ERITH** *A sad concrete 1960s shopping centre with a horrible multi-storey car-park above. The High Street is due to be pedestrianised which might improve things slightly but it won't change the small cheap shops and chains. The Town Square is enlivened a bit by a twice-weekly clothes and food market. Large William Morrison superstore recently built on former industrial riverside site* • **THAMESMEAD** *New shopping centre built in answer to complaints that there were no shops nearer than Woolwich. Handsome new Safeway but otherwise small unremarkable shops.*

RESTAURANTS *

Generally a bit of a culinary desert. Old Bexley has a couple of brasseries and tavernas. Elsewhere it's the usual choice of variable High Street Indian, Chinese, take-aways and other local restaurants.

CRIME RATES * * * * *

79 crimes per 1000 of the population. Position in Metropolitan Police league table: 29th out of 32 (where 1 is worst and 32 best).

THE COUNCIL * * *

POLITICAL AFFILIATION *No overall control* • **MINUS POINTS** *Has been upbraided by residents for not repairing roads and pavements quickly enough* • **PLUS POINTS** *Good schools. One of the most efficient boroughs in London at turning round property searches quickly. Fortnightly door-to-door recycling collections and a scheme for recycling householders' garden compost* • **PROPERTY SEARCHES CARRIED OUT IN 10 WORKING DAYS** *99.9%* • **STANDARD SEARCH FEE** *£105* • **COUNCIL TAX COLLECTED** *96.2%*

● **COUNCIL TAX 1998-99**

BAND	PROPERTY VALUE	CHARGE	BAND	PROPERTY VALUE	CHARGE
A	up to £40,000	£463.47	E	£88,001-£120,000	£849.68
B	£40,001-£52,000	£540.71	F	£120,001-£160,000	£1,004.18
C	£52,001-£68,000	£617.96	G	£160,001-£320,000	£1,158.67
D	£68,001-£88,000	£695.20	H	over £320,000	£1,390.40

BRENT

Brent is a bit schizophrenic. It's technically outer London but its eastern half is as inner city as anywhere, a melting pot of races living in a jumble of Victorian terraces and council blocks criss-crossed by tube and train tracks and busy, polluted roads. By contrast, its western half is suburban, mostly unsmart but mostly respectable.

In the 1980s Brent had the dubious distinction of being the only "loony left" outer London borough, with high council tax and adminstrative and political chaos much more characteristic of the uncontrolled inner city than polite suburbia. The borough's wild reputation put off many who might otherwise have moved there and until recently, it was often a last resort for people who couldn't afford smarter areas like Notting Hill, Maida Vale or West Hampstead or even the better suburbs of Barnet or Harrow. Now council tax has fallen even though it's still struggling financially. The council's not perfect but getting better and more people are discovering that there are plentiful stocks of solid Victorian property to buy or rent. The area is reasonably central and transport to town is quick.

Brent starts in the east with the Victorian terraces of Kilburn, long colonised by the Irish and more recently by West Indians. (The borough is one of the most multiracial with nearly half the population from an ethnic minority. There are large Indian and Jewish communities as well as Irish and Afro-Caribbeans). To the west are the larger Victorian houses of Brondesbury and Willesden Green before the miles of red suburban roofs of Neasden and Dollis Hill take over to the north and west. Beyond the North Circular lies Wembley, with its large and colourful Indian community, and the council blocks of Stonebridge. On the hills beyond Neasden is the respectable 1930s suburb of Kingsbury.

The borough is nowhere near as poor as many other inner London boroughs but is on the cusp between inner city and suburb, coming near the top of the deprivation leagues for outer London. Unemployment is the second highest in outer London at 8% and it's the 29th most deprived area in England. There's widespread joblessness and poor housing, particularly in Harlesden in the south. However large sums of public and private money are being spent on training and job creation as well as environmental improvements and crime reduction in busy shopping areas like Kilburn High Road.

One of the chief beneficiaries of regeneration funds will be Wembley, whose drab High Road and graffiti-covered stations are set to benefit from the building of a new £200 million national sports stadium and the upgrading of surrounding areas with shops, leisure facilities and better parking. Residents whose lives are regularly disrupted by up to 80,000 visitors arriving for events (and trying to park) are desperate to see improvements.

PROPERTY AND ARCHITECTURE

KILBURN & QUEENS PARK

Roads of small late Victorian terraces predominate around Willesden Lane cemetery with larger three- and four-storey Victorian houses around Queens Park to the west and up towards Brondesbury Park in the north. Lots of conversion flats which give you more space for your money than anywhere nearer Hampstead, cheaper parking and an entree into one of London's up and coming areas. (For West Kilburn, see Westminster).
ATTRACTS *First-time buyers; young professionals; people who can't afford West Hampstead or North Kensington; families; people moving from Maida Vale or Ladbroke Grove to get more space for their money* •
CONSERVATION AREAS *Queens Park; Paddington Cemetery; North Kilburn; Kilburn* • **AVERAGE PRICES** *Flats: studio: £65,000-£80,000; 1-bed: £75,000-£100,000; 2-bed: £90,000-£120,000; 3-bed: £120,000-£190,000 Houses: 3-bed: £160,000-£300,000; 4-bed: £200,000-£340,000; 5-bed: £500,000+* • **AVERAGE RENTS (MONTHLY)** *Flats: studio: £650-£900; 1-bed: £750-£1200; 2-bed: £900+; 3-bed: £1200+ Houses: 3-bed: £1200+; 4-bed: £1300+; 5-bed: £1500+.*

BRONDESBURY & WILLESDEN GREEN

Has benefited hugely from buyers rippling west from West Hampstead and is now the most expensive part of Brent. Large red brick Victorian terraces in tree-lined roads, many converted into flats although there are still some single houses. Some of the most sought-after properties are in the Mapesbury Conservation area north of Willesden Lane, where the large houses make handsome conversions. The large houses around Aylestan and Milverton Avenues are popular with diplomats whose countries can't afford St. John's Wood. Incongruous among the modern apartment blocks and interwar semis and detached houses in Willesden Lane is the Shree Swaminavaga Temple, sprouting cupolas, minarets, domes and trellises.
ATTRACTS *First-time buyers; flat-hunters; people who can't afford West Hampstead or Maida Vale; families* • **CONSERVATION AREAS** *Mapesbury; Willesden; Brondesbury* • **AVERAGE PRICES** *Flats: 1-bed: £105,000-£115,000; 2-bed: £120,000-£170,000 Houses: 4-bed: £300,000+; 5-bed: £400,000+* • **AVERAGE RENTS (MONTHLY)** *Flats: studio: £560;*

1-bed: £700+; 2-bed: £900+; 3-bed: £1300+ Houses: 3-bed: £1300+;
4-bed: £1600+; 5-bed: £2000+.

WILLESDEN & CRICKLEWOOD

Less exalted than Brondesbury but still solid. Cricklewood suffers from
being a bit "in between" with residents keen to label the area Hampstead
Borders or Brondesbury. It's also carved up with railway lines and the busy
A5 main through-road. But it has a mix of most types of property from
Victorian terraces and villas to 1930s semis and flats in modern blocks.
A good hunting area for Victorian conversion flats. Small Victorian terraces
around Willesden itself.

ATTRACTS *First-time buyers; professional couples and families who can't
afford West Hampstead* • **CONSERVATION AREAS** *None* • **AVERAGE PRICES**
*Flats: studio: £50,000-£60,000; 1-bed: £55,000-£70,000; 2-bed:
£70,000-£100,000; 3-bed: £80,000-£100,000 Houses: 3-bed:
£150,000; 4-bed: £160,000-£190,000; 5-bed: £170,000+* • **AVERAGE
RENTS (MONTHLY)** *Flats: studio: £500+; 1-bed: £600-£650; 2-bed:
£700-£780; 3-bed: £1100 Houses: 2-bed: £900; 3-bed: £1300+;
4-bed: £1300-£1400; 5-bed: £1450+.*

NEASDEN & DOLLIS HILL

Neasden's been the butt of more scornful metropolitan jokes than almost
any other part of London. Yes, it's suburban and not very exciting, although
it does have some good views to relieve the monotony and the largest
Hindu temple outside India, carved in marble by local residents. Mainly
1930s semis with few conversions. More up-market Dollis Hill also has
good views and enclaves of Edwardian property around Gladstone Park
as well as 1930s semis and modern blocks with a good choice of flats.

ATTRACTS *Families; members of the Asian community; people who can't
afford Willesden* • **CONSERVATION AREAS** *Homestead Park; Neasden
Village; St Andrews* • **AVERAGE PRICES** *Flats: studio: £40,000; 1-bed:
£55,000-£60,000; 2-bed: £75,000 Houses: 2-bed: £90,000; 3-bed:
£120,000+; 4-bed: £180,000+* • **AVERAGE RENTS (MONTHLY)** *Flats:
studio: £410-£470; 1-bed: £500-£540; 2-bed: £650 Houses: 3-bed:
£780-£1080; 4-bed: £1080-£1510.*

WEMBLEY

The largest commercial and retail area of Brent, with Wembley Stadium
to the east. A large stretch of middling 1930s semis sprawling up and
down hills, with the occasional stone lion or wrought iron gate to assert
individuality and superiority. Deep eaves, half-timbering and large curved
bays – they're all here. North Wembley is the poshest part of Wembley
with the Sudbury Court estate around East Lane and Watford Road one of
the most sought-after parts. Roads round Wembley Park station could be
worth watching – some of the tower blocks on the nearby Chalkhill estate
are being demolished and Wembley Park station and surroundings are
being upgraded as part of the national stadium improvements. Mostly
family houses, some ex-council. The few flats here tend to be in new
developments.

ATTRACTS *Families; members of the Asian and Afro-Caribbean communities*
• **CONSERVATION AREAS** *Barn Hill; Preston Park; Lawns Court; Wembley
Hill Garden Suburb* • **AVERAGE PRICES** *Flats: studio: £45,000-£50,000;
1-bed: £60,000-£70,000; 2-bed: £75,000-£90,000 Houses: 2-bed:*

£100,000+; 3-bed: £100,000-£200,000; 4-bed: £160,000-£250,000; 5-bed: £300,000-£500,000 • **AVERAGE RENTS (MONTHLY)** *Flats: studio: £500; 1-bed: £550-£600; 2-bed: £700 Houses: 2-bed: £700; 3-bed: £850-£900; 4-bed: £1200+; 5-bed: £2000+.*

KINGSBURY & KENTON

Parts of Kingsbury are the nearest thing Brent has to smart suburbia. Some handsome detached houses in tree-lined roads with leaded light windows and large gardens by the wonderful open space of Fryent Country Park. Elsewhere mostly fairly standard 1930s semis and some small neo-Georgian town houses on Fryent Way. Middling semis in Kenton.

ATTRACTS *Families; members of the Jewish community (Kingsbury); members of the Asian community (Kenton)* • **CONSERVATION AREAS** *Roe Green; Slough Lane; Buck Lane; Manor Close* • **AVERAGE PRICES** *Flats: studio: £50,000; 1-bed: £55,000-£60,000; 2-bed: £70,000+ Houses: 2-bed: £90,000-£100,000; 3-bed: £115,000-£125,000; 4-bed: £170,000+; 5-bed: £200,000* • **AVERAGE RENTS (MONTHLY)** *Flats: studio: £450-£500; 1-bed: £500-£600; 2-bed: £600-£700 Houses: 2-bed: £700; 3-bed: £650-£900.*

BEST POSTCODES

The part of West Hampstead NW6 which is in Brondesbury Park is undoubtedly the best postcode, appreciated by residents who can quite truthfully say they live in West Hampstead. Cricklewood NW2 (see also Barnet) is better than Willesden NW10 which includes the council estates of Harlesden.

AMENITIES

SCHOOLS★★★

Not as bad as you might expect given the borough's unfortunate image. State primary and secondary schools are far from scraping the bottom. Good level of pre-school provision for under-fours in both state and private nurseries. Two private Asian schools.

PRE-SCHOOL PROVISION *90 private and voluntary nurseries; 4 state nursery schools; 50 state primary, church and Jewish schools with nursery places. Proportion of under-fives in state nurseries: 72%* • **STATE PRIMARY SCHOOLS** *Overall position in league table: 70th out of 150. Top scorers: North West London Jewish Day School (with nursery unit), Willesden; Leopold School (with nursery unit), Willesden; Michael Sobell Sinai, Harrow* • **STATE SECONDARY SCHOOLS** *Overall position in league table: 65th out of 150. Best scorers: Preston Manor (mixed), Wembley; Convent of Jesus and Mary Language College (girls, mixed in sixth) Harlesden; Claremont High (mixed), Kenton* • **PRIVATE SCHOOLS** *Swaminarayan (mixed from 2); Islamia Girls High (from 11).*

TRANSPORT★★★★

An even spread of tubes and trains throughout the borough. Brent has long stretches of the generally efficient Jubilee and Bakerloo lines for quick journeys to the centre of town and Wembley is particularly well served by both tubes and trains.

TRAINS Brondesbury: *Zone 2. Cost of annual season ticket: £704. No of trains per hour: North London line 3.* Willesden Junction: *No of trains per hour: to Euston 3; North London line 3; to Clapham Junction 2; Fastest journey: to Euston 16 minutes.* Wembley Stadium: *Zone 4. Cost of annual season ticket: £1068. No of trains per hour: to Marylebone 2; Fastest journey: 11 minutes* • **TUBES** Kilburn: *Zone 2. Frequency: Jubilee line to Charing Cross every 3-5 minutes; Fastest journey: 19 minutes.* Willesden Junction: *Zone 2. Frequency: Bakerloo to Oxford Circus every 5 to 10 minutes; Fastest journey: 24 minutes.* Wembley Park: *Zone 4. Frequency: Jubilee line to Charing Cross every 5 minutes; Fastest journey: 27 minutes* • **BUSES** *A good choice to town although journeys can be slow, particularly at rush hour along the borough's many main roads. Services include the 6 to Piccadilly Circus via Willesden and Queen's Park, the 16 via Kilburn High Road and Brondesbury to Victoria, the 18 via Wembley and Harlesden to Euston and the 52 from Willesden to Victoria* • **TRAFFIC BLACKSPOTS** Kilburn: *The High Road. Traffic clogged, blocked with delivery vans, buses and people trying to do U turns in a road that's too narrow.* Neasden: *The horrible spaghetti junction of dual carriageways around the North circular is always busy, which begs the urgent question of why the borough has seen fit to put its local history museum in the middle of one of the largest roundabouts on this road system.* Harrow Road: *Particularly bad (and that's saying something) round the junctions with the North Circular Road* • **PARKING** *Until last year Brent was one of only two London boroughs not charging for residents' parking permits unless they have more than one car. The cost of parking a second car was £26. But as part of the council's efforts to curb car use, you'll now have to pay £50 when you move into the borough or renew your permit. From January 2000 a second car will cost £100 and a third £150. Currently there are controlled parking zones in the centre of Wembley, Harlesden and around the Hindu temple in Neasden but there are plans for new zones in Kilburn and Willesden and around Kingsbury Station to discourage commuter parking and protect residents from cross border sorties by motorists trying to avoid paying heavily to park in more expensive Westminster or Camden.*

LEISURE FACILITIES * * *

THEATRES & CONCERT HALLS *One repertory theatre, the Tricycle in Kilburn High Road, which has recovered from a devastating fire 10 years ago and filled a large gap in provision of theatres in this part of north-west London. New and off-the-wall plays (often exploring multiracial themes) and theatre for children in a clean modern building (look up at the ceiling in the entrance hall to see the intriguing moving arrangement of tricycle wheels and chains), a complete contrast to the grubby Kilburn High Road. Live music at Wembley Arena and at the Mean Fiddler in Harlesden. Classical concerts at the Stables Gallery and Arts Centre, Dollis Hill* • **CINEMAS** *The Tricycle cinema specialises in art films although it's been struggling to raise enough cash for a new 250 seat cinema and visual arts studio. More mainstream films at Willesden Green Belle Vue, part of a recently-built complex with café, bookshop and the borough's flagship library around a spacious atrium. A new mulitplex cinema is being planned for Wembley* • **MUSEUMS & GALLERIES** *Not a huge choice. The Stables Gallery and Arts Centre at Dollis Hill has exhibitions of paintings, sculpture and pottery. Local history at the Grange Museum of Community History, (the one marooned on a traffic roundabout). Tours of Wembley Stadium at Wembley* • **SPORTS FACILITIES** *Three sports centres at Wembley, Willesden and Kilburn.*

All have recently been refurbished and the council has put in a bid for lottery funds to revamp tired changing rooms at Wembley. All have fitness suites and pools. Sailing at the Welsh Harp Reservoir (see also Barnet). Athletics stadium at Willesden Green. International football (watching not playing) at Wembley Stadium. Tennis courts and other sports in parks across the borough • **LIBRARIES** *Average use, although Willesden Green in particular deserves better because it's spacious and well-equipped. Reasonable opening hours with some long evenings and all branch libraries have accessible hours. Many libraries are closed on Wednesdays. 7.7 library visits per head. Position in library-use league table: 15th out of 32 (where 1 is best and 32 worst).*

OPEN SPACES * * *

Brent doesn't have great swathes of green belt land but it's well-endowed with green space particularly in the north, as well as a section of the Grand Union Canal (although this flows almost unremittingly through dreary warehouses and industrial parks). Parks in the south tend to be small and a bit municipal although Queens Park is popular with local residents. **WIDE OPEN SPACES** *Fryent Country Park. A wonderful surprise in the midst of suburbia with rolling fields, framed by wooded hills in the distance. It's rural enough for the locals to harvest hay here in summer •* **RIVERS & WATER** *The Welsh Harp Reservoir and surrounding open space. The reservoir was formed in 1835 from damning the river Brent to provide a source for the Grand Union canal and it's now a sailing and wildlife haven. The rural effect of the water itself is marred by the gantries of the North Circular Road visible in the distance but it doesn't take long to lose yourself in the grass and woodland around.*

SHOPS * * *

KILBURN & HARLESDEN *Kilburn High Road has the same collection of chains, cheap high fashion clothes shops, discount stores, electrical goods, whole-salers and ethnic supermarkets as many inner London high streets. A number of boarded-up shops. Afro hairdressers and Jamaican and Irish newspapers displayed prominently are reminders of the area's multiracial makeup as is the shop devoted to Our Lady of Fatima complete with kitsch statues of Jesus and Mary in the window. Sainsbury's. Mostly local shops in Harlesden with big Afro-Caribbean influence (bakers, hairdressers and supermarkets)*
• WILLESDEN & BRONDESBURY *Mostly local shops, wholesalers and Halal butchers in Willesden High Road, another of London's Victorian shopping streets turned into a traffic jam. But cleaner and more litter-free than Kilburn High Road. Suffers from being within easy reach of Brent Cross (see Barnet)*
• NEASDEN *Dreary parades of small shops around Neasden Lane and Blackbird Hill. Large Tesco at Brent Park •* **WEMBLEY** *The borough's main shopping centre, set for a badly needed face-lift as part of the revamp of Wembley Stadium and surroundings. Currently the High Road has medium-size cheap chain stores and a handful of depressing shops in a 1960s outdoor shopping precinct near Wembley Central Station. There are plans to redevelop this area with a cinema and "other leisure facilities". Ealing Road just off the High Road is by contrast a riot of colour and interest, with Indian sari and wedding shops, jewellers, Asian supermarkets and sweet-shops selling delectable sweets and cakes full of coconut and nuts. Sainsbury's in the High Road •* **KINGSBURY** *Busy roads around the roundabout at Kingsbury Circus lined with half-timbered and brick 1930s parades. Lots of discount and charity shops, halal butchers and an Aldi superstore.*

RESTAURANTS ✱ ✱ ✱

KILBURN, WILLESDEN & HARLESDEN *A couple of good Indian restaurants and a recommended Japanese and Spanish restaurant in Willesden. Thai restaurant in Harlesden* • **WEMBLEY** *The place to go in Brent for a good choice of Indian restaurants* • **ELSEWHERE** *Nothing of note. Huge range of ethnic restaurants of varying quality.*

CRIME RATES ✱ ✱ ✱

113 crimes per 1000 of population. Position in Metropolitan Police league table: 18th out of 32 (where 1 is worst and 32 best).

THE COUNCIL ✱ ✱ ✱

POLITICAL AFFILIATION *Labour* • **MINUS POINTS** *Often sloppy at street-sweeping and litter collection (lots of old litter in main streets)* • **PLUS POINTS** *Trying to extricate itself from the adminstrative and political chaos of past years. Couldn't be more efficient at turning around property searches. Council tax currently one of the lowest rather than one of the highest although it may rise sharply this coming year because of the council's financial problems. Door-to-door recycling* • **PROPERTY SEARCHES CARRIED OUT IN 10 WORKING DAYS** *100%* • **STANDARD SEARCH FEE** *£100* • **COUNCIL TAX COLLECTED** *87.6%* • **COUNCIL TAX 1998-99**

BAND	PROPERTY VALUE	CHARGE	BAND	PROPERTY VALUE	CHARGE
A	up to £40,000	£392.62	E	£88,001-£120,000	£719.81
B	£40,001-£52,000	£458.05	F	£120,001-£160,000	£850.68
C	£52,001-£68,000	£523.50	G	£160,001-£320,000	£981.55
D	£68,001-£88,000	£588.93	H	over £320,000	£1,177.86

BROMLEY

Bromley has never really wanted to be part of London. Successive local councils have made that much clear ever since they resisted pressure to re-house poor people from inner London in the 1960s and then took the Greater London Council to court in the 1980s over the GLC's attempts to cut tube fares using rate payers' money. With half its area designated as Green Belt land, Bromley's mostly affluent residents in their detached commuter belt homes prefer to think they really live in Kent rather than south-east London.

But Bromley has its fair share of Victorian suburbia as well as 1930s developments and Kentish villages. It's the largest borough in London, with Crystal Palace Park and the once fashionable Victorian villas and terraces of Anerley and Penge at its north-west tip. Detached 1930s houses with gardens start to take over further east on the outskirts of Bromley and Beckenham, giving way again to handsome Victorian houses and stockbroker-belt mock-Tudor around sought-after Chislehurst. Further south, roads of well-kept semi-detached and detached houses mixed with salubrious modern developments radiate from the stations and shopping centres of Hayes, Petts Wood and Orpington and tempting paths disappear through woods and commons to the villages of Keston and Farnborough.

Much of the borough is affluent commuterland, built up during the housing booms of the first three decades of the century. Given the daily flows of workers to town and back, it's not surprising that unemployment is low, even by outer London standards, at 3.1%. Residents are mostly white (only 5% of the borough is from an ethnic minority), middle class families, seduced by the prospect of good schools, large gardens, lots of green space and well stocked, if undramatic, shops.

But the north-west corner around Crystal Palace feels as if it belongs more to neighbouring inner city Lewisham or Lambeth than Bromley, with boarded-up and down-at-heel shops and Victorian houses which have seen better days. It's here, in Penge, Anerley and around Crystal Palace Park that £150 million is being invested by the council, central government and the private sector to regenerate town centres, provide employment and training and improve public transport.

Ambitious plans to build a £55 million leisure centre on the site of the old Crystal Palace are however being bitterly opposed by an unlikely alliance of local amenity groups and self-styled Eco warriors, who argue the proposed centre (with multiplex cinema, sports facilities and restaurant) will create huge amounts of extra traffic and congestion. The Eco warriors, many veterans of past road and building-site battles, set up camp around the Crystal Palace TV mast in April last year and so far show no sign of retreating, despite attempts by Bromley council to evict them.

PROPERTY AND ARCHITECTURE

ANERLEY & PENGE

Both areas are mainly slightly down-at-heel Victorian with some roads of terraces of varying sizes and some of Victorian cottages. Some large villas still survive in roads around Crystal Palace Park, reminders of the days when Crystal Palace was one of the wonders of London. Now they've mostly been converted into large flats. There are smaller detached and semi-detached Victorian houses mixed with 1930s houses off Lennard Road. A mixture of Edwardian and 1930s terraces and council blocks can be found around the shopping parades of Elmers End further south.
ATTRACTS *First-time buyers; people who can't afford Beckenham or Streatham; those wanting lots of space for their money* • **CONSERVATION AREAS** *Crystal Palace Park; Penge High Street; Cator Road* • **AVERAGE PRICES** *Flats: studio: £30,000-£40,000; 1-bed: £40,000-£50,000; 2-bed: £50,000-£80,000 Houses: 1-bed: £58,000-£60,000; 2-bed: £50,000-£80,000; 3-bed: £80,000-£120,000; 4-bed: £120,000+; 5-bed: £160,000+* • **AVERAGE RENTS (MONTHLY)** *Flats: studio: £350+; 1-bed: £400+; 2-bed: £500+; 3-bed: £550+ Houses: 1-bed: £650; 2-bed: £650+; 3-bed: £750+; 4-bed: £1000+; 5-bed: £1100+.*

BECKENHAM & BROMLEY

Several steps up from Anerley or Penge. Despite its current image as twentieth century suburbia par excellence Bromley was a thriving market town by the nineteenth century. So there's a lot of Victoriana in and around Bromley, particularly in Plaistow to the north (a mixture of terraces and detached family homes) and Shortlands (cottages and terraces among the 1930s semis). Shortlands was aptly once home to Enid Blyton who doubtless relished its pleasant suburban atmosphere. Elsewhere Bromley is mainly detached Edwardian and 1930s houses of all shapes and sizes with lots of fake Tudor beams, wood fronts and deep sloping roofs, well maintained with cared-for front gardens in tree-lined roads. Flats are mostly in purpose-built blocks. Beckenham is also Victorian in the middle with some large detached houses on the main Beckenham Road, now mostly flats, and roads of Victorian terraces. Its smartest area is Park Langley with roads of large detached Edwardian and 1930s homes.

ATTRACTS *Families wanting good schools and gardens; City workers wanting good transport links; some first-time buyers* • **CONSERVATION AREAS** *Beckenham St George's; Beckenham Kelsey Square; Chancery Lane; Manor Way Beckenham; Park Langley; Bromley Town Centre; Bromley Common; Shortlands; Garden Road; Durham Avenue; Garden Road; Sundridge Avenue* • **AVERAGE PRICES** *Flats: studio: £35,000-£50,000; 1-bed: £55,000-£65,000; 2-bed: £70,000-£90,000 Houses: 1-bed: £65,000-£70,000; 2-bed: £85,000-£110,000; 3-bed: £100,000-£150,000; 4-bed: £150,000-£300,000; 5-bed: £200,000-£350,000* • **AVERAGE RENTS (MONTHLY)** *Flats: studio: £400; 1-bed: £500; 2-bed: £600-£800 Houses: 1-bed: £550; 2-bed: £700-£800; 3-bed: £700-£950; 4-bed: £900-£2000; 5-bed: £1800-£2750.*

CHISLEHURST & PETTS WOOD

Some of the best parts of the borough, surrounded by commons and green space on all sides. Chislehurst is slightly grander and has more of a buzz than Petts Wood. Some large Victorian houses round Chislehurst Common, mixed with 1980s neo-Georgian "executive homes" and stockbroker mock-Tudor with leaded lights in roads around. Some pleasant estates of 1970s detached houses in Bickley to the south mixed in with 1930s half-timbered houses. The best parts of Petts Wood are east of the railway line with wide roads of detached Edwardian and 1930s homes each intentionally different from its neighbours. Flats mainly in purpose-built blocks.

ATTRACTS *Families looking for good schools (roads in Petts Wood in the Bullers Wood school catchment area are much sought after); City workers; professional couples moving out from south-east London areas like Blackheath for more space* • **CONSERVATION AREAS** *Chislehurst; The Chenies, Petts Wood; Station Square, Petts Wood; Chislehurst Road, Petts Wood* • **AVERAGE PRICES** *Flats: studio: £40,000-£50,000; 1-bed: £60,000-£85,000; 2-bed: £75,000-£110,000; 3-bed: £100,000-£125,000 Houses: 2-bed: £105,000-£140,000; 3-bed: £130,000-£200,000; 4-bed: £210,000-£400,000; 5-bed: £280,000-£600,000* • **AVERAGE RENTS (MONTHLY)** *Flats: studio: £425; 1-bed: £500-£850; 2-bed: £650-£850 Houses: 1-bed: £550; 2-bed: £700-£850; 3-bed: £750-£1000; 4-bed: £1000-£2250; 5-bed: £1800-£2750.*

ORPINGTON & ST PAUL'S CRAY

More detached houses around Orpington with some of the best in roads off Crofton Road. Some roads of smaller Victorian terraces and cottage-style houses in roads off the main shopping streets around the old priory, now the local museum and library. A lot of St Paul's Cray is ex-council bought by tenants under the Right-to-Buy scheme and now back on the market but there are bargains to be had. Local advice is to stay well north of the railway line and west of the A224.

ATTRACTS Families wanting to get children into sought-after schools (Orpington); first-time buyers (St. Paul's Cray) • **CONSERVATION AREAS** Broomhill; Orpington Priory; St Paul's Cray; St Mary Cray • **AVERAGE PRICES** Flats: 1-bed: £45,000; 2-bed: £55,000-£60,000 Houses: 1-bed: £58,000; 2-bed: £70,000; 3-bed: £85,000-£130,000; 4-bed: £170,000-£220,000; 5-bed: £250,000-£300,000 • **AVERAGE RENTS (MONTHLY)** Flats: 1-bed: £500; 2-bed: £600; 3-bed: £700 Houses: 1-bed: £550; 2-bed: £650; 3-bed: £800; 4-bed: £1100+; 5-bed: £1800+.

WEST WICKHAM & HAYES

A step up from Beckenham or Bromley. More roads of large early twentieth century detached and semi-detached houses built as London spilled out into the fields of Kent round the new commuter stations. Every style known to builders from mock-Tudor to brick and some satisfyingly crunchy gravel drives. Some of the best roads are near the wooded Hayes Common in Hayes and Spring Park in West Wickham. Flats are mostly in purpose-built blocks.

ATTRACTS Families wanting to be near good schools; professionals; people moving out from south-east London • **CONSERVATION AREAS** Hayes Village; Nash • **AVERAGE PRICES** Flats: 1-bed: £60,000-£65,000; 2-bed: £80,000-£140,000; 3-bed: £100,000+ Houses: 2-bed: £80,000-£135,000; 3-bed: £120,000-£220,000; 4-bed: £140,000-£350,000; 5-bed: £250,000+ • **AVERAGE RENTS (MONTHLY)** Flats: 2-bed: £550-£600 Houses: 2-bed: £700; 3-bed: £750-£1000; 4-bed: £1000+; 5-bed: £1400+.

KESTON & FARNBOROUGH

These Kentish villages feel as if they've been included in London by mistake. Keston is surrounded on three sides by wooded commons (one of the most attractive features of the area) and centres on a pub and village green, overlooked by some attractive and well-maintained Victorian semi-detached cottages. A mixture of everything from Victorian to modern in other roads. Few flats. Farnborough is more suburban, with mostly 1930s semis and detached to the north but with lovely open fields to the south. The biggest houses (detached 1930s) are in the private estates of Keston Park and Farnborough Park. Again, few flats.

ATTRACTS Families; City workers • **CONSERVATION AREAS** Keston Park; Keston Village; Farnborough Village; Farnborough Park • **AVERAGE PRICES** Flats: 2-bed: £80,000 Houses: 3-bed: £150,000-£250,000; 4-bed: £400,000+; 5-bed: £550,000-£1.5 million • **AVERAGE RENTS (MONTHLY)** Flats: 2-bed: £550-£600 Houses: 2-bed: £700; 3-bed: £750+; 4-bed: £1100-£3000; 5-bed: £1500+.

BEST POSTCODES

Not a major issue. Most of the borough has out-of-London postcodes with only the not-very-smart postcodes of Upper Norwood SE19 and Anerley SE20 in London. The borough boundary is more important, as people are prepared to pay thousands of pounds more for the privilege of living in low-cost, efficient Bromley rather than in Lewisham, Lambeth or Southwark, where schools are poor and council tax higher.

AMENITIES

SCHOOLS * * * *

State schools' performance is excellent in league tables and they are widely praised by parents. They are coveted by the less fortunate in neighbouring boroughs and almost all heavily over-subscribed, particularly at secondary level. In true Tory spirit, all but one of the borough's secondary schools is grant-maintained. Two, Newstead Woods and St Olave's, are selective. Some other schools have also been reserving up to 25% of their places for the children who do best in academic tests but under pressure from parents, this looks set to stop by next year. Little state provision for children under-four so expect to pay for pre-school. A good selection of private prep and secondary schools.

PRE-SCHOOL PROVISION *9 primary schools with part-time nursery classes, 146 private day nurseries and playgroups; 6 independent schools with nursery units. Proportion of under-fives in state nurseries: 35%* • **STATE PRIMARY SCHOOLS** *Overall league table position: 15th out of 150. Top scorers: St Mary's RC, Beckenham; Farnborough, Orpington; St Mark's C of E, Bromley* • **STATE SECONDARY SCHOOLS** *Overall league table position: 9th out of 149. Top scorers: Newstead Woods (girls), Orpington; St Olave's and St. Saviour's (boys), Orpington; Bullers Wood (girls), Chislehurst (operates tight catchment area)* • **PRIVATE PREP SCHOOLS** *Bishop Challoner (mixed to 18), Shortlands; Eden Park (mixed), Elmers End; Elmhurst Prep (mixed) Beckenham; Greenhayes (boys), West Wickham; St Christopher's, (mixed) Beckenham; St David's College (mixed), West Wickham; Ashgrove (mixed), Bromley; Baston (girls to 18), Hayes; Bickley Park Prep (boys), Bickley; Braeside Prep (mixed), Bromley; Holy Trinity Convent Prep (mixed to 5, girls to 11), Bromley; Babington House (boys to 6, girls to 16), Chislehurst; Eltham College Junior (boys), Mottingham; Faringtons and Stratford House (girls to 18), Chislehurst* • **PRIVATE SECONDARY SCHOOLS** *Chart-toppers Bromley High (girls), Bromley; Eltham College (boys, girls in 6th), Mottingham; Holy Trinity College (girls), Bromley.*

TRANSPORT * * *

Trains only throughout the borough. Stations are fairly evenly spread out but commuter services to the east, particular to Orpington, which is on two different lines, are the most frequent.

TRAINS *Anerley: Zone 4. Cost of annual season ticket: £1068; No of trains per hour: to London Bridge 2; Fastest journey: 21 minutes. Beckenham Junction: Zone 4. No of trains per hour: to London Bridge 1; to Victoria 3; Fastest journey: to London Bridge 30 minutes; to Victoria 20 minutes. Bromley South: Zone 5. Cost of annual season ticket: £1280; No of trains per hour: to Victoria 8; Fastest journey: 17 minutes. Chislehurst:*

Zone 5. No of trains per hour: to London Bridge 3; to Charing Cross 1; Fastest journey: to London Bridge 20 minutes; to Charing Cross 28 minutes. Petts Wood: Zone 5. No of trains per hour: to London Bridge 3; to Charing Cross 1; Fastest journey: to London Bridge 23 minutes; to Charing Cross 30 minutes. Hayes: Zone 5. No of trains per hour: to London Bridge 2; to Charing Cross 2; Fastest journey: to London Bridge 33 minutes; to Charing Cross 41 minutes • **BUSES** Quite a lot of them – especially in Bromley and Crystal Palace but they're almost all suburban with few going anywhere more central than Lewisham. The exception is the 176 from Penge to Oxford Circus. Only at night can you get back from town directly by bus. Night buses include the N3 to Crystal Palace and Penge from Trafalgar Square; the N21 to Chislehurst from Trafalgar Square and the N47 from Victoria to Orpington via Petts Wood and Farnborough • **TRAFFIC BLACKSPOTS** Crystal Palace: Four roads converge at the end of Crystal Palace Parade by the Park with uncontrolled zebra crossings on each road. Long tail-backs frequent on Westow Hill, Crystal Palace Parade and Anerley Hill. Bromley: Busy around the entrances to car-parks and roads around the Glades shopping centre where several main roads converge. Chislehurst: Trafficky in roads around the common and around the main shopping areas particularly on Saturdays with long queues to get into Sainsbury's car-park. Orpington: The High Street is often busy and traffic can build up around the mini roundabout near the bottom of the street • **PARKING** Not too bad in most parts of the borough because of wide roads and lots of space, although it can get sticky around Crystal Palace and in shopping centres on Saturdays. Currently only one controlled parking zone, in Bromley itself. Three zones: inner around the main shopping centre (cost of annual permit: £30); north and south (cost of annual resident's permit: £15).

LEISURE FACILITIES***

THEATRES & CONCERT HALLS A good selection. The Churchill Theatre in Bromley town centre has an eclectic choice of touring West End shows, dance, music and amateur theatre productions. The Studio in Beckenham has workshops (including stand-up comedy and dance), live music, comedy and theatre. Open-air concerts now with permanent stage at the Crystal Palace Bowl in Crystal Palace Park, with a mixture of nostalgic rock and pop and middle-of-the-road classical, with a back-drop of some of the best views in London • **CINEMAS** Only two, the Odeon in Bromley and the ABC in Beckenham, both showing mainstream films. There are plans for a multiplex cinema in Crystal Palace Park (but see introduction) • **MUSEUMS & GALLERIES** A small but interesting choice. The Bromley Museum in Orpington is housed in an attractive 700 year-old mullion-windowed priory next to the library with a rather thin collection of local history (although the mock-up of a 1930s breakfast room is fun). The beautiful house and gardens in Downe where Charles Darwin wrote The Origin of Species. Regular tours of Chislehurst Caves, used as an shelter by thousands of Londoners during the Blitz. The Crofton Roman villa at Orpington • **SPORTS FACILITIES** Well-resourced and used. Four leisure centres in use all year round at Beckenham (being refurbished), Orpington, Bromley and West Wickham. Also during evenings and weekends, use of school facilities at Orpington, Biggin Hill, Mottingham and Beckenham. Golf at High Elms Country Park, Farnborough and Bromley. Athletics track and sports centre at Crystal Palace Park. Indoor bowls at Orpington • **LIBRARIES** Good, particularly the central library in Bromley, housed in a spacious three-storey building overlooking *the lake in Church House Gardens. Good, long, opening hours in libraries throughout the borough although all branch libraries close either Wednesday or Thursday and there's no Sunday opening. Surprisingly only just above-average library use at 7.7 visits per head. Position in library-use league table: 16th out of 32 (where 1 is best and 32 worst).*

OPEN SPACES *****

A good variety of green space and lots of it. Almost half the borough is green-belt land. The bits that aren't have some wonderful commons and woods as well as more formal parks of all sizes, and tree-lined streets and well-looked-after gardens add their own dash of colour. The borough's conservation department offers guided walks around conservation areas taking in listed buildings.

VIEWS Crystal Palace Park. Great views over London from the Crystal Palace site above the crumbling stone terraces and lions which are all that remains of the original glass palace, burnt down in 1936. There are plans to "restore the park to its former glory" but many people prefer it as it is. Also High Elms Country Park on top of the North Downs with views over Kent • **WOODS** Hayes Common with mature oak trees, bracken undergrowth and nature trail. Petts Wood for lovely rural walks between Petts Wood and Chislehurst • **FAMILIES** The frighteningly realistic Victorian model dinosaurs on the lake at Crystal Palace. The world's first theme park. Crystal Palace Zoo and mini railway. Nature trails at High Elms Park.

SHOPS ****

PENGE & ANERLEY Run-down Victorian parades of mostly local shops at the moment but there are plans for environmental improvements to Penge High Street and the down-at-heel car-park at Blenheim Road. There are also plans to rejuvenate the rather sad street market at Maple Road. Sainsbury's in Penge High Street. Costcutter in Anerley Road • **ELMERS END & BECKENHAM** Elmers End has a series of dull Tudorbethan local shopping parades around a busy roundabout, with the usual take-aways, newsagents and hardware stores. There's a pretty raised section of High Street at Beckenham by the church with pleasant branches of all the usual chain stores further along. Big Waitrose by Beckenham Junction Station. Safeway in the High Street • **BROMLEY** Excellent variety of shopping, drawing in people from all over south-east London and Kent. The Glades shopping centre tolled the death knell for many smaller shopping centres when it opened in 1991. Its French chateau-style twin towers manage to merge skilfully (at least at the front – the back's a bit of a mess) with the pedestrianised High Street and Market Square. Lots of hanging baskets and pavement cafés help to jolly shoppers along. Good branches of all chains, including more up-market ones like Habitat, and two department stores, the Army & Navy and Allders, as well as a large M&S and several bookshops. Waitrose • **CHISLEHURST** Mostly decorative rather than useful shops in attractive Royal Parade next to the common including antiques, designer clothes, and a shop where you paint your own pots. Bank branches, a couple of chains and Sainsbury's in the high street • **PETTS WOOD & ORPINGTON** Good shopping centre at Orpington although it's overshadowed by Bromley. The main street has mostly small branches of chains but with up-market stock, mixed with a couple of second-hand bookshops and charity shops. There's a lively food and clothes market in the square of the Walnut Shopping Centre. Sainsbury's. Duller parade-style shopping at Petts Wood. Safeway.

RESTAURANTS ★ ★

The culinary desert that is outer south-east London continues, with the honourable exception of Chislehurst, now something of an oasis for restaurant-goers. Maybe not top of the critics' list but a pleasant place for a stroll. Good choice of restaurants including Indian, Italian, Pizza Express, Café Rouge and a range of pubs and brasseries.

CRIME RATES ★ ★ ★ ★

81 crimes per 1000 of population. Position in Metropolitan Police league table: 26th out of 32 (where 1 is worst and 32 best).

THE COUNCIL ★ ★ ★

POLITICAL AFFILIATION *No overall control* • **MINUS POINTS** *Poor state nursery provision for under-fours. Very competitive entry to borough schools which could leave the less academic or unorganised floundering (although this looks set to change). Slow in carrying out property searches while charging a higher fee than neighbouring boroughs* • **PLUS POINTS** *Excellent academic results in schools. Active programme of leisure and arts activities. Generally clean and tidy streets and efficient rubbish collection* • **PROPERTY SEARCHES CARRIED OUT IN 10 WORKING DAYS** *75%* • **STANDARD SEARCH FEE** £105 • **% OF COUNCIL TAX COLLECTED** *97.2%*

- **COUNCIL TAX 1998-99**

BAND	PROPERTY VALUE	CHARGE	BAND	PROPERTY VALUE	CHARGE
A	up to £40,000	£406.38	E	£88,001-£120,000	£745.03
B	£40,001-£52,000	£474.11	F	£120,001-£160,000	£880.49
C	£52,001-£68,000	£541.84	G	£160,001-£320,000	£1,015.15
D	£68,001-£88,000	£609.57	H	over £320,000	£1,219.14

CAMDEN

There's scarcely a corner of Camden which isn't up-and-coming, already trendy or seriously rich, if you believe everything you read in the press. Its blend of metropolitan sophistication, seething energy and in-your-face wealth cheek-by-jowl with poverty and deprivation have proved irresistible to London commentators. It does the borough's image no harm that it harbours large numbers of journalists, broadcasters and writers within its borders (encouraged by a council keen to attract media and communications companies away from their traditional Soho haunts), as well as scores of academics at London University.

At Camden's southern tip lie the Georgian terraces of Holborn and Bloomsbury, home of London's top lawyers and the University of London respectively. West of Bloomsbury and brash Tottenham Court Road is the small enclave of Georgian and Victorian streets known as Fitzrovia. Across the Euston Road, with the skyline dominated by the red Gothic spires of the restored St Pancras station are the shabby flat-fronted Georgian terraces of Kings Cross. The council blocks of Somers Town contrast starkly with the Nash terraces of Regent's Park and the grand Georgian terraces and Victorian crescents of west Camden Town. To the north-west are the large white stucco and multicoloured Italianate villas of Primrose Hill and Belsize Park, giving way to more modest terraces and mansion blocks at West Hampstead and Kilburn (see Brent). High on Hampstead Heath, with majestic views over London, sit Hampstead and some of the most beautiful Georgian parts of Highgate. Victoriana takes over again to the east of Hampstead Heath beyond the council blocks of Gospel Oak, with the large terraces of Kentish Town and Dartmouth Park.

Camden has some of the wealthiest people in London but it's also the 15th most deprived area in England. Unemployment is lower at 9.2% than that of any of its immediate inner London neighbours but there are still significant pockets of poverty and joblessness particularly in the areas around Kings Cross, Euston and Somers Town. Race relations have been uneasy over the past few years, creating tensions for the fifth of the population which comes from an ethnic minority, although the significant African, Afro-Caribbean, Asian and Turkish communities, along with large numbers of Jewish and Irish residents, help make Camden one of the most cosmopolitan areas of central London.

One of the biggest question marks over Camden is still the future of Kings Cross, dogged by government stop-and-go over the Channel Tunnel rail link and blighted by uncertainty. Plans to re-route traffic and create a piazza with shops, living space and offices between Kings Cross and St Pancras stations are on hold because no-one knows how much of the area will have to be dug up to accommodate the rail link and regenerate the stations. But £253 million of public and private money is still earmarked for the area over seven years (1999 is the fourth year) and is already being used to improve housing, community health, job prospects and security, with better street-lighting and CCTV.

PROPERTY AND ARCHITECTURE

HOLBORN & BLOOMSBURY

Both areas have benefited hugely from Londoners' renewed enthusiasm for central London living, encouraged by a government under pressure to stop new housebuilding on greenfield sites. Houses are rare and usually change hands by word of mouth. Flats are either in converted office blocks or in the area's characteristic flat-fronted Georgian terraces around Grays Inn Road, the British Museum and London University. Lots of ex-council property. There are also flats above shops and restaurants or in former council blocks in Covent Garden (see Westminster) as well as the ever more buzzing enclave of Fitzrovia around Charlotte Street and Fitzroy Street.

ATTRACTS *Singles wanting to be at the centre of things; young professionals* • **CONSERVATION AREAS** *Bloomsbury; Charlotte Street; Covent Garden; Kingsway* • **AVERAGE PRICES** *Flats: studio: £65,000-£75,000; 1-bed: £95,000+; 2-bed: £130,000+; 3-bed: £165,000+* • **AVERAGE RENTS**

(MONTHLY) *Flats: studio: £780-£860; 1-bed: £1170-£1300; 2-bed: £1300-£1730 Houses: 3-bed: £2810-£3030; 4-bed: £3030.*

KINGS CROSS

Traditionally known for sleazy bed and breakfast hotels, prostitution, drug-taking, pickpockets and drunks, none of which are a recommendation if you're looking for a place to live. But the council and the police claim they've stamped out much of the worst drug-taking. Some of the B & Bs in attractive Georgian terraces in streets round the station are gradually closing as tighter housing benefit rules for single people start to bite. The area has great potential if you don't mind living on the edge and not knowing exactly what the place's future is going to be. A lot of ex-council property but houses are rare (most have been converted to flats). The borough has injected £40 million into the area round Argyll Street south of the Euston Road. Developers have converted warehouses along the Regents Canal into one- and two-bedroom apartments which sell for anything up to £250,000 (technically in Islington rather than Camden but will be mentioned here).

ATTRACTS *Creative people (artists, photographers, architects and media people) who like a central location with a bit of bite; young professionals; single people* • **CONSERVATION AREA** *Kings Cross and St Pancras* • **AVERAGE PRICES** *Flats: 1-bed: £80,000-£85,000; 2-bed: £100,000-£250,000+; 3-bed: £160,000+* • **AVERAGE RENTS (MONTHLY)** *Flats: studio: £630; 1-bed: £730-£1300 (new development); 2-bed: £860-£1840 (new development).*

CAMDEN TOWN

Almost a victim of its own success as tourists start mixing with the grunge crowds and New Agers at the ever-expanding weekend market. A mixture of every type of property from smart Georgian terraces off Parkway and tucked away rus in urbe Nash villas at Park Village West and East to handsome Victorian houses in Gloucester Crescent, big semi-detached mid-Victorian houses in streets off Camden Road and Victorian flat conversions. A lot of council blocks round Mornington Crescent.

ATTRACTS *Young professionals; young singles; creative types; media people; families who can't afford or don't want to live in Hampstead* • **CONSERVATION AREAS** *Camden Town; Regents' Canal; Jeffrey's Street; Camden Square* • **AVERAGE PRICES** *Flats: studio: £80,000-£120,000; 1-bed: £90,000-£150,000; 2-bed: £120,000-£250,000; 3-bed: £165,000-£375,000 Houses: 2-bed: £200,000-£325,000; 3-bed: £280,000-£500,000; 4-bed: £350,000-£750,000; 5-bed: £450,000-£1m+* • **AVERAGE RENTS (MONTHLY)** *Flats: studio: £520-£820; 1-bed: £600-£1450; 2-bed: £1080-£1510; 3-bed: £1300-£1730 Houses: 3-bed: £1300-£2380; 4-bed: £1950-£2810; 5-bed: £2810+.*

PRIMROSE HILL & BELSIZE PARK

Lots of four- and five-storey white stucco Victorian houses in both areas although Primrose Hill's are better looked after and fewer are converted into flats. Pretty multicoloured houses around Chalcot Square in Primrose Hill, one of the area's best addresses. Last year it was threatened with the removal of its lifeline bridge over the railway to Chalk Farm Road while Railtrack upgraded main line track. The area is still facing years of disruptive night working because of the upgrading. There are flats in mansion blocks and tall red brick Victorian terraces in Primrose Gardens, Belsize Park. There is white stucco around Belsize Avenue and some attractive mews cottages tucked away off Belsize Lane.

ATTRACTS *Families; well-off couples; people who can't afford Hampstead* • **CONSERVATION AREAS** *Primrose Hill; Belsize Park; Eton* • **AVERAGE PRICES** *Flats 1-bed: £120,000-£180,000; 2-bed: £200,000-£350,000; 3-bed: £225,000-£450,000 Houses: 2-bed: £300,000-£500,000; 3-bed: £300,000-£550,000; 4-bed: £550,000-£850,000; 5-bed: £800,000-£1.75m* • **AVERAGE RENTS (MONTHLY)** *Flats 1-bed: £1080+; 2-bed: £1300+; 3-bed: £1730+ Houses: 2-bed: £1950-£2160; 3-bed: £1950+; 4-bed: £2160+.*

WEST HAMPSTEAD

Hampstead's poor cousin, on the wrong side of the Finchley Road but popular with its many supporters who argue that it's less smug and self-satisfied and friendlier than Hampstead. Others go further and say it's set to be the next Notting Hill with solid Victorian properties, good transport and shops. Streets of handsome red brick mansion blocks and houses divided into generously-sized flats and maisonettes just off the Finchley Road, some with beautiful hidden communal gardens at the back. Well-kept two- and three-storey Victorian terraces with small front gardens in roads off Fortune Green. Lots of conversion flats but beware the problem of short leases.

ATTRACTS *Families; people who can't afford Hampstead; people who've come up in the world from Kilburn; young professionals; members of the Jewish community* • **CONSERVATION AREAS** *Swiss Cottage; West End Green and Parsifal Road* • **AVERAGE PRICES** *Flats: studio: £75,000-£85,000; 1-bed: £125,000; 2-bed: £160,000-£200,000+; 3-bed: £180,000-£275,000+; 4-bed: £250,000-£400,000 Houses: 3-bed: £280,000-£400,000; 4-bed: £400,000+; 5-bed: £650,000+* • **AVERAGE RENTS (MONTHLY)** *Flats: studio: £650; 1-bed: £860; 2-bed: £1190; 3-bed: £1625; 4-bed: £1950 Houses: 3-bed: £1730+; 4-bed: £2160; 5-bed: £2600.*

HAMPSTEAD

One of the places in London where you live if you've arrived. Home of opinion-formers and chatterati of all sorts including actors, successful writers and artists, media magnates and editors as well as the seriously rich and simply well off. Active community organisations fiercely defend the village and heath from unwanted shops and developments (although they failed to halt McDonalds). There's a good mix of property, with everything from more modest Victorian terraces south of the heath, large Victorian houses converted into flats and mansion blocks overlooking the heath and Georgian cottages and houses in winding lanes near the centre of the village. Beautiful individual early nineteenth century houses in Downshire Road leading to the Heath. Just a walk away across the Heath to the east, a small but perfect slice of Highgate Village includes the Georgian red brick town houses of the Grove and the wide tree-lined roads of the half-timbered Edwardian Holly Lodge estate (see Haringey for the rest of Highgate).

ATTRACTS *The creative and those who like to think they're creative; wealthy families; wealthy first-time buyers; Americans; members of the Jewish community* • **CONSERVATION AREAS** *Hampstead Village; Fitzjohns and*

Netherhall; Redington and Frognal; South Hill Park; Mansfield; Holly Lodge Estate; Highgate Village • **AVERAGE PRICES** *Flats: studio: £80,000-£120,000; 1-bed: £100,000-£180,000; 2-bed: £150,000-£300,000; 3-bed: £250,000-£500,000; 4-bed: £350,000+ Houses: 2-bed: £275,000-£400,000; 3-bed: £375,000-£750,000; 4-bed: £550,000-£1m; 5-bed: £750,000-£1.5m* • **AVERAGE RENTS (MONTHLY)** *Flats: studio: £860; 1-bed: £1120-£1300; 2-bed: £1300-£1730; 3-bed: £1950 Houses: 3-bed: £2380-£2600; 4-bed: £3460-£4330; 5-bed: £5200.*

KENTISH TOWN & DARTMOUTH PARK

More poor relations of Hampstead (but then, where isn't?). Kentish Town has a slightly more raffish feel than Dartmouth Park, with main roads lined with once handsome early Victorian terraces now crumbling. Much more gentrified in roads off the main road with well looked after, carefully restored two- and three-storey terraces in roads off Fortess Road. Mostly grim council estates with tower blocks in Gospel Oak, west of Kentish Town Road (although the council is set to spend £6 million regenerating and possibly demolishing some of the worst examples). But even here there are some surprises with small, pretty, flat-fronted and bay window Victorian terraces in roads by Gospel Oak Station. Dartmouth Park is an enclave of mostly well looked after large three- and four-storey Victorian terraces with tidy gardens. **ATTRACTS** *Families wanting good schools (some good peformers nearby); people who can't afford Hampstead or Highgate* • **CONSERVATION AREAS** *Dartmouth Park; Kentish Town; Kelly Street* • **AVERAGE PRICES** *Flats: studio: £65,000-£75,000; 1-bed: £115,000-£130,00; 2-bed: £135,000-£160,000; 3-bed: £170,000-£220,000 Houses: 2-bed: £180,000-£200,000; 3-bed: £250,000-£300,000; 4-bed: £325,000-£425,000; 5-bed: £350,000-£600,000* • **AVERAGE RENTS (MONTHLY)** *Flats: studio: £600; 1-bed: £820; 2-bed: £950+; 3-bed: £1120 Houses: 4-bed: £2169-£2380; 5-bed: £2600-£2810.*

BEST POSTCODES

Hampstead NW3 is one of the prime postcodes of London, let alone Camden and people are prepared to pay significantly more for the coveted code. Elsewhere areas are so mixed that it's difficult to rank codes. Parts of Camden Town NW1 are smart but the code also includes the council blocks of Kings Cross and Somers Town. Similarly, Kentish Town NW5 is slightly better than West Hampstead NW6 because it includes Dartmouth Park but it also includes the council blocks of Gospel Oak.

AMENITIES

SCHOOLS★★★★

Camden seems to have achieved what few other inner London boroughs have managed – schools which attract middle class parents rather than sending them fleeing to the nearest outer London borough in search of a decent education for their children. Good overall results, particularly at secondary level and some sought-after state schools including the upfront Camden School for Girls, which has spawned writers, MPs and journalists. A good selection of private prep and secondary schools as well as private nurseries. Expect to have to pay for nursery schools for under-fours as provision is below average.

PRE-SCHOOL PROVISION *112 private or voluntary nurseries and playgroups; 5 state nursery schools; 39 nursery classes in state primary and church schools. Proportion of under-fives in state nurseries: 49%* • **STATE PRIMARY SCHOOLS** *Overall place in league tables: 80th out of 150. Top scorers: St Paul's C of E, Hampstead; New End, Hampstead; Christ Church C of E (Redhill Street) (with nursery unit), Camden* • **STATE SECONDARY SCHOOLS** *Overall place in league tables: 54th out of 150. High scorers: Jews Free School (mixed), Camden Town; La Sainte Union RC (girls), Dartmouth Park; Camden School for Girls, Camden Town* • **PRIVATE PREP SCHOOLS** *Devonshire House (mixed), Hampstead; The Hall (boys), Hampstead; Hereward House (boys), Hampstead; Lyndhurst House (boys), Hampstead; St Anthony's, (boys), Hampstead; St Christopher's (girls), Belsize Park; St Margaret's (girls to 16), Hampstead; St Mary's (mixed) Hampstead; Sarum Hall (mixed), Hampstead; University College Junior (boys), Hampstead* • **PRIVATE SECONDARY SCHOOLS** *Chart-toppers South Hampstead High (girls from 4), Hampstead and University College School (boys) Hampstead; also North Bridge House (mixed), Camden Town; St Margarets (girls), Hampstead; The Royal School (girls) Hampstead.*

TRANSPORT * * * * *

Excellent connections to all parts of London, particularly in the south of the borough. Plentiful tubes, trains and buses.

TRAINS *Gospel Oak: Zone 2. Cost of annual season ticket: £704. No of trains per hour: North London line 3. West Hampstead: No of trains per hour: Thameslink to Kings Cross 4; North London line 3; Fastest journey (Thameslink): 9-11 minutes. Kentish Town: No of trains per hour: Thameslink to Kings Cross 4; Fastest journey: 7 minutes* • **TUBES** *Central locations Zone 1. Cost of annual season ticket: £572. Holborn: Central and Piccadilly; Russell Square: Piccadilly; Euston Square: Metropolitan, Circle; Warren Street: Northern, Victoria; Kings Cross: Victoria, Northern, Circle, Metropolitan, Hammersmith and City. Camden Town: Zone 2. Cost of annual season ticket: £704; Frequency: Northern line to Charing Cross every 3-4 minutes; to London Bridge every 4-5 minutes; Fastest journey: to Charing Cross 10 minutes; to London Bridge 15 minutes Kentish Town: Zone 2. Frequency: Northern line to Charing Cross every 10-14 minutes; to London Bridge every 6-8 minutes; Fastest journey: to Charing Cross 14 minutes; to London Bridge 19 minutes. Hampstead: Zone 2. Frequency: Northern Line to Charing Cross every 6-7 minutes; to London Bridge every 6-7 minutes; Fastest journey: to Charing Cross 18 minutes; to London Bridge 22 minutes. West Hampstead: Zone 2. Frequency: Jubilee to Charing Cross every 3-4 minutes; Fastest journey: 16 minutes* • **BUSES** *Lots of buses into town and out to the suburbs with the biggest choice round Camden Town and Mornington Crescent. Services include the 24 from Hampstead to Pimlico via Camden Town; the 13 to Oxford Circus via Finchley Road and Swiss Cottage; the 113 to Oxford Circus via Finchley Road and Swiss Cottage; the 29 via Camden Town to Trafalgar Square* • **TRAFFIC BLACKSPOTS** *Holborn and Bloomsbury: Central – so most streets are busy during the day. Long daytime queues along Southampton Row heading up towards Russell Square across Theobalds Road. Kings Cross and St Pancras: The Euston Road is a main west to east through-road and always clogged with several lanes of traffic each way. There are often jams at the junction of Pentonville Road, Caledonian Road and Euston Road. Camden: The one-way High Street is often jammed up to the lights by Camden Town tube and at weekends pedestrians visiting the markets do*

*their best to pretend that the High Street and Chalk Farm Road are
pedestrianised. Camden, one of the most avidly anti-car boroughs, is
carrying out a study and consulting with residents and traders in a bid
to cut traffic and has recently proposed closing off the High Street. But
residents fear this will mean more traffic is forced down side streets.
Hampstead: The narrow high street often has long queues stretching back
from the lights at the junction with Heath Street. Heath Street coming down
to the tube is also busy* • **PARKING** *Difficult throughout the whole borough.
Wardens are zealous and Camden is experimenting with the reduction or
eradication of car parking spaces on new developments. Almost the whole
borough, except parts of Kilburn and the Camden section of Highgate, is
in a controlled parking zone. Opponents of a controlled parking zone in
Belsize Park lost their battle last year. Cost of annual resident's permit: £82.*

LEISURE FACILITIES * * * * *

THEATRES & CONCERT HALLS *With part of the West End within the borough
boundaries, there is an excellent choice although it helps to like musicals
or long-running murder mysteries. The Roundhouse at Camden Town
(converted from an old railway engine turner) has off-West-End plays,
repertory and ambitious plans to become a creative centre of studios and
workshops. The Hampstead Theatre shows a lot of new works. Open-air
concerts at Kenwood House on Hampstead Heath and Lauderdale House
in Waterlow Park, Highgate. Good selection of other live music venues in
pubs and clubs* • **CINEMAS** *Nine cinemas including several in the West
End, showing everything from mainstream to arty films. Also the eight
screen Odeon in Camden Town (replacing the much-lamented Parkway)
and two repertory cinemas in Hampstead, the Everyman, recently
revamped, and Screen on the Hill. The former Scala cinema at Kings Cross
is set to reopen later this year with a cinemas, arts spaces and live music
facilities.* • **MUSEUMS & GALLERIES** *A huge range from the famous (the British
Museum) to the eclectic (the Jewish Museum, Camden Town, Freud's House
in Hampstead, Dickens House in Bloomsbury, the Sir John Soane collection
in Lincoln's Inn Fields, the London Canal Musuem in Kings Cross in an old
ice warehouse). Art collection at Kenwood House; Hampstead history
museum at Burgh House, Hampstead* • **SPORTS FACILITIES** *Four sports
centres at Swiss Cottage, Covent Garden, Kentish Town and Mornington
Crescent, Camden, run in partnership with Holmes Place and all recently
refurbished. New sports hall at Somers Town. Outdoor heated pool at
Covent Garden. Outdoor swimming on Hampstead Heath at Highgate
Pond (men), Kenwood Pond (women), Hampstead Pond (mixed) and
Parliament Hill lido. Tennis, bowls, athletics and other sports at parks across
the borough. Discount card scheme in operation* • **LIBRARIES** *£15 million
has been invested over the past couple of years in repairs and technology.
But residents are angry about cutbacks in opening hours. All libraries
are closed on Wednesday and Sunday and opening hours in smaller
branch libraries are patchy. Below-average use although the council says
membership rose recently for the first time in 10 years. 7.2 library visits
per head. Place in library-use league table: 20th out of 32 (where 1 is
best and 32 worst).*

OPEN SPACES * * * *

A built-up borough but it still manages to have a interesting and varied
selection of open space from small hidden gardens to the wooded acres of

Hampstead Heath (owned by the Corporation of London). Camden rises steeply to the north and there are some wonderful views of London.
TOWN SQUARES AND SPACES *Grays Inn Gardens with long lawns overlooked by barristers' chambers – a haven away from the busy Theobalds Road (restricted opening hours); Bloomsbury Square, which is more intimate than the larger Russell Square •* **VIEWS AND KITE-FLYING** *Primrose Hill, an otherwise featureless grassy mound but excellent views over the West End and City; Parliament Hill Fields, Hampstead Heath, a wide open space framed with extensive woods; Waterlow Park, with lush lawns and ponds leading down to Highgate cemetery •* **WOODS** *Hampstead Heath, easy to lose yourself and think you're nowhere near London •* **CEMETERIES** *Highgate, the mother of all mysterious overgrown Victorian cemeteries with lots of trailing ivy and broken angels.*

SHOPS * * * * *

HOLBORN, BLOOMSBURY & WEST END *Everything from small arty shops and New Age-type places in the cluster of shops around Seven Dials, Covent Garden to the hi-fi, electronics and computer shops of Tottenham Court Road alongside the furniture shops of Heal's and Habitat. Hatton Garden, the jewellery quarter of London, is set for a £2 million revamp in a bid to improve the currently tired, trafficky street and neighbouring Leather Lane market. Mostly dull chain stores along High Holborn but could perk up if the former Liverpool Victoria building becomes the HQ of the new Greater London Authority as is possible. Big new Safeway in Bloomsbury at the Brunswick Shopping Centre next to a trendy new laundrette complete with coffee bar •* **KINGS CROSS** *Can only improve. Currently run-down shops along Pentonville and Caledonian Road, many boarded up because of uncertainty over the Channel Tunnel Rail Link. Lots of burger bars and discount stores and used car dealers under the arches. But there are plans for new shops and a superstore as part of developments around Kings Cross station. •* **PRIMROSE HILL & BELSIZE PARK** *An attractive villagey street of local shops in Primrose Hill with delis, interior design shops including a minimalist bathroom shop, clothes shops and a second-hand bookshop. More local shops in Englands Lane, Belsize Park including interior design shops and galleries and a clutch of shops around Belsize Crescent •* **CAMDEN TOWN** *Has ballooned in recent years as Camden Market spread along Regents Canal at Camden Lock, and Chalk Farm Road followed by shops selling Doc Martens, grunge clothes, leather jackets and records. Huge choice of records, books, clothes, antiques and food and crowded with tourists as well as locals at weekends. The south end of the High Street has good branches of Boots, Waterstones and other chains. Sainsbury's in bizarre metal building on Camden Road. Safeway in Chalk Farm Road •* **HAMPSTEAD** *A network of streets tumbling down the hill from the tube station in Hampstead village. Lots of good patisseries and delis, a big Waterstones, designer clothes shops, a real butchers and a second-hand bookshop among the collection of interesting local shops. Spoilt by traffic •* **WEST HAMPSTEAD & FINCHLEY ROAD** *Massive improvements here over the past few years as the middle classes ripple out from Hampstead, although Finchley Road is the main road to the M1. Several patisseries, popular meeting places for the area's East European and Jewish communities, have disappeared. Habitat and large Waitrose. Sainsbury's has recently opened as part of the B2 development with multiscreen Warner village and leisure facilities, although residents are worried the development will make traffic on Finchley Road worse. West End Lane is* *more interesting than it used to be with a lot of furniture shops, a second-hand bookshop and music shop among other local shops •* **KENTISH TOWN** *Rather run-down shops lining the busy Kentish Town Road with a lot of discount shops, off-licences and ethnic supermarkets.*

RESTAURANTS*****

BLOOMSBURY, HOLBORN & WEST END *A huge choice, particularly in Covent Garden and Fitzrovia around Charlotte Street (Greek, Italian, Korean and Japanese just for starters). Holborn's a bit dead in the evening but Bloomsbury is more interesting, especially in the streets round the British Museum and around Great Ormond Street Hospital in the pedestrian Lambs Conduit Street •* **CAMDEN TOWN** *Everything from brasseries to Scandinavian with Chinese, Indian, Vietnamese and Italian in between. The best selection is round Regents Park Road and Parkway just off Camden High Street. Very lively in the evening and if you live here there's no need to leave your own patch to have a good time •* **HAMPSTEAD & WEST HAMPSTEAD** *Better choice in West Hampstead with wine bars, sushi bars, Italian and East European in West End Lane. Lots of pavement cafés and people braving the traffic for a wine or coffee after work. Brasseries, cafés and some modern European in Hampstead and friendly branch of Café Rouge •* **ELSEWHERE** *A couple of notable African restaurants and pubs in Kentish Town, as well as a Pizza Express and locally praised Italian.*

CRIME RATES*

221 crimes per 1,000 population, the second highest in London. But the council argues that this figure is distorted by the huge daytime influx of population. Position in Metropolitan Police league table: 2nd out of 32 (where 1 is worst and 32 best).

THE COUNCIL****

POLITICAL AFFILIATION *Labour •* **MINUS POINTS** *Residents complain that the planning department can be inconsistent and tricky to deal with. Not enough ongoing supervision in playgrounds so that they're vulnerable to vandalism •* **PLUS POINTS** *Generally efficient to deal with. Litter collection and street-sweeping much improved around Camden Town although still poor around Tottenham Court Road and in areas like Kentish Town. Much praised, efficient, twice weekly rubbish collection. Good schools. Energetic promotion of regeneration sites like Kings Cross •* **PROPERTY SEARCHES CARRIED OUT IN 10 WORKING DAYS** *97% •* **STANDARD SEARCH FEE** *£100 •* **COUNCIL TAX COLLECTED** *87.7%*

• **COUNCIL TAX 1998-99**

BAND	PROPERTY VALUE	CHARGE	BAND	PROPERTY VALUE	CHARGE
A	up to £40,000	£585.98	E	£88,001-£120,000	£1,074.32
B	£40,001-£52,000	£683.66	F	£120,001-£160,000	£1,269.66
C	£52,001-£68,000	£781.31	G	£160,001-£320,000	£1,464.97
D	£68,001-£88,000	£878.99	H	over £320,000	£1,757.98

CITY OF LONDON

This is where London began. From this small square mile on the north bank of the Thames, the capital grew in wealth and influence from Roman times onwards, stretching its tentacles ever further into the outlying countryside, halted only by the twin deterrents of Adolf Hitler and the green belt. For centuries, people lived as well as worked in the City, which was the centre of political, intellectual, economic and social life. But as the habit of travelling to work took off in the eighteenth century, the City's residential population dwindled to a few thousand, swollen by thousands more workers every weekday morning.

The City is still primarily commercial, a world centre of global banks and finance houses, blinking computer screens and plate glass office blocks rearing up on every side. From Monday to Friday, its pavements seethe with smart suits. At weekends, it's dead, with shops, restaurants and pubs closed. Despite this it's seen a residential renaissance in the last couple of years as developers have responded to government pressure to build on previously used inner city sites, converting office blocks and warehouses to smart new apartments. Most of the purchasers have been City workers who spend long hours in the office and don't want the hassle of a commute or investors buying to rent.

The City begins in the west at Temple and the attractive collegiate gardens and buildings of the Inns of Court, home of London's barristers. To the east are Fleet Street, once the home of the newspaper industry, and St Paul's, with its sublime cathedral buildings still blighted by the ugly, empty 1960s office blocks surrounding it (fortunately set to be replaced by a slightly more congenial development after years of wrangling). North of St Paul's is the Barbican, a series of tower blocks sticking up like jagged teeth, and the City's largest concentration of private housing. Travel along London Wall, the route of the City's old Roman wall and cut south, and you reach the financial heart of the city around the Bank of England and Lloyd's of London. At its eastern boundary by the Tower of London and Aldgate, the wealth of the city starts to recede, giving way abruptly to the beginning of the East End.

Until recently, there was no challenge to the City's financial and economic pre-eminence. But the 1990s haven't altogether been a success story. For a start, Canary Wharf (see Tower Hamlets), which looked dead in the water at the beginning of the decade, revived with the last economic upturn and has taken some of the City's best corporate tenants. On top of this, there's been a lot of looking over shoulders at European pretenders to the City's financial throne. Physically the heart of the City has been twice devastated by bombing, leading to the creation of a "ring of plastic" to control traffic movement and crime.

On the plus side for the City, it's managed to survive the government's centralising attempts at London government reform in return for radical reforms in its much criticised "jobs for the boys" electoral system. It's also been an active player in regeneration initiatives across east London and a staunch keeper of some of London's most treasured green spaces.

PROPERTY AND ARCHITECTURE

FLEET STREET & ST PAUL'S

A number of luxury developments have sprung up, tucked away behind street facades along Fleet Street and Ludgate Hill up towards St Paul's. There are fabulous views of St Paul's now that the horrible blue railway bridge to Holborn Viaduct has been taken down.

ATTRACTS *People who want to be in the centre of things; City workers; investors; older people wanting a pied-à-terre* • **CONSERVATION AREAS** *Dyers Buildings; Chancery Lane; Fleet Street; Temples; Whitefriars; Ludgate Hill* • **AVERAGE PRICES** *Flats: studio: £80,000-£125,000; 1-bed: £140,000-£190,000; 2-bed: £220,000-£260,000; 3-bed: £275,000-£325,000; Penthouse: £400,000-£600,000* • **AVERAGE RENTS (MONTHLY)** *Flats: studio: £700-£860; 1-bed: £1080; 2-bed: £1400-£1950; 3-bed: £1730-£2380; Penthouse: £3030-£4330.*

BARBICAN

Built in the 1970s on a site almost completely razed by bombing during the blitz and originally intended as council flats. Some 10% of residents are still council tenants. You either love the Barbican or you hate it. It has all the worst architectural accoutrements of the 1970s – huge towers, walkways, dead walls and concrete that soaks in the rain. It's so confusing to find your way around that there's a yellow line painted on the pavement to mark the route. But once you penetrate the complex, the centre has gardens, fountains, flats with large windows and balconies. And of course, the Barbican Arts centre is right in the middle, along with the Guildhall School of Music and Drama and City of London Girls School. Increasingly popular as the City livens up. Residents pay premiums for south- and west-facing flats or apartments on high floors of tower blocks and often buy after renting. Beware high service charges.

ATTRACTS *Singles; City workers; people wanting pieds-à-terre* • **CONSERVATION AREAS** *Postman's Park; The Brewery, Chiswell Street* • **AVERAGE PRICES** *Flats: studio: £75,000-£100,000; 1-bed: £95,000-£180,000; 2-bed: £150,000-£240,000; 3-bed: £240,000+; Penthouse: £450,000+* • **AVERAGE RENTS (MONTHLY)** *Flats: studio: £730-£860; 1-bed: £975-£1300; 2-bed: £1300-£1730; 3-bed: £1730-£2160; Penthouse: £2600+.*

BEST POSTCODES

City postcode areas are so small that you hardly notice when you're walking from one to another. Fenchurch EC3 is primarily commercial, with most of the residential action in Queen Victoria Street EC4 and Moorgate EC2 which includes the Barbican. Postcodes have little snob value. For Clerkenwell EC1 see Islington.

AMENITIES

SCHOOLS * * *

The City counts several good private schools within its boundaries. No state secondary schools. One primary school, Sir John Cass's Foundation School, which performs well above average in league tables. Below-average proportion of under-fives in state nurseries.

PRE-SCHOOL PROVISION *1 state-run nursery (for residents only, not open to day time workers from outside the borough); 1 nursery class in a state primary school; 6 private or voluntary playgroups or day nurseries (more available in surrounding boroughs, for example Islington or Westminster). Proportion of under-fives in state nurseries: 31%* • **STATE PRIMARY SCHOOLS** *Overall position of borough in league tables: 2nd out of 150* • **PRIVATE PREP SCHOOLS** *St Paul's Cathedral School (boys)* • **PRIVATE SECONDARY SCHOOLS** *City of London Girls (from 7) (Barbican); City of London Boys, EC4.*

TRANSPORT * * * * *

You can't get much more central. All Zone 1. Cost of annual season ticket: £572. There are three main-line stations within its boundaries (Liverpool Street, Fenchurch Street and Cannon Street), as well as 11 tube and DLR lines and countless buses. London Bridge station isn't in the City but thousands of commuters stream across London Bridge every weekday morning to the City and back across to head out to the southern suburbs in the evening.

TRAFFIC *After the IRA bomb which hit Bishopsgate in 1993, the City reacted by encompassing the whole City with barriers and police checkpoints. The idea was to block off smaller streets and keep traffic flowing only through the City's main arteries. There was much grumbling at first as the restrictions caused huge jams, particularly when travelling east to west (to get across London Bridge from east of Tower Hill means elaborate detours round the Aldgate one-way system or south of the river), but the ring of plastic, as it quickly became known, has reduced traffic and cut crime, according to City police* • **BLACKSPOTS** *Aldgate: Several main roads converge, all carrying heavy traffic which then has to manoeuvre to change lanes to get on to other main roads. Upper Thames Street: The alternative to Aldgate to get out of the City going west. Once you're stuck in it there's no way out. Moorgate: Clogged with traffic going north to Islington. Particularly bad at the junction with London Wall* • **PARKING** *Don't even think about parking on the streets unless you want to keep popping out to feed the meter. No residents' parking permits but you can get a concessionary rate in car parks: £145 for 12 weeks. Is it worth it? Developments with underground parking are understandably popular.*

LEISURE FACILITIES * * * *

THEATRES & CONCERT HALLS *A wealth of venues and activity. The Barbican Centre has managed to shake off its initial image of being miles from anywhere* with nothing much going on, although it's still a bit confusing to find your way around. Now the London home of the Royal Shakespeare Company but there's plenty besides Shakespeare, both in the more formal theatre and the more intimate Pit. There's also music of all sorts from classical and choral to jazz and rock 'n roll. Next door at the Guildhall School of Music and Drama there's a steady flow of plays, opera and orchestral music. One of the City's other musical pleasures is the wide range of organ, piano and other recitals in the sublime setting of its churches. More intimate drama, with both new and existing plays, at the Bridewell theatre, Fleet Street, a former Victorian bath house • **CINEMAS** Two cinemas at the Barbican showing both the latest films and more arty films and classics • **MUSEUMS & GALLERIES** A large selection packed into a small area, including the excellent Museum of London, charting the history of London from Roman times to the present. Unprepossessing from the outside with no proper street entrance but worth it once you're in. Lots of small museums run by churches, livery companies and city firms, as well as the Bank of England (coins, banknotes and a peep behind the scenes of a modern bank). Dr Johnson's house is tucked away behind Fleet Street. Art galleries at the Barbican and the Guildhall, the fifteenth century headquarters of the Corporation of London (worth visiting for the splendour of both its exterior and interior, despite the ugly modern office buildings of the Corporation overshadowing it) • **SPORTS FACILITIES** Just one publicly funded leisure centre at Golden Lane, with a swimming pool, badminton, tennis and classes. Other boroughs' facilities close by. Otherwise the City is choc-a-bloc with private gyms and pools for workaholic bankers who need to use up adrenalin • **LIBRARIES** Specialist reference collections open to the public as well as lending libraries. The City Business Library, Guildhall (great for London obsessives) and St Bride's Printing Library are some of the collections available. Good music collection as well as general library at the Barbican. Opening hours reflect City's tendency to close down at weekends, with the Barbican the only library to open on Saturday (mornings only). Libraries are also facing cuts in hours. Huge numbers of visits per head of population because of daily influx of workers. 229 library visits per head. Not included in library-use league tables because its figures aren't comparable with other boroughs.

OPEN SPACES * * (* * *)

A tricky area to judge, at least within the borough structure of this book, because the Corporation of London owns and cares for some of London's best known open spaces. But they're all outside the City boundary. Hence the three extra stars in brackets, for Hampstead Heath (Camden), Highgate Wood (Haringey), Queen's Park (Brent), West Ham Park (Newham), Epping Forest (Waltham Forest), West Wickham Common (Bromley), Coulsdon Common (Croydon) and Bunhill Fields, the dissenters' burial ground in Islington. The City itself is densely built up and populated. You don't live here for wide open space and this can be wearing, particularly in summer. At summer lunch-times, green spaces are crowded with City workers. Most of Finsbury Circus, the City's largest public garden, is taken up with the bowling green, which looks lovely but cuts down sitting or walking room for everyone else. But there are some lovely small spaces. **CHURCHYARDS** St Paul's. One of the largest with lots of good places to sit and have a sandwich. Can be crowded in the summer though because St Paul's is such a tourist honeypot. The small churchyard of St Olave's, where Samuel Pepys is buried, is a welcome retreat from the city crowds, as are the churchyards of St Bride's Fleet Street and St Botolph's Bisphopsgate.

SHOPS***

Lots of shops are still closed at weekends and by early evening.

CHEAPSIDE, BISHOPSGATE, MOORGATE & FENCHURCH STREET *The main shopping drags of the City, with small branches of middle market and smarter chains and (inevitably) lots of sandwich bars, coffee houses and City menswear shops. All are trafficky with motorcycle couriers an ever-present hazard and more for desperate last minute rushes than a leisurely shop. Lunchtimes are hell. Tesco Metro in Cheapside, huge M&S in Moorgate and recently opened food M&S at St Mary Axe* • **LEADENHALL & LIVERPOOL STREET** *Good and interesting shopping in the restored Victorian Leadenhall Arcade, several streets of pedestrianised covered shopping. Lots of restaurants and sandwich bars of course, but also a real fishmonger, hardware and independent leather goods shops as well as large Waterstones. The Liverpool Street arcade, until recently fairly sorry for itself, has been given a new lease of life with expensive designer clothes shops, cafés and restaurants* • **PETTICOAT LANE** *One of London's best known markets, particularly for clothes and leather goods, on the City's eastern boundary, where it starts turning into the East End.*

RESTAURANTS***

During the week, a huge choice of wine bars and coffee bars as well as Thai, Chinese, Japanese, French, Italian, British and anything else you can think of. Many are stuffed to the gunnels at weekday lunch-times, as are pubs. Don't believe all you read about the death of City lunches. But most are restaurants closed at weekends. The City also closes down early in the evening as workers stop for a quick drink after work and then move on elsewhere.

CRIME RATES

There are no comparable figures because the City has its own police force and isn't under the jurisdiction of the Metropolitan Police.

THE COUNCIL****

POLITICAL AFFILIATION *Independent. The City has its own electoral system, with annual elections where each ward returns representatives to the court of common council. All common councillors face elections every year. Each ward also has an alderman, who is currently elected for life but under reforms being proposed, will face regular elections. There's nothing to stop the court of common council from being elected on party lines but in practice it's been independent for some years* • **MINUS POINTS** *Small or non-existent choice of state schools meaning children of secondary school age have to cross the borough boundary. Low nursery provision. Many services (eg libraries) only function during working hours* • **PLUS POINTS** *Generally clean streets and well maintained roads. One of the quickest in London at turning round property searches. The highest levels of council tax collected in London. Well maintained green space. Low council tax* •

PROPERTY SEARCHES CARRIED OUT IN 10 WORKING DAYS *99%* • **STANDARD SEARCH FEE** *£10* • **COUNCIL TAX COLLECTED** *98.1%*

• **COUNCIL TAX 1998-99**

BAND	PROPERTY VALUE	CHARGE	BAND	PROPERTY VALUE	CHARGE
A	up to £40,000	£342.00	E	£88,001-£120,000	£627.00
B	£40,001-£52,000	£399.00	F	£120,001-£160,000	£741.00
C	£52,001-£68,000	£456.00	G	£160,001-£320,000	£855.00
D	£68,001-£88,000	£513.00	H	over £320,000	£1,026.00

CROYDON

Croydon is more familiar to many people as a series of train stations on journeys to the south coast or Gatwick airport than as a place to live, and what they see looks dire. Ugly 1960s office slabs mixed with more recent red brick towers and blocks of every shape and size suddenly rise on all sides as trains pull into East Croydon station, then just as quickly disappear as the view from the window gives way to a sea of suburbia, tatty on the way into London and smarter on the way out. It's easy to dismiss Croydon as at best, dull and at worst, a bit of a dump.

But appearances can be deceptive. The tower blocks of Croydon itself hide not only some excellent shopping but also some beautiful restored nineteenth century public buildings. And Croydon town centre is geographically a tiny part of Croydon borough, which stretches from the inner suburbs of South London down to the Surrey green belt. In the north, it touches four other boroughs (Bromley, Lambeth, Southwark and Lewisham) at Crystal Palace before plunging down the hill to Upper Norwood, whose huge detached Victorian villas still manage to look gracious despite being mostly converted into flats. In next door South Norwood, the large villas show signs of neglect and shabby conversions mix with Edwardian semis and modern houses. To the east and north of Croydon town centre are the mostly dreary Victorian terraces of Woodside, Addiscombe and Thornton Heath and the 1930s semis of Norbury. East and south of Croydon and in parts of Purley, things get grand with detached stockbroker-belt houses set in large gardens with backdrops of wooded hills. Smaller detached and semi-detached houses from Edwardian to modern line the suburban crescents of Sanderstead, Selsdon, and Coulsdon.

Predictably the more suburban parts of Croydon are popular with families who want access to houses with gardens, good schools, good transport links and green space. But it's more cosmopolitan than neighbouring Bromley, for example, with significant Asian and West Indian communities. Nearly a fifth of the population is from an ethnic minority. Unemployment is relatively low for outer London at 4.8% with large numbers of people working locally in white collar jobs (particularly financial services) or commuting to central London.

The borough is energetically marketing Croydon town centre as the dynamic, modern commercial centre for a huge swathe of south London and the south east, trying to rid the area of its reputation as a boring set of office blocks. Alongside its ever expanding shopping centres (£23 million already spent with another £8.5 million to come), roads in and around Croydon are being dug up and laid with tram tracks in preparation for Tramlink, the first modern train system in London. This will link the southern suburbs with the south west at Wimbledon and the south east at Beckenham for the first time and give travellers access to a wide range of train services into London. After initial suspicion, many local residents support Tramlink but there've been complaints about delays, mess, and confusing changes to bus routes while the work's done.

PROPERTY AND ARCHITECTURE

UPPER NORWOOD

Grand, detached red brick Victorian villas with gables, wooden carved balconies and other lush original features in roads running down from Crystal Palace and Westow Hill into Upper Norwood. The most elevated corner of Upper Norwood, bordered by Westow Hill, Church Road and Westow Street, is known as the Westow Hill triangle and has attracted an interesting mix of middle class residents claiming village status for the area, artists and New Agers (some drawn by the ongoing protest over plans for Crystal Palace-see Bromley). Elsewhere there are roads of 1930s semi-detached and detached properties mixed with modern blocks and council property.

ATTRACTS *First-time buyers; flat-hunters of all descriptions; some families* • **CONSERVATION AREA** *Harold Road; Upper Norwood Triangle; Church Road* • **AVERAGE PRICES:** *Flats: studio: £30,000; 1-bed: £40,000-£45,000; 2-bed: £55,000-£65,000 Houses: 2-bed: £70,000-£75,000; 3-bed: £100,000+; 4-bed: £150,000+; 5-bed: £250,000+* • **AVERAGE RENTS (MONTHLY)** *Flats: studio: £400-£425; 1-bed: £450-£550; 2-bed: £600+ Houses: 2-bed: £700; 3-bed: £800+; 4-bed: £1000; 5-bed: £1500+.*

SOUTH NORWOOD & WOODSIDE

More down-market than Upper Norwood. Some large detached Victorian houses in South Norwood, most of which has been converted into flats and seen better days, alongside roads of Edwardian semis, half-timbered 1930s semis and low-rise council houses. Depressing rows of pebble-dashed, louvred windowed houses fronted with scrubby trees off Portland and Morland Roads in Woodside, relieved by the open space of Woodside Green lined with some handsome semi-detached Victorian villas.

ATTRACTS *First-time buyers; local locals; families wanting a lot of space for their money* • **CONSERVATION AREAS** *South Norwood* • **AVERAGE PRICES** *Flats: studio: £30,000-£40,000; 1-bed: £40,000+; 2-bed: £55,000-£65,000; 3-bed: £70,000 Houses: 2-bed: £65,000-£80,000; 3-bed: £80,000-£140,000; 4-bed: £130,000+; 5-bed: £140,000+* • **AVERAGE RENTS (MONTHLY)** *Flats: studio: £350; 1-bed: £400-£450; 2-bed: £500-£550 Houses: 2-bed: up to £650; 3-bed: £650-£750; 4-bed: £700+.*

THORNTON HEATH & NORBURY

Mostly streets of two- and three-storey Victorian terraces, Edwardian and 1930s semis in Thornton Heath, many of which have been "improved" by their owners with louvred windows and modern doors. This is fruitful flat-hunting territory with flats in conversions or modern blocks. Norbury's slightly more up-market, with a lot of 1930s semis in roads off London

Road. Some attractive individual 1930s and modern detached houses in Gibson's Hill, with beautiful views over London and Surrey.

ATTRACTS *First-time buyers; loyal locals* • **CONSERVATION AREAS** *None* • **AVERAGE PRICES** *Flats: studio: £30,000; 1-bed: £40,000-£45,000; 2-bed: £55,000-£65,000 Houses: 2-bed: £75,000; 3-bed: £110,000+; 4-bed: £160,000+* • **AVERAGE RENTS (MONTHLY)** *Flats: studio: £320-£420; 1-bed: £400-£450; 2-bed: £500-£550; 3-bed: £600-£620 Houses: 2-bed: £550-£650; 3-bed: £700-£750; 4-bed: £800-£1000.*

SOUTH CROYDON, EAST CROYDON & ADDISCOMBE

East Croydon is the town's best side, closely followed by South Croydon (where a lot of the most sought-after schools are). East Croydon's where commuter belt takes over from London sprawl and Croydon starts to feel part of Surrey. The grandest roads are on the Whitgift estate by Lloyd Park. Wide, handsome but slightly bleak roads of big 1930s detached houses with gardens, in every style from stockbroker Tudor to overgrown rustic cottage with exaggaratedly deep eaves. As a definite sign that the owners have arrived, houses have names not numbers. More large detached and semi-detached houses in parts of South Croydon, especially round the Waldrons conservation area. Smaller Victorian terraces and detached and semi-detached 1930s in more affordable Addiscombe.

ATTRACTS *Commuters wanting to be near East Croydon station; families wanting good schools and green space* • **CONSERVATION AREAS** *The Waldrons; Parish Church; central Croydon* • **AVERAGE PRICES** *Flats: studio: £30,000-£50,000; 1-bed: £40,000-£75,000; 2-bed: £50,000-£100,000 Houses: 2-bed: £60,000-£120,000; 3-bed: £75,000-£160,000; 4-bed: £130,000-£500,000; 5-bed: £160,000-£500,000* • **AVERAGE RENTS (MONTHLY)** *Flats: studio: £350-£500; 1-bed: £400-£700; 2-bed: £450-£900 Houses: 2-bed: £450-£900; 3-bed: £525-£1200.*

SHIRLEY & SELSDON

Mostly 1930s houses of various shapes and sizes in more popular Shirley. South of the Wickham Road is posher than north and the poshest part of all is Shirley Hills, private roads of large detached houses sandwiched between Addington Golf Course on one side and Addington Hills on the other. Much of Selsdon by contrast was built in the 1960s and 1970s on three estates, Forestdale, Ashendale and Selsdon Dale. Lots of small houses and blocks of flats in cul-de-sacs. Property values here could rise with the arrival of Tramlink.

ATTRACTS *Commuters; families* • **CONSERVATION AREA** *Addington Village* • **AVERAGE PRICES** *Flats: studio: £35,000-£40,000; 1-bed: £45,000-£60,000; 2-bed: £65,000-£80,000 Houses: 2-bed: £85,000-£130,000; 3-bed: £95,000-£180,000; 4-bed: £150,000-£250,000+; 5-bed: £350,000+* • **AVERAGE RENTS (MONTHLY)** *Flats: studio: £375; 1-bed: £450; 2-bed: £550 Houses: 2-bed: £575; 3-bed: £650-£750; 4-bed: £700-£1200; 5-bed: £950-£2000.*

PURLEY

Just like its reputation, Purley is safe and predictable, inhabited by regular commuters who catch the same train to town every day. More turn of the century and interwar suburbia set in green belt land with a generous supply of golf courses. Pleasant but unremarkable residential streets. The grandest part of Purley is the Webb estate to the south west of Purley town centre. Here there are tree-lined private roads (with firm notices telling the *hoi polloi* to keep out), with huge detached houses, many behind high hedges or with elaborate entrance gates and money no object.

ATTRACTS *The wealthy; commuters of more modest means; professional couples; families wanting good schools and green space* • **CONSERVATION AREA** *Webb Estate and Upper Woodcote Village* • **AVERAGE PRICES** *Flats: studio: £40,000-£45,000; 1-bed: £50,000-£60,000; 2-bed: £65,000-£80,000 Houses: 2-bed: £80,000-£90,000; 3-bed: £95,000-£160,000; 4-bed: £200,000+; 5-bed: £250,000+* • **AVERAGE RENTS (MONTHLY)** *Flats: studio: £400-£500; 1-bed: £500-£700; 2-bed: £600-£900 Houses: 2-bed: £700-£900; 3-bed: £700-£1200; 4-bed: £1500-£3000; 5-bed: £3000+.*

COULSDON

The further away you are from the main Brighton Road the better. Mainly 1930s semis and some Victorian terraces in Coulsdon itself, with larger semis and detached houses in grander West Coulsdon. Up the hill, Old Coulsdon has a more villagey atmosphere, helped by views over the surrounding Downs, a village green, shops and some good pubs.

ATTRACTS *Families; professional couples* • **CONSERVATION AREA** *Bradmore Green* • **AVERAGE PRICES** *Flats: studio: £38,000-£40,000; 1-bed: £55,000-£65,000; 2-bed: £64,000-£70,000 Houses: 2-bed: £85,000; 3-bed: £105,000-£185,000; 4-bed: £150,000-£250,000; 5-bed: £250,000-£320,000* • **AVERAGE RENTS (MONTHLY)** *Flats: studio: £400-£500; 1-bed: £500-£700; 2-bed: £600-£900 Houses: 2-bed: £700-£900; 3-bed: £700-£1200; 4-bed: £1500-£3000; 5-bed: £3000+.*

BEST POSTCODES

Largely irrelevant as most of the area has Croydon rather than London postcodes. Of the two areas with London postcodes, Norwood SE19 and South Norwood SE25, neither is considered particularly smart, even by South London standards.

AMENITIES

SCHOOLS ***

Some excellent and sought-after state schools at both primary and secondary level. Primary schools perform creditably in league tables but secondary schools are more disappointing despite some good schools. A good choice of private prep and secondary schools. Slightly below-average state pre-school provision but there are a number of private nurseries in the borough.

PRE-SCHOOL PROVISION *4 state nursery schools; 32 nursery classes in state primary or church schools; 121 private and voluntary day nurseries. Proportion of under-fives in state nurseries: 55%* • **STATE PRIMARY SCHOOLS** *Overall league table position: 76th out of 150. Top scorers: Greenvale, South Croydon; Coulsdon C of E, Coulsdon; St John's C of E, Croydon* • **STATE SECONDARY SCHOOLS** *Overall league table position: 92nd out of 150. High scorers: Coloma Convent RC (girls), Croydon; Archbishop Tenison's C of E (mixed), Croydon; St. Andrews C of E (mixed), Croydon* • **PRIVATE PREP SCHOOLS** *The Lodge (girls to 18), Purley; St David's (mixed), Purley;*

*West Dene (mixed), Purley; Sanderstead Junior (mixed), Sanderstead;
Croham Hurst (girls to 18), South Croydon; Croydon High (girls to 18),
South Croydon; Cumnor House (boys), South Croydon; Elmshurst (boys),
South Croydon; Old Palace (girls to 18), Croydon; Royal Russell Prep
(mixed), Croydon* • **PRIVATE SECONDARY SCHOOLS** *Royal Russell (mixed)
Croydon; Trinity (boys), Croydon; Whitgift (boys), South Croydon*

TRANSPORT* * *

Rail only throughout the borough until the arrival of the £200 million
Tramlink in 2000 which will provide much needed east-west links.
Connections to Croydon, particularly East Croydon, are excellent, with
fast trains to and from London, Gatwick and the south coast often stopping
only at East Croydon. Trains from here go to Victoria and London Bridge,
Blackfriars and Kings Cross on the Thameslink and an estimated 600 trains
a day pass through East Croydon. But services are more patchy to outlying
parts of the borough, particularly in the east where large tracts are
nowhere near a station.

TRAINS Thornton Heath: *Zone 4. Cost of annual season ticket: £1068;
No of trains per hour: to Victoria: 5-6; to London Bridge: 2; Fastest
journey: to Victoria 21 minutes; to London Bridge 30 minutes.* Norwood
Junction: *Zone 4; No of trains per hour: to London Bridge 4-5; to Victoria
2; Fastest journey: to London Bridge 14 minutes; to Victoria 30 minutes.*
East Croydon: *Zone 5. Cost of annual season ticket: £1280; No of trains
per hour: to Victoria 10-15; to London Bridge 13-19; to Blackfriars 4;
Fastest journey: to London Bridge 20 minutes; to Victoria 20 minutes.*
Purley: *Zone 6. Cost of annual season ticket: £1396; No of trains per
hour: to Victoria 4; to London Bridge up to 8; Fastest journey: to London
Bridge 25 minutes; to Victoria 30 minutes.* • **BUSES** *On the outer limits of
the bus network. Good links to and from Croydon and Purley to the rest
of the borough but again buses are less frequent in more far-flung areas.
Routes out of the borough normally link suburbs in neighbouring south
London rather than going to the centre of town. Only the109 goes from
Purley via Croydon, Thornton Heath and Norbury to Trafalgar Square.
Night buses include the N109 from Purley to Trafalgar Square and the
N70 from Trafalgar Square to Norwood Junction* • **TRAFFIC BLACKSPOTS**
Purley: *The main A23 between Croydon and Purley is trafficky all down the
Purley Way culminating in tail-backs at the junction where four main roads
meet at Purley. Notorious for trapping irate motorists desperate to get to
the coast or Gatwick airport. Residents claim traffic in Purley itself has got
worse since the arrival of a new Tesco.* Croydon: *Long tail-backs in central
Croydon with cars waiting to get into shopping centre carparks.* South
Norwood: *Long tailbacks at the lights at the junction of Portland Road and
the High Street* • **PARKING** *Not generally a problem in the south of the
borough where there's lots of space and wide roads but can get tricky
around shopping centres and stations. There are six controlled parking
zones in Croydon (broken into five sub zones), South Norwood, Thornton
Heath, Purley, Coulsdon and Sanderstead. Cost of annual resident's
permit: £26, valid only in the zone for which it's issued.*

LEISURE FACILITIES* * *

THEATRES & CONCERT HALLS *Much improved since the arrival of the Croydon
Clocktower arts centre, a stunning conversion of the town centre's
clocktower and town hall into a light modern theatre, cinema and library
behind a beautiful nineteenth century facade. The Braithwaite Hall at the*

Clock Tower has fringe theatre, jazz and live music and dance. The Ashcroft Theatre at the Fairfield Halls shows musicals and plays by touring companies. New plays at the Warehouse Theatre. Classical, jazz and rock concerts at the Fairfield Halls, home of the London Mozart players. Community shows at Stanley Halls, South Norwood • CINEMAS Currently four film venues including the David Lean cinema at the Clocktower showing a mix of mainstream and more off-the-wall films; Fairfield Halls (mostly mainstream); the ABC in Purley and the Warner Multiplex on Purley Way. There are plans for a 14 screen multiplex as part of a huge leisure and shopping development in Croydon town centre behind the florid nineteenth century façade of the former Grants department store. • MUSEUMS & GALLERIES A small selection. Lifetimes, a new interactive local history museum at the Clocktower. Galleries at the Clocktower. Croydon Old Palace (now a school but once the mediaeval home of the Archbishops of Canterbury) and Addington Palace (now the Royal School of Church Music but once the eighteenth century home of the Archbishops of Canterbury) are both open to visitors • LEISURE FACILITIES Sports and fitness centre at Selsdon. Swimming pools at New Addington, Purley, South Norwood and Thornton Heath. Well-provided-for golf courses with two public ones at Addington and Coulsdon alongside the seven private ones. Boating and fishing on the lake at South Norwood Country Park and athletics on the recently refurbished running track. Tennis, football and other outdoor sports in various parks. There are plans for a 15,000 seater arena on the long empty site next to East Croydon station. Crystal Palace has its ground at Selhurst Park • LIBRARIES Improving all the time. An impressive new three-storey library at the Clocktower with active childrens library, music library and local history archive. Thirteen branch libraries, 8.6 library visits per head. Position in library-use league table: 10th out of 32 (where 1 is best and 32 worst).

OPEN SPACES ★ ★ ★ ★

A quarter of the borough's area is Green Belt land and there are plentiful parks, open spaces and woods, particularly in the south. But there are some unexpected treats in the north, including Norwood Grove, a white seventeenth century mansion set in beautiful grounds with sloping lawns, flower gardens and wonderful views over south London and Surrey. A complete surprise in suburban Upper Norwood.

VIEWS Addington Hills. Wooded hills rising south of the open space of Lloyd Park with views to Croydon and beyond to Windsor and Epping (on a good day). A satisfying finish to a walk across Lloyd Park (see below) • RURAL SPACES Lloyd Park is one of many open spaces in Croydon with wild grass and heathland, framed by trees and a backdrop of hills that remove you instantly from built-up suburbia. If you're desperate to escape from the tower blocks of Croydon town centre, Lloyd Park is nearest • DOWNLAND The ring of open spaces around Coulsdon, Whyteleafe and Kenley including Happy Valley Park, Coulsdon Common and Riddlesdown are part of the Surrey Downs with lovely views and walks • WATERSPORTS & ACTIVITIES South Norwood Country Park. Only 10 years old and not as rural as its name suggests (there are always views of suburban streets through the trees). But an interesting open space in an otherwise built-up area, with mature trees and a large boating and fishing lake.

SHOPS ****

CRYSTAL PALACE & UPPER NORWOOD *Don't be put off by boarded-up shops at the Park end of Church Row. There are a couple of interesting shops including a second-hand bookshop further up. Interesting individual shops in Westow Street. Safeway in Westow Street (see also Lambeth)*

• **SOUTH NORWOOD & THORNTON HEATH** *Typically inner London suburban high streets, with mostly local shops – newsagents, take-aways and discount shops are prominent. Depressing and a bit run-down, on roads often clogged with traffic. Both have suffered from being too near Croydon, which dominates the borough, although the council is targeting both districts with grants for shop face-lifts as part of efforts to regenerate areas in the north of the borough. Safeway in South Norwood; Sainsbury's in Thornton Heath* • **CROYDON TOWN CENTRE** *Excellent shopping, if a bit predictable. There can't be a chain store that's not got a branch either in the pedestrianised North End or in the Whitgift or Drummond indoor shopping centres. Large branches of national chains, Allders department store and a definite American feel to the galleried malls with quietly moving escalators and glass ceiling. Like Bromley, probably its nearest competitor, new shopping centres are well-integrated with existing streets. But more soulless than Bromley with fewer pavement cafés. The sixteenth century Whitgift almshouses at the corner of North End are a poignant antidote to the consumerism raging on all sides. Fruit and veg market at Surrey Street, mainly Fridays and Saturdays.* • **PURLEY** *Another town centre suffering from the spread of Croydon. Several streets of shops centring on a busy one-way system. Mostly banks, building societies, chainstores and charity shops. Purley Way, one of the main roads between Purley and Croydon is now lined with out-of-town superstores, DIY, computer and white goods stores, causing big traffic jams on weekends and bank holidays. Big new Tesco.*

RESTAURANTS **

CRYSTAL PALACE & UPPER NORWOOD *Westow Street, one edge of the Westow Hill triangle (see also Lambeth) is attracting a number of good restaurants, including Italian, American, Chinese, Thai and Vegetarian. This area is an evening magnet for residents of less interesting parts of south London* • **CROYDON** *Struggling to get over its reputation as being dead in the evening. More pubs and restaurants are opening and it's becoming less of a joke among younger people to say they're going out on the town in Croydon. The usual pizza, pasta and other chains and a good vegetarian restaurant in the High Street* • **ELSEWHERE** *A couple of restaurants in Purley popular with locals and good pubs in Old Coulsdon. The rest of the borough has nothing of note.*

CRIME RATES ***

103 crimes per 1000 of population. Position in Metropolitan Police league table: 20th out of 32 (where 1 is worst and 32 best).

THE COUNCIL ***

POLITICAL AFFILIATION *Labour* • **MINUS POINTS** *Residents report uneven record on rubbish collection which the council blamed on unreliable contractors. Central recycling bins aren't emptied often enough although there are plenty of them. No door-to-door recycling* • **PLUS POINTS** *Good schools. Enthusiastic promotion of a borough whose attractions aren't* *immediately obvious to outsiders. One of the cheapest outer London boroughs for property searches* • **PROPERTY SEARCHES CARRIED OUT IN 10 WORKING DAYS** 97% • **STANDARD SEARCH FEE** £98 • **COUNCIL TAX COLLECTED** 92.1%

• **COUNCIL TAX 1998-99**

BAND	PROPERTY VALUE	CHARGE	BAND	PROPERTY VALUE	CHARGE
A	up to £40,000	£461.80	E	£88,001-£120,000	£864.63
B	£40,001-£52,000	£538.77	F	£120,001-£160,000	£1,000.57
C	£52,001-£68,000	£615.73	G	£160,001-£320,000	£1,154.50
D	£68,001-£88,000	£692.70	H	over £320,000	£1,385.40

EALING

The title of Queen of the Suburbs is hotly contested, it seems, with Ealing and Surbiton (see Kingston) both laying claim to the accolade. Without any set criteria it's tricky to judge the real winner (maybe the government should get on to it) but if it means having a good mix of historically interesting suburban architecture, a variety of shops to suit all moods, excellent links to town and country and lots of parkland and rural green space, then Ealing wins hands down. Even if the contest is a bit David and Goliath with a whole borough pitted against a single area. Sorry, Surbiton.

A walk from east to west in Ealing is as good a lesson in the outward spread of London's development as you're likely to get. At the bottom east end is the exclusive enclave of Bedford Park (see Hounslow). Separated from Bedford Park only by a railway line is Victorian Acton. To the west are the grander Victoriana of Ealing and the more modest cottages and terraces of Hanwell. North Ealing, on the hills above Ealing itself is Edwardian, with its own pioneering garden suburb at Brentham built in the heyday of such social experiments before the First World War. To the east of Brentham is up-market 1930s suburbia; to the west and north towards Southall and Greenford, speculative 1930s terraces and semis chucked up hurriedly during the 1930s building boom.

Ealing is mostly middle class and white collar, popular with young professionals who value a quick trip to the City and more space for their money than they'd get in cramped and expensive Fulham or Hammersmith. But it also has London's largest Indian community and the largest Sikh community outside India, clustered in Southall on the borough's western border, as well as a large Afro-Caribbean community. Nearly a third of Ealing's population is from an ethnic minority, the fifth highest in London. Unemployment is middling for outer London at 5.3% although there are blackspots in poorer areas like South Acton and Southall.

Ealing itself has perked up considerably since its shopping centre was opened more than 10 years ago but as is often the way, neighbouring areas have suffered. Acton High Street and neighbouring roads are still shabby despite the building of a small shopping mall but there are plans for a further revamp of the town centre as part of a larger regeneration scheme taking in the council estates of South Acton. In a bid to encourage owners to improve their town centre properties the council is also offering grants to pay for repairs of original features.

PROPERTY AND ARCHITECTURE

ACTON

Just a step to the west of Bedford Park (see Hounslow) but substantially cheaper. Historically, Acton is second best to Ealing, blighted by ugly council blocks around Acton Town station. But now people are starting to discover the area's large stock of Victorian houses and conversion flats. The group of streets known as Poets Corner (including Shakespeare, Milton and Cowper Roads) has hit the headlines recently as a hitherto undiscovered enclave of pretty Victorian terraces and large flat conversions (not to be confused with roads of the same name in Hanwell). On the other side of the tracks around West Acton, there is a total change architecturally with distinctive half-timbered houses and flats disguised as Tudor houses on the Hanger Hill Garden estate (known locally as the Tudor estate).

ATTRACTS *Young professionals; people who can't afford Ealing, Hammersmith or Fulham; Japanese wanting to be near the Japanese school* • **CONSERVATION AREAS** *Acton Town Centre; Acton Park; Creffield Road; Hanger Hill Garden Estate* • **AVERAGE PRICES** *Flats: studio: £45,000-£60,000; 1-bed: £70,000-£85,000; 2-bed: £85,000-£110,000 Houses: 2-bed: £150,000-£170,000; 3-bed: £160,000-£210,000; 4-bed: £220,000-£300,000; 5-bed: £250,000+* • **AVERAGE RENTS (MONTHLY)** *Flats: studio: £600+; 1-bed: £650+; 2-bed: £860 Houses: 1-bed: £650+; 2-bed: £860+; 3-bed: £1300+; 4-bed: £1510+.*

EALING & NORTH EALING

A popular middle class family area with a good range of solid Victorian and Edwardian property. Mostly medium and large Victorian terraces and semis with some roads of detached villas in roads round the attractive open space of Walpole Park. Victorian villas, some converted into flats, around Ealing Common. Larger and grander Victorian and Edwardian houses mixed with some modern blocks around Castlebar and Montpelier Park in North Ealing and on the Hanger Hill Haymills estate. Brentham, north of Montpelier Park, part of what estate agents now call Pitshanger Village, was built to provide cottage homes for working people in the early years of this century. Now there are expensive and attractive whitewashed homes with small paned windows and neatly clipped hedges. A strong community atmosphere, sought after for good schools. The best choice of flats is in central Ealing.

ATTRACTS *Families* • **CONSERVATION AREAS** *Brentham Garden Estate; Grange and White Ledges; Ealing Green; Haven Green; Montpelier Park; Mount Park; Ealing Town Centre; Ealing Common; Hanger Lane (Haymills) estate* • **AVERAGE PRICES** *Flats: studio: £60,000; 1-bed: £80,000-£120,000; 2-bed: £120,000-£180,000 Houses: 2-bed: £170,000; 3-bed: £180,000+; 4-bed: £250,000-£300,000; 5-bed: £350,000+*

• **AVERAGE RENTS (MONTHLY)** *Flats: studio: £600-£675; 1-bed: £850-£1000; 2-bed: £1100-£1200; 3-bed: £1300-£1500 Houses: 2-bed: £1000-£1100; 4-bed: £1800-£2000; 5-bed: £2000-£3000.*

WEST EALING & HANWELL

West Ealing is the cheapest part of Ealing, with grids of Victorian and Edwardian terraces, many pebble-dashed and "improved" in stark contrast to the carefully preserved original features further north. Hanwell is a mix of large Victorian houses around Golden Manor near the Brent Valley, smaller terraces and cottages in roads round the station and later 1930s terraces, many with hideous modern windows and pebble-dashing.

ATTRACTS *Families; people who can't afford Ealing (especially Hanwell, becoming increasingly popular); first-time buyers (especially West Ealing)*
• **CONSERVATION AREAS** *Cuckoo Estate; Hanwell Clock Tower; Hanwell Village Green* • **AVERAGE PRICES** *Flats: studio: £45,000-£55,000; 1-bed: £65,000-£95,000; 2-bed: £90,000-£120,000 Houses: 2-bed: £90,000-£160,000; 3-bed: £120,000+; 4-bed: £150,000-£300,000* • **AVERAGE RENTS (MONTHLY)** *Flats: studio: £550-£600; 1-bed: £650-£700; 2-bed: £750-£850; 3-bed: £1000-£1200 Houses: 2-bed: £850-£950; 3-bed: £1000-£1200; 4-bed: £1300-£1400; 5-bed: £1500-£1600.*

GREENFORD & NORTHOLT

Mostly roads of "improved" small and medium-sized 1930s semis with more modern estates of small houses and blocks of flats. Architecturally some of the dullest parts of Ealing, carved up by the busy A40, tube and train lines. The Westway Cross retail park has been built on the site of former factories around the Grand Union Canal. A good area for cheap family homes and fairly good transport links (especially Greenford). Northolt is cheaper than Greenford and there's a lot of ex-council property.

ATTRACTS *First-time buyers; bargain hunters; families; investors*
• **CONSERVATION AREAS** *Northolt Village Green* • **AVERAGE PRICES** *Flats: studio: £40,000+; 1-bed: £50,000-£62,000; 2-bed: £55,000-£70,000 Houses: 2-bed: £80,000-£90,000; 3-bed: £90,000-£140,000; 4-bed: £140,000-£150,000* • **AVERAGE RENTS (MONTHLY)** *Flats: studio: £480-£500; 1-bed: £550-£600; 2-bed: £600+ Houses: 2-bed: £600+; 3-bed: £800+; 4-bed: £1000+.*

SOUTHALL

Predominantly Asian. A few shabby Victorian terraces near the main shopping streets but otherwise mostly 1930s semis and terraces huddled together in bleak streets. Norwood Green is popular because it's closest to green space but a lot of the housing stock in Southall is in poor condition and much of it is rented, often to people on benefits who can't find anything to rent elsewhere. Some modern blocks of flats and flats above shops.

ATTRACTS *Members of the Asian community* • **CONSERVATION AREAS** *None*
• **AVERAGE PRICES** *Flats: studio: £44,000; 1-bed: £50,000; 2-bed: £60,000 Houses: 2-bed: £75,000; 3-bed: £95,000; 4-bed: £115,000* • **AVERAGE RENTS (MONTHLY)** *Flats: studio: £430-£450; 1-bed: £495-£540; 2-bed: £540-£620 Houses: 2-bed: £540-£620; 3-bed: £720+; 4-bed: £900+.*

BEST POSTCODES

Ealing W5 is the best postcode, covering the smartest parts of North Ealing. But Acton W3 is becoming more acceptable, as is Hanwell W7. West Ealing W13 is less smart. Middlesex postcodes around Southall and Greenford.

AMENITIES

SCHOOLS ★ ★ ★

Not a startling overall performance either at primary or secondary level but certainly not scraping the bottom of the barrel. The best schools are highly sought after and operate tight catchment areas. Quite generous state nursery provision for pre-schoolers. A number of private prep and secondary schools.
PRE-SCHOOL PROVISION *104 private day nurseries and playgroups; 50 nursery classes in state and church primary schools; 9 state-run nurseries. Proportion of under-fives in state nurseries: 68%* **STATE PRIMARY SCHOOLS** *Overall position in league tables: 73rd out of 150; Top scorers: Havelock (with nursery unit), Southall; North Ealing (with nursery unit), Pitshanger Village; Mant Carmel (with nursery unit), Ealing* • **STATE SECONDARY SCHOOLS** *Overall position in league tables: 66th out of 150; Best scorers: Twyford C of E High (mixed) Acton; Ellen Wilkinson (girls), Acton; Drayton Manor High (mixed), Drayton Bridge* • **PRIVATE SCHOOLS** *Barbara Speake Stage School (mixed 4 to 16), East Acton; King Fahad Academy (Muslim, mixed from 4-18), Acton; Notting Hill and Ealing High, (girls 5-19), Ealing; Harvington (girls 2-17), Ealing* • **PRIVATE SECONDARY SCHOOLS** *St Augustine's Priory (girls), Ealing; Ealing College Upper School, Ealing; St Benedict's (boys, girls in sixth), Ealing.*

TRANSPORT ★ ★ ★ ★

One of the area's big draws. Generally excellent – especially around Ealing and Acton, with trains and tubes, so if one mode of transport isn't working you can use something else. And if one tube line isn't working, it's usually a fairly short walk to an alternative. Hanwell and Southall come off less well, with trains only.
TRAINS *Hanwell: Zone 4. Cost of annual season ticket: £1068. No of trains per hour: to Paddington 2; Fastest journey: 13 minutes. Southall: Zone 4. No of trains per hour: to Paddington 4; Fastest journey: 15 minutes* • **TUBES** *Acton Town: Zone 3. Cost of annual season ticket: £860; Frequency: District line to Embankment every 10 minutes. Piccadilly line to Piccadilly Circus every 2-3 minutes; Fastest journey: District: 30 minutes; Piccadilly: 20 minutes. Ealing Broadway: Zone 3. Frequency: District line to Embankment: every 10 minutes; Central line to Oxford Circus: every 6-10 minutes; Fastest journey: District line: 34 minutes; Central line: 25 minutes. Greenford: Zone 4. Cost of annual season ticket: £1068; Frequency: Central line to Oxford Circus: every 6-10 minutes; Fastest journey: 28 minutes* • **BUSES** *One or two to town or at least more central areas of London including the 7 from Russell Square to Acton and the 70 from South Kensington Station to Acton. Other than that, buses go to local destinations, shopping centres like Kingston or Brent Cross and Heathrow Airport. Night buses include the N23 to Northolt via Ealing Broadway and Greenford from Trafalgar Square and the N207 from Victoria to Uxbridge via Ealing and Hanwell* • **TRAFFIC BLACKSPOTS** *Ealing: The shopping areas around the Broadway are separated by busy roads which doesn't enhance otherwise good shopping. Often snarled up with buses and lorries. The*

section of the Uxbridge Road between Ealing and Acton can be particularly bad round Ealing Common at the junction with the North Circular. Southall: Bad traffic around the crossroads of the central shopping area. Main Roads: Brilliantly convenient for escaping from town to the west when they're not jammed. Ealing is home to the infamous Hanger Lane gyratory system linking the North Circular to the A40. The A40, the main road to Oxford and Birmingham, is often solid and plans to widen it have been put on ice, leaving gaping holes where homes along the route have been demolished or left boarded up. • **PARKING** Two controlled parking schemes in the borough, in Perivale around the industrial park just north of the A40, and around Thames Valley University just south of Ealing Broadway. Cost of annual resident's permit in Perivale: £15 per vehicle; cost of annual resident's permit around Thames Valley University: £45 per vehicle.

LEISURE FACILITIES * * *

THEATRES & CONCERTS Plays and stand-up comedy at Drayton Court, Ealing. The Questor Theatre in Ealing, which describes itself as "Britain's most exciting non-professional theatre" has lots of plays by well-known writers (Ayckbourn and Stoppard to name but two). Plays also at Pitshanger Manor, an elegant Regency Manor House on the edge of Walpole Park in Ealing restored by Sir John Soane. Live music in the summer in Walpole Park and year round in Pitshanger Manor, halls and venues across the borough • **CINEMAS** Lots of screens although unfortunately they usually show many of the same predictable mainstream films. Warner Village at Park Royal and Virgin at Ealing Broadway. The BelleVue in West Ealing has Asian films • **MUSEUMS & GALLERIES** An eclectic little collection. Pitshanger Manor has art galleries and workshops, displays of pottery and period furniture. Southall has the railway centre, a trainspotter's dream with collections of rolling stock and engines. Weekends only. Also the archives of the Guinness company at Park Royal • **SPORTS FACILITIES** Well provided for. Eight leisure centres at Acton (three), Southall, Hanwell, Greenford, Ealing and Northolt. Pools at Acton (restored Victorian swimming baths), Southall, Ealing and Northolt. Golf at Brent Valley (Hanwell) and Horsenden Hill (Perivale) • **LIBRARIES** The most under-used and some of the most poorly resourced in outer London despite a large central library in Ealing, integrated into the Broadway shopping centre and pleasant branch libraries. All libraries closed on Mondays with several smaller branches closed one or two other days as well. A dearth of long evening opening hours even in the central library. 4.6 visits per head. Position in library-use league table: 28th out of 32 (where 1 is best and 32 worst).

OPEN SPACES * * * *

An excellent variety of space with woods, rivers, meadowland and high viewpoints all within easy striding distance of each other, as well as greenery on a more domestic scale in gardens and tree-lined streets. **GOOD VIEWS** Horsenden Hill. One of the high points of suburban west London with views over to Harrow on the Hill and beyond to metroland over a spread of tidy red 1930s roofs below. Part of a wide swathe of open space in the north of the borough including Horsenden Wood and golf course • **RIVER WALKS** The Brent Valley walk. Created as a linear riverside park in the 1970s to rescue the river from dereliction. You can now walk from Brentham to Brentford High Street along seven miles of river and canal passing through meadows, parkland and woods as well as getting a spectacular view of Brunel's Wharncliffe Viaduct built to take the

Great Western Railway to Bristol across Ealing's fields • **PARKS** *Walpole Park. Lush park in the centre of Ealing adorned by Pitshanger Manor and surrounded by salubrious Victorian villas.*

SHOPS * * * *

ACTON Uninspiring, trafficky high street, with mostly small chains and local shops, take-aways and discount stores. The Oaks shopping centre has more chains and an indoor market. There are plans for better pedestrian crossings and other environmental improvements but Acton's main problem is that it's overshadowed by Ealing. Safeway • **EALING** Big choice of well-stocked chains including large M&S and more off-the-wall shops. Two indoor shopping malls on either side of the Broadway, the Broadway and Arcadia. The Broadway has the main library and Safeway. Good middle of the road shopping centre with an attractive entrance via a pedestrianised street of shops and restaurants with Victorian shop fronts. More specialised shops and restaurants in Bond Street and the High Street round the green. The trafficky Broadway is the main detraction. A well-used local high street in Brentham. • **SOUTHALL** If you ever need Indian spices, saris, jewellery or Indian sweets, this is the place to come. Two main streets of almost exclusively Asian shops including a huge supermarket with shelves of spices, sacks of rice and drums of cooking oil. Lots of traders spill on to the street with fruit, vegetables, material and jewellery. Dull shopping street transformed into Eastern bazaar • **GREENFORD & HANWELL** Small broadways of chains and local shops. Hanwell is suffering from Ealingitis. Tesco and Sainsbury's at Greenford and retail park by the A40. Tesco in fabulous art deco former Hoover building on the A40, with green lighting at night.

RESTAURANTS * * *

ACTON & EALING Thai and East European restaurants in Acton. Ealing has Cafe Rouge, Caffe Uno and all the other ubiquitous restaurant chains you'd expect in a middle class area plus Chinese, Italian, East European and Japanese (for the large Japanese community) • **SOUTHALL** A wide choice of Indian restaurants, Tandoori grills and kebab shops. Take-aways with naan bread rolled in front of your eyes.

CRIME RATES * * *

118 crimes per 1000 of population. Position in Metropolitan Police league table: 16th out of 32 (where 1 is worst and 32 best).

THE COUNCIL * * *

POLITICAL AFFILIATION Labour • **MINUS POINTS** Litter in the street not always dealt with quickly. Underused libraries • **PLUS POINTS** Door to door recycling being extended across the borough. Active promotion of Ealing as tourist and business destination. Generous state nursery provision. Generally judged by residents to be friendly and efficient • **PROPERTY SEARCHES CARRIED OUT IN 10 WORKING DAYS** 99% • **STANDARD SEARCH FEE** £96 • **COUNCIL TAX COLLECTED** 94%

● **COUNCIL TAX 1998-99**

BAND	PROPERTY VALUE	CHARGE	BAND	PROPERTY VALUE	CHARGE
A	up to £40,000	£428.67	E	£88,001-£120,000	£785.89
B	£40,001-£52,000	£500.11	F	£120,001-£160,000	£928.78
C	£52,001-£68,000	£571.56	G	£160,001-£320,000	£1,071.67
D	£68,001-£88,000	£643.00	H	over £320,000	£1,286.00

ENFIELD

"Golf clubs on one side and deprivation on the other" is Enfield's director of housing's verdict on London's northernmost borough. Like other London boroughs, created by administrative mergers, Enfield is an uneasy mix of affluent and even grand suburbia in the west and, just a short bus ride away, brutal-looking council estates and run-down shopping areas which can compete with London's worst.

The industrial east side stretches up the banks of the River Lea from the tower blocks and Victorian terraces of Edmonton and Ponders End to the suburban sprawl of outer Enfield. But cross the A10 and you're in middle class territory, from the large Edwardian terraces of Palmers Green in the south, reaching up through leafy villagey Winchmore Hill and elegant Enfield Town to Southgate and the respectable suburbs of Oakwood and Cockfosters. This is where the tube line ends and the fields of Hertfordshire begin, protected by the Green Belt before they could be engulfed in a sea of speculative semis. Tucked away in the countryside is Hadley Wood, favoured haunt of celebrities who like its big houses and greenery.

To look at places like Hadley Wood and Winchmore Hill, it's difficult to believe than unemployment in Enfield is quite high for outer London at 5.7%. It's also difficult to believe that Enfield has significant Afro-Caribbean and Indian communities. Although the borough isn't as multiracial as any of its neighbours, 14% of its population is from an ethnic minority.

But the poorest areas around Edmonton and Ponders End are now receiving large injections of funds from Europe as well as private and public sector money to regenerate former industrial sites along the River Lea, to create new jobs particularly in high tech indsutries and bring derelict areas back into use. Between 1995 and 2002, £120 million will be spent on the area. On top of this, some of the tower blocks dominating the skyline over Edmonton are set to be demolished while others are refurbished, and the depressing Edmonton Green shopping centre given a much needed overhaul. The promise is that Edmonton Green will be unrecognisable in 10 years time, a welcome prospect.

PROPERTY AND ARCHITECTURE

EDMONTON & PONDERS END

Apart from tower blocks, this stretch of the borough has a mixture of small late Victorian terraces (it was built as a workmen's suburb near the Great Eastern railway line which offered workers cheap fares) and messed about 1930s semis with the usual complement of "improvements" in the shape of modern windows, biliously-coloured stained glass and ugly porches. Flats in purpose-built blocks and lots of ex-council property. Good for small (nothing much larger than three bedrooms), cheap houses. A first-time buy after which you move out as quickly as you can. Ponders End is slightly more expensive than Edmonton.

ATTRACTS *First-time buyers; loyal locals* • **CONSERVATION AREAS** *Church Street, Edmonton; Ponders End Flour Mills; Turkey Street; Enfield Lock; Montague Cemeteries* • **AVERAGE PRICES** *Flats: studio: £33,000; 1-bed: £42,000-£50,000; 2-bed: £50,000-£62,000; 3-bed: £60,000-£65,000 Houses: 2-bed: £65,000+; 3-bed: £75,000-£85,000* • **AVERAGE RENTS (MONTHLY)** *Flats: studio: £390-£430; 1-bed: £430+; 2-bed: £500; 3-bed: £540 Houses: 2-bed: £585-£630; 3-bed: £650; 4-bed: £860.*

ENFIELD TOWN

More like an attractive county town than part of London, with a high profile local amenity society. This is the beginning of the middle class half of Enfield, with a mix of most styles of property from modest Victorian terraces to larger Edwardian semis around the centre of town and in roads off Chase Side and modern blocks near the grammar school. The jewel in Enfield's crown is Gentlemen's Row, a street of assorted Georgian and early Victorian houses, some set in large gardens, overlooking a grassy sward planted with mature trees. The large detached houses of The Ridgeway to the north west and west of Bush Hill Park station are also sought after. The nearer you are to the A10 the cheaper it is.

ATTRACTS *Families; City workers* • **CONSERVATION AREAS** *Enfield Town; extension to Enfield Town; Bush Hill Park; Forty Hill; Clay Hill* • **AVERAGE PRICES** *Flats: studio: £50,000; 1-bed: £60,000; 2-bed: £75,000+ Houses: 1-bed: £75,000; 2-bed: £105,000+; 3-bed: £110,000-£125,000+; 4-bed: £180,000-£235,000; 5-bed: £200,000+* • **AVERAGE RENTS (MONTHLY)** *Flats: studio: £410; 1-bed: £520; 2-bed: £650+ Houses: 2-bed: £750+; 3-bed: £900+; 4-bed: £1000+; 5-bed: £1210+.*

WINCHMORE HILL & SOUTHGATE

Winchmore Hill is chic and self-consciously villagey, perched on a hill with far-reaching views from the village green. Mostly Victorian terraces and cottages in roads off the centre with larger, up-market Edwardian and interwar semis in roads towards Southgate. Broad Walk is the grandest part of Winchmore Hill, with large detached houses, some vulgar and brash, some hidden behind discreet shrubbery. Popular with celebrities as well as the merely wealthy. Southgate is up-market suburbia, an attractive mix of solid Edwardian semis and half timbered 1930s houses with deep eaves, tall Tudor-style chimneys and neat gardens. You pay more for flats than houses in Southgate because of the tube, but more for houses in Winchmore Hill. Cockfosters and Oakwood are slightly more expensive than Southgate proper because they're nearer the country but still have tubes.

ATTRACTS *Families keen to be close to good schools; young professionals wanting to be close to tubes; minor celebs* • **CONSERVATION AREAS** *Winchmore Hill Green; Bush Hill Park; Southgate Green: Trent Park* • **AVERAGE PRICES** *Flats: studio: £50,000+; 1-bed: £70,000+; 2-bed: £90,000+ Houses: 2-bed: £110,000-£125,000; 3-bed: £150,000-£270,000; 4-bed: £265,000-£300,000* • **AVERAGE RENTS (MONTHLY)** *Flats: studio: £430; 1-bed: £560+; 2-bed: £700+ Houses: 2-bed: £800; 3-bed: £1000; 4-bed: £1120; 5-bed: £1210+.*

PALMERS GREEN

Once an elegant Edwardian suburb and still mostly Edwardian in roads off the central triangle. Many of the four- and five-bedroom family homes have survived being converted into flats (although this is good flat-hunting territory as well). Further away from the centre, 1930s semis take over. Palmers Green is cheaper than Southgate or Winchmore Hill (no tube and less village atmosphere) but more expensive than Enfield Town (closer to London). South of the north circular, there are smaller Victorian terraces around Bowes Park.

ATTRACTS *Families; first-time buyers* • **CONSERVATION AREAS** *None* • **AVERAGE PRICES** *Flats: studio: £35,000-£50,000; 1-bed: £60,000-£80,000; 2-bed: £70,000-£110,000 Houses: 2-bed: £90,000-£120,000; 3-bed: £100,000-£200,000; 4-bed: £180,000-£250,000* • **AVERAGE RENTS (MONTHLY)** *Flats: studio: £400-£430; 1-bed: £520+; 2-bed: £650+ Houses: 2-bed: £700; 3-bed: £900; 4-bed: £1080+.*

HADLEY WOOD

The most expensive part of Enfield. Large detached houses on the edge of green belt land yet attached to London by the umbilical cord of the railway line to Moorgate. Surrounded by the greenery and grand Georgian houses of Hadley Common, Hadley Wood looks mostly towards Barnet (see Barnet). Another area popular with minor celebrities, footballers and pop stars. (According to one local agent there are enough footballers to make a team) The most expensive, mostly 1930s houses, are south of Camlet Way and Beech Avenue, known locally as millionaires' row, with smaller 1960s houses to the north. Few flats.

ATTRACTS *Wealthy families; celebrities* • **CONSERVATION AREA** *Hadley Wood* • **AVERAGE PRICES** *Flats: 2-bed: £140,000+; 3-bed: £200,000+ Houses: 2-bed: £150,000+; 3-bed: £280,000-£300,000+; 4-bed: £350,000; 5-bed: £425,000* • **AVERAGE RENTS (MONTHLY)** *Houses: 3-bed: £1300+; 4-bed: £1730+; 5-bed: £2160+.*

BEST POSTCODES

There are lots of London postcodes here, considering this is outer London. Winchmore Hill N21 is the best code, closely followed by Southgate N14, both of which carry premiums of between 10% and 15% on prices in neighbouring Palmers Green N13. But N13's a good deal better than N9 or N18 (Edmonton and Ponders End). Middlesex codes to the north but EN1 and EN2 are much better than EN3 (east of the A10). Everywhere proximity to tubes (rather than trains) adds to prices.

AMENITIES

SCHOOLS***

Middling performance in school league tables with secondary schools doing better than primary schools, helped by some good selective state and private schools. Some parents send their children over the border to Hertfordshire or Barnet. Below average state provision for pre-schoolers but a wide choice of private nurseries and playgroups. A small number of private prep and secondary schools.

PRE-SCHOOL PROVISION *120 private day nurseries and playgroups; 24 nursery classes in state primaries and church schools. Proportion of under-*

fives in state nurseries: 52% • **STATE PRIMARY SCHOOLS** *Overall league table position: 89th out of 150. Top scorers: Grange Park, Winchmore Hill; St Andrew's C of E (with nursery unit), Enfield; St Monica's RC, Southgate* • **STATE SECONDARY SCHOOLS** *Overall league table position: 84th out of 150. Best scorers: Latymer School (selective, mixed), Edmonton; Enfield County School (girls), Enfield; Southgate School (mixed), Cockfosters* • **PRIVATE PREP SCHOOLS** *Keble Prep (boys), Winchmore Hill; Salcombe Prep (mixed from 2), Southgate* • **PRIVATE SECONDARY SCHOOLS** *Palmers Green High (girls), Palmers Green; St John's Preparatory and Senior School (mixed from 4), Enfield.*

TRANSPORT***

Tubes only in the far west of the borough, with the last three stops of the Piccadilly Line linking Southgate, Arnos Grove and Cockfosters with the centre of town. Not only is the tube a vital transport link but its distinctive 1930s tube stations at the Enfield end of the Piccadilly line are a reminder of the days when London Underground took station architecture seriously. Southgate's circular station with its peculiar space-age mast and integrated shopping parade is particularly distinguished. In the south and east of the borough it's trains only, not always very frequent outside rush hour.
TRAINS *Edmonton Green: Zone 4; Cost of annual season ticket: £1068; No of trains per hour: to Liverpool Street 4; Fastest journey: 30 minutes. Ponders End: Zone 5; Cost of annual season ticket: £1280; No of trains per hour: to Liverpool Street 2; Fastest journey: 25 minutes. Enfield Town: Zone 5; No of trains per hour: to Liverpool Street 2; Fastest journey: 30 minutes. Winchmore Hill: Zone 4; No of trains per hour: to Moorgate 3; Fastest journey: 30 minutes* • **TUBES** *Cockfosters: Zone 5; Frequency: to Piccadilly Circus every 6 minutes; Fastest journey: 35 minutes. Southgate: Zone 4; Frequency: to Piccadilly Circus every 6 minutes; Fastest journey: 31 minutes* • **BUSES** *The 149 runs from Edmonton Green to London Bridge but be prepared for a struggle through some of North London's most trafficky roads (Tottenham High Road and Kingsland Road to name but two). The 29 from Palmers Green to Trafalgar Square is a similar travelling experience. Otherwise buses mostly link different parts of the borough, providing vital west to east services as railway lines run north to south. Night buses include the N29 from Trafalgar Square to Palmers Green, Winchmore Hill and Enfield Town, the N91 from Trafalgar Square to Southgate and Cockfosters and the N279 from Trafalgar Square to Endmonton and Ponders End* • **TRAFFIC BLACKSPOTS** *Edmonton: The junction of the North Circular road which slashes through the borough from East to West, particularly at the junction with the A10, one of the main roads through North London to the City. Major roadworks along the North Circular where flyovers are planned* • **PARKING** *Five controlled parking zones in the borough at Enfield Town, Bush Hill Park, Grange Park, Oakwood and Arnos Grove. Cost of annual resident's parking permit: £10.*

LEISURE FACILITIES***

THEATRES & CONCERT HALLS *Two theatres. The Millfield Theatre in Edmonton has family shows, middle of the road plays, the annual Christmas panto, musicals and live music. Plays, opera and so on also at the Gladys Child theatre on the campus of Southgate College. Summer open-air concerts and plays in parks round the borough* • **CINEMA** *Improved since the arrival of the Lea Valley Leisure Centre by the River Lea with 12 screen UCI cinema. Mainstream viewing on all 12 screens* • **MUSEUMS & GALLERIES**

Small collection. Forty Hall Museum has exhibitions of furniture, ceramics and glass in a handsome seventeenth century manor house. Collection of early vehicles in the former New River pump house at the Whitewebbs Museum of Transport and Industry in Enfield. Watch truncated opening hours. If you're into gardens, Capel Manor in Enfield is the HQ of the Greater London College of Horticulture and Countryside Studies, with themed gardens, demonstrations and classes. Try also the plant collection at Myddleton House Gardens, Enfield • **SPORTS FACILITIES** Leisure centres at Enfield, Edmonton, Southgate and Picketts Lock in the Lea Valley. Pools at Enfield, Arnos Grove, Edmonton and Southgate. Golf at the Lea Valley regional centre. Tennis, football and other sports in open spaces across the borough. Discount programme in operation • **LIBRARIES** Under-used and one of the most under-resourced library services in London. Spending per head dropped slightly last year. Even the central library in Enfield is small and cramped compared with the modern palaces of learning and culture built by some other boroughs. But staff are pleasant and helpful. Opening hours are patchy, with some branch libraries closed more than they're open, although the central library keeps reasonable hours. No Sunday opening. 6.5 visits per head. Position in library-use league table: 21st out of 32 (where 1 is best and 32 worst).

OPEN SPACES ★ ★ ★ ★

No shortage of open space, as London suddenly turns into fields in the startling way it has along its outer edge, demonstrating that the Green Belt, put in place to stop London's growth, really does work. A good choice of parkland and woods, as well as a general feel of green in more built-up areas. Lots of new open space is also opening up along the Lea Valley with the creation of the Lea Valley Park along what were once the derelict banks of the River Lea. The park stretches right down from Hertfordshire through Enfield and down into Docklands (see also Haringey, Hackney and Newham). **PARKLAND** Trent Country Park. Rolling hills, woodland (muddy in winter as countryside should be). Only the glimpse of the ugly office block on the skyline at Cockfosters and the whistle of tubes spoils the rural idyll. Try also Forty Hall, the borough's other country park near Enfield • **RIVER WALKS** The towpath along the River Lea. Great if you like industrial walks right under electricity pylons with the roar of factories on the other side of the river. Frustratingly, there are massive reservoirs just next to the towpath but they're hidden by grass mounds, making the towpath a bit claustrophobic. The New River, which used to bring water supplies to London from Hertfordshire is also being given a face-lift of its loop around Enfield Town with £18 million of lottery money over five years.

SHOPS ★ ★ ★

EDMONTON, PONDERS END & ENFIELD OUTSKIRTS One of the nastiest 1960s shopping centres in London at The Broadway, Edmonton Green, with small, tired shops and greasy spoons along concrete corridors, opening out into a hangar-like central marketplace with stalls selling fruit, vegetables and clothes. Bargain stores and cheap chains predominate. Tesco. Easy to get lost and disoriented, and emerge onto a urine-smelling staircase. Due for a big overhaul and about time. More human-scale local shops in Upper Edmonton and Ponders End. Tesco in Ponders End, Safeway by A10 • **ENFIELD TOWN** Instantly likeable town centre, just the right size for a stroll around the market (clothes, food, second-hand books) and along the high street. Mostly chains but with attractive shop fronts. More up-market chains *and large M&S in Palace Gardens, the pedestrianised open-air shopping centre tucked so subtly behind the high street that it takes some finding. Antique shops, frame shops and clothes exchanges on Chase Side. Tesco by station, Sainsbury's in shopping centre* • **WINCHMORE HILL, SOUTHGATE & PALMERS GREEN** *Winchmore Hill is mostly beautiful not useful. Victoriana, antiques and bedsteads are among the attractive cottagey shops on the green. The dull, sensible shops are in Southgate and Palmers Green. Southgate is sprawling and trafficky and some residents complain, with some justification, that most of the shops seem to have turned into charity shops, restaurants and building societies. Palmers Green's Edwardian shopping streets feel more gracious although the shops aren't very exciting. Tesco in Palmers Green.*

RESTAURANTS**

Not very thrilling. A recommended Spanish restaurant in Southgate, Pizza Express and Caffe Uno in Enfield Town (the stamp of a middle class neighbourhood) and a smart-looking Italian restaurant in Winchmore Hill. Otherwise, chains and the usual collection of local restaurants of varying quality.

CRIME RATES****

96 crimes per 1000 of population. Position in Metropolitan Police league table: 23rd out of 32 (where 1 is worst and 32 best).

THE COUNCIL***

POLITICAL AFFILIATION *Labour* • **MINUS POINTS** *No door-to-door recycling collections. Poorly resourced library service* • **PLUS POINTS** *Some of the cheapest residents' parking permits in London. Couldn't be quicker at turning round property searches. Enthusiastic participant in regenerating the Lea Valley. Generally good at rubbish collection and street-sweeping*

- **PROPERTY SEARCHES CARRIED OUT IN 10 WORKING DAYS** *100%*
- **STANDARD SEARCH FEE** £*105* • **COUNCIL TAX COLLECTED** *91.8%*
- **COUNCIL TAX 1998-99**

BAND	PROPERTY VALUE	CHARGE	BAND	PROPERTY VALUE	CHARGE
A	up to £40,000	£453.33	E	£88,001-£120,000	£831.11
B	£40,001-£52,000	£528.89	F	£120,001-£160,000	£982.22
C	£52,001-£68,000	£604.44	G	£160,001-£320,000	£1,133.33
D	£68,001-£88,000	£680.00	H	over £320,000	£1,360.00

GREENWICH

No London borough can boast of more newspaper column inches in the last few years than Greenwich, home of the controversial Millennium Dome. But the Greenwich Peninsula, where the masts and canopy of the Dome are rising inexorably on the site of a former gasworks, is only a tiny part of the borough. Greenwich's boundaries stretch east along the river for eight miles beyond the Thames Barrier at Woolwich to the Victorian terraces of Plumstead and the 1960s tower blocks of Thamesmead. From the Peninsula eastwards, crumbling warehouses, rusting machinery and weed-choked open spaces are the only reminder of the area's industrial past.

To the south lie the ancient woodlands of Oxleas Woods and the open spaces and golf courses of suburban Eltham. In West Greenwich, known to millions from glossy guidebooks, the wonderful Royal Naval College buildings (soon to be home to Greenwich University) open out on to the Thames and back on to the sweep of Greenwich Park; nearby, tourists throng the streets and markets. A steep climb through Greenwich Park brings you to the plateau of Blackheath and some of its grandest Georgian houses on the fringes of the Heath (see also Lewisham).

But despite all the tourist attractions of West Greenwich, the borough as a whole is the 14th most deprived in the UK. There is high unemployment, particularly in the blackspots of Woolwich and Thamesmead, hard hit by the decline of traditional manufacturing industry. Greenwich borough has one of the smallest ethnic communities in inner London with only 16 per cent of the population coming from an ethnic minority, but racial tensions have flared,culminating in the murder of black teenager Stephen Lawrence in Eltham six years ago.

The government has been pouring money into the area for several years in a bid to stem the tide of deprivation, rejuvenate the town centres of Greenwich and Woolwich and improve poor transport facilities. The Dome may be criticised as a waste of £750 million but it's put Greenwich on the map, attracting the attention of cynical north Londoners who can't believe how much cheaper property is south of the river. Previously derelict land next to Deptford Creek is also being turned into luxury flats with shops, a hotel, a 12 screen cinema and a cruise liner terminal. The arrival of the Docklands Light Railway later this year with a station at Cutty Sark will finally provide a direct link with Docklands, elimininating the need for a 15 minute walk under the eerily dripping Greenwich foot tunnel. The Jubilee line extension, also supposedly due this year but dogged with technical and financial difficulties, will link north Greenwich with the West End in 15 minutes. But for locals, the big question is, will this be enough to handle the expected influx of visitors during the Millennium?

PROPERTY AND ARCHITECTURE

WEST GREENWICH & BLACKHEATH

Architecturally the most impressive, with four-storey Georgian terraces in roads west of Greenwich Park. For Victorian cottages, try roads off Royal Hill. Blackheath Standard (on the opposite side of the A2 from Blackheath Village and duller) has large Victorian houses, many converted into flats. Near Blackheath Village itself, look for large stucco early Victorian houses, Georgian cottages or modern Span houses on the Cator estate, the poshest part of Blackheath (see also Lewisham). Anything on the left side of the A102M motorway (looking north) is better than anything on the right. **ATTRACTS** *Professional couples; families; history lovers and people who like* *to boast that they discovered the area ages ago* • **CONSERVATION AREAS** *West Greenwich; Greenwich Park; Ashburnham Triangle* • **AVERAGE PRICES** *Flats: studio: £55,000-£60,000; 1-bed: £85,000+; 2-bed: £110,000-£120,000; 3-bed: £150,000-£200,000 Houses: 2-bed: £150,000-£200,000; 3-bed: £250,000+; 4-bed: £325,000-£400,000* • **AVERAGE RENTS (MONTHLY)** *Flats: studio: £500; 1-bed: £600-£650; 2-bed: £750-£800; 3-bed: £950-£1000 Houses: 2-bed: £800+; 3-bed: £1,100+; 4-bed: £1,300+.*

EAST GREENWICH

Mostly small two- and three-storey Victorian terraces and council blocks fanning out either side of the traffic-choked Trafalgar and Woolwich Roads. A total contrast to the West Greenwich which tourists see but good for cheaper property in Greenwich including ex-council stock. The further east you go, the more the area is dominated by the concrete monstrosity of the northbound A102M flyover. Hardly any property on the Greenwich peninsula yet but there are plans for an ambitious urban Millennium Village, which will be a model of sustainable and energy efficient development with 1,400 homes.
ATTRACTS *First-time buyers; people who can't afford West Greenwich; investors; loyal locals* • **CONSERVATION AREAS** *East Greenwich* • **AVERAGE PRICES** *Flats: studio: £45,000; 1-bed: £60,000+; 2-bed: £65,000-£85,000; 3-bed: £120,000 Houses: 2-bed: £120,000+; 3-bed: £160,000-£180,000; 4-bed: £200,000-£250,000* • **AVERAGE RENTS (MONTHLY)** *Flats: studio: £450; 1-bed: £525; 2-bed: £600; 3-bed: £700 Houses: 2-bed: £650-£750; 3-bed: £750-£800; 4-bed: £850-£900.*

KIDBROOKE & CHARLTON

The best roads are nearest Blackheath and Greenwich to the west, with mainly Victorian houses. But otherwise, detached and semi-detached 1920s and 1930s family houses predominate, interspersed with large scale council estates and ex-council property. More of a centre at Charlton (generally considered better than Kidbrooke) with a village street of small cottagey shops and a church. Roads of Victorian terraces to the north of Charlton Road slope steeply down towards the Thames giving some stunning views of Docklands and the remnants of a once busy working river.
ATTRACTS *Working families who can't afford Blackheath or West Greenwich; loyal locals; first-time buyers* • **CONSERVATION AREAS** *Rectory Field; Charlton Village* • **AVERAGE PRICES** *Flats: studio: £30,000-£40,000; 1-bed: £40,000-£50,000; 2-bed: £50,000-£70,000 Houses: 2-bed: £65,000-£100,000; 3-bed: £70,000-£130,000; 4-bed: £160,000+* • **AVERAGE RENTS (MONTHLY)** *Flats: studio: £350; 1-bed: £500; 2-bed: £550-£600; 3-bed: £700-£750 Houses: 2-bed: £550-£600; 3-bed: £700-£750; 4-bed: £800+.*

WOOLWICH & PLUMSTEAD

A mess of warehouses, council blocks and two- and three-storey Victorian terraces at riverside Woolwich . There's only one way for it to go and that's up. A total of £100 million is being spent on regenerating the area, including more than £43 million developing the handsome listed buildings of the former Royal Arsenal, recently vacated by the Ministry of Defence. Go up to Shooters Hill Road and Woolwich Common for Victorian houses or huge flat conversions in Royal Herbert Pavilions, formerly a mental

hospital. Plumstead has mostly Victorian terraces, with the best to be found round Plumstead Common and the chain of green spaces to the east.
ATTRACTS *First-time buyers; people moving further out of London; people who can't afford Bexleyheath; investors; loyal locals* • **CONSERVATION AREAS** *Woolwich Common; Plumstead Common; Sun in the Sands; Royal Arsenal Woolwich* • **AVERAGE PRICES** *Flats: studio: £25,000-£30,000; 1-bed: £35,000-£45,000; 2-bed: £45,000+ Houses: 2-bed: £55,000-£65,000; 3-bed: £65,000; 4-bed: £70,000-£90,000* • **AVERAGE RENTS (MONTHLY)** *Flats: studio: £300-£375; 1-bed: £380-£430; 2-bed: £450-£475; 3-bed: £500-£550 Houses: 2-bed: £450-£500; 3-bed: £550-£650; 4-bed: £650-£700.*

ABBEY WOOD & THAMESMEAD

Thamesmead is a dispiriting collection of 21 brutal concrete tower blocks built on reclaimed marshland by the GLC in the 1960s as a massive rehousing project. A rash of housebuilding started to the east after the town was taken over by a resident-controlled trust after the abolition of the GLC in the 1980s. The nicest new homes (many starter homes) are near the river at Thamesmead North (see also Bexley). There are plans to build 2500 more homes at Gallion's Reach on the river at a cost of £200 million. But still an area out on a limb despite the arrival of a new Safeway. Further inland, Abbey Wood has some good turn of the century homes on the Co-op Estate but large tracts of council property. One of the cheapest parts of London.
ATTRACTS *First-time buyers; families looking for low-cost housing or part exchange* • **CONSERVATION AREAS** *None of note* • **AVERAGE PRICES** *Flats: studio: £22,000-£28,000; 1-bed: £30,000-£35,000; 2-bed: £40,000-£50,000 Houses: 1-bed: £35,000-£40,000; 2-bed: £55,000-£60,000; 3-bed: £60,000-£85,000; 4-bed: £85,000-£120,000* • **AVERAGE RENTS (MONTHLY)** *Flats: studio: £300-£350; 1-bed: £350-£400; 2-bed: £425-£475; 3-bed: £450-£550 Houses: 2-bed: £450-£550; 3-bed: £500-£600; 4-bed: £525-£650.*

ELTHAM & NEW ELTHAM

Mostly 1930s suburbia, sliced through by busy main roads carrying traffic to Kent and the channel ports. But there are roads of handsome family homes round Eltham Palace (see Museums) and the Royal Blackheath Golf Club, and smaller cottage-style homes on the Progress Estate, built in 1915 to house munitions workers. Also worth checking out is the Corbett Estate with Edwardian homes of up to six bedrooms near Oxleas Woods. New Eltham is mostly 1930s suburbia interspersed with newer properties and has less of a centre than Eltham although afficiandos claim it has a good community spirit.
ATTRACTS *Families with children (who want to be near good schools); commuters* • **CONSERVATION AREAS** *Progress Estate; Eltham Palace; Eltham Green; Well Hall Pleasaunce* • **AVERAGE PRICES** *Flats: studio: £40,000; 1-bed: £45,000-£55,000; 2-bed: £50,000-£70,000 Houses: 2-bed: £70,000-£90,000; 3-bed: £80,000-£150,000; 4-bed: £150,000-£320,000* • **AVERAGE RENTS (MONTHLY)** *Flats: studio: £350-£400; 1-bed: £400-£550; 2-bed: £500-£700; 3-bed: £550-£750 Houses: 2-bed: £650-£750; 3-bed: £750-£900; 4-bed: £850-£1,000.*

BEST POSTCODES

Best postcodes (in descending order): Blackheath SE3, Eltham SE9, Greenwich SE10, Charlton SE7. Kidbrooke's inclusion in SE3 slightly pushes up prices in parts of Kidbrooke but other factors (large council estate, no centre) are against it. The largest differential is between SE7 and SE18 (Woolwich) where a two-bed house in SE18 can cost £10,000 less than an almost identical one in SE7.

AMENITIES

SCHOOLS**

Consistently indifferent performance by state schools in national league tables, particularly at primary level. But a bleak picture is partly redeemed by a good selection of private schools and relatively generous state nursery provision

PRE-SCHOOL PROVISION *44 state primary schools with nursery classes; 6 state nursery schools; 90 private and voluntary nurseries and playgroups. Proportion of children in state nurseries: 66%* • **STATE PRIMARY SCHOOLS** *Overall league table position: 143rd out of 150; High scorers: Our Lady of Grace RC, Charlton; St Mary's RC, Eltham; Brooklands (with nursery unit), Blackheath* • **STATE SECONDARY SCHOOLS** *Overall league position: 127th out of 150; High scorers: St Ursula's Convent (girls), Greenwich; St Thomas More RC (girls), Greenwich; St. Paul's RC (mixed), Abbey Wood* • **PRIVATE PREP SCHOOLS**: *Colfe's Prep, Lee (boys from 3); St Olave's Prep, New Eltham (mixed); Riverston (mixed from 2), Lee* • **PRIVATE SECONDARY SCHOOLS**: *chart-toppers Blackheath High (girls), Colfe's (boys, mixed in sixth).*

TRANSPORT**

No tubes anywhere in Greenwich borough until the Jubilee line and DLR arrive next year and some areas are better served than others by the rail network. Thamesmead has no station nearer than Abbey Wood, two and a half miles miles distant.

TRAINS *Abbey Wood: Zone 4; Cost of annual season ticket: £1068; No of trains per hour: to London Bridge 7; to Charing Cross 4; Fastest journey: 25 minutes. Woolwich Arsenal: Zone 4; No of trains per hour: to London Bridge 7; to Charing Cross 4; Fastest journey: 23 minutes. Charlton: Zone 3; Cost of annual season ticket: £860; No of trains per hour: to London Bridge 7; to Charing Cross 4; Fastest journey: 18 minutes. Greenwich: Zone 2/3; Cost of annual season ticket: £704; No of trains per hour: to London Bridge 5; to Charing Cross 2; Fastest journey: 20 minutes. Eltham: Zone 4; No of trains per hour: to London Bridge 2; to Charing Cross 2; to Victoria 3; Fastest journey: 28 minutes* • **BUSES** *Not well served with buses to town, particularly from West Greenwich where buses are often crowded with tourists. Services include: 188 from Greenwich to Euston; 53 from Plumstead Common via Woolwich and Charlton to Oxford Circus; 21 from Sidcup via Eltham and Kidbrooke to Moorgate. Planned: a bus link from Charlton Station to the Dome site* • **BOATS** *Pleasure boats to and from Westminster and down to the Thames Barrier. Also planned: a new river bus service from piers at Waterloo, Westminster, Millbank and Blackfriars and a shuttle boat from Greenwich Pier to a new pier at the Millennium Site on Greenwich Peninsula. At Woolwich, the Woolwich free ferry crosses regularly to and from North Woolwich on the north bank of the river* • **TRAFFIC BLACKSPOTS** *Greenwich town centre: Packed with pedestrians visiting the sites and markets and choked with cars queuing as* streams of people use the zebra crossings. Plans for bypass tunnelling under the foreshore in front of the Royal Naval College are on ice for lack of funding. As a compromise there's a ban on heavy lorries through Greenwich. The A2. Where the heavy lorries go instead. Carves up Blackheath just outside Greenwich Park. Eltham High Street: Often blocked with traffic waiting at the lights at the junction with Well Hall Road. The A102. The dual carriageway is being widened to take traffic to the Dome and there are long queues at the Blackwall Tunnel • **PARKING** There are controlled parking zones around Greenwich Town Centre; Eltham Station and Woolwich Town Centre. A controlled parking zone within 2.5 miles of the Dome around East Greenwich and Charlton is under discussion. Greenwhich is almost impossible to park in at weekends because of the influx of tourists and visitors to the market. Cost of annual resident's permit: £42 in Greenwich and Woolwich; £10 around Eltham Station.

LEISURE FACILITIES ★ ★ ★ ★

THEATRES & CONCERT HALLS Greenwich Theatre closed in March for lack of funding but local residents are fighting for it to be re-opened. The Prince Theatre is now the only theatre in Greenwich itself. The Bob Hope Theatre in Eltham offers a mixture of amateur drama, musicals and jazz nights. Stand-up comedy at Up the Creek in Greenwich. For Blackheath venues, see Lewisham • **CINEMAS** Three, including Greenwich Odeon, Well Hall Coronet and Woolwich Coronet. All show mainly blockbuster films although Greenwich sometimes has brief showings of more interesting or obscure films • **MUSEUMS & STATELY HOMES** Well provided for. West Greenwich has the National Maritime Museum, the Royal Naval College, the Old Royal Observatory, with its meridian line, the Queen's House and the Rangers House (on Blackheath) containing portraits and a collection of early musical instruments. Eltham Palace just off Eltham High Street surrounded by trees and a moat, was a royal palace until the time of Charles 1. It's now undergoing a major refurbishment by English Heritage and expected to open in Spring 1999. Charlton House, built in 1612, is now a library and community centre. Part of the Royal Military academy in Woolwich houses a museum of artillery history • **SPORTS FACILITIES** Seven sports centres including the popular Arches in Greenwich in a refurbished 1920s building with pools, gym and baby gym. Other centres at Eltham, Kidbrooke, Plumstead, Thamesmead and Woolwich. Sailing, fishing and birdwatching on lakes at Thamesmead. Open-air lido at Charlton. Tennis and other sports in parks across the borough • **LIBRARIES** The main library and reference library are in Woolwich, open reasonable hours. Truncated opening hours at many branch libraries. Library system underused: only 4.5 library visits per head. Place in library-use league table: 29th out of 32 (where 1 is best and 32 worst).

OPEN SPACES ★ ★ ★ ★

Excellent for parks, woods and open spaces which cover a quarter of the borough's space. Greenwich rises steeply from the Thames and many of its parks have stunning river views **GOOD VIEWS** Greenwich Park. One of the best Royal Parks with excellent views over the Isle of Dogs, Canary Wharf and the Millennium Dome from hills rising above the Thames and the Royal Naval College. Point Hill (Blackheath) has panoramic views over the city. Maryon Park in Charlton is another good viewpoint • **WOODS** Oxleas Woods, one of London's most ancient woodlands, recently reprieved from destruction when plans to build a road through it were abandoned

• **BIG SPACES** Blackheath, (see Lewisham); Avery Hill, Eltham, home of the Avery Hill campus of Greenwich University.

SHOPS * * *

WEST GREENWICH Some tourist tat but also some interesting shops including several second-hand bookshops, an antique map shop, second-hand clothes shops and New Age shops and stalls in the covered market. Expanding and lively weekend market opposite and around St Alfege's Church selling books, records, clothes, furniture. But only small local foodshops. Safeway at Blackheath Standard and Asda by the river between Charlton and Woolwich are a bus-ride away. East Greenwich has mostly small local shops • **BLACKHEATH** See Lewisham • **WOOLWICH** Described by the council as the borough's main shopping area but currently a sad collection of mostly small chain stores and discount shops. Daily, uninspiring market selling mostly fish, fruit and vegetables in a pedestrianised square. The whole town centre is set for a face-lift as part of the Woolwich Revival Programme. Sainsbury's and Somerfields in Woolwich. Safeway at Thamesmead • **ELTHAM** Shops line a wide, fairly featureless high street and spread into streets on either side. Mostly chain stores although some interesting local shops in the Arcade including a second-hand classical record shop. Sainsbury's in Eltham; Asda in Bexleyheath • **OTHER AREAS** Small shops in Charlton Village; parades at New Eltham and Plumstead. Large electrical goods and DIY stores in Bugsby's Way, Charlton by the river.

RESTAURANTS * * *

GREENWICH A good choice in West Greenwich including smart Chinese and Thai restaurants, Vietnamese, Indian and a number of pubs serving good food and/or providing entertainment • **BLACKHEATH** See Lewisham • **ELTHAM** A couple of local wine bars plus the usual line-up of Indian Tandooris and Chinese take-aways • **OTHER AREAS** Nothing of note.

CRIME RATES * *

139 crimes per 1,000 of population. Position in Metropolitan Police league table: 12th out of 32 (where 1 is worst and 32 best).

THE COUNCIL * * *

POLITICAL AFFILIATION Labour • **MINUS POINTS** Poor performing schools. More expensive council tax than surrounding boroughs • **PLUS POINTS** Energetic encouragement for Millennium developments which will bring much needed regeneration money to Greenwich and Woolwich

• **PROPERTY SEARCHES CARRIED OUT WITHIN 10 WORKING DAYS** 99%
• **STANDARD SEARCH FEE** £95 • **COUNCIL TAX COLLECTED** 91.4%
• **COUNCIL TAX 1998-99**

BAND	PROPERTY VALUE	CHARGE	BAND	PROPERTY VALUE	CHARGE
A	up to £40,000	£588.90	E	£88,001-£120,000	£1,079.95
B	£40,001-£52,000	£687.05	F	£120,001-£160,000	£1,275.95
C	£52,001-£68,000	£785.20	G	£160,001-£320,000	£1,472.25
D	£68,001-£88,000	£883.35	H	over £320,000	£1,766.70

HACKNEY

Hackney is bloody but unbowed. It's cursed with some of the worst poverty in Europe – according to the council, parts of the east of the borough are poorer than Bosnia. It has the highest unemployment in London (more than 15% of its residents are out of work) and is the third most-deprived area in England. Nearly half its residents live in council-owned property, many on grim sink estates. The council has been mired in scandals including child abuse and housing fraud and its schools were so bad they were taken over by a government hit squad and are now threatened with privatisation. But Hackney is doggedly reinventing itself as a lively, culturally exciting and challenging place to be. Warehouses and factories are being turned into studios and workshops for small, creative businesses. Middle class homeowners are moving in, not just because it's cheaper than Islington or Tower Hamlets (although it still is) but because it's less self-consciously hip than Islington and not full of modern yuppie ghettos like Docklands. And Hackney Council regularly blows up the worst tower blocks on its council estates (remember the documentary about the cockroach-infested tower block on the Kingshold Estate in South Hackney?) to cheers from tenants already rehoused in human-scale, small houses with gardens.

At its southern tip, Hackney starts where the wealthy City of London ends, at the clothing factories and warehouses of Shoreditch and Hoxton. North of the Regent's Canal are the Victorian terraces and council blocks of Hackney and some of the borough's best Georgian and Victorian architecture around Victoria Park in the east and de Beauvoir town in the west. Past the enclaves of small cottagey Victorian terraces of Dalston and Shacklewell among the council blocks is recently yuppified Stoke Newington. To the north are the large late Victorian and turn-of-the-century houses favoured by the Orthodox Jewish communities of Stamford Hill and Clapton.

One of the reasons why Hackney has been slow to take off as a place to live is that there's no tube link (apart from Old Street, almost in the City). Residents have been campaigning for one for years and hopes are high that this omission (bizarre for such a central location) will soon be rectified with the extension of the East London line north from Shoreditch. After years of stalling and refusing to open the public purse, there were hopeful signs at the end of last year that the project could finally get some public funding, although the future elected Mayor of London will have to give the go-ahead. The extension, which will use existing track, will connect Hoxton, Haggerston and Dalston to the tube network for the first time.

But successive governments and the private sector have invested millions of pounds in the borough for other projects in an attempt to iron out some of Hackney's most pressing problems of derelict properties, menacing streets and unemployment. They include £37.5 million on improving Dalston, with investment in housing, jobs and the environment and better streetscaping, £10 million in neighbouring Haggerston, one of the poorest parts of the borough, and £64 million over seven years in Hackney Wick. Hackney itself will get a face-lift with a new town hall square, dominated by a futuristic technology and learning centre. There will be funds to stimulate more artistic and cultural activity around Shoreditch and Hoxton on the city fringes and to improve streetscapes and shop fronts (see also Islington).

PROPERTY AND ARCHITECTURE

SHOREDITCH & HOXTON

Loft-living is taking off around here in a big way as former warehouses and factories are converted into live and work spaces or simply huge lofts which make the most of the large windows of former industrial buildings, although artists and others who moved here when it was cheap now complain the area is being gentrified. A lot of council property both here, in Hoxton and in Haggerston east of Kingsland Road, some bought under the Right-to-Buy scheme and now being resold. Big price differences between ex-council and trendy loft spaces. Very few houses.

ATTRACTS *Creative types; young single people; some young professionals*
• **CONSERVATION AREAS** *South Shoreditch; Shoreditch High Street; Underwood Street; Hoxton Street* • **AVERAGE PRICES** *Flats: 1-bed: £40,000-£130,000; 2-bed: £50,000-£150,000; 3-bed: £80,000-£200,000* • **AVERAGE RENTS (MONTHLY) (EXCLUDES EX-COUNCIL)** *Flats: 1-bed: £750+; 2-bed: £1170-£2160.*

DE BEAUVOIR TOWN

The closest part of Hackney to Islington, with prices to match the more expensive Islington. An attractive enclave of roads of two- and three-storey early Victorian houses centring on de Beauvoir Square with its unusual gabled- and diamond-paned semi-detached houses round a central square. A peaceful spot because many roads are cut off from traffic. This area had a narrow escape from planners in the 1960s – if they'd had their way the whole place would now be covered with council blocks as the southern half of de Beauvoir Town is. Mostly houses.

ATTRACTS *Professionals; families* • **CONSERVATION AREA** *de Beauvoir* • **AVERAGE PRICES** *Houses: 3-bed: £250,000+; 4-bed: £300,000+; 5-bed: £300,000-£400,000* • **AVERAGE RENTS (MONTHLY)** *Houses: 3-bed: £1300+; 4-bed: £1730+; 5-bed: £2160*

HACKNEY & VICTORIA PARK

Hackney itself has council estates mixed with standard Victorian two- and three-storey terraces and smaller terraces of cottages. But it also has some lovely Georgian and early Victorian streets and squares, particularly in the triangle of roads between Lower Clapton Road, Dalston Lane and Pembury Road. Victoria Park to the south is more expensive than central Hackney, forever up-and-coming but never quite making it into the Islington league, in spite of the lovely green space of Victoria Park, the Regent's Canal, some leafy streets of large Victorian terraces, large detached Victorian houses and an elegant pedimented Georgian terrace of four-storey houses in Cassland Road. As ever, council blocks are around most corners but not as dominant here as in one of the poorest parts of this borough, Hackney Wick to the east. The towers of the New Kingshold estate (of cockroach fame) are being demolished.

ATTRACTS *Families; young professionals; City workers* • **CONSERVATION AREAS** *Clapton Square; Town Hall Square; Clapton Pond* • **AVERAGE PRICES** *Flats: studios: £30,000-£70,000; 1-bed: £50,000-£85,000; 2-bed: £70,000-£120,000; 3-bed: £90,000-£125,000 Houses: 2-bed: £85,000-£180,000; 3-bed: £125,000-£200,000; 4-bed: £150,000-£250,000; 5-bed: £200,000+* • **AVERAGE RENTS (MONTHLY)** *Flats: Studio: £560; 1-bed: £500-£600; 2-bed: £600-£700 Houses: 2-bed: £650-£1300; 3-bed: £860-£1430; 4-bed: £1040-£1300; 5-bed: £1300-£1730.*

DALSTON & LONDON FIELDS

Parts of Dalston are still pretty scruffy but it will get a big boost if and when it sets its own tube station, so you may get a bargain. Lots of roads of attractive mid-Victorian terraces, particularly west of Hackney Downs and north of Dalston Lane. The Nightingale estate, another grim set of tower blocks is set to be demolished. Roads to the west of the small but lush green space of London Fields are increasingly favoured by the middle classes who like the manageably-sized Victorian terraces and smaller cottages. Some of the most coveted houses are in Albion Square, which has early Victorian terraces around a grassy square. Like most areas of Hackney, nineteenth century terraces are cheek-by-jowl with council estates. But the Holly Street estate, which hit the headlines last year as the venue for the launch of Tony Blair's plans to improve Britain's council estates, has been expensively revamped, most of its hated towers pulled down and replaced with new low-rise flats.

ATTRACTS *First-time buyers; people who can't afford Stoke Newington* • **CONSERVATION AREAS** *Albion Square; Graham Road and Mapledene; Broadway Market* • **AVERAGE PRICES** *Flats: 1-bed: £45,000-£75,000; 2-bed: £68,000-£130,000; 3-bed: £80,000-£140,000 Houses: 2-bed: £140,000+; 3-bed: £150,000-£230,000; 4-bed: £150,000-£350,000; 5-bed: £250,000+* • **AVERAGE RENTS (MONTHLY)** *Flats: 1-bed: £630+; 2-bed: £860+ Houses: 2-bed: £860+; 3-bed: £1300; 4-bed: £1510.*

STOKE NEWINGTON

One of London's trendiest areas, despite having no decent public transport apart from the 73 bus. Streets of small two- and three-storey Victorian terraces off Stoke Newington Church Street, all sought-after, more expensive and smaller than anything further south. Mostly houses, with few flats and some loft apartments. Larger Victorian semis and detached houses north of Clissold Park, around the reservoirs and towards Finsbury Park, many divided into flats (see Haringey).

ATTRACTS *Middle-class families wanting to get their children into one of the borough's few good schools; young singles; young professionals; people who can't afford Islington; loyal locals* • **CONSERVATION AREAS** *Stoke Newington; Clissold Park; Stoke Newington Reservoirs, Filter-beds and New River* • **AVERAGE PRICES** *Flats: Studio: £55,000; 1-bed: £70,000-£90,000; 2-bed: £80,000-£150,000; 3-bed: £130,000-*

£160,000 *Houses: 2-bed: £145,000-£165,000; 3-bed: £180,000-
£205,000; 4-bed: £200,000-£250,000; 5-bed: £250,000-£300,000*
• **AVERAGE RENTS (MONTHLY)** *Flats: Studio: £560; 1-bed: £600+; 2-bed:
£780+; 3-bed: £1000 Houses: 2-bed: £860+; 3-bed: £1300+; 4-bed:
£1510+.*

STAMFORD HILL & CLAPTON

Home to many of North London's Orthodox Jewish community. Properties
here are much larger than in Stoke Newington (five bedrooms isn't
unusual). Roads of late Victorian red brick and Edwardian terraces off
Stamford Hill and down towards the marina at the River Lea. Although the
houses are large, they're quite densely packed together and the area's still
urban rather than suburban. It's been plagued with prostitutes hanging
around on street corners (particularly offensive to Orthodox sensibilities)
but the council has pledged to clamp down. Properties often change hands
privately rather than through agents.

ATTRACTS *Members of the Orthodox Jewish community; families*
• **CONSERVATION AREAS** *Clapton Common* • **AVERAGE PRICES** *Flats: 1-bed:
£55,000-£60,000; 2-bed: £65,000-£75,000; 3-bed: £90,000+
Houses: 3-bed: £130,000+; 4-bed: £150,000+; 5-bed: £200,000+*
• **AVERAGE RENTS (MONTHLY)** *Flats: 1-bed: £540-£560; 2-bed: £600-
£780; Houses: 2-bed: £715-£860; 3-bed: £1080-£1300; 4-bed:
£1510-£2160.*

BEST POSTCODES

Stoke Newington N16 and the small corner of Finsbury Park N4 in
Hackney are the best postcodes in the borough. Hackney E8 suffers from
not being neighbouring Islington N1 but is better than Clapton E5.

AMENITIES

SCHOOLS *

Hackney's local education department has been chaotic for the last few
years, as councillors fell out with officials, a succession of senior officials
left or were sacked and a government hit squad was brought in to take
over. The results are painful to see as the borough languishes near the
bottom of the league tables, particularly at primary level. On the plus side,
there's (just) above-average provision for state nursery school places for
three and four year-olds and a range of private and voluntary nurseries.
There is a handful of private selective schools run by the Jewish Community
PRE-SCHOOL PROVISION *12 council nursery schools and day nurseries;
43 nursery classes in state primary and church schools; 91 private and
voluntary day nurseries and playgroups. Proportion of under-fives in state
nurseries: 59%* • **STATE PRIMARY SCHOOLS** *Overall position in league table:
146th out of 150; Top scorers: Simon Marks (with nursery unit), Stoke
Newington; Laurista School (with nursery unit), Victoria Park; Colvestone
(with nursery unit), Hackney* • **STATE SECONDARY SCHOOLS** *Overall position
in league table: 145th out of 150; Best scorers: Our Lady's Convent High
RC (girls), Stoke Newington; Stoke Newington School (mixed), Stoke
Newington; Cardinal Pole RC (mixed), South Hackney* • **PRIVATE SCHOOLS**
*Mechinah Liyeshivah Zichron Moshe (boys), Stamford Hill; Yesodey
Hatorah (mixed from 2), Stamford Hill; Beis Malka (girls from 2), Stamford*

Hill; Beis Rochel d'Satmar (girls from 5), Stamford Hill; Lubavitch House (mixed from 2) Stamford Hill.

TRANSPORT * *

Currently transport is poor for an inner London borough, although this should change with the arrival of the new tube line. For now, there are trains only and stations are unevenly scattered, with the west side south of Dalston the most poorly served. The south is best off with access to Old Street tube (zone 1) and a good choice of buses.

TRAINS London Fields: Zone 2. Cost of annual season ticket: £704; No of trains per hour: to Liverpool Street 2; Fastest journey: 9 minutes Hackney Central and Dalston Kingsland: Zone 2. No of trains per hour: North London line: 3. Stoke Newington: Zone 2. No of trains per hour: to Liverpool Street 4; Fastest journey: 15 minutes • **BUSES** A good choice with plenty of buses to the city and West End (there need to be as buses are the borough's lifeline). Services include the 38 to Victoria via Hackney Central and Dalston, the 30 to Hackney Wick from Kings Cross via Hackney Central, Hackney Downs and Dalston, the 48 via Clapton Pond and Hackney Central to London Bridge and the 55 via Clapton and Hackney to Oxford Circus • **TRAFFIC BLACKSPOTS** Shoreditch: A horrible tortuous one-way system which leaves even seasoned eastenders confused at times. Lots of traffic, buses and lorries delivering locally (the narrow cobbled streets are often blocked) and heading for the eastern motorways and docks. Dalston Junction: Kingsland High Street, the main street, is another of London's main through roads disguised (not very well) as a shopping street. Too narrow for the amount of traffic it has to carry, backed up with buses valiantly trying to provide transport for Hackney residents and cluttered with delivery and market vans from Ridley Road market. Stoke Newington: The High Street is the continuation of Kingsland High Street and just as trafficky. And don't try driving down Stoke Newington Church Street on a Saturday night – it's jammed with restaurant-goers. • **PARKING** Controlled parking in most of the south of the borough. Parking in the north around Stoke Newington and Stamford Hill is still not impossible, because most of the properties are houses. There are five controlled parking zones: zones A and B around Shoreditch and Old Street, zone C around Dalston Junction, zone D in central Hackney and zone F around Hoxton (zone E has mysteriously disappeared). Cost of annual resident's permit: zones A and B: £40; zones C, D and F: £30.

LEISURE FACILITIES * * * *

THEATRES & CONCERT HALLS The much loved but still struggling Hackney Empire in Mare Street is a variety theatre which stages everything from cabaret to musicals and circuses in a wonderfully florid Victorian building full of red plush, carved wood and marble pillars. Its terracotta exterior was refurbished with lottery money but last year it failed to get more funds for new restaurant facilities. Also live circus performances at the Circus Space, a training school and performance venue in a converted electricity generating station in Shoreditch. Concerts at the Tudor Sutton House in Hackney and the Round Chapel, Clapton • **CINEMAS** As you'd expect in this arts-mad borough, the Lux cinema in a grey industrial style building in Shoreditch and the Rio in Dalston both have repertory and sometimes obscure arthouse films • **MUSEUMS & GALLERIES** A good variety. Galleries in Hackney tend towards the informal. The borough claims to have Europe's largest concentration of artists who open up their studios for public

consumption (and purchasing) on a regular basis and several artists
have opened galleries, particularly around Dalston and Shoreditch. The
Hackney Museum, an excellent local history museum with well-labelled and
arranged exhibitions, is temporarily "on tour" until its new headquarters
in the Technology and Learning building in Hackney is finished. But the
Geffrye Museum chronicling the history of the front room in almshouses in
Dalston has just been refurbished. Sutton House, a Tudor town house now
owned by the National Trust has original furniture and panelling • **SPORTS
FACILITIES** Four leisure centres in Hoxton, Stoke Newington, Haggerston and
Clapton all with pools, gyms and other indoor sports facilities. Riding at
Lea Valley. Tennis, cricket and other sports in parks round the borough.
Stoke Newington West Reservoir is being converted into a £3.2 million
watersports centre. The pumping station in a turreted Victorian castle on
Green Lanes (no hiding away industrial marvels in concrete boxes for the
Victorians) is now a climbing centre • **LIBRARIES** Under-used although
facilities are improving. A new modern library at Shoreditch will be joined
by the new library in the Technology and Learning Centre to be built by
2001. Opening hours are long with libraries across the borough open until
8 pm during the week. All libraries are closed Wednesdays and Sundays.
5.5 library visits per head. Position in library-use league table: 26th out of
32 (where 1 is best and 32 worst).

OPEN SPACES***

A much better range than Islington. Victoria Park, one of the area's largest
open spaces and firmly attached to Hackney in the public mind, is actually
just over the border in Tower Hamlets because Hackney and Tower Hamlets
councils couldn't agree to run it jointly. Whoever runs it, it's still treasured
by Hackney residents. Large swathes of lawn, a huge ornate Victorian
drinking fountain and the Regents Canal running along the bottom make
this a special space in an otherwise built-up area.
CEMETERIES Abney Park with overgrown Victorian cemetery full of crumbling
gravestones with a looming derelict chapel in the middle • **RIVER & CANAL
WALKS** The eastern edge of Hackney Marshes after the Lea navigation
canal and River Lea divide. Gentle walk along the river, overgrown with
reeds and overhung with weeping willows. (Hackney Marsh itself is now
a dull, drained expanse used as football pitches). Also the Regents Canal
from De Beauvoir Town to Victoria Park – more reminders of Hackney's
industrial past • **CHILDREN** Clissold Park, which has deer and ducks as well
as a recently refurbished playground.

SHOPS***

HACKNEY A mixture of small chains including M&S (which recently
stopped selling mens' underwear to the fury of male residents), Boots and
Woolworths, and a motley collection of discount stores along the partly
pedestrianised Narroway at the north end of Mare Street, central
Hackney's main drag. Trafficky south Mare Street has tatty local shops, a
couple of bank branches and some take-aways. Tesco tucked behind St
John at Hackney church • **VICTORIA PARK** A small clutch of craft and pottery
shops, antique shops, furniture shops, one or two restaurants and branches
of estate agents, all signs of some middle class colonisation • **DALSTON &
KINGSLAND** Dalston has the borough's only indoor shopping centre, the
Dalston Cross. Clean and warm with small branches of mostly cheaper
chain stores. A total contrast to Ridley Road market next door where
butchers haul carcasses, chickens hang complete with heads and stalls sell

*ethnic food (particularly Turkish – there's a large Turkish community here),
clothes and fruit. Sainsbury's in the shopping centre •* **STOKE NEWINGTON**
*The high street has the usual collection of take-aways, Turkish supermarkets
and cheap discount stores where everything's £1. Church Street's much
more interesting. Lots of New Age shops selling incense, candles, jewellery
and cards, several second-hand and new bookshops, a violin shop
(even if you can't play, the window display of old and new instruments
is interesting). Interior design and furniture shops testify to middle class
presence •* **STAMFORD HILL** *Boring parades around the main junction of
Stamford Hill and Amhurst Road, enlivened by Jewish bakers, bagels
and kosher butchers' shops. Safeway.*

RESTAURANTS * * *

SHOREDITCH *Has seen an explosion of new restaurants and bars over the
past few years as it moved from being a dump no-one wanted to walk
round at night to a hip place to be seen. Good Vietnamese and vegetarian,
some new bars (often filled with city workers) and restaurants with
entertainment, although the Blue Note club was forced to move to Islington
after complaints from residents about noise •* **HACKNEY & VICTORIA PARK**
*Surprisingly central Hackney's not as good as you'd like, particularly at
weekend lunchtimes. But there is good Turkish and Chinese food and a
couple of bars. Restaurants in Lauriston Road by Victoria Park •* **DALSTON**
Good for Turkish restaurants, as well as bagels • **STOKE NEWINGTON** *The
restaurant capital of the borough. A huge choice including Indian, African,
Far Eastern, Turkish, Spanish and Thai all grouped in and around Church
Street. Good in the daytime too with cafés and patisseries selling delicious
cakes and pubs managing more than a curled-up cheese sandwich for
lunch.*

CRIME RATES * *

Crime is a problem. The third worst borough in London for burglary and
robbery and the fourth worst for sex crimes. 179 crimes per 1000 of
population. Position in Metropolitan Police league table: 6th out of 32
(where 1 is worst and 32 best).

THE COUNCIL * * *

POLITICAL AFFILIATION *Labour* • **MINUS POINTS** *Terrible schools. Collects less
council tax than any other London borough. Standards of street-sweeping
and litter collection variable. Still trying to disentangle itself from the
problems caused by years of political infighting on the council •* **PLUS
POINTS** *Actively working to improve sink estates. Door-to-door recycling
collections throughout the borough. Active in seeking regeneration funds
and lobbying for tube services. One of the cheapest boroughs in inner
London for land searches •* **PROPERTY SEARCHES CARRIED OUT IN 10
WORKING DAYS** *99%* • **STANDARD SEARCH FEE** £90 • **COUNCIL TAX
COLLECTED** *79.4%*

• **COUNCIL TAX 1998-99**

BAND	PROPERTY VALUE	CHARGE	BAND	PROPERTY VALUE	CHARGE
A	up to £40,000	£526.40	E	£88,001-£120,000	£965.07
B	£40,001-£52,000	£614.13	F	£120,001-£160,000	£1,140.53
C	£52,001-£68,000	£701.87	G	£160,001-£320,000	£1,315.99
D	£68,001-£88,000	£789.60	H	over £320,000	£1,579.20

HAMMERSMITH AND FULHAM

It's been hard for Hammersmith and Fulham having such grand neighbours on its eastern boundary. Until the 1980s Fulham, let alone Hammersmith, was beyond the pale for thousands of people who refused to consider living anywhere west of Chelsea or South Kensington. Criss-crossed by main roads heading out of London, with large tracts of industrial land, lacking elegant parks or smart shops, it was a distinct second best. Then suddenly in the mid-1980s parts of it became fashionable. Nice girls and boys fresh up in London from public school or university colonised the pubs and bought converted flats in the Victorian terraces. Wine bars and shops followed them. Now the fickle young have moved on to pastures new in Clapham and Battersea but have left Hammersmith and Fulham firmly established.

Most of the borough is Victorian, built up as London spread out over fields and market gardens in the nineteenth century. The grids of small two- and three-storey Victorian houses give some parts of Fulham in particular a claustrophobic and slightly monotonous feel despite attempts to liven things up by painting houses bright colours in some streets. From the elaborate terracotta mansion blocks of Hurlingham by the river, Hammersmith and Fulham reaches west along the river and north to the Victorian terraces of Fulham and the slightly grander red brick terraces of Parson's Green. North of Parson's Green lies the large white, slightly shabby stucco and elaborate brick terraces of West Kensington and beyond the office blocks and fly-over of Hammersmith to the west, more Victorian terraces and cottages round Ravenscourt Park and Shepherds Bush. The few roads of Victorian semis and terraces around Wormwood Scrubs and White City in the north are dominated by the grim walls of the prison and the Westway.

There may be wine bars and well-heeled people in Fulham (always more middle class than Hammersmith) but the borough also ranks as the 16th most deprived area of England. It has higher unemployment, with 7.4% of the population out of work, than all its immediate neighbours except Brent. But millions of pounds are going into regeneration schemes to improve employment and training prospects in the poorest parts of the borough, particularly White City, which is to have an extra £15.2 million spent on it in the next seven years. There are plans to revamp traffic-clogged central Fulham, the Lyric Theatre in Hammersmith and give Shepherd's Bush a new station, shops and leisure facilities. The borough is working with the Architecture Foundation on a project to improve some of the grimmest areas of the borough through consultation with local people. Target areas include Wormwood Scrubs, underpasses across the Great West road, the Hammersmith riverside, North End Road market, Eel Brook Common and Lillie Road.

Many of these areas suffer from heavy traffic, a major concern for local residents and made worse by the two year closure of Hammersmith Bridge for structural repairs. Fulham suffered most as extra traffic poured through from nearby Putney Bridge. Now the bridge is set to open again this year at the request of residents despite the lobbying of a sizeable minority who liked the peace and quiet of the closed bridge.

PROPERTY AND ARCHITECTURE

CHELSEA HARBOUR

Despite its name, Chelsea Harbour's just in Hammersmith and Fulham (to the disgust of some of its residents who did their darnedest to get the boundary moved so that they could be in Kensington and Chelsea). A slightly tired-looking 1980s development of flats and town houses and hotel around a glass and marble shopping centre now converted into a one stop-shop interior design centre after the shopping centre failed to take off with a 20-storey tower as its centrepiece. Popular with well-off professionals and city workers who like its river views and burgeoning collection of restaurants and shops nearby.

ATTRACTS *Young professionals; City workers* • **CONSERVATION AREAS** *None* • **AVERAGE PRICES** *Flats: 1-bed: £240,000-£280,000; 2-bed: £320,000-£550,000; 3-bed: £475,000-£1.75 million; 4-bed: £1.2m-£2 million Houses: 5-bed: £850,000-£1.1 million* • **AVERAGE RENTS (MONTHLY)** *Flats: 1-bed: £1950-£2160; 2-bed: £2380; 3-bed: £3460; 4-bed: £5630 Houses: 5-bed: £5630.*

FULHAM & PARSONS GREEN

The two- and three-storey bay-windowed Victorian terrace reigns supreme in Fulham. Many are still houses with some converted into two or three flats. Some streets, off Fulham Palace Road, for example, have gone multicoloured with houses painted yellow, pink, blue and terracotta to relieve the red brick. Some larger Victorian terraces in Parsons Green with some of the pleasantest overlooking Eel Brook Common. Roads of large red brick four-bedroom terraces complete with gables and stone lions on the sought-after Peterborough Estate and large mansion blocks, some ornate terracotta and some plainer, by the river at Hurlingham. Once-industrial Sands End has 1990s developments of flats and workshops with a massive development proposed for the site of the old Imperial gas works. In nearby roads, large red brick Victorian terraces, many converted to flats, are mixed with smaller terraces and council blocks. Sands End is now nearly as expensive as the rest of Fulham despite being a long way from public transport.

ATTRACTS *Families; young well-heeled professionals; first-time buyers* • **CONSERVATION AREAS** *Hurlingham; Putney Bridge; Bishops Park; Studdridge Street; Parsons Green; Fulham Park Gardens; Crabtree Estate; Walham Green; Sedlescombe Road; Central Fulham; Colehill Gardens;*

Snads End Riverside; Imperial Square • **AVERAGE PRICES** *Flats: studio: £65,000-£90,000; 1-bed: £95,000-£165,000; 2-bed: £145,000-£230,000; 3-bed: £175,000-£270,000 Houses: 2-bed: £210,000-£300,000; 3-bed: £300,000-£500,000; 4-bed: £385,000-£600,000; 5-bed: £450,000-£700,000* • **AVERAGE RENTS (MONTHLY)** *Flats: studio: £560+; 1-bed: £820-£1300; 2-bed: £1080-£1950; 3-bed: £1510+ Houses: 2-bed: £1510-£1950; 3-bed: £1510-£2600; 4-bed: £1950-£4330; 5-bed: £3250+.*

WEST KENSINGTON & BARONS COURT

Much more similar in character to Kensington or Earls Court than Fulham. Large white stucco houses with pillared porches or tall four- and five-storey Victorian brick houses with elaborate carved facings. Mostly divided into flats with many rented out on short lets. A lot of the properties are slightly unkempt, particularly around West Kensington station and the area has a transient feel, not helped by the main A4 carving through the middle of the area carrying four lanes of traffic. But just a few roads away are the grand red brick mansion blocks of Queen's Club Gardens overlooking private gardens and tennis courts and the pretty multicoloured terraces in roads off North End Road known as The Villes to estate agents.

ATTRACTS *Young professionals; people who can't afford Kensington; investors looking for rental income* • **CONSERVATION AREAS** *Queen's Club Gardens; Turneville and Chesson; Barons Court; Gunter Estate; Dorcas Estate; Fitzgeorge and Fitzjames* • **AVERAGE PRICES** *Flats: 1-bed: £110,000+; 2-bed: £140,000+; 3-bed: £180,000-£260,000 Houses: 2-bed: £230,000+; 3-bed: £260,000+* • **AVERAGE RENTS (MONTHLY)** *Flats: 1-bed: £950; 2-bed: £1380; 3-bed: £1625-£1730 Houses: 2-bed: £1510.*

HAMMERSMITH & RAVENSCOURT PARK

The residential roads of Hammersmith are a pleasant contrast to the giant traffic roundabout that is Hammersmith Town Centre. To the east is a mixture of mansion blocks, cottages, large and small Victorian terraces and conversions round Olympia, Brook Green and what residents and estate agents call Blythe Village, centred on Blythe Road. North of the town centre there are roads of small Victorian terraces around Brackenbury Road, in Brackenbury Village (another place you'll never find on the A-Z). Victorian cottages and mid-nineteenth century multicoloured terraces in roads around Ravenscourt Park. The riverside at Hammersmith is uncomfortably close to the flyover but there are some lovely Georgian houses overlooking the river. Mansion blocks facing the flyover.

ATTRACTS *Families who can't afford a house in Kensington or Chelsea; professionals; first-time buyers; French people wanting to be near the French school at Brook Green* • **CONSERVATION AREAS** *Brook Green; Lakeside, Sinclair, Blythe Road; Hammersmith Odeon; The Mall; Hammersmith Broadway; King Street (East); Bradmore; Ravenscourt Park; Melrose; Hammersmith Grove* • **AVERAGE PRICES** *Flats: studio: £75,000; 1-bed: £85,000-£135,000; 2-bed: £120,000-£190,000; 3-bed: £185,000-£265,000 Houses: 2-bed: £235,000; 3-bed: £250,000-£300,000; 4-bed: £350,000-£400,000; 5-bed: £450,000-£500,000* • **AVERAGE RENTS (MONTHLY)** *Flats: studio: £605-£695; 1-bed: £825-£1210; 2-bed: £860-£1510; 3-bed: £1300 Houses: 2-bed: £1300-£1510; 3-bed: £1730-£1950; 4-bed: £2160; 5-bed: £2600.*

SHEPHERDS BUSH

Shepherds Bush is popular with first-time buyers for the large choice of big Victorian houses converted into flats between the Uxbridge and Goldhawk Roads. Larger Victorian and turn-of-the-century family houses to the west of Askew Road feel more like neighbouring Chiswick than Shepherds Bush. Further north a mixture of Victorian terraces, conversions, council and ex-council houses in the bleak roads around Wormwood Scrubs, with the ugly blocks of the White City council estate and the ever-spreading offices of the BBC by the main A40.

ATTRACTS First-time buyers; young professionals; families who can't afford a house in Notting Hill or Kensington; investors buying for rental income • **CONSERVATION AREAS** Coningham Road; Limes Grove; Shepherd's Bush: Ingersoll and Arminger; Cleverly Estate; Old Oak and Wormholt; Wood Lane; St Marys • **AVERAGE PRICES** Flats: studio: £45,000-£65,000; 1-bed: £85,000-£120,000; 2-bed: £120,000-£180,000; 3-bed: £170,000-£230,000 Houses: 3-bed: £250,000+; 4-bed: £300,000+; 5-bed: £400,000+ • **AVERAGE RENTS (MONTHLY)** Flats: studio: £605-£695; 1-bed: £735-£860; 2-bed: £950-£1126; 3-bed: £1300-£1645; 4-bed: £1820 Houses: 3-bed: £1645; 4-bed: £1950; 5-bed: £2380-£2510.

BEST POSTCODES

The best postcode is Fulham SW6, followed by West Kensington W14 and Hammersmith W6. But the key issue affecting price is how far away you are from a tube station, because tube provision is patchy, particularly in Fulham. Roads in Sands End (east of Wandsworth Bridge Road) within walking distance of Fulham Broadway tube are just as expensive as anything in Fulham although the area as a whole is still cheaper.

AMENITIES

SCHOOLS * * *

State secondary schools perform creditably in league tables, although primary schools are more disappointing. There is a choice of private prep and secondary schools in the borough itself, including some famous names like St Pauls Girls, with more in neighbouring boroughs (see Kensington & Chelsea and Wandsworth). Good provision for three and four year-olds in state nursery schools and private nurseries.

PRE-SCHOOL PROVISION 5 council-run nursery schools; 27 nursery classes in state primary or church schools; 72 private and voluntary day nurseries and playgroups. Proportion of under-fives in state nurseries: 62% • **STATE PRIMARY SCHOOLS** Overall position in league tables: 101st out of 150. Top scorers: London Oratory, Fulham; John Betts, Hammersmith; Holy Cross RC (with nursery unit), Parsons Green • **STATE SECONDARY SCHOOLS** Overall league table position: 77th out of 150. High scorers: London Oratory School (boys, girls in sixth) (choice of the Blairs), Fulham; St, Margarets (girls), Parsons Green; Sacred Heart High School (girls, the Blairs' other choice), Hammersmith • **PRIVATE PREP SCHOOLS** Bute House (girls), Hammersmith; Latymer Prep (boys), Hammersmith • **PRIVATE SECONDARY SCHOOLS** St Paul's Girls, Brook Green; Godolphin and Latymer (girls), Hammersmith; Latymer Upper School (boys), Hammersmith.

TRANSPORT***

The tube reaches to most parts of the borough but looks better on the map than it actually is. The centre and west are best served, by both District and Piccadilly lines but the south relies on the less frequent and more crowded Wimbledon branch of the District line. Sands End and Chelsea Harbour are a long way from a tube. The central line serves the north of the borough. **TUBES** Fulham Broadway: Zone 2. Cost of annual season ticket: £704 Frequency: District: every 4-8 minutes; Fastest journey: to Embankment 18 minutes. Putney Bridge: Zone 2. Frequency: District: every 4-9 minutes; Fastest journey: to Embankment 22 minutes. Hammersmith: Zone 2. Frequency: District, Piccadilly: every 3-6 minutes; Hammersmith and City line: every 4 -9 minutes; District: every 4-9 minutes; Fastest journey: to Embankment 17 minutes; to Piccadilly Circus 12 minutes; to Paddington 9 minutes. Shepherd's Bush: Zone 2. Frequency: Central: every 3-6 minutes; Fastest journey: to Oxford Circus 12 minutes • **BUSES** Lots of buses both to town and neighbouring suburbs, with Hammersmith bus station a key interchange and terminus. Services to town include the 9 from Hammersmith to Aldwych, the 11 from Fulham Broadway to Trafalgar Square and Liverpool Street, the 14 via Fulham Broadway to Tottenham Court Road and the 74 via Fulham Palace Road to Baker Street • **TRAFFIC BLACKSPOTS** Fulham: The junction of Fulham Road, Dawes Road and Fulham Broadway is often choked with traffic including heavy lorries and buses. The end of Fulham Road by Stamford Bridge is trafficky on football match days. In central Fulham, driving along the south part of the North End Road is a nightmare because of the daily market. The junction of Fulham Palace Road and Lillie Road is slow because of blockages further up by the hospital. Hammersmith: A junction of several major main roads including the A4 out of London and a fiendish one-way system through the central shopping area, which was improved by the closure of Hammermsith Bridge. Shepherds Bush: The Shepherd's Bush roundabout is usually crowded with traffic from the M41 motorway. Roads round Shepherds Bush Common are also busy • **PARKING** Controlled parking zones cover most of the borough and parking regulations are strictly enforced. A new system of PVC cards is being introduced to replace paper permits. Residents can apply for a new permit through a machine when they change their car, which immediately issues them with a temporary permit to tide them over until the new card is issued. Cost of annual resident's permit: £50.

LEISURE FACILITIES***

THEATRES & CONCERT HALLS Three main theatres, mostly well-known to Londoners. Fringe theatre and new plays at The Lyric in Hammersmith, (which could soon be set for a £12 million revamp if a lottery application succeeds), and at Riverside Studios in Hammersmith. There's also the Bush Theatre at Shepherds Bush and live music and musicals at the Apollo, Hammersmith • **CINEMAS** One mainstream cinema – the Virgin at Hammersmith. Riverside Studios also has a repertory cinema, showing classic and arts films • **MUSEUMS & GALLERIES** A bit thin on the ground. Museums include the Fulham Palace Museum housed in Fulham Palace, the borough's oldest building, dating from the sixteenth century with a peaceful courtyard and fountains, set in riverside gardens. Local activities and guided tours of the palace. William Morris's former house by the river in Hammersmith opens to the public a couple of days a week • **SPORTS FACILITIES** Three leisure centres at Hammersmith, Shepherds Bush and

central Fulham – all with fitness centres and indoor sports facilities.
Swimming pools at Fulham and Shepherds Bush. Football, cricket, tennis
and athletics in various combinations at Hurlingham Park, Ravenscourt Park
and Wormwood Scrubs. Three major league football clubs – Chelsea,
Fulham and QPR – have their grounds in Fulham (all in residential areas
which can make Saturdays tricky for parking or even walking down the
street) • **LIBRARIES** Two main libraries (Fulham, and Hammersmith, in a
beautiful building with a carved staircase and stained glass windows), and
four branch libraries. Good long opening hours, although don't think of
using any borough library on Thursday (all closed). No Sunday opening.
Under-used, with only 6 library visits per head. Position in library-use
league table: 23rd out of 32 (where 1 is best and 32 worst).

OPEN SPACES***

A bit short of open space, especially in comparison with neighbouring
boroughs. But the long, mostly residential, river frontage is a pleasure,
although some of the choicest river front is privately owned by the posh
Hurlingham Club with no access from the public Hurlingham Park (graffiti-
scrawled grandstand and scrubby grass).

RIVERSIDE WALKS Prior Bank Gardens and Bishops Park, with a long grassy
tree-lined walkway and riverside path looking over to the boathouses of
Putney on the south bank. Fulham Palace and grounds are in the park
• **WIDE OPEN SPACE** Wormwood Scrubs, a huge featureless flat expanse of
common. A good place to stand in and scream without disturbing anyone
• **FAMILIES** Ravenscourt Park with several play areas, pretty ornamental
lake and mature trees.

SHOPS***

CHELSEA HARBOUR & SANDS END Up-market and often almost empty
galleried shopping centre at Chelsea Harbour filled with the exotic rather
than the practical (hot competition among designer clothes shops).
Sainsbury's at Sands End • **FULHAM** Several shopping drags. Smart antique
shops on the new Kings Road. A handful of antique shops, clothes shops
and lots of estate agents around Fulham Broadway but some of it looks
down-at-heel, with shops boarded up and heavy traffic. Safeway in North
End Road. There is a market at the south end of North End Road six days
a week selling mostly fruit, vegetables and cheap clothes. Struggling and
universally considered a blot on the landscape (particularly by residents
who have to suffer market lorries and litter at the end of their roads and
constant traffic jams) • **HAMMERSMITH** The borough's main shopping centre
is here along with two indoor malls and several streets of shops. But the
experience is marred by heavy traffic from all directions which can make
shopping tricky and unpleasant (lots of waiting to cross the road). The
Broadway incorporating the revamped bus station is new and smart with a
Tesco Metro, bookshop and up-market chocolate shop among the chains.
Kings Mall is older and shabbier with chains and a large Safeway. King
Street has small tired, chain stores. The area should improve when plans to
create a new pedestrianised square and home for Hammersmith Grove
market round the Lyric theatre are implemented • **SHEPHERDS BUSH** Another
traffic roundabout masquerading as a shopping centre. Mostly local shops
round the three sides of Shepherds Bush Common with a small partially-
covered shopping centre. A bankruptcy and salvage trading shop strikes
a sombre note. More ethnic shops (restaurants, bureaux de change and
supermarkets around Goldhawk Road) and a six-day market under the

railway arches off Goldhawk Road. Safeway. The whole area should get a big face-lift because of plans for a new £450 million shopping and leisure complex with housing as well as a new bus and train station by the Westway.

RESTAURANTS***

FULHAM & PARSONS GREEN *A good choice – particularly round the ends of the Fulham and Kings Roads. Wine bars, pubs and all sorts of restaurants including Italian, Spanish and Thai* • **HAMMERSMITH & SHEPHERDS BUSH** *A range for most tastes including Scandinavian and East European, mainly grouped around King Street. A number of up-market restaurants have also sprung up in middle class enclaves like Brackenbury Village and around the south park of Shepherds Bush Road near Blythe Village. A handful of European and Far Eastern restaurants around Goldhawk Road.*

CRIME RATES**

163 crimes per 1000 of population. Position in Metropolitan Police crime league table: 9th out of 32 (where 1 is worst and 32 best).

THE COUNCIL***

POLITICAL AFFILIATION *Labour* • **MINUS POINTS** *The third slowest borough for inner London in carrying out property searches. Not always punctilious enough about clearing litter from the streets* • **PLUS POINTS** *Council tax frozen for 1998/99. Has made a big effort to restructure the council to make it more responsive and open to local residents. Energetic programme of weekly door-to-door recycling and free weekend skips (sorely needed in an area where people are constantly doing up their homes). A majority of residents in the latest annual survey said the council was doing a good job*

- **PROPERTY SEARCHES CARRIED OUT IN 10 WORKING DAYS** *76%*
- **STANDARD SEARCH FEE** *£100* • **COUNCIL TAX COLLECTED** *87.6%*
- **COUNCIL TAX 1998-99**

BAND	PROPERTY VALUE	CHARGE	BAND	PROPERTY VALUE	CHARGE
A	up to £40,000	£526.67	E	£88,001-£120,000	£965.56
B	£40,001-£52,000	£614.44	F	£120,001-£160,000	£1,141.11
C	£52,001-£68,000	£702.22	G	£160,001-£320,000	£1,316.67
D	£68,001-£88,000	£790.00	H	over £320,000	£1,580.00

HARINGEY

No borough has trendier neighbours than Haringey, with Camden, Islington and Hackney encamped on its southern boundary. But so far similar fashionableness appears to have eluded much of Haringey, possibly because it's a longer commute to town and has fewer attractive Georgian squares. Blighted more than 13 years ago by the horrific riots on the Broadwater Farm Estate in Tottenham which resulted in the brutal murder of a policeman, Haringey has been keeping a low profile, trying to rebuild bridges between its disparate ethnic communities (nearly a third of residents are from ethnic minorities. Afro-Caribbeans are the largest single group but there are also large communities of Turks, Greeks and Asians).

Officials have never been able to decide whether Haringey is inner or outer London. But most residents would classify it as inner London psychologically, because it has the inner city's sharp contrasts between rich and poor and the cosmopolitan mix of races and cultures. It contains some of London's richest people in some of its most beautiful houses, as well as some of its poorest who live on alienating 1960s council estates. It stretches from the wooded heights of (parts of) Highgate and the Edwardian splendour of Muswell Hill, Alexandra Palace and Crouch End in the west through to the Victorian railway suburbs of Finsbury Park and Hornsey in the south. Further north on the axis of Victoriana which bisects the borough is Wood Green. Towards the flat expanse of marsh marking the beginning of the Essex flatlands are the council blocks, council houses and small terraces of Tottenham.

The hilly western parts of the borough around Muswell Hill and Crouch End include enough journalists among their middle class residents to ensure a good flow of coverage in the national and regional press about how marvellous the shops are, how friendly the people and how spacious the family homes.

But Haringey is also the 10th most deprived area in England and 11.4% of its residents are out of work for which reasons public and private sector money is flowing in to improve some of the borough's derelict and troubled areas, improve training and job prospects and attract business to the area. By 2002 more than £120 million is set to be invested in new shops, leisure facilities and housing on the former railway and gasworks sites between Alexandra Palace and Wood Green. Money will also go towards measures to calm the busy traffic along Wood Green High Road. In Tottenham, funds have been used to improve Tottenham Hale station. There are plans to stimulate the setting up of new businesses in the moribund Upper Lea Valley along the River Lea, as well as for enviromental improvements and incentives for shops to move into the boarded-up shops along Tottenham High Road.

PROPERTY AND ARCHITECTURE

HIGHGATE

One of London's most desirable areas, much sought after for its views over London, its villagey (although trafficky) high street and its cosy community feel. An area of active middle class residents' associations and strong amenity groups. Some of its loveliest Georgian houses are in roads just off the High Street. The Edwardian half-timbered houses of the Holly Lodge estate are outside the borough (see Camden) but there is also a good mixture of property with everything from mews cottages to large Victorian houses, modern blocks and a wide choice of conversion flats.

ATTRACTS *Families; well-off first-time buyers; people who can't afford Hampstead but want to be near the Heath* • **CONSERVATION AREA**

Highgate • **AVERAGE PRICES** *Flats: studio: £55,000-£85,000; 1-bed: £75,000-£125,00; 2-bed: £125,000-£250,000; 3-bed: £175,000-£300,000 Houses: 2-bed: £200,000+; 3-bed: £250,000-£350,000; 4-bed: £300,000+; 5-bed: £450,000+* • **AVERAGE RENTS (MONTHLY)** *Flats: studio: £650-£860; 1-bed: £700+; 2-bed: £825+; 3-bed: £1080+ Houses: 2-bed: £860+; 3-bed: £1190+; 4-bed: £1510+; 5-bed: £2160+.*

MUSWELL HILL & CROUCH END

Muswell Hill is a good middle class suburb, sought after for its elegant shops, green space and handsome red brick Edwardian houses with lots of carved wooden balconies and porches, many on steep hills sloping downwards from the Broadway or wide tree-lined streets. Some of the best houses are in roads between Highgate and Muswell Hill. A good range of conversion flats. More modest semis and Victorian terraces towards Alexandra Park. Plainer Edwardian houses around Bounds Green to the north and some ex-council. Muswell Hill's main drawback is that it's a bus ride (or an extremely brisk walk) to a station. Such enforced self-containment is possibly a reason for residents' community enthusiasm (they even have their own Inside Guide to all the best shops and facilities in the area). Crouch End used to be a part of London that people only knew from the outside of buses but it has grown increasingly fashionable over the past 10 years. Its large Edwardian houses are sought after both as family homes and as generously-sized conversion flats. Like Muswell Hill, the residents pride themselves on being a distinct community.

ATTRACTS *Families; first-time buyers; young professionals* • **CONSERVATION AREAS** *Alexandra Palace and Park; Bowes Park; Muswell Hill; Fortis Green* • **AVERAGE PRICES** *Flats: studio: £50,000; 1-bed: £55,000-£120,000; 2-bed: £60,000-£200,000; Houses: £110,000-£190,000; 3-bed: £130,000-£250,000; 4-bed: £220,000-£500,000* • **AVERAGE RENTS (MONTHLY)** *Flats: studio: £560-£650; 1-bed: £650-£860; 2-bed: £700-£1080 Houses: 2-bed: £740; 3-bed: £1080; 4-bed: £1560; 5-bed: £1730.*

WOOD GREEN & HORNSEY

Much of Wood Green consists of Victorian terraces in various stages of repair and "improvements". No comment on the house painted pink with orange window frames just off Westbury Avenue. The most historically interesting part of Wood Green (but the cheapest) is Noel Park. Built as model housing for workers, this is an enclave of dead straight avenues between Westbury Avenue and Lordship Lane, lined with red brick Victorian terraces, broken regularly with Dutch or cottage-style gables. To the south of Wood Green are the rows of late Victorian terraces known locally as the Ladder, as this is what the street pattern looks like on the map. Hornsey is more expensive than Wood Green, with a mixture of big Victorian houses, smaller Victorian terraces and modern blocks. The most expensive houses are closest to Crouch End.

ATTRACTS *First-time buyers; loyal locals* • **CONSERVATION AREAS** *Noel Park; Wood Green Common; Lordship Lane; Hornsey High Street; Hornsey Water Works and Filter Beds* • **AVERAGE PRICES** *Flats: studio: £30,000-£40,000; 1-bed: £65,000-£90,000; 2-bed: £75,000-£120,000 Houses: 3-bed: £140,000-£200,000; 4-bed: £160,000-£230,000; 5-bed: £180,000-£300,000* • **AVERAGE RENTS (MONTHLY)** *Flats: studio: £430; 1-bed: £540; 2-bed: £650 Houses: 2-bed: £715; 3-bed: £860; 4-bed: £1300; 5-bed: £1625.*

FINSBURY PARK

Fifteen years ago few people would have been seen dead around here. The unsavoury reputation of the south end of Seven Sisters Road as a poor and vicious place long predated the grim council estates built to replace slums. But the 1980s boom had a lasting effect, with developers eagerly dividing up the larger Victorian houses round the park into spacious flats and young professionals discovering how good its transport links were. Lots of conversions. Large houses are rare. Some of the area is still run-down and the area round the station particularly is a bit sleazy. But socially Finsbury Park is more like parts of Islington or Camden (indeed parts of it fall into both these boroughs). More expensive Stroud Green has mostly Victorian terraces, often divided into flats.

ATTRACTS *Young single people working in town; young professional couples* • **CONSERVATION AREAS** *None* • **AVERAGE PRICES** *Flats: studio:£40,000-£60,000; 1-bed: £70,000-£95,000; 2-bed: £100,000-£140,000; 3-bed: £150,000-£200,000 Houses: 2-bed: £175,000-£220,000; 3-bed: £150,000-£250,000; 4-bed: £250,000-£350,000* • **AVERAGE RENTS (MONTHLY)** *Flats: studio: £430-£520; 1-bed: £650-£860; 2-bed: £780- £1080; 3-bed: £1080+ Houses: 2-bed: £860; 3-bed: £1080-£1300; 4-bed: £1510-£1730.*

TOTTENHAM

Tottenham spreads across the east side of the borough and is its cheapest part. There is a mixture of Victorian and Edwardian terraces in the middle around Bruce Grove and towards Seven Sisters as well as roads of 1930s semis with modern council infill further north around White Hart Lane and Northumberland Park. The notorious Broadwater Farm estate, now revamped, is just west of Bruce Grove. The nearer you get to the marshes and the run-down warehouses lining the canal near the reservoirs, the bleaker the roads are. South Tottenham near Seven Sisters tube is one of the most expensive parts of Tottenham because of good transport links. Downhills Park near Turnpike Lane tube is also popular. Around White Hart Lane is the cheapest.

ATTRACTS *First-time buyers; people who can't afford Highbury, Islington or Finsbury Park; investors* • **CONSERVATION AREAS** *Bruce Castle; Campsbourne Cottage Estate; Clyde Circus; North Tottenham; Tottenham Bruce Grove; Tottenham Cemetery; Tottenham Green; Tottenham High Road and Scotland Green; Peabody Cottages* • **AVERAGE PRICES** *Flats: studio: £35,000-£40,000; 1-bed: £50,000-£60,000; 2-bed: £60,000-£70,000 Houses: 2-bed: £75,000-£85,000; 3-bed: £80,000-£120,000; 4-bed: £110,000-£130,000* • **AVERAGE RENTS (MONTHLY)** *Flats: studio: £390; 1-bed: £476; 2-bed: £600 Houses: 2-bed: £650; 3-bed: £715-£820; 4-bed: £860-£950.*

BEST POSTCODES

Highgate N6 and Muswell Hill N10 are, not surprisingly, the smartest postcodes in Haringey. Hornsey N8 is generally considered better than the part of Finsbury Park N4 which is in Haringey. N15 South Tottenham is smarter than Tottenham N17. Good transport links affect property prices more than postcodes.

AMENITIES

SCHOOLS**

Dismal performance by secondary schools, only partially redeemed by slightly better performance at primary level and well-above-average state nursery provision. A handful of private prep and secondary schools.
PRE-SCHOOL PROVISION *3 state nursery centres; 41 nursery classes in state primary and church schools; 82 private and voluntary nurseries and playgroups. Proportion of under-fives in state nursery schools: 77%* ● **STATE PRIMARY SCHOOLS** *Overall position in league tables: 138th out of 150; Top Scorers: St Martin of Porres RC (with nursery unit), Bounds Green, St James C of E (with nursery unit), Muswell Hill; Tetherdown, Muswell Hill* ● **STATE SECONDARY SCHOOLS** *Overall position in league tables: 144th out of 150; Best scorers: Fortismere (mixed), Muswell Hill; Hornsey School (girls), Hornsey; Highgate Wood School (mixed), Hornsey* ● **PRIVATE PREP SCHOOLS** *Channing (girls to 18), Highgate; Highgate Junior School (boys), Highgate* ● **PRIVATE SECONDARY SCHOOL** *Highgate (boys), Highgate.*

TRANSPORT***

Unevenly spaced with some areas (Muswell Hill, parts of Hornsey, parts of South Tottenham) a long way from a station. It's worth being near a tube because two of the best lines (Victoria and Piccadilly) go through the centre of the borough. Finsbury Park almost certainly has the best transport, with excellent tube, bus and rail links, and mainline trains often stop there on their way north and east. Tottenham has three railway stations.
TRAINS *Finsbury Park: Zone 2. Cost of annual season ticket: £704. No of trains per hour: to Kings Cross 4; Fastest journey: 7 minutes. Alexandra Palace: Zone 3. Cost of annual season ticket: £860. No of trains per hour: to Old Street 6; Fastest journey: 15 minutes. Bruce Grove (Tottenham): Zone 3. No of trains per hour: to Liverpool Street 4; Fastest journey: 20 minutes* ● **TUBES** *Finsbury Park: Zone 2. Frequency: to Victoria every 3-4 minutes; to Piccadilly Circus every 2-3 minutes; Fastest journey: to Oxford Circus 15 minutes; to Piccadilly Circus 15 minutes. Wood Green: Zone 3. Frequency: to Piccadilly Circus every 2-3 minutes; Fastest journey: to Piccadilly Circus 21 minutes. Tottenham Hale: Zone 3. Frequency: to Victoria every 3-4 minutes; Fastest journey: 19 minutes* ● **BUSES** *Pretty good although buses from town can get tied up in traffic, giving you more time to absorb Archway Road, Wood Green High Road or Tottenham High Road than you'd ever need. Services to town include the 43 via Muswell Hill and Highgate to London Bridge, the 29 via Wood Green, Turnpike Lane and Green Lanes to Trafalgar Square and the 171A from Northumberland Park via Tottenham and Green Lanes to Waterloo* ● **TRAFFIC BLACKSPOTS** *Finsbury Park: A tortuous one-way system through mostly once-quiet residential roads. Always clogged with buses and cars around the station. Highgate: Often long queues on Highgate Hill into Highgate Village with lots of buses and lorries struggling up the Hill from Archway. The village itself has far more traffic than its narrow main street can manage, with lots of parked delivery vans and buses. The Archway Road can also be a long haul, particularly in the rush hour. Wood Green: Expect long waits at the junction of Station Road and the High Road around the tube station. Lots of buses, shoppers and cars. Turnpike Lane can also be busy, with parked cars on both sides and late-night shoppers at the Asian supermarkets.*

Tottenham: *The High Road doubles as the main A10. Another of London's depressingly polluted, traffic-dominated shopping streets with several lanes of traffic each way* • **PARKING** *So far, there's only one controlled parking zone in Haringey, around Wood Green High Road stretching out to Turnpike Lane. Cost of annual resident's permit: £30.*

LEISURE FACILITIES**

THEATRES & CONCERT HALLS *No dedicated indoor theatre but two theatres, the Mountview Conservatoire for the Performing Arts (Hornsey) and Jackson's Lane Community Centre (Highgate) have regular performances of a mix of professional and amateur productions. The North London Performing Arts Centre in Muswell Hill has theatre courses and performances. The Pit Open Air Theatre in Finsbury Park has summer performances. No permanent concert venue but rock concerts and annual Irish Fleadh in Finsbury Park (much to the disgust of some residents who object to the noise and litter)* • **CINEMAS** *There are two, the Turnpike Lane Coronet and the Muswell Hill Odeon, both showing mainstream films. There are plans for a multiplex cinema in Wood Green* • **MUSEUMS & GALLERIES** *Not a huge choice. Local history museum at Bruce Castle, a handsome Grade 1 listed Tudor building in lush grounds, a startling contrast to the roads of small Tottenham terraces around it. Art and craft exhibitions in the Alexandra Gallery at Alexandra Palace, the massive Edwardian pile which dominates Alexandra Park and whose television mast winks at its counterpart in faraway Crystal Palace. 'Ally Pally', as it's called locally has had a chequered history. It has suffered two fires, the most recent in 1980 which gutted half the building and from which it's still recovering. Behind the terrace with its wonderful views across London, you can still see smoke-blackened brick work, boarded-up openings and skips full of rubble and black rubbish sacks* • **SPORTS FACILITIES** *Three leisure centres at Wood Green, Tottenham and Hornsey. Swimming pools at Hornsey and Tottenham. Hornsey has indoor and outdoor pools. Ice-skating at Alexandra Palace. Football matches at White Hart Lane (Tottenham Hotspur's home ground – residents who aren't fans dread match days). Tennis courts and other facilities at parks throughout the borough* • **LIBRARIES** *Under-funded and under-used. Even the borough's largest library in Wood Green hasn't been refurbished for a long time and it shows. Branch libraries are small and struggling. Opening times are among the most truncated of any borough with some branches closed almost as often as they're open. 5.2 library visits per head. Position in library-use league table: 27th out of 32 (where 1 is best and 32 worst).*

OPEN SPACES****

Everything from woods to marshes to parks and no area is too far from an interesting space. Finsbury Park, one of the largest open spaces in the borough and the largest run directly by the council, could get a much-needed face-lift to its silted-up lake and vandalised cricket pavilion if a £1.5 million lottery bid is successful.

VIEWS *Alexandra Park, no contest. When it's clear, you can see to the hills of Crystal Palace and beyond and there are excellent views of the City, West End and Canary Wharf* • **WOODS** *Highgate Woods. A treasure of mature woodland between Highgate and Muswell Hill (although the woods do make coming out of Highgate Station late at night a bit creepy). Run by the Corporation of London. The Parkland Walk, along the old railway line from Finsbury Park to Alexandra Palace runs from the woods* to Finsbury Park. Good views of people's back gardens • **RIVER WALKS** The towpath on the River Lea. The river runs through the Lea Valley Regional Park, an area of grassy marshland dominated by electricty pylons. The towpath runs alongside the canal which is a diversion of the River Lea with locks and rows of moored houseboats (none of your posh Islington stuff here though – these houseboat owners have broken-down old cars parked on the bank and washing hanging out to dry).

SHOPS * * *

HIGHGATE Attractive villagey shops in the High Street including several bookshops (the second-hand one is deceptively spacious), clothes shops and local grocery and food shops, among others. But a constant flow of traffic up and down the hill blights an otherwise pleasant shopping experience • **MUSWELL HILL & CROUCH END** Muswell Hill manages to combine the interesting and the practical, making this one of the best shopping areas in the borough. Local bookshops, the sort of toy shop with real wooden toys rather than computer games, furniture and interior design shops with items you can actually imagine living with and reasonably-priced clothes shops are mixed with the dull but necessary banks, building societies and other chains. Sainsbury's. Crouch End has some similarly interesting shops north of the Clocktower – the Broadway itself is fairly predictable. Budgens • **WOOD GREEN & HORNSEY** Wood Green is the borough's official flagship shopping centre which is fine if you like indoor malls full of chain stores (mostly at the cheaper end of the potential choice). Shopping City, an ugly red brick building with multistorey carpark looms above on either side of the High Road, joined by a pedestrian bridge. Sainsbury's. The High Road itself has local shops, mostly take-aways and small supermarkets. Turnpike Lane is much more interesting, with mostly Indian-run shops, full of bright saris and materials, exotic bakeries, halal butchers and boxes of fruit and vegetables spilling onto the pavement. Hornsey has antique shops along the High Street and Middle Lane. Residents are fighting plans for a big Sainsbury's • **FINSBURY PARK & TOTTENHAM** Mostly local shops along wide trafficky roads. Ethnic supermarkets, including a lot of Turkish shops around Green Lanes in Finsbury Park. Sainsbury's by Harringay and Green Lanes station. Lots of Afro-Caribbean shops in Tottenham including hairdressers and soul record shops. Tesco in Tottenham High Road. A new retail park by Tottenham Hale station is part of the area's regeneration, with office and electrical goods stores.

RESTAURANTS * * *

HIGHGATE Up-market chains like Cafe Rouge alongside locally popular French and Italian restaurants and winebars • **MUSWELL HILL & CROUCH END** A good choice of everything from pizza and pasta chains to individual winebars and brasseries • **ELSEWHERE** Lots of Turkish and Greek restaurants of varying quality, particularly in Finsbury Park, Wood Green and Hornsey. The best are often little more than cafés from the outside but offer good value and freshly-cooked food.

CRIME RATES * *

The fourth highest robbery rate in London. 140 crimes per 1000 of population. Position in Metropolitan Police league table: 11th out of 32 (where 1 is worst and 32 best).

THE COUNCIL★★

POLITICAL AFFILIATION *Labour* • **MINUS POINTS** *Some of the worst primary schools in London. Poorly resourced and used libraries. Not always thorough at sweeping the streets (lots of old black refuse sacks with rubbish bursting out of them across the borough). The slowest in the whole of London at turning round property searches* • **PLUS POINTS** *Experimenting with a door-to-door recycling scheme. Energetic promotion of the borough to businesses and government and encouragement of regeneration*

- **PROPERTY SEARCHES CARRIED OUT IN 10 WORKING DAYS** *56%*
- **STANDARD SEARCH FEE** *£85.50* • **COUNCIL TAX COLLECTED** *84.7%*
- **COUNCIL TAX 1998-99**

BAND	PROPERTY VALUE	CHARGE	BAND	PROPERTY VALUE	CHARGE
A	up to £40,000	£570.66	E	£88,001-£120,000	£1,046.23
B	£40,001-£52,000	£665.77	F	£120,001-£160,000	£1,236.45
C	£52,001-£68,000	£760.89	G	£160,001-£320,000	£1,426.66
D	£68,001-£88,000	£865.00	H	over £320,000	£1,712.00

HARROW

Harrow (to people who don't live there) means Harrow School, alma mater to prime ministers, poets and peers, whose buildings sprawl up and down the narrow streets of Harrow on the Hill and whose uniform of dark blazers and straw boaters would be instantly recognisable to the Victorians who presided over the school's nineteenth century expansion.

But Harrow on the Hill is one of the borough's high points, both physically and architecturally. Walk down the Hill and you plunge into miles of streets of anonymous mostly interwar suburbia across the south part of the borough around Harrow itself and in Wealdstone, Harrow Weald and South Harrow. To the north around Pinner in the west and Stanmore in the east, however, the densely packed houses start to thin out, giving way to the large detached houses, well preserved high streets and open space of Harrow's metroland, before London rises up over its northern hills to meet Hertfordshire.

This is the beginning of the north-west London commuter belt, with more than half the borough's residents travelling outside the borough to go to work every morning. They're mostly a solid lot, big in white collar industries like banking, finance and public administration. Not surprisingly, the council's keen to tempt others in and has been enthusiastically pressing the attractions of Harrow (good transport links and schools, green space) on the service and manufacturing sectors. Unemployment is low at 3.5 %.

As in neighbouring Hillingdon and Ealing, Harrow's large Indian community has made its mark, particularly on otherwise fairly uninspiring local shopping parades, although Harrow has nothing to compare with Southall (see Ealing). More than a quarter of the borough's population is from an ethnic minority, with Indians the largest single group. A large Jewish population, particularly round

Stanmore adds to a melting pot of cultures which preserves Harrow from being merely a bland tract of suburbia.

The borough's main shopping centre in Harrow got a big face-lift two years ago with the addition of the St George's shopping and entertainment complex to complement the existing St Ann's centre at the other side of the pedestrianised shopping street. Designers eschewed the obvious glass ceiling and lifts in favour of a vaulted church-like roof with arched brick window surrounds and a series of iron railinged walkways on upper floors rising from the ground floor like tiers of theatre balconies. Harrow now has one of the largest shopping centres for miles around, to compete with the lure of Brent Cross just over the border in Barnet, with the council claiming Harrow as one of the top 10 retail centres in Greater London.

PROPERTY AND ARCHITECTURE

HARROW ON THE HILL

Spectacularly set on a wooded hill with church spire, overlooking a sea of red suburban roofs below and a dramatic point of reference for miles around. In contrast to surrounding areas Harrow on the Hill is mostly Victorian and Edwardian mixed with some beautiful Georgian town houses. The picturesque main streets of the Hill, as locals call it, are dominated by the buildings of Harrow School (small notices indicating Matron's Entrance are a give-away that a building is a boys' boarding house rather than a desirable residence) so most of the properties for mere mortals are in roads running up to the village street at the top. A good mix of flats (many in new developments) and houses but don't expect a bargain.

ATTRACTS *Wealthy families; young professionals* • **CONSERVATION AREAS** *Roxeth Hill; Harrow School; Harrow Park; Harrow on the Hill village; South Hill Avenue; Mount Park Estate; Roxborough Park* • **AVERAGE PRICES** *Flats: studio: £40,000+; 1-bed: £70,000+; 2-bed: £100,000+; 3-bed: £130,000-£250,000 Houses: 2-bed: £150,000-£180,000; 3-bed: £200,000+; 4-bed: £260,000-£550,000; 5-bed: £450,000+* • **AVERAGE RENTS (MONTHLY)** *Flats: studio: £520; 1-bed: £650; 2-bed: £750-£1500; 3-bed: £1750+ Houses: 2-bed: £800-£1000; 3-bed: £1300; 4-bed: £2000+; 5-bed: £2500-£3000.*

HARROW & WEALDSTONE

On paper Harrow has a number of different parts – North Harrow, South Harrow, Harrow Weald and Harrow itself. But they're all more or less suburban, with streets of mostly 1930s semis further away from Harrow, mixed with Victorian and Edwardian two-storey terraces around Wealdstone. Harrow has a good choice of modern blocks of flats. The pecking order of desirability is roughly: Harrow (good shops and transport), North Harrow (because it borders on smarter Pinner), Wealdstone and South Harrow. Harrow Weald is the smarter part of Wealdstone (or the more down-market end of Stanmore if you prefer).

Some bargains to be had in South Harrow and Wealdstone if you want a cheap house.

ATTRACTS *First-time buyers; families; members of the Asian communities (especially Wealdstone)* • **CONSERVATION AREAS** *Brookshill, Harrow Weald; West Drive, Harrow Weald* • **AVERAGE PRICES** *Flats: studio: £40,000-£50,000; 1-bed: £55,000-£75,000; 2-bed: £70,000-£95,000 Houses: 2-bed: £85,000-£105,000+; 3-bed: £100,000-£160,000; 4-bed: £140,000-£200,000; 5-bed: (Harrow) £250,000* • **AVERAGE RENTS (MONTHLY)** *Flats: studio: £400-£500; 1-bed: £500-£700; 2-bed: £650-£1000 Houses: 2-bed: £650-£800; 3-bed: £800+; 4-bed: £1200-£1500.*

PINNER & HATCH END

Superior metroland, with well-spaced detached and semi-detached 1930s houses built in what their first owners were happy to believe was a "country" style – Tudor beams, leaded lights, tall chimneys and deep sloping eaves. Now on the edge of green belt land, maybe the speculative builders were more accurate than they knew. Modern estates of small 1960s and 1970s town houses and new blocks in roads leading to the centre of Pinner, which, with its attractive hilly Tudor high street, could certainly pass muster as a prosperous Hertfordshire or Buckinghamshire town. Cosy village community in Pinner if you want to get involved.

ATTRACTS *Families; commuters; young professionals; members of the Jewish Community* • **CONSERVATION AREAS** *Pinner High Street; Tookes Green; Pinnerwood Park Estate; Waxwell Lane; Waxwell Close, East End Farm; Pinnerwood Farm; Moss Lane; Pinner Hill Estate; West Towers* • **AVERAGE PRICES** *Flats: 1-bed: £60,000-£75,000; 2-bed: £80,000-£120,000 Houses: 2-bed: £100,000+; 3-bed: £150,000-£300,000; 4-bed: £200,000-£230,000+; 5-bed: £300,000+* • **AVERAGE RENTS (MONTHLY)** *Flats: 1-bed: £600-£700; 2-bed: £800+; 3-bed: £950-£1000 Houses: 2-bed: £850-£900; 3-bed: £1100-£1400; 4-bed: £2000+; 5-bed: £2000+.*

STANMORE

Blessed with some of the borough's most attractive green space, Stanmore includes some of the grandest houses in Harrow in the private roads between Stanmore Common and Bentley Priory open space. Huge houses with iron gates, double drives and houses with bewildering numbers of wings, gables and entrances. Just to make it clear who's top dog, some of the grass verges outside the houses warn anyone who's odd enough not to be in a car to keep off the grass. A mixture of well-kept Edwardian, 1920s and 1930s semis and detached houses further south in roads off Uxbridge Road, around the Broadway and around Canons Park.

ATTRACTS *Families wanting good schools and green space; members of the Jewish community; members of the Asian community* • **CONSERVATION AREAS** *Little Common; Stanmore Hill; Old Church Lane; Kerry Avenue; Canons Park Estate* • **AVERAGE PRICES** *Flats: 1-bed: £60,000-£80,000; 2-bed: £110,000-£250,000; 3-bed: £200,000+ Houses: 2-bed: £120,000+; 3-bed: £135,000-£200,000; 4-bed: £200,000-£275,000; 5-bed: from £350,000* • **AVERAGE RENTS (MONTHLY)** *Flats: studio: £470; 1-bed: £560+; 2-bed: £700-£860; 3-bed: £780+ Houses: 2-bed: £1000; 3-bed: £860-£1950; 4-bed: £1000; 5-bed: £1510-£2380.*

BEST POSTCODES

Postcodes are largely irrelevant as the whole borough is in Middlesex. Proximity to transport links has a significant impact on prices.

AMENITIES

SCHOOLS★★★★

Harrow's school system works differently from all the other London boroughs (with the exception of Merton) in that it operates a three-tiered school system with primary, middle and high school. Harrow's high schools finish at 16 and there are no council-run sixth form colleges. There's also a system of "links" between primary and middle schools and high schools to control entry. Not everyone approves of these unusual arrangements and the council is reviewing its procedures as part of a general overhaul. But there are no signs that they work to Harrow's detriment, with very good results both at primary and secondary school level. A good selection of top performing private schools. Below average provision for under-fives in state nurseries but a decent choice of private nurseries.

PRE-SCHOOL PROVISION *68 private nurseries and playgroups; 25 state primary and church schools with nursery places. Proportion of under-fives in state nurseries: 46%* • **STATE PRIMARY SCHOOLS** *Overall position in league tables: 16th out of 150. Top scorers: St Anselms RC, Harrow; Newton Farm (with nursery unit), South Harrow; Pinner Park (with nursery unit), Pinner* • **STATE SECONDARY SCHOOLS** *Overall position in league tables: 20th out of 150. Best scorers: Bentley Wood High School (girls), Stanmore; Harrow; Nower Hill High School, (mixed) Pinner; Park High (mixed), Stanmore* • **PRIVATE PREP SCHOOLS** *Alpha Prep (mixed), Harrow; Inellan House (mixed) Pinner; Reddiford (mixed), Pinner; Quainton Hall (boys), Harrow; Orley Farm (mixed with girls to 8); Harrow on the Hill* • **PRIVATE SECONDARY SCHOOLS** *Harrow School (boys); John Lyon (boys), Harrow; Buckingham College (boys, girls in sixth), Harrow; Heathfield (girls from 3), Pinner; Peterborough and St Margaret's, Stanmore; North London Collegiate (girls), Canons Park.*

TRANSPORT★★★★

Well served by tube (as you'd expect in a borough which largely exists as a result of tube line building) with Jubilee, Metropolitan and Bakerloo lines running through it. These are all good tube lines but the Metropolitan line is a better bet than the Bakerloo from Harrow for a fast trip into town – only about half the Bakerloo line trains come out as far as Harrow and Wealdstone and the train stops at every station, unlike the fast trains from Harrow on the Hill. Trains only around Hatch End in the far north of the borough unless you fancy a brisk walk to Pinner.

TRAINS *Hatch End: Zone 6. Cost of annual season ticket: £1396 No of trains per hour: to Euston 3; Fastest journey: 35 minutes* • **TUBES** *Harrow on the Hill: Zone 5. Cost of annual seasonal ticket: £1280. Frequency: Metropolitan to Baker Street: 10 trains an hour; Fastest journey: 16 minutes Pinner: Zone 5. Frequency: Metropolitan to Baker Street: 5-6 trains an hour; Fastest journey: 23 minutes. Harrow and Wealdstone: Zone 5. Frequency: Bakerloo to Charing Cross: every 10 minutes; Fastest journey: 43 minutes. Stanmore: Zone 5. Frequency: Jubilee line to Charing Cross: every 7 minutes; Fastest journey: 36 minutes* • **BUSES** *Brent*

Cross is about as near as you'll get to the glittering lights of town during the day on a bus from Harrow. But links between different parts of the borough are generally good, particularly around Harrow itself. Services tail off a bit around Stanmore and there can be long waits. Night buses include the N18 from Trafalgar Square via Harrow and Harrow Weald, the N98 from Trafalgar Square to Stanmore • **TRAFFIC** Rare among outer London boroughs in that it escapes the blight of motorways and dual carriageways which turn into motorways. But its main shopping areas don't escape traffic, particularly as the borough has a lot of 1930s parades built directly onto busy roads • **BLACKSPOTS** Harrow & Harrow on the Hill: There can be long waits at the lights at the bottom of Harrow on the Hill heading for the main shopping centre. The shopping centre itself is pedestrianised which inevitably means more traffic building up in roads immediately outside it. Pinner: The streets around the station and Sainsbury's can get clogged with traffic • **PARKING** There are controlled parking zones in Pinner; Rayners Lane; Harrow; Harrow on the Hill; Wealdstone and Stanmore. Cost of annual resident's permit: £20. Permits only valid for zone for which they're issued.

LEISURE FACILITIES * * *

THEATRES & CONCERT HALLS Of local appeal. The Travellers Theatre and Elliot Concert Hall are both housed in the Harrow Arts Centre, an attractive Queen Anne-style red brick building in Hatch End. Travellers Theatre has a mixture of plays by visiting companies, childrens' shows, drama workshops and live music. Elliot has middle-of-the-road concerts and Mum and Gran's favourite stars. Concerts and Sunday bands at Headstone Manor (see below). Gilbert and Sullivan evenings at Grim's Dyke House, Harrow Weald, once owned and lived in by W S Gilbert • **CINEMAS** Much improved choice since the arrival of the 8 screen Warner Village cinema at the St George's Centre, Harrow, although if black and white arts cinema's your thing, you'd better head for the tube station. The Safari Cinema in Harrow shows Asian films only • **MUSEUMS & GALLERIES** A small selection but there are plans for a big expansion of the local history museum and heritage centre at Headstone Manor with a £1.5 million lottery grant. The manor, a fourteenth century manor house with barns and a granary already has some local history displays (including mock-ups of 1930s front rooms) but the borough plans a whole historical sweep of displays from medieval to present day. Cat obsessives should head for the Cat Museum in Harrow on the Hill (antique porcelain and glass rather than warm fur). Art gallery in the Old Speech Room at Harrow School (limited opening hours) • **SPORTS FACILITIES** One leisure centre in Harrow. Tennis, football, basketball, cricket in parks throughout the borough • **LIBRARIES** Under-used although the central library at the Civic Centre is large and well laid out. Opening hours are erratic around the borough with several opening in the middle of the afternoon. Everything's closed on Wednesdays and half the borough's branch libraries are closed on Fridays, with those that open in the morning closing in the afternoon. No Sunday opening. 7 library visits per head. Position in library-use league table: 19th out of 32 (where 1 is best and 32 worst).

OPEN SPACES * * * *

Fields, woods, hills, parks – you want it, it's here. As in other outer London boroughs, the northernmost reaches are the greenest, as built-up London gives way to green belt but there are excellent views from Harrow on the Hill in the south as well.

VIEWS The lawns by the library at Harrow School (if you're permitted access – this is private property). Beautiful views across to London from one of the area's most prominent hills. Also the top of the climb by the deer park in Bentley Priory Open Space (if the views aren't obscured by trees). Cattle with villainous-looking horns grazing by the path help the rural effect. Bentley Priory is otherwise a bit of a disappointment because much of it's now owned by the Ministry of Defence and fenced off • **ELEGANT GARDENS** Canons Park – once the grounds of a grand mansion which is now the North London Collegiate School. Peaceful gardens (despite tubes passing regularly) with poplars, weeping willows and a walled garden with formal flower beds • **WOODS** Stanmore and Harrow Weald Commons. Good walks through mature woods (although attempts to cut across the grounds of Bentley Priory from one to the other don't work).

SHOPS***

HARROW ON THE HILL Pretty High Street of whitewashed cottages and Victorian shopfronts, including the inevitable Harrow School outfitters, as well as antique shops, a few restaurants, estate agents and other local shops. Beautiful rather than useful • **HARROW** Just at the bottom of the Hill and a total contrast. Harrow itself is visually nothing to look at – a mess of office blocks and shops of different vintages – but there's a large choice of decent chains both in the pedestrianised St Ann's Road and in the St Ann's and St George's shopping centres, once you've crossed the nasty busy road by the station. Nothing startlingly original but a pleasant place to shop. Tesco • **WEALDSTONE** Down the road from Harrow and suffering for it. A partially pedestrianised street of small shabby shops. Cheap clothes, halal butchers and pile 'em high, sell 'em cheap discount stores, occupying empty shops until someone catches up with them. Asda withdrew plans last year (1998) for a superstore which traders hoped would help regenerate the area • **PINNER** Very up-market and Home Counties. The best shops gleam discreetly from under the overhanging Tudor eaves of the high street (and some of this is real Tudor, not Tudorbethan). Designer clothes, jewellery, galleries, a bookshop and (of course) estate agents. Sainsbury's by the station and more ordinary local shops in roads off the high street. Safeway at Hatch End • **STANMORE** Disappointing shops for such a smart area. Mostly local shops including a real butcher, a baker and a couple of clothes shops but mysteriously, a Lidl discount store, normally found in more down-market areas than this. Sainsbury's planned.

RESTAURANTS***

A couple of good Indian restaurants in Harrow as well as Thai and Chinese. Otherwise local brasseries and restaurants in Harrow on the Hill and up-market bar and pizza chains (Pizza Express, All Bar One) in Pinner. WS Gilbert's former home at Grim's Dyke House is now a hotel with a restaurant.

CRIME RATES*****

The third lowest crime rate in London. 79 crimes per 1,000 of population. Position in Metropolitan Police league table: 30th out of 32 (where 1 is worst and 32 best).

THE COUNCIL ****

POLITICAL AFFILIATION *Labour, for the first time in living memory. To the amazement of local residents, true blue Harrow on the Hill returned a Labour member, turning the council from Tory to Labour with one vote* • **MINUS POINTS** *One of the most expensive boroughs in London for property searches* • **PLUS POINTS** *Excellent schools. Generally efficient and effective. Door-to-door recycling (pilot scheme). Has begun residents feedback scheme on council policies* • **PROPERTY SEARCHES CARRIED OUT IN 10 WORKING DAYS** *100%* • **STANDARD SEARCH FEE** £120 • **COUNCIL TAX COLLECTED** 96.4%

• **COUNCIL TAX 1998-99**

BAND	PROPERTY VALUE	CHARGE	BAND	PROPERTY VALUE	CHARGE
A	up to £40,000	£482.34	E	£88,001-£120,000	£884.29
B	£40,001-£52,000	£562.73	F	£120,001-£160,000	£1045.07
C	£52,001-£68,000	£643.12	G	£160,001-£320,000	£1205.47
D	£68,001-£88,000	£723.51	H	over £320,000	£1,447.02

HAVERING

If you're one of the many people who thinks there's no life east of Islington, you've probably never heard of Havering. London's easternmost borough is a large chunk of Essex fields, marshland, big skies and industrial Thames which suburban sprawl hasn't yet managed to overwhelm. Its built-up areas are mostly the prosaic result of decades of speculative development round tube and train lines but there's more open space in relation to built-up areas than in almost any other London borough. Or at least it feels that way.

At Havering's western boundary is Romford, the main shopping and administrative centre, surrounded by the attractive garden suburb of Gidea Park. To the east of Romford is the post-war council estate of Harold Hill before countryside takes over around Havering Atte Bower right in the north. To the south are Upminster and Hornchurch, once distinctive towns in their own right but engulfed in waves of building at the beginning of the century. Surrounded by marshland and fields in the south of the borough are the industrial estates of Rainham, reaching down to the Thames.

This is where multiracial London finally dies out as Essex takes over. Only three per cent of Havering's population is from an ethnic minority, the lowest in London. Its other vital statistics are low too: crime rates are the second lowest in the capital and unemployment stands at just 2.9%, the fourth lowest in London. Statistically it has most in common with wealthy western and northern boroughs like Richmond, Sutton and Barnet. But Havering doesn't drip prosperity. It's not part of the commuter belt. Its suburbs don't have the cachet even of old East London suburbs like Woodford or Wanstead, although there are some large houses lived in by people not short of a bob or two. This is solid, semi-detached Essex, still making more than a tenth of its money from manufacturing, although the borough is keen to push its credentials (good transport links, space) to white collar industries.

But despite lots of manufacturing activity on the Thames waterfront, vast tracts of marshland lie derelict. There was once talk of building a theme park on Rainham Marshes but these haven't come to anything (yet). Now there are plans for a major industrial development and creation of a country park by the river on the 1,100 acre site as part of the government's efforts to regenerate East London. Improved road access should take through-traffic out of Rainham Village although some residents are worried about increased noise.

Inland there are plans to revamp Romford Town centre with a big development on the site of the Romford Brewery in the High Street which closed in 1992. The latest proposals for the £118 million development include a Savacentre hypermarket, 16 screen multiplex cinema, health and fitness centre and new museum. This should perk up a part of Romford which is currently looking a bit tired.

PROPERTY AND ARCHITECTURE

ROMFORD

Romford grew up around the railway which reached it in the 1850s and bears all the familiar traits of suburban building although there are still a few reminders of its past as a market town. A mix of Victorian terraces and more recent 1930s terraces round the centre, many bearing the mark of ubiquitous "improvements". 1930s semis and bungalows predominate in Collier Row to the north. Some blocks of modern flats and a good choice of conversion flats.

ATTRACTS First-time buyers; loyal locals; City workers • **CONSERVATION AREAS** Romford • **AVERAGE PRICES** Flats: studio: £38,000-£42,000; 1-bed: £45,000+; 2-bed: £50,000+ Houses: 1-bed: £58,000; 2-bed: £68,000-£72,000; 3-bed: £70,000+; 4-bed: £145,000-£225,000; 5-bed: £250,000+ • **AVERAGE RENTS (MONTHLY)** Flats: studio: £375+; 1-bed: £400+; 2-bed: £475+ Houses: 1-bed: £430+; 2-bed: £500+; 3-bed: £575+; 4-bed: £650+; 5-bed: £900+.

GIDEA PARK

Gidea Park was developed as a garden suburb at the beginning of this century. The most sought-after part around the golf course is called the Exhibition Estate, after an architectural competition and exhibition in 1911 which resulted in 100 individually designed houses. Handsome Edwardian half-timbered detached houses in tree-lined streets, private drives and a big contrast to Romford just a few minutes drive away. An established area. More modest mostly 1930s houses south of Main Road are popular for proximity to the station.

ATTRACTS Families; wealthy commuters • **CONSERVATION AREA** Gidea Park and Railway Extension • **AVERAGE PRICES** Flats: 2-bed: £68,000-£72,000 Houses: 3-bed: £125,000-£175,000; 4-bed: £170,000-£240,000+; 5-bed: £300,000 • **AVERAGE RENTS (MONTHLY)** Flats: 2-bed: £440; 3-bed: £520 Houses: 2-bed: £540+; 3-bed: £620+; 4-bed: £700+; 5-bed: £950+.

HAROLD HILL

A sprawling council estate started after the Second World War to house overspill tenants from London. A fussy series of cul-de-sacs, crescents and loop roads lined with low red brick barrack-like terraces. A good bus ride away from decent shops and without a car you could be marooned, with Harold Wood station on the other side of the A13. But local estate agents estimate that 65% of the estate is now private after many were sold to tenants under the Right-to-Buy scheme and sold on. A good area for cheap houses and lots of space for your money.

ATTRACTS *Bargain hunters; local first-time buyers; people from the East End; people who can't afford Romford* • **CONSERVATION AREAS** *none* • **AVERAGE PRICES** *Flats: studio: £27,000; 1-bed: £40,000; 2-bed: £47,000 Houses: 2-bed: £62,000+; 3-bed: £68,000+* • **AVERAGE RENTS (MONTHLY)** *Flats: 1-bed: £375-£400; 2-bed: £450 Houses: 2-bed: £475-£500; 3-bed: £550.*

HAVERING ATTE BOWER

Pronouced Havering Atty Bower. No more than a cluster of (mostly large) houses, a couple of pubs and a church but set very attractively on the edge of undulating fields and Havering Country Park. Large gardens and a feeling of being in the middle of the country rather than in London are powerful attractions. A car is vital. Lettings are rare and so are flats.

ATTRACTS *Wealthy people with cars; families; people moving out of Romford or Gidea Park to be nearer the country* • **CONSERVATION AREAS** *Havering atte Bower* • **AVERAGE PRICES** *Flats: 2-bed: £75,000 Houses: 3-bed: £125,000+; 4-bed: £200,000+; 5-bed: £500,000+.*

HORNCHURCH

A respectable suburb with a proper town centre. Ordinary 1930s semis along the main road to Hornchurch and in Hornchurch itself, mixed with some Victorian and modern blocks. A good choice of flats and maisonettes south of the high street. The largest houses are in Emerson Park north of the railway line (it has its own station) with every combination of half timbering, red brick, sloping roofs and large gardens. This is where the new money is in Havering.

ATTRACTS *Families; new money* • **CONSERVATION AREAS** *St Leonards; RAF Hornchurch; also south of South Hornchurch: Rainham* • **AVERAGE PRICES** *Flats: 1-bed: £55,000-£75,000; 2-bed: £65,000-£170,000 Houses: 2-bed: £60,000-£85,000; 3-bed: £90,000-£180,000+; 4-bed: £150,000-£200,000+; 5-bed: £150,000-£300,000* • **AVERAGE RENTS (MONTHLY)** *Flats: studio: £375+; 1-bed: £400+; 2-bed: £475+ Houses: 1-bed: £430-£450; 2-bed: £500+; 3-bed: £575+; 4-bed: £650+; 5-bed: £900+.*

UPMINSTER

Familiar to most people as the destination at the end of the eastbound District line, Upminster is a step above Hornchurch, partly because of the good transport links (District line and trains) and partly for its good schools. North of the tube and railway line lies another of the garden suburbs built for the professional middle classes at the beginning of the century, with a mix of large Edwardian houses in wide roads round the golf course. More modest houses south of the railway line.

ATTRACTS *Families wanting good schools and good transport links; City workers; people progressing up from Dagenham and East Ham*

- **CONSERVATION AREAS** Cranham; North Ockenden; Corbets Tey.
- **AVERAGE PRICES** Flats: 1-bed: £55,000-£65,000; 2-bed: £63,000-£100,000 Houses: 2-bed: £85,000+; 3-bed: £100,000-£160,000; 4-bed: £180,000-£200,000; 5-bed: £300,000+ • **AVERAGE RENTS (MONTHLY)** Flats: 1-bed: £400+; 2-bed: £400+ Houses: 2-bed: £600+; 3-bed: £800+; 4-bed: £1000+.

BEST POSTCODES
Irrelevant as the whole borough has Essex postcodes.

AMENITIES

SCHOOLS***
Good performance overall in league tables by both primary and secondary schools. Above-average state provision for under-fives. No independent schools.

PRE-SCHOOL PROVISION 11 nursery classes in state primary schools; 95 private day nurseries and playgroups. Proportion of under-fives in state nursery schools: 63% • **STATE PRIMARY SCHOOLS** Overall position in league tables: 24th out of 150. Top scorers: St Josephs RC, Upminster; Gidea Park, Romford; Upminster Junior, Upminster • **STATE SECONDARY SCHOOLS** Overall position in league tables: 31st out of 150. Top scorers: Coopers Company and Cobourn (mixed), Upminster; Campion (boys, girls in sixth), Hornchurch; Sacred Heart of Mary (girls), Upminster.

TRANSPORT***
Upminster and Hornchurch are best served, by the fairly reliable district line as well as trains at Upminster. Trains only (although fast and quite frequent) to Romford. Fewer trains to Rainham.

TRAINS Romford: Zone 6. Cost of annual season ticket: £1396. No of trains per hour: to Liverpool Street every 10 minutes; Fastest journey: 24-27 minutes • **TUBES** Upminster: Zone 6. Frequency: District line to Embankment every 5-10 minutes; Fastest journey: 50 minutes. Hornchurch: Zone 6. Frequency: District line to Embankment every 5-10 minutes; Fastest journey: 48 minutes • **BUSES** No buses to town (tubes and trains do it much better) unless you're travelling at night when there's the N15 to Romford from Trafalgar Square and the N25 to Romford and Harold Hill from Trafalgar Square. Buses criss-cross the borough, although travel to outlying parts can be tricky, and there are regular buses to the huge Lakeside shopping centre at Thurrock. A car is possibly the most useful form of transport, unenvironmental though it may be, particularly as the M25 is so close • **TRAFFIC BLACKSPOTS** Gallows Corner: Where four main roads meet, bringing traffic from Romford in one direction and the M25 in the other. The council recently sparked anger among residents in salubrious Gidea Park when it proposed a bus lane and a number of bans on right turns into Main Road in a bid to ease congestion. Residents say their roads are becoming rat-runs and fear worse. Hornchurch High Street: Too narrow for the amount of traffic travelling down it, along with buses and delivery vans • **PARKING** Two controlled parking zones at Romford (divided into six sectors of which two need residents' permits); and Harold Wood. Cost of annual resident's permit: £3.

LEISURE FACILITIES * *

THEATRES & CONCERT HALLS The Queen's Theatre, Hornchurch has a good reputation for staging new plays as well as West End shows, live music and jazz, pantomimes and childrens' shows • **CINEMAS** Two, an ABC and an Odeon, in Romford, both multiscreen. With this many screens already, it's not quite clear why developers think the town needs 16 more on the planned Brewery site • **MUSEUMS & GALLERIES** Museums are thin on the ground with nothing run by the borough itself. The fifteenth century thatched Upminster tithe barn has a display of local history exhibits and the early nineteenth century Upminster Windmill is open to the public. Run by local historical society. Opening hours limited. Rainham Hall, an elegant Georgian house in Rainham is owned by the National Trust • **SPORTS FACILITIES** Two leisure centres at Rainham and Hornchurch, both with swimming pools and fitness centres. Pool at Harold Hill with weight training and health and beauty suite. Public golf course at Romford, skating rink at Romford, greyhound racing at Romford and tennis, football, cricket and other games in parks across the borough • **LIBRARIES** Under-used and a bit under-resourced. The main library in Romford is a good size with helpful staff although it's separated from the main shopping areas by busy roads and accesible via subways, not the best way of tempting people in. Patchy and inconsistent opening hours, with lots of closing for lunch and on various days during the week. Romford central library has the best opening hours. 6.2 library visits per head. Position in library-use league table: 22nd out of 32 (where 1 is best and 32 worst).

OPEN SPACES * * * * *

Half the borough's area is Green Belt land, with gentle fields stretching out on either side of narrow country lanes in the north and flat marshland in the south. There are also country parks which are more country than park and miles of river frontage.

PARKS Havering Country Park. Tucked into fields by Havering Atte Bower with mature woodland and glimpses of nothing but rural countryside. Great for rides and walks in the park or across the fields to Hainault Forest Country Park (see Redbridge). Hornchurch Country Park at the edge of fields at Hornchurch has walks through the meadows by the River Ingrebourne. Once an airfield for Battle of Britain spitfires, it still has concrete reminders of the old defence system • **RIVER WALKS** The Havering Riverside Pathway Project, a path along part of Havering's three mile industrial river frontage. Views of bleak beauty on a sunny day across to Thamesmead and Erith (see Bexley) while mechanical diggers bite into the piles of aggregate behind you. There is talk of building a new pier and starting riverbus crossings to Erith and commuter services to London.

SHOPS * *

ROMFORD Where most of Havering's shopping's at. Seriously unpromising approaching from the outside, with a mess of concrete multistorey car parks, office blocks and a gaping hole where most of the brewery used to be. But more interesting than you'd expect in the centre, with a couple of Essex clapboard cottages and pedestrianised marketplace. Once this was a livestock market, now there's an all-purpose market on Wednesday, Friday and Saturday. For permanent shopping, there's less of a single shopping mall and more of a series of arcades all linking up with each other although this only becomes obvious when you've passed the same shop several times. Mostly chain store shopping here and in the newer Liberty shopping centre. Indoor shopping hall and local shops overlooking the market place. Sainsbury's • **HORNCHURCH & UPMINSTER** Hornchurch is nothing spectacular but at least it's a proper high street with local shops including toy shop, baker and local shoe repair shop. Some attractive cottages in the centre but spoilt by heavy traffic. Sainsbury's. Dull chains and parades of off licences, banks and take-aways around Upminster Station • **RAINHAM** Some more villagey shops around the centre including an antique shop. Otherwise small local shops. The borough has recently spent £320,000 on environmental improvements to give it a more "historic look". Tesco.

RESTAURANTS*
Of strictly local appeal.

CRIME RATES*****
78 crimes per 1,000 of population, the second lowest crime rate in London. Position in Metropolitan Police league table: 31st out of 32 (where 1 is worst and 32 best).

THE COUNCIL***
POLITICAL AFFILIATION No overall control • **MINUS POINTS** One of the most expensive for property searches • **PLUS POINTS** Quick at turning round property searches. Good schools. Playing its part in regeneration. Door-to-door recycling in most parts of the borough. Some of the cheapest residents' parking in London • **PROPERTY SEARCHES CARRIED OUT IN 10 WORKING DAYS** 99% • **STANDARD SEARCH FEE** £122.40 • **COUNCIL TAX COLLECTED** 96.7%

● **COUNCIL TAX 1989-99**

BAND	PROPERTY VALUE	CHARGE	BAND	PROPERTY VALUE	CHARGE
A	up to £40,000	£482.66	E	£88,001-£120,000	£884.89
B	£40,001-£52,000	£563.11	F	£120,001-£160,000	£1,045.78
C	£52,001-£68,000	£643.56	G	£160,001-£320,000	£1,206.66
D	£68,001-£88,000	£724.00	H	over £320,000	£1,448.00

HILLINGDON

It can be a good thing to have the world's busiest airport on your doorstep. No struggling through the traffic or sitting on the tube at the beginning of your trip, a bewildering choice of destinations and a quick pop home when you arrive back exhausted. But for residents of Hillingdon who don't want to go anywhere and don't depend on Heathrow for their livelihood, the presence of the airport spreading over the bottom third of their borough is a mixed blessing. Low-flying aircraft, constant traffic jams in roads round the airport and the prospect of a fifth terminal make Heathrow a noisy and disagreeable neighbour. As if one airport wasn't enough, Hillingdon is also home to Northholt Aerodrome, scene of many wartime sorties and arrivals.

But Metroland, that 1930s dream of comfortable suburban living and escape from the city smog, still survives almost unscathed in many parts of a borough which looks more to the rolling hills of the Chilterns and the Thames Valley than London, 14 miles to the east. Hillingdon is London's second biggest borough. Around Heathrow, the air throbs with the roar of planes. Further north, warehouses and factories cluster round the Grand Union Canal and stretch up to Hayes (Middlesex and not to be confused with Hayes, Kent (see Bromley)). To the west are the Victorian terraces of Uxbridge opening out into fields and hills and the village of Ickenham to the north. Salubrious Ruislip and Eastcote give way to wealthy Northwood, spiritually in Hertfordshire and only a few steps from the edge of London. Large properties, abundant green space and children in neat school uniforms breathe prosperity.

Northwood, Northwood Hills and Ruislip are Hillingdon's metroland, linked umbilically to London by the rattling Metropolitan line tube bringing thousands of commuters to town every morning. Many more work at Heathrow, a major employer. The south around Hayes and West Drayton, once a busy manufacturing area, is now reinventing itself as a magnet for high tech, retail and other white collar service industries looking for space and good transport links. Not surprisingly, the unemployment rate is low at 2.8% but more than £21 million of public and private money has been injected into improving employment prospects and the environment, and cutting crime in the area.

Uxbridge, the borough's retail and adminstrative centre, and currently a bit of an acquired taste, is also set for a massive face-lift. The north side of the High Street may now be a gaping hole but in three years' time a completely new high street of shop facades will rise up with a Debenhams, 75 other new shops and a nine screen multiplex cinema. If the £150 million centre looks somehow familiar when it's done, it's not necessarily that you're getting jaded about the predictability of outer London shopping (although this would be quite understandable). The company working on Uxbridge was also responsible for The Glades in Bromley and Lakeside in Thurrock.

PROPERTY AND ARCHITECTURE

HAYES

Hayes falls into two parts, the more commercial Hayes Town to the south around the station and the more villagey Hayes proper around the thirteenth century church to the north. 1930s semis mixed with modern blocks, small estate houses and council houses predominate around Hayes Town. Hayes itself has some Victorian terraces and cottages grouped round the church but the few shops on Church Road have given up the unequal struggle with Hayes Town shopping centre and the area's a bit forlorn. A good area to buy a cheap house although Hayes is a bus ride away from the station. 1930s semis, many "improved" with pebble-dash and picture windows in West Drayton.

ATTRACTS *First-time buyers; families; members of the Asian community* • **CONSERVATION AREAS** *Hayes Village; Botwell (East and West walk); Bulls Bridge; West Drayton Green* • **AVERAGE PRICES** *Flats: studio: £35,000; 1-bed: £45,000; 2-bed: £60,000 Houses: 1-bed: £60,000; 2-bed: £80,000; 3-bed: £90,000; 4-bed: £130,000* • **AVERAGE RENTS (MONTHLY)** *Flats: studio: £400+; 1-bed: £450-£500; 2-bed: £600+ Houses: 1-bed: £550; 2-bed: £650; 3-bed: £700-£800; 4-bed: £1000+; 5-bed: £1100+.*

UXBRIDGE & HILLINGDON

The centre of Uxbridge is almost completely commercial, a mix of narrow winding streets and ugly 1960s multistorey carparks. Roads of mostly Victorian and Edwardian terraces predominate around the centre of this once important market town with some modern apartment blocks on main roads. 1930s semis take over on the fringes. Hillingdon has its share of 1930s semis but also some large detached houses.

ATTRACTS *Families, loyal locals; first-time buyers who want to be close to tubes and shops* • **CONSERVATION AREAS** *Old Uxbridge; The Greenway; Cowley Lock; Cowley Church* • **AVERAGE PRICES** *Flats: studio: £50,000; 1-bed: £60,000; 2-bed: £70,000-£75,000 Houses: 1-bed: £70,000; 2-bed: £90,000; 3-bed: £120,000; 4-bed: £200,000; 5-bed: £300,000-£350,000* • **AVERAGE RENTS (MONTHLY)** *Flats: studio: £450+; 1-bed: £500+; 2-bed: £650+ Houses: 1-bed: £600; 2-bed: £700; 3-bed: £750; 4-bed: £1000+.*

RUISLIP & EASTCOTE

This is where things get more up-market as industry and built-up streets give way to green belt land. All these areas were mostly built up in the 1930s but with middling and large detached houses rather than semis, giving them a more spacious feel than other suburban parts of London. Well-cared-for family houses in every kind of style known to the 1930s speculative builder (half-timbered, diamond-paned windows, small wooden panes with shutters, red brick manorial). Attempts at a Ruislip Garden Suburb petered out but the results are still there around Manor Way just off Eastcote Road, with characteristic cottage-style houses grouped round green space. The grandest houses in Ruislip are just by the Common, while Eastcote's most sought-after area is the Eastcote Park Estate. Mostly family houses rather than flats.

ATTRACTS *Families* • **CONSERVATION AREAS** *Ruislip Village; Manor Way Ruislip; Eastcote Village* • **AVERAGE PRICES** *Flats: studio: £45,000; 1-bed: £65,000-£75,000; 2-bed: £80,000-£100,000 Houses: 1-bed: £75,000-£85,000; 2-bed: £80,000-£120,000; 3-bed: £115,000-£260,000; 4-bed: £160,000-£350,000; 5-bed: up to £500,000* • **AVERAGE RENTS (MONTHLY)** *Flats: studio: £425-£450; 1-bed: £550; 2-bed: £650-£700 Houses: 1-bed: £600; 2-bed: £700; 3-bed: £850+; 4-bed: £1500.*

ICKENHAM

Suspended on a band of green belt north of Uxbridge and south of Ruislip, Ickenham likes to think of itself as superior to the sea of suburbia around it although it too was mostly built up in the 1930s. But it does still have a village pump and pond and a discernible centre with a handful of shops and cottages. More akin in most respects to Ruislip, it also has some roads grand enough to compete with anything posher Northwood can offer. The area west of Long Lane is most sought-after for its large houses and because it comes within the catchment area of one of the borough's best schools, Vyners.

ATTRACTS *Families wanting good schools and green space* • **CONSERVATION AREA** *Ickenham Village* • **AVERAGE PRICES** *Flats: studio: £40,000; 1-bed: £60,000; 2-bed: £75,000-£90,000 Houses: 2-bed: £100,000-£120,000; 3-bed: £145,000-£260,000; 4-bed: £200,000-£325,000* • **AVERAGE RENTS (MONTHLY)** *Flats: studio: £420; 1-bed: £500-£600; 2-bed: £900; 3-bed: £1200 Houses: 1-bed: £500-£600; 2-bed: £750-£800; 3-bed: £1400+; 4-bed: £2000.*

NORTHWOOD

Includes the crème-de-la crème of the borough's property, particularly in the roads between the golf course and Ruislip Common. Wide roads lined with mature trees and houses which aren't ashamed to be huge. Neo-Georgian, stockbroker Tudor, Hacienda style – it's all there. Houses have names like Wildwood and Oak Lodge and there are lots of wrought iron gates and olde worlde carriage lamps. Slightly less exalted houses around the centre of Northwood and Northwood Hills, which sounds as though it should be posher than Northwood but isn't.

ATTRACTS *The wealthy; families wanting good schools and green space; wealthy internationals* • **CONSERVATION AREAS** *Northwood* • **AVERAGE PRICES** *Flats: 1-bed: £80,000; 2-bed: £120,000+; 3-bed: £220,000+ Houses: 2-bed: £130,000; 3-bed: £150,000-£250,000; 4-bed: £300,000+; 5-bed: £450,000+* • **AVERAGE RENTS (MONTHLY)** *Flats: studio: £500; 1-bed: £500-£650; 2-bed: £1000-£1500; 3-bed: £1000-£2000 Houses: 1-bed: £550-£650; 2-bed: £900+; 3-bed: £1800+; 4-bed: £2500+; 5-bed: £3000+.*

BEST POSTCODES

Hillingdon is all well beyond the reach of London postcodes.

AMENITIES

SCHOOLS★★★

Overall league table performance is quite good, particularly at primary level, without being startling. No selective state schools at secondary level. A number of excellent private schools around Northwood. Below-average provision of nursery places for under-fives but a reasonable choice of private and voluntary day nurseries.

PRE-SCHOOL PROVISION *1 state nursery school; 6 state primary and church schools with nursery classes; 103 private day nurseries and playgroups. Proportion of under-fives in state nurseries: 45%* • **STATE PRIMARY SCHOOLS** *Overall position in league tables: 39th out of 150. Top scorers: St Swithern Wells RC, Ruislip; Breakspear, Ickenham; Newnham, Ruislip* • **STATE SECONDARY SCHOOLS** *Overall position in league table: 71st out of 150. Best scorers: Vyners School (mixed), Ickenham; Bishop Ramsey C of E (mixed), Ruislip; Haydon School (mixed), Eastcote* • **PRIVATE PREP SCHOOLS** *St John's (boys), Northwood; St Martins (boys) Northwood* • **PRIVATE SECONDARY SCHOOLS** *Chart-topper St Helens Northwood (girls from 4); Northwood*

College (girls from 4) Northwood; Merchant Taylors (boys) Northwood;
Guru Nanak Sikh College (mixed from 3), Hayes.

TRANSPORT***

Much better in the middle and north of the borough than the south, where
large tracts of residential areas in Yeading and Hayes are a bus ride away
from a not terribly good rail service. The north has the Metropolitan and
Piccadilly lines, both fairly reliable although it's a bit of a slog to the end of
the line, stopping at every station, and not all trains go that far.
TRAINS Hayes and Harlington: Zone 5. Cost of annual season ticket:
£1280; No of trains per hour: to Paddington 4 or 5; Fastest journey: 20
minutes • **TUBES** Ruislip: Zone 6. Cost of annual season ticket: £1396
No of trains per hour: Metropolitan line to Baker Street 7; Piccadilly line to
Piccadilly Circus 5; Fastest journey: Metropolitan 32 minutes; Piccadilly
line 47 minutes. Uxbridge: Zone 6. No of trains per hour: Metropolitan
line to Baker Street 7; Piccadilly line to Piccadilly Circus 4; Fastest journey:
Metropolitan 39 minutes; Piccadilly line 57 minutes. Northwood: Zone 6.
No of trains per hour: Metropolitan line to Baker Street 8; Fastest journey:
28 minutes • **BUSES** Good choice of services to Heathrow, as you'd
expect. But otherwise buses mostly link suburbs and there are no regular
daytime services all the way into central London. It's difficult to get from
one end of the borough to the other without changing buses. Night buses
include the N97 to Heathrow from Trafalgar Square and the N207 from
Trafalgar Square to Uxbridge via Hayes and Hillingdon • **TRAFFIC
BLACKSPOTS** Heathrow: The A4 alongside the airport perimeter. Always
several lanes of traffic, often sitting in tailbacks from traffic lights and
roundabouts trying to get on to other main roads. Uxbridge: A depressing
confluence of main roads meets at a large roundabout just south of the
town's main shopping area. Often jammed with traffic waiting at a series
of confusing traffic lights. Uxbridge town centre itself isn't too bad for traffic-
a pleasant contrast to some other London shopping streets • **PARKING**
There are three controlled parking zones: north of Uxbridge Town Centre;
Yiewsley and West Drayton town centre; and the Heathrow fly-drive area.
Cost of annual resident's permit: £20 for the first car; £30 for the second,
£50 for the third and £100 for a fourth or subsequent.

LEISURE FACILITIES***

THEATRES & CONCERT HALLS Two theatres, the Beck theatre in Hayes, and
the Compass theatre in Ickenham, with a mix of plays, childrens' shows,
bands and music recitals. Plays also at the Winston Churchill Hall, Ruislip.
Theatre groups meet at Southlands Arts Centre in West Drayton, started
by local residents in the 1960s in despair that there was nothing to do in
Hillingdon • **CINEMAS** A poor show. Only one, the Uxbridge Odeon,
strictly mainstream • **MUSEUMS & GALLERIES** Local art galleries at the Cow
Byre Gallery, Ruislip and the Atrium Gallery in Uxbridge's large and
impressive central library, as well as exhibitions at the Southlands Arts
Centre and Brunel University. Only one museum, of local history in
Uxbridge Central Library. RAF Uxbridge occasionally allows the public a
glimpse of the underground control centre used to direct the Battle of Britain
• **SPORTS FACILITIES** Well provided for. Five leisure centres in Hayes (two),
Ruislip, Harefield and Northwood. Pools at Hayes, Harlington and Ruislip.
Four public golf courses at Northwood, Ruislip, Uxbridge and Stockley
Park, West Drayton. Water sports at Ruislip Lido, an attractive 40 acre lake
surrounded by Ruislip Woods and golf courses. Dry ski slope at Uxbridge.

Discount leisure card scheme in operation • **LIBRARIES** *Used less than average which Uxbridge, at least, doesn't deserve, as it's well organised, with helpful staff. Ruislip also has a small but beautiful library in a sixteenth century barn with hammer-beamed roof and stained glass windows. But opening hours across the borough are gappy, which could account for lower usage. Lots of lunchtime closing in smaller branch libraries. All libraries, with the strange exception of Harlington (why?) are closed on Wednesdays. 6.8 library visits per head. Position in library-use league table: 20th out of 32 (where 1 is best and 32 worst).*

OPEN SPACES ★★★★

This is where Hillingdon really scores. It has large tracts of rolling green belt land within its boundaries particularly in the north west, where it borders on to the beginnings of the Chilterns, as well as some excellent woodland walks between Ruislip and Northwood. Many of its houses have large gardens and roads are lined with mature trees. Even though the south is more built-up it still has woods, open space and rivers running along past the backs of houses, although some of its parks could do with some TLC. The Victorian mansion of Barra Hall in Barra Hall Park. Hayes for example is sorely in need of a coat of paint although it's set for a face-lift and the open-air theatre is derelict. Hillingdon's section of the Grand Union Canal is industrial for most of its length.

WOODS Ruislip Woods. Now a national nature reserve. The council claims this is the single largest unbroken stretch of mature woodland in London, which is easy to believe if you set off for a walk there just before lunch with no provisions, then get slightly lost. Beech trees and mud, just like a real Chiltern walk. Ruislip lido is just through the trees and a miniature steam railway runs round the lido.

SHOPS ★★★

HAYES One of Hillingdon's two main shopping centres. Pedestrianised shopping centre and shopping in streets around Hayes Town. Fairly predictable, with mostly chains at the cheap end of the market, take-aways and burger bars. More shops along Uxbridge Road, again predictable (but useful). Sainsbury's in Hayes Town. Waitrose in Uxbridge Road • **UXBRIDGE** Where it's at for Hillingdon shopping. The pedestrianised area outside the handsome art deco Uxbridge station with a couple of pavement cafés is a good welcome for new arrivals. Chain stores and indoor market stalls selling cheap clothes and leather bags at the Pavilions Shopping Centre. The centre is looking a bit tired and it's questionable whether the planned new shopping centre will be much help to its future (although it should perk up Uxbridge). Much more interesting small shops in the narrow old Windsor Road including antique shops, jewellers, evening dress hire and, defiantly, a sex shop. Look back at the bottom of Windsor Road for a depressing view of the back of the Pavilions and horrible 1960s multi-storey car park. Sainsbury's • **RUISLIP** More like the high street of a Buckinghamshire town than London with a good mix of the useful (chains) and the individual (long established local shops). Tidy streets lined with half-timbered and red brick parades on both sides, including a real butcher and baker, a couple of old-fashioned clothes shops and furniture and interior design shops. Waitrose • **NORTHWOOD** A sloping high street of mostly well-manicured local shops and charity shops promised ex-fashion show stock. Lots of estate agents and a large Waitrose. Shabbier shops in Northwood Hills.

RESTAURANTS*
A bit of a culinary desert although there are one or two recommended Indian restaurants in Hayes. The usual collection of local restaurants, brasseries, pizza and pasta chains and take-aways.

CRIME RATES***
103 crimes per 1000 of population. Position in Metropolitan Police league table: 21st out of 32 (where 1 is worst and 32 best).

THE COUNCIL***
POLITICAL AFFILIATION No overall control • **MINUS POINTS** Residents have complained about the state of some of the parks and open spaces. One of the slowest boroughs in London at turning round property searches quickly while charging a lot for the privilege • **PLUS POINTS** Piloting a door-to-door recycling scheme. Generally acknowledged by residents to be acceptably friendly and efficient • **PROPERTY SEARCHES CARRIED OUT IN 10 WORKING DAYS** 87% • **STANDARD SEARCH FEE** £125 • **COUNCIL TAX COLLECTED** 94.3%
• **COUNCIL TAX 1998-99**

BAND	PROPERTY VALUE	CHARGE	BAND	PROPERTY VALUE	CHARGE
A	up to £40,000	£469.22	E	£88,001-£120,000	£860.25
B	£40,001-£52,000	£547.43	F	£120,001-£160,000	£1,016.66
C	£52,001-£68,000	£625.64	G	£160,001-£320,000	£1,173.06
D	£68,001-£88,000	£703.84	H	over £320,000	£1,407.68

HOUNSLOW

The transport planners haven't been kind to Hounslow. Not only is the northern part of the borough carved up by the M4 and the A4 (both running almost parallel to each other, just to turn the knife) but the sleep of its residents is regularly shattered by incoming planes landing at Heathrow. The prospect of a fifth terminal at Heathrow is chilling for those with homes under the flight path although like their fellow sufferers in Richmond, their fight threatens to run into the sand through lack of funds. Hounslow has some of the best westward road and air connections of any borough but this is cold comfort to people who live there and want to stay put rather than force their way out.

But is Hounslow worth staying in? Yes and no. It has miles of frankly dull suburbs thrown up during London's westward expansion in the 1930s, as a glance out of the window of a Heathrow-bound tube over a sea of tiled roofs will confirm. But it also has some of the prettiest riverside in London, some elegant parks and some good schools.

Its boundaries stretch from middle class Victorian Chiswick in the East down to the Thames, across to once-industrial Brentford and the pretty riverside village of Isleworth. To the north are the large family homes of Osterley by Osterley Park and to the west from Hounslow outwards are the amorphous 1930s suburbs of Feltham and Heston.

Hounslow has some posh bits but it's more a white collar worker enclave than part of the stockbroker commuter belt. Unemployment is comfortably low by London standards at 3.6%, with many residents employed at nearby Heathrow or British Airways or at the BBC in neighbouring White City to the East. Nearly a quarter of the population is from an ethnic minority, the vast majority of whom are Indian. Although the Indian community adds interest to what is otherwise a fairly staid area, it hasn't made as much of an obvious mark as in nearby Southall (see Ealing).

Middle class homeowners have been colonising Chiswick for years, attracted by its closeness to the river and good tube links. Now they're turning their attention to neighbouring Brentford, which is set for a series of major face-lifts over the next five years in a bid to improve the town centre, rehabilitate rivers and canals from industrial dereliction and bring life to the area in the evening. New luxury riverside developments have risen from the debris of old scrap metal sites and there are plans for a £37 million development at Brentford Lock, on land now contaminated by coal deposits. The rusting warehouses will be turned into restaurants, pubs, flats and a hotel. At the other end of the High Street, more riverside industrial sites will be turned into a mixture of housing, shops and offices with a large element of the affordable housing the council wants to encourage. And there are plans to demolish some of the dullest buildings in Brentford High Street to open it up to the river behind in an £80 million mixed development.

PROPERTY & ARCHITECTURE

CHISWICK & GUNNERSBURY

Streets of well-kept Victorian cottages and terraces and later Edwardian terraces in roads off and around Chiswick High Road. Mansion blocks on the High Road. Much larger Victorian semi-detached and detached houses nearer the river in Grove Park near Chiswick Station in wide tree-lined roads. Some of the houses are now flats but many still have original stained glass windows and ornate woodwork porches and balconies. Along Strand on the Green on the river towpath is a lovely mix of Georgian and early Victorian cottages and larger houses, some of the most sought-after in Chiswick. Equally sought-after is Bedford Park, a suburb of Queen Anne-style detached houses and smaller cottages built as an artists' colony in the 1870s. Bedford Park's active local amenity society has angered some residents who resent their zealous guardianship of the conservation area.
ATTRACTS *Young professionals; families; first-time buyers; people who are disenchanted with Fulham; workers from the BBC* • **CONSERVATION AREAS** *Old Chiswick; Chiswick House; Strand on the Green; Turnham Green; Stamford Brook; Bedford Park; Gunnersbury Park* • **AVERAGE PRICES** *Flats: studio: £80,000; 1-bed: £110,000-£150,000; 2-bed: £160,000-£300,000; 3-bed: £250,000+ Houses: 2-bed: £260,000-£275,000; 3-bed: 325,000+; 4-bed: £350,000+; 5-bed: £450,000+* • **AVERAGE RENTS (MONTHLY)** *Flats: studio: £860; 1-bed: £780-£1300; 2-bed: £950-£1950; 3-bed: £1210 Houses: 2-bed: £1300-£1730; 3-bed: £1510+; 4-bed: £1950+; 5-bed: £2380+.*

BRENTFORD, ISLEWORTH & OSTERLEY

Brentford still bears many traces of its industrial past, with factories and riverside warehouses, more recently joined by tower blocks. But there are some roads of attractive small terraces and cottages off the main road, particularly in the conservation areas around St Pauls recreation ground. The area has improved a lot in the last 10 years. The best part of Brentford is The Butts, large Victorian houses set back from a wide road leading to an almost-perfect square of Georgian townhouses (many of which are now offices). Old Isleworth around Church Road feels more like part of an old seaside town with the Thames on one side and a street of white painted and brick houses and cottages on the other. Further inland there's a mix of modern estate houses and Victorian terraces. A good choice of small flats. Osterley, the best part of Isleworth around the park, has some large Victorian and Edwardian houses among 1930s houses in Jersey Road.

ATTRACTS *Young professionals (including employees of the BBC); families* • **CONSERVATION AREAS** *Isleworth Riverside; St Pauls Brentford; The Butts; Osterley Park* • **AVERAGE PRICES** *Flats: studio: £55,000; 1-bed: £65,000+; 2-bed: £75,000-£100,000 Houses: 1-bed: £70,000+; 2-bed: £85,000+; 3-bed: £115,000-£140,000; 4-bed: £160,000+; 5-bed: £185,000+* • **AVERAGE RENTS (MONTHLY)** *Flats: studio: £450; 1-bed: £550; 2-bed: £700+ Houses: 1-bed: £550; 2-bed: £800; 3-bed: £950; 4-bed: £1200; 5-bed: £1500.*

HOUNSLOW, FELTHAM & HANWORTH

A lot of central Hounslow is Victorian, with roads of large and small terraces near the shopping centre. West Hounslow is mostly 1930s semis as is the area around Hounslow Heath. Further south, almost the only good thing that can be said about Feltham and Hanworth is that they're cheap. Shabby 1930s semis on wide, treeless, rather bleak roads broken by parades of uninspiring local shops predominate and there are a couple of local council estates which should be avoided. Local agents say the area has become an airport workers' colony. Lots of local authority flats. The best parts of Hanworth are near the border with Hampton (see Richmond) where parents can send their children to schools just over the border in Richmond.

ATTRACTS *Families; airport workers; loyal locals (a recent survey found that more than half the people questioned had lived in Feltham 10 years or more); investors (Hounslow)* • **CONSERVATION AREAS** *St Pauls Hounslow; St Stephens Hounslow; Hounslow Cavalry Barracks; Feltham Town Centre; Hanworth Park* • **AVERAGE PRICES** *Flats: studio: £45,000-£50,000; 1-bed: £50,000-£65,000; 2-bed: £60,000-£75,000 Houses: 1-bed: £60,000; 2-bed: £75,000-£85,000; 3-bed: £80,000-£115,000; 4-bed: £100,000-£145,000* • **AVERAGE RENTS (MONTHLY)** *Flats: studio: £425; 1-bed: £525; 2-bed: £650 Houses: 1-bed: £550; 2-bed: £700; 3-bed: £850; 4-bed: up to £1000.*

BEST POSTCODES

Largely irrelevant as most of the borough is technically in Middlesex. Chiswick W4 is one of London's sought-after postcodes.

AMENITIES

SCHOOLS ★ ★ ★

Both primary and secondary schools perform creditably overall in league tables. But there are several chart topping state schools all of which are oversubscribed. Primary schools all operate catchment areas (called Priority Admissions areas) to keep schools local. Above-average provision of state nursery school places. A couple of private schools in the borough itself but there's also a good choice in neighbouring boroughs (see Richmond and Ealing).

PRE-SCHOOL PROVISION *42 nursery units in state and church primary schools; 64 private nurseries and playgroups. Proportion of under-fives in state nurseries: 70%* • **STATE PRIMARY SCHOOLS** *Overall league table position: 82nd out of 150. Top scorers: St Michael and St Martin RC, (with nursery unit), Hounslow; St Mary's RC (with nursery unit), Chiswick; Our Lady and St John RC (with nursery unit), Brentford. Expect grillings about church attendance, backed up with baptismal certificates* • **STATE SECONDARY SCHOOLS** *Overall league table position: 50th out of 149. Top scorers: Green School (girls), Isleworth; Gumley House Convent (girls), Isleworth; Heathland School (mixed), Hounslow* • **PRIVATE SCHOOLS** *Arts Educational School (mixed to 16), Chiswick; Ashton House (mixed from 3), Isleworth; Hounslow College (boys from 9), Hounslow.*

TRANSPORT ★ ★ ★

Good tube services in the centre and east of the borough with Chiswick and Hounslow particularly well served, although the travelling in on the Piccadilly line from Heathrow with the gangways cluttered by the unwieldy suitcases of long-haul air passengers can be tedious. In the west and south some areas (parts of Hanworth for example) are a long way from a station.

TRAINS *Brentford: Zone 4. Cost of annual season ticket: £1068. No of trains per hour: to Waterloo 2 (one every half hour); Fastest journey: 29 minutes. Feltham: Zone 6. Cost of annual season ticket: £1396; No of trains per hour: to Waterloo 6; Fastest journey: 27 minutes* • **TUBES** *Turnham Green (Chiswick): Zone 2. Cost of annual season ticket: £704; Frequency: District to Embankment every 6-10 minutes; Fastest journey: 23 minutes. Gunnersbury: Zone 3. Cost of annual season ticket: £860; Frequency: District to Embankment every 6-10 minutes; Fastest journey: 25 minutes. Hounslow Central: Zone 4. Frequency: Piccadilly to Piccadilly Circus every 3-6 minutes; Fastest journey: 38 minutes* • **BUSES** *Mostly linking one suburb with another, particularly shopping suburbs like Kingston. The nearest you'll get to town without a change is Shepherds Bush or Hammersmith. But there are good links to Heathrow. The N97 nightbus goes from Trafalgar Square via Turnham Green, Brentford, Isleworth and Hounslow* • **TRAFFIC BLACKSPOTS** *Chiswick: The A4 Great West Road and Hogarth Roundabout. One of the oldest and still one of the nastiest pieces of road in London. Fast, merciless traffic. No one has yet worked out an alternative to the makeshift-looking bridge carrying traffic over the roundabout. The A4 carves Chiswick into two, creating an ugly barrier between the centre and the river. Chiswick High Road is also often chock-a-block. Hounslow: The main London Road west into Hounslow can be very slow, particularly at rush hour and school times, as can roads connecting Hounslow with Isleworth. Feltham: Traffic bottlenecks can build up during* the rushhour around the railway bridge and at the junction of Hounslow and Harlington Roads • **PARKING** Controlled parking zones operate in Hounslow West, Hounslow Central, Brentford around The Butts, East Chiswick and Twickenham Road, Isleworth. A controlled parking zone could be implemented in Bedford Park, Chiswick if residents agree. Cost of annual resident's permit: Hounslow West: £30; Hounslow Town Centre: £30; East Chiswick: £75; The Butts: £50; Isleworth: £30.

LEISURE FACILITIES * * * *

THEATRES & CONCERT HALLS Two theatres in the borough, the Paul Robeson in Hounslow which has a lot of family shows, pantomimes and regular Asian shows (attended by Asians from all around West London), and the Watermans Art Centre on the riverside at Brentford which has a wide variety of theatre, contemporary dance and live music. Regular plays and shows also at Feltham Assembly Hall. Summertime concerts organised by the Paul Robeson theatre in the amphitheatre in the grounds of Chiswick House • **CINEMAS** Repertory cinema at the Watermans Art Centre; 14 screen cineworld at Feltham showing mainstream films • **MUSEUMS & GALLERIES** A surprisingly good choice. Hounslow was once a favoured choice as a country seat for the aristocracy and rich merchants and several of their stately homes survive as reminders that the borough wasn't always a mere extension of London. They include: Chiswick House, the elegant white Palladian house of Lord Burlington; Gunnersbury House, once the home of the Rothschilds and now a local history museum (often seen by motorists from the vantage point of the Chiswick flyover; the slightly forbidding grey mass of Syon House in Brentford, home of the Duke of Northumberland; and Osterly Park House. If stately homes pall, there's the Kew Bridge Steam museum in a Victorian pumping station with water tower. There are also the weird and wonderful automatic musical instruments at the Musical Museum and tours of Fullers Brewery at Chiswick • **SPORTS FACILITIES** Five leisure centres at Brentford, Feltham, Isleworth, Chiswick and Heston. Pools at Chiswick and Heston. Golf at Heston, Osterley and Hounslow Heath as well as tennis, football and other outdoor sports in parks across the borough. Leisure card system offering discounts • **LIBRARIES** Well used. The central library in Hounslow is conveniently situated in the main Treaty shopping centre just next to the Paul Robeson theatre. But opening hours are patchy with most libraries closed on Wednesday and some on Friday. No Sunday opening. Few long evening openings. 9.5 library visits per head. Position in library-use league table: 7th out of 32 (where 1 is best and 32 worst).

OPEN SPACES * * * *

One of the borough's best features despite all attempts by traffic planners to site motorways next to or across beautiful parks like Gunnersbury or Osterley. A good choice of parks with manicured lawns, noble trees, elegant conservatories and so on.

RIVER WALKS The section of the Thames Path running along most of the borough's waterfront. Takes in the riverside "villages" of Strand on the Green and Old Isleworth as well as the warehouses of Brentford with views over some of the Thames' most rural stretches. Also the tangle of islets around Brentford leading to the towpath along the Grand Union Canal, a canalised section of the river Brent. Overgrown with tall grass and with houseboats moored under the trees, its industrial past has faded. But the concrete pillars of the raised M4 motorway rearing up overhead still come as a shock • **WILD HEATHLAND** Hounslow Heath. Once one of the dodgiest *areas around London, stalked by highwaymen. Now a tangle of woods, brambles and open heathland, a welcome break in the surrounding suburbia. Paths along the Crane River to the west are being restored and improved.*

SHOPS * * *

CHISWICK *Where most of the borough's most interesting shops are. An up-market collection of antiques, furniture shops (futons and minimalism rather than World of Leather), bookshops, designer clothes and respectable chains like M&S and Dillons. Spoilt by several lanes each way of horrible and constant traffic, a serious disincentive to energetic shopping. Sainsbury's* • **BRENTFORD & ISLEWORTH** *Brentford is dull, as even its supporters admit, which is why there are plans to gee it up by knocking some of it down. A dispiriting collection of take-aways, small cafés and local shops with lots of empty shops in modern and 1950s parades. Somerfields* • **HOUNSLOW** *The official flagship, with a large indoor shopping centre at The Treaty and more shops in the adjoining pedestrianised shopping street. A good shopping environment, generally clean and litter-free and The Treaty's large atrium saves it from being overwhelming or claustrophobic. Mostly chain stores although some of the branches are of good size. Some stores have been occupied by quick-turn-around traders. Safeway* • **FELTHAM** *So dull that it's depressing even to be there. A long street of chain stores and local shops, broken by a 1960s concrete and glass shopping precinct overlooked by slab blocks of offices and flats. Fortunately there are plans to revamp the town centre under the Feltham First regeneration initiative.*

RESTAURANTS * * *

CHISWICK *Any yuppie restaurant chain that hasn't yet set up a branch in or around Chiswick High Road yet will doubtless soon get in on the act. The usual suspects – All Bar One, Pitcher & Piano et al are already there and there's a huge choice of other brasseries, wine bars, pubs with large picture windows and restaurants including several good Thais* • **HOUNSLOW** *The usual pizza and pasta chains and All Bar One among other local places* • **ELSEWHERE** *Nothing of note.*

CRIME RATES * *

One of the highest crime rates of any outer London borough. 126 crimes per 1000 of population. Position in Metropolitan Police league table: 13th out of 32 (where 1 is worst and 32 best).

THE COUNCIL * * *

POLITICAL AFFILIATION *Labour* • **MINUS POINTS** *Not always thorough in litter collection and street-sweeping (old litter particularly obnoxious by the Thames Path); has annoyed traders and residents with unco-ordinated digging up of roads* • **PLUS POINTS** *Door-to-door recycling; 100% efficiency in turning round property searches within target times (although it charges for it)*
- **PROPERTY SEARCHES CARRIED OUT WITHIN 10 WORKING DAYS** *100%*
- **STANDARD SEARCH FEE** *£120* • **COUNCIL TAX COLLECTED** *92.7%*
- **COUNCIL TAX 1998-99**

BAND	PROPERTY VALUE	CHARGE	BAND	PROPERTY VALUE	CHARGE
A	up to £40,000	£460.67	E	£88,001-£120,000	£844.57
B	£40,001-£52,000	£537.45	F	£120,001-£160,000	£998.13
C	£52,001-£68,000	£614.23	G	£160,001-£320,000	£1,151.68
D	£68,001-£88,000	£691.01	H	over £320,000	£1,382.02

ISLINGTON

Until the 1960s, Islington was beyond the pale to the middle classes. It was poor, full of run-down, crumbling rented terraces, surrounded by other poor areas and worst of all, on the wrong (ie not west) side of London. Now, 30 years later, in one of the subtle shifts in which London specialises, Islington itself has been colonised by City and West End workers, politicians and opinion formers, who covet its elegant Georgian and Victorian terraces, its proximity to the centre, shops, bars, restaurants and innovative arts scene. So complete has the takeover been in people's minds that the very word Islington has become shorthand for a certain type of self-consciously New Labour middle class hipness, the "sun-dried tomato effect" as one cynic calls it. In retrospect, Islington was the only place where Tony and Cherie Blair could have lived. Those who can't afford Islington's rocketing house prices have turned their attention north to Tufnell Park, signalled by the inexorable appearance of antique fireplace shops in the Holloway Road.

But like its surrounding neighbours, Camden, Hackney and Haringey, the borough of Islington is more complex than the rather one-sided media coverage would suggest. It's not all trendy chatterers seeing and being seen in the eateries of Upper Street. It's a melting pot of races (nearly a fifth of the population is from an ethnic minority). The poor haven't left Islington; they live next door to the rich. Unemployment is the fourth highest in London at 11.7% and the borough ranks as the fourth most deprived in England. Islington Council, still trying to jettison its reputation as one of the loony left councils of the 1980s, is spending millions on refurbishing some of its worst estates.

The borough of Islington stretches from the newly trendy warehouses and workshops of Clerkenwell up through the council blocks of Finsbury, touching Kings Cross before reaching the beautiful Georgian terraces of Islington itself. North of Islington are the elegant squares and terraces of Barnsbury, Canonbury and Highbury. They then give way to the densely packed Victorian terraces of Archway to the east of Holloway Road and the more salubrious Victorian enclave of Tufnell Park to the west.

The past few years have seen large injections of private and public money into the borough to regenerate Kings Cross (see Camden) and the crumbling city fringe areas of Clerkenwell, Shoreditch and Hoxton (see Hackney) and Spitalfields (see Tower Hamlets). Islington, Hackney, Tower Hamlets and their private sector partners are spending up to £15 million over eight years to help the unemployed and small businesses and to revamp streetscapes and lighting. In Islington, Cowcross Street by Farringdon Station and Exmouth Market will be the chief beneficiaries of new streetscaping. They are included in proposals by Railtrack to improve the cross-London Thameslink line with new platforms and a smart new ticket office for Farringdon Station. Public money is also helping to fund a new "cultural quarter", encouraging the use of urban spaces (warehouses, streets) for public art and cultural events, cutting traffic and making it pleasanter to walk round the area.

PROPERTY AND ARCHITECTURE

CLERKENWELL & FINSBURY

A hotchpotch of council blocks, Georgian terraces and former warehouses converted into dramatically spacious loft apartments. Ten years ago this area was full of boarded-up and bombed-out industrial buildings, deserted by the printers and watchmakers who used to work in them. Then it took off in a big way as loft-living caught on. Developers bought up the warehouses and the yuppies moved into spaces (not flats, please) full of exposed brick and industrial steel fittings. There are some beautiful Georgian terraces in Clerkenwell in the triangle between St John's Street and Farringdon Road, particularly in Sekforde Street. Humbler but still attractive Georgian properties in Finsbury. Warehouses and lofts mostly in and around main roads including St Johns Street and Clerkenwell Road.

ATTRACTS *Young well-off single people; creative types; City workers wanting to be central; members of the Italian community* • **CONSERVATION AREAS** *Clerkenwell Green; Charterhouse Square; Hat and Feathers; Bunhill Fields and Finsbury Square; Moorfields; St Lukes; Northampton Grove* • **AVERAGE PRICES** *Flats: studio: £90,000+; 1-bed: £140,000+; 2-bed: £180,000+; 3-bed: £210,000+ Houses: 2-bed: £300,000; 3-bed: £400,000; 4-bed: £450,000+* • **AVERAGE RENTS (MONTHLY)** *Flats: studio: £860; 1-bed: £1080; 2-bed: £1510 Houses: 2-bed: £1730; 3-bed: £2160.*

ISLINGTON & HIGHBURY

One of the most sought-after and expensive parts of the borough. Islington and its satellite Barnsbury have delectable streets of tall Georgian and early Victorian flat-fronted terraces and cottages, many carefully restored with their owners leaving the curtains open at dusk so that passers-by can admire their exquisite taste. Canonbury has some large Victorian villas with large gardens alongside terraces. Cheaper Highbury has some splendid houses overlooking Highbury Fields, with a mixture of mansion blocks and Victorian terraces, many converted into flats in roads around. Progressively shabbier four-storey Victorian houses and smaller terraces towards Arsenal football ground, favoured by adventurous souls who hope the boarded-up shops may open up as something wonderful.

ATTRACTS *The right-on, wealthy New Labour; young professionals; City workers; well-off families who can afford to send their children to private school* • **CONSERVATION AREAS** *Duncan Terrace and Colebrooke Row; The Angel; Chapel Market and Penton Street; Arlington Square; East Canonbury; Canonbury; Upper Street North; Barnsbury* • **AVERAGE PRICES** *Flats: studio: £60,000-£100,000; 1-bed: £90,000-£145,000; 2-bed: £155,000-£240,000 Houses: 2-bed: £220,000-£350,000; 3-bed: £250,000-£500,000; 4-bed: £425,000-£650,000; 5-bed: £500,000-£650,000* • **AVERAGE RENTS (MONTHLY)** *Flats: studio: £650; 1-bed: £650-£1300; 2-bed: £1080-£1730 Houses: 2-bed: £1080-£1730; 3-bed: £1510+; 4-bed: £1730+; 5-bed: £2810+.*

TUFNELL PARK

Once an obscure web of Victorian residential streets west of the Holloway Road but now considered an acceptable alternative by people who've been priced out of Islington or Highbury. Wide tree-lined roads with Victorian terraces (cleverly designed to look like semis with separate gabled roofs) set back from the street in small gardens. Wooden slatted blinds and freshly painted exteriors are evidence of middle class colonisation. The further away you are from the Holloway Road the better.
ATTRACTS *First-time buyers; young professionals; families* • **CONSERVATION AREAS** *Tufnell Park; Hillmarton; Mercers Road and Tavistock Terrace* • **AVERAGE PRICES** *Flats: studio: £85,000+; 1-bed: £90,000-£120,000; 2-bed: £125,000-£160,000 Houses: 3-bed: £160,000-£210,000; 4-bed: £200,000-£250,000; 5-bed: £240,000-£270,000* • **AVERAGE RENTS (MONTHLY)** *Flats: studio: £520-£600; 1-bed: £650-£780; 2-bed: £1040-£1300 Houses: 2-bed: £1300+; 3-bed: £1730+; 4-bed: £2000+.*

UPPER HOLLOWAY

This segment of streets to the east of Holloway Road and Archway Road is a mixture of potentially posh and pretty shabby. Large Victorian family houses further north in roads off Archway Road in the Whitehall conservation area would be seriously expensive if they were picked up and placed over the postcode border into Highgate N6, so they're an excellent buy if you can put up with the indignity of N19 on your letterhead. They give way further south to narrow streets of tall, densely packed Victorian terraces divided into flats in streets east of the Holloway Road (although this is good flat-hunting ground). This area is home to wholesale clothing stores and factories and there are several council estates.
ATTRACTS *First-time buyers; young professionals; families who can't afford Highgate* • **CONSERVATION AREAS** *Whitehall; Highgate Hill and Hornsey Lane; St Johns Grove* • **AVERAGE PRICES** *Flats: 1-bed: £70,000-£90,000; 2-bed: £95,000-£100,000; 3-bed: £160,000-£180,000 Houses: 2-bed: £170,000; 3-bed: £215,000-£220,000; 4-bed: £200,000-£240,000; 5-bed: £240,000-£280,000* • **AVERAGE RENTS (MONTHLY)** *Flats: studio: £430-£520; 1-bed: £560-£690; 2-bed: £780-£1250; 3-bed: £1100-£1250 Houses: 2-bed: £900; 3-bed: £1250; 4-bed: £1600; 5-bed: £2000+.*

BEST POSTCODES

Islington N1 is generally the best, although it includes some of the sleazy areas of Kings Cross, followed by Highbury N5. The relative social cachet of postcodes further north then get seriously confusing. To quote a local estate agent: "The part of Tufnell Park that's in N7 is better than Archway N19 (near Highgate), which in turn is better than Upper Holloway N19. This is better than Lower Holloway N7." Got that? Good.

AMENITIES

SCHOOLS*

A generally dismal performance, with secondary schools among the worst in the country, let alone London. Parents of secondary school age children flee to other boroughs rather than suffer their children to be educated in

Islington. Primary schools don't do quite as badly but this isn't saying much. No private prep schools and only one secondary school in the borough itself although there are several in neighbouring Highgate (see Haringey). A relatively small range of private nursery schools but an above-average number of places in state nursery schools.

PRE-SCHOOL PROVISION *3 state nursery schools; 38 nursery classes in state primary and church schools; 91 private or voluntary nurseries and playgroups. Proportion of under-fives in state nurseries: 68%* • **STATE PRIMARY SCHOOLS** *Overall place in league table: 131st out of 150. Top scorers: St Peter's and St Paul's RC (with nursery unit), Clerkenwell; St Joan of Arc RC (with nursery unit), Highbury; Price Weston, Clerkenwell* • **STATE SECONDARY SCHOOLS** *Overall place in league tables: 147th out of 150. Best scorers: Highbury Fields (girls), Highbury; Islington Green (mixed), Islington; St. Aloysius' College (boys), Highgate* • **PRIVATE SECONDARY SCHOOL** *Italia Conti Academy of Dance Theatre, Clerkenwell (top of Islington league table).*

TRANSPORT * * * *

Very good transport links to most parts of the borough although the north-west has to rely on the unpleasant Northern line tube from High Barnet. The east has the much better Piccadilly line. A good choice of buses.

TUBES Central services: *Zone 1. Cost of annual season ticket: £572. Clerkenwell: Farringdon; Circle and Metropolitan. Islington: Angel; Northern. Highbury and Islington: Victoria. Holloway Road: Zone 2. Cost of annual season ticket: £704; Frequency: Piccadilly: every 5 minutes; Fastest journey: Piccadilly Circus: 15 minutes. Finsbury Park: (see Haringey). Tufnell Park: Zone 2. Frequency: Northern line every 6 minutes; Fastest journey: to Charing Cross 20 minutes* • **BUSES** *A good selection of services to the northern suburbs, into town and beyond. The best choice is at Upper Street and Archway (the terminus for many buses from town). Services include the 19 via Highbury and Islington to Piccadilly Circus and Battersea, the 38 via Islington to Victoria, the 43 via Archway, Holloway and Islington and the 10 from Archway via Tufnell Park to Kings Cross* • **TRAFFIC BLACKSPOTS** Islington: *The junction of roads near Angel tube station at the south end of Upper Street. Often long tail-backs up Upper Street because of short traffic lights.* Holloway Road: *The main A1 out of London. Several lanes of traffic in each direction, often jammed.* Archway: *The continuation of the A1 with a massive ugly traffic roundabout, clogged with buses and lorries which then have problems hauling themselves up the hill at Archway Road. Frequent attempts to widen the Archway Road have floundered in the face of huge opposition by residents whose property would be demolished* • **PARKING** *Not quite as bad as in neighbouring boroughs although bad enough. Traffic wardens are tightening up. There are controlled parking zones around Old Street, Clerkenwell, Angel and Highbury and an extension is being discussed for Barnsbury. Parking permits are the most expensive in London at £95 a year. Residents around Arsenal football ground can pay £10 for proof of residency to avoid their cars being towed away on match days.*

LEISURE FACILITIES * * * *

THEATRES & CONCERT HALLS *A good choice. Sadlers Wells, the borough's best-known theatre, re-opened last October after a long closure for a complete overhaul and specialises in dance and opera. Islington is also one of the best places for fringe theatre and off-the-wall theatre in London.*

The Almeida theatre in Islington specialises in new plays and productions. New plays, music and exhibitions at the refurbished Victorian music hall Rosemary Branch theatre. The Courtyard at Kings Cross has fringe plays. The Kings Head pub in Islington has an upstairs theatre. Lots of other smaller theatre groups • **CINEMAS** Currently not a huge choice in the borough itself but there are plenty of cinemas in the West End and neighbouring boroughs. Screen at the Green Islington shows a mixture of mainstream and fringe films. The Holloway Odeon is definitely mainstream, although the art deco exterior of the building is stunning. But there are plans for a nine-screen cinema as part of a huge new shopping development at Angel behind Upper Street. Clerkenwell could also get its first cinema if a planned development of shops, offices, apartments and cinema on the former Allied Domecq warehouse site in St Johns Street goes ahead • **MUSEUMS & GALLERIES** A small, eccentric but fascinating selection, ranging from the House of Detention in Clerkenwell, an underground prison which was the site of the last public execution, to the Museum of Methodism in City Road with the chapel and house of Methodism's founder, John Wesley. The London Canal Museum is in a nineteenth century ice house on the Kings Cross canal basin. Art exhibitions in Berry House, a former warehouse in St John's Street in Clerkenwell's "cultural quarter" • **SPORTS FACILITIES** Well provided for with seven leisure centres in Archway, Kings Cross, Finsbury, Highbury, Clerkenwell, Upper Holloway and Islington. Pools at Archway, Caledonian Road and Highbury; gyms at Archway, Finsbury, Highbury, Clerkenwell and Islington. Tennis at Islington and skating at the Sobell Centre, Upper Holloway. Tennis and football at parks across the borough. Highbury is home to Arsenal FC (can be hell on matchdays for residents in nearby streets who aren't football fans – and Arsenal is trying to expand its facilities) • **LIBRARIES** Well-used libraries (the daytime population is swollen by workers and there are a lot of students). Good long opening hours at the central library in Highbury but more patchy elsewhere with an annoyingly inconsistent pattern so that it's easy to get caught out. Threats of cuts in the library budget are angering residents. 10.5 library visits per head. Position in library-use league table: 2nd out of 32 (where 1 is best and 32 worst).

OPEN SPACES*

Less open space than any other borough in London. Densely built-up and populated, Islington can be awful on a hot day. But as a compensation, the cool oasis of the Regents Canal flows through Islington itself. **CANAL WALKS** The Regents Canal. Excellent walks along the towpath from the canal basin at Kings Cross, then through the streets of Islington as the canal goes through a long early nineteenth century tunnel, and then joins the towpath again below the Georgian houses of Colebrooke Row. Great views of people's back gardens stretching down to the water and colourfully painted houseboats moored by the bridge • **URBAN RELIEF** Highbury Fields, gently sloping grass and mature trees bring welcome relief from hard tarmac. Tennis courts and swimming pool.

SHOPS***

CLERKENWELL & FINSBURY Short on shops at the moment although restaurants are burgeoning (see below). Small parades of shops including some useful shops, like hardware shops, around Farringdon station and more small shops in Exmouth Market. Clerkenwell, traditionally home to a large Italian community, has good Italian delis. But there are plans to build shops as part of developments on two large sites in Cowcross Street and St John's Street. Daily market at Exmouth Market • **ISLINGTON** Great for small, unusual shops especially furniture, interior design, antiques (Camden Passage off Upper Street with its furniture, silver and jewellery shops is a haven for antiqueophiles). Upper Street with pavements at the south end conveniently raised to separate shoppers from the remorseless traffic, is a pleasant place to shop with small branches of chains and bookshops opening late. But a bit of a dearth of larger, national chains, a gap which should be filled by the new Angel shopping development. Daily fruit, veg and clothes market in Chapel Market just off Upper Street. Large Sainsbury's in Liverpool Road • **HOLLOWAY & ARCHWAY** Holloway Road is trafficky and depressing – boarded-up shops are frequent, and there's the usual motley collection of fast food joints, cafés, small newsagents and shops offering international phone calls, testifying to the large numbers of residents with overseas links. The building which used to house Jones Bros, Holloway's department store, now has a selection of smaller shops and a Waitrose. Big Safeway further up the street. Some signs of gentrification around Tufnell Park with a smart kitchen shop and fireplace shop. Residents and traders are being consulted on proposals to build an indoor shopping mall near the Archway roundabout which should improve shopping in an area which desperately needs it. No sign yet though of what everyone would really like – the demolition of the eyesore tower block by the roundabout.

RESTAURANTS * * * *

CLERKENWELL New winebars and restaurants springing up, particularly around Cowcross Street and Exmouth Market (one reason why the latter was such a culinary desert until recently was that council planners had a policy of restricting restaurants). Now a total volte-face, encouraged by the re-opening of Sadlers Wells and the prospect of lots of pre- and post-theatre diners. Good Spanish, Korean and pie and mash as well as the Quality Chop House, once the purveyor of Noted Cups of Tea and stodgy puddings to nearby postal workers and now serving up-market British food • **ISLINGTON** If you can't find something to eat in Upper Street, you're very fussy. Residents complain there are too many restaurants but it's great for visitors. Every sort of restaurant from chains like Pizza Express, the Dome and Cafe Flo to Turkish, Vietnamese and Granita, scene of the famous leadership meeting between Tony Blair and Gordon Brown. The pavements are thronged with people and diners eating and drinking at outside tables. One of London's best attempts at café society – even the traffic becomes an exciting part of urban living rather than a drag after a couple of glasses of wine • **HOLLOWAY** Some good ethnic restaurants around the Holloway Road including Middle Eastern, Korean and Jewish, as well as Spanish and pie and mash.

CRIME RATES *

176 crimes per 1000 of population (although daytime population can distort the figure). Position in Metropolitan Police league table: 7th out of 32 (where 1 is worst and 32 best). 4th out of 32 for violent crime and 5th for car crime.

THE COUNCIL *

POLITICIAL AFFILIATION Labour • **MINUS POINTS** The most expensive council tax in London. The most expensive parking permits in London. The worst

schools in London. No door-to-door recycling service. Very lax at street-sweeping and emptying bins. Threatening deep cuts to library services.
• **PLUS POINTS** *The second quickest inner London borough at turning round property searches quickly* • **PROPERTY SEARCHES CARRIED OUT IN 10 WORKING DAYS** 99.5% • **STANDARD SEARCH FEE** £100 • **COUNCIL TAX COLLECTED** 83%
• **COUNCIL TAX 1998-99**

BAND	PROPERTY VALUE	CHARGE	BAND	PROPERTY VALUE	CHARGE
A	up to £40,000	£608.00	E	£88,001-£120,000	£1,114.67
B	£40,001-£52,000	£709.33	F	£120,001-£160,000	£1,317.33
C	£52,001-£68,000	£810.67	G	£160,001-£320,000	£1,520.00
D	£68,001-£88,000	£912.00	H	over £320,000	£1,824.00

KENSINGTON & CHELSEA

Kensington and Chelsea is the borough with everything – beautiful and varied architecture (70 per cent of its territory is a conservation area), properties to die for, excellent transport links, a wealth of museums, galleries, parks and gardens, a range of shops from the eclectic to the practical and some of the most up-to-the-minute bars and restaurants. So what's the downside? It's one of the most expensive parts of London, it tends to get crowded with tourists and coaches especially in summer, it can compete with anywhere else for the most traffic-clogged roads, and the simple act of parking outside your own front door can be a nightmare.

Up from the river and at its southern boundary, the borough stretches from the red-bricked Dutch-gabled elegance of Chelsea's Cadogan estate in the east around Sloane Square tube station past the artists' studios, early-Victorian stucco terraces and cottages of central Chelsea to Chelsea Harbour in the south west corner, built on a former industrial site next to Lots Road power station (see Hammersmith & Fulham). Further north, West Chelsea gives way to the shabbier, hotel-lined roads of transient Earls Court before smartening up again around the museums and porticoed streets of South Kensington and moving north to the white stucco and multi-coloured cottages of Notting Hill. Beyond the Westway, built when cars were in and conservation and the environment were out, lie the more modest brick and stucco terraces of North Kensington, mixed with council estates.

Kensington and Chelsea appears to be one of the most affluent boroughs of London. Its residents are not just domestic but international, from businessmen to diplomats. The south of the borough is the preferred home of well-off middle class families and well-off young professionals, many armed with fat bonuses from the City. It's the home of royalty at Kensington Palace (although this didn't prevent it from supporting its formidable and articulate residents in a campaign against the proposal for a memorial garden for the late Diana, Princess of Wales, in Kensington Gardens).

Unemployment is the third lowest in inner London at 5.6%. But there is still widespread deprivation, particularly in the north, and it ranks as the 19th most deprived borough in England.

Popular areas like South Kensington, Kensington and the Sloane Square end of Chelsea have never fallen from grace and their popularity has rippled out over the years to the far western reaches of Chelsea and to Notting Hill, once both considered near slums. North Kensington, the poorest part of the borough, is the latest to feel the effect as more people venture north of the Westway to discover some of the cheapest property in Kensington. North Kensington has also received £35 million of government regeneration money since 1993, matched by £127 million from the public and private sectors. An area which people used to have to nerve themselves up to visit is now more stimulatingly cosmopolitan than threatening. Kensington and Chelsea has one of the smallest ethnic minority populations of inner London at 16% but many members of the West Indian community live in North Kensington. The south of the borough is popular with expatriates from other parts of Europe.

PROPERTY AND ARCHITECTURE

CHELSEA & WEST CHELSEA

A long east-west swathe of some of the most desirable real estate in London. 30 years ago, Chelsea was considered raffish and arty. Rising prices and increasingly international clientele have smartened it up but it's still less staid than Kensington. Flats in imposing red brick mansion blocks with elaborate gables and carving in streets around Sloane Street and Pont Street, owned by the Cadogan Estate. West of Sloane Square and in streets off Kings Road, there are small but expensive Victorian terraces. Larger, more formal houses around the Royal Hospital and big red brick family homes north of Kings Road. Streets opposite the Worlds End council estate in West Chelsea have four-bedroom white stucco family houses which were once beyond the pale because of the council estate and the distance from transport – but no more.

ATTRACTS *Well off, mainly English buyers including young professionals and families; those wanting pieds-à-terre; glitterati* • **CONSERVATION AREAS** *Royal Hospital; Cheyne; Chelsea Park and Carlyle; Sloane and Stanley; Chelsea; Hans Town; Sloane Square* • **AVERAGE PRICES** *Flats: studio: £120,000-£200,000; 1-bed: £175,000-£300,000; 2-bed: £250,000-£500,000; 3-bed: £500,000-£800,000; 4-bed: £650,000+ Houses: 2-bed: £300,000+; 3-bed: £650,000-£900,000; 4-bed: £900,000+; 5-bed+: £1.2 million* • **AVERAGE RENTS (MONTHLY)** *Flats: studio: £650; 1-bed: £1300-£2160; 2-bed: £2160-£3030; 3-bed: £3500+ Houses: 2-bed: £3250+; 3-bed: £4300+; 4-bed: £5200+.*

SOUTH KENSINGTON

Where all mothers would like their children to live when they come to London. Safe, smart and respectable as well as fun. Gracious streets of four- and five-storey stucco wedding cake houses, many converted to flats, off Old Brompton Road and Gloucester Road. Many have private garden squares. Much of South Kensington is owned by the Wellcome Trust Estate, which has strict rules about what people can do with property. Some huge grand houses between the Fulham and Brompton Roads where houses change hands for millions. South Kensington has more flats than Chelsea but is getting too expensive for first-time buyers. Some smaller houses in streets north of Fulham Road.

ATTRACTS *Expatriate Europeans, particularly French wanting to be near the French lycée; English families and professionals; people wanting a pied-à-terre* • **CONSERVATION AREAS** *The Boltons; Thurloe; Wellcome; Brompton* • **AVERAGE PRICES** *Flats: studio: £100,000-£180,000; 1-bed: £150,000+; 2-bed: £250,000+; 3-bed: £400,000+; 4-bed: £700,000+ Houses: 2-bed: £400,000+; 3-bed: £650,000+; 4-bed: £850,000+* • **AVERAGE RENTS (MONTHLY)** *Flats: studio: £650; 1-bed: £1300-£2160; 2-bed: £2160-£3030; 3-bed: £3500+ Houses: 2-bed: £3250+; 3-bed: £4300+; 4-bed: £5200+.*

EARLS COURT

Traditionally the scruffy bit between South Kensington and Kensington proper. But improving all the time as seedy hotels are replaced by luxury flat conversions or turned back into houses. East of Earls Court road, tall red brick gabled terraces and squares of large stucco houses are almost as smart as Kensington. More transient to the west with backpackers, tourists and short-stay tenants but still less shabby than it was. Victorian cottages in and around Kenway Road off Earls Court Road.

ATTRACTS *People who can't afford Kensington or Chelsea; well-off first-time buyers* • **CONSERVATION AREAS** *Courtfield; Earls Court Square; Nevern Square; Philbeach; Earls Court Village* • **AVERAGE PRICES** *Flats: studio: £90,000; 1-bed: £160,000; 2-bed: £180,000-£350,000; 3-bed: £375,000+ Houses: 2-bed: £275,000; 3-bed: £350,000-£450,000; 4-bed: £450,000+* • **AVERAGE RENTS (MONTHLY)** *Flats: studio: £860; 1-bed: £1080-£1110; 2-bed: £1300-£1700; 3-bed: £1950-£2160 Houses: 2-bed: £1950-£2160; 3-bed: £2380-£2600; 4-bed: £3460+.*

KENSINGTON & HOLLAND PARK

Like South Kensington, safe, pretty and fun. Less hip than Notting Hill. Streets of white stucco three- and four-storey terraces, many still family homes, in roads both sides of Kensington High Street, alongside some streets of red brick Queen Anne terraces. Mansion blocks and luxury apartments in and around Kensington High Street. Further up around Holland Park there are some massive Victorian houses, now mostly converted into flats and some attractive terraces up around Campden Hill Square. Family houses in roads around Addison Avenue.

ATTRACTS *Wealthy British and internationals; families* • **CONSERVATION AREAS** *Edwardes Square, Scarsdale and Abingdon; Lexham Gardens; Kensington Square; Kensington Court; de Vere; Holland Park; Kensington; Kensington Palace* • **AVERAGE PRICES** *Flats: studio: £120,000-£200,000; 1-bed: £170,000+; 2-bed: £225,000; 3-bed: £385,000 Houses: 3-bed: £550,000+; 4-bed: £1m+; 5-bed: £1m+* • **AVERAGE RENTS (MONTHLY)** *Flats: studio: £650; 1-bed: £1300-£2160; 2-bed: £2160-£3030; 3-bed: £3,500+ Houses: 2-bed: £3250+; 3-bed: £4300+; 4-bed: £5200+.*

NOTTING HILL

Currently the hippest part of the borough – sufficiently daring without being dangerous to attract well-off young single professionals, celebrities and trustafarians – rich young things living off family trust money. A magnet for people who want to see and be seen in one of the area's many new restaurants. 30 years ago, Notting Hill was cheap and scruffy, populated with immigrants forced into crumbling overcrowded terraces. Now it's expensive and beautiful. Lots of white stucco and some lovely multicoloured terraces and cottages around Portobello Road. Lots of private garden squares.

ATTRACTS *The young; the well-off buying with their own or other people's money; glitterati* • **CONSERVATION AREAS** *Norland; Ladbroke; Pembridge* • **AVERAGE PRICES** *Flats: studio: £110,000-£120,000; 1-bed: £220,000-£225,000; 2-bed: £300,000-£550,000; 3-bed: £400,000-£650,000 Houses: 2-bed: up to £550,000; 3-bed: £650,000+; 4-bed: £750,000+; 5+bed: £1.2+* • **AVERAGE RENTS (MONTHLY)** *Flats: studio: £860; 1-bed: £1080-£1300; 2-bed: £1300-£2160; 3-bed: £2160-£4330 Houses: 2-bed: £2600; 3-bed: £2600-£3460; 4-bed: £4760; 5+bed: £5200+.*

NORTH KENSINGTON

Still a bit down-at-heel north of the Westway but improving as it gets attention from people looking for cheap(ish) property in Kensington. Three- and four-bedroom Victorian terraces in streets off Ladbroke Grove just north of the Westway. Large terraces around St Charles Square. Council estates further east but even some of these have become trendy, particularly Trellick Tower, a massive tower block now apparently great to live in but still monstrous from the outside.

ATTRACTS *Young professionals wanting to live on the front line; families* • **CONSERVATION AREAS** *Oxford Gardens; Kensal Green Cemetary* • **AVERAGE PRICES** *Flats: studio: £70,000-£100,000; 1-bed: £100,000-£160,000; 2-bed: £150,000-£300,000; 3-bed: £300,000+ Houses: 3-bed: £300,000+; 4-bed: £350,000+; 5+bed: £1m+* • **AVERAGE RENTS (MONTHLY)** *Flats: studio: £650; 1-bed: £860; 2-bed: £1190+; 3-bed: £1300 Houses: 2-bed: £2160+; 3-bed: £4760; 4-bed: up to £6500.*

BEST POSTCODES

Several pecking orders within the borough. In South Kensington SW7 is best, followed by SW10 then SW5 (Earls Court). In Chelsea, SW3 is better than SW10. In Kensington and Notting Hill, W8 is better than W11 which is better than W14. Some huge price anomalies, particularly around the boundary of W11 and W14.

AMENITIES

SCHOOLS * * *

State primary schools score well but there's a slight falling off at secondary level possibly because of some creaming off to private schools. There are only four state secondary schools. Lower than average provision for pre-school children in state nurseries although there's a good choice of private nurseries and nursery classes linked to voluntary-aided or grant-maintained schools. Good for prep schools and there are a number of private secondary schools.

PRE-SCHOOL PROVISION 4 state nursery schools; 21 nursery classes in state primary or church schools; 66 private nurseries and playgroups. Proportion of under-fives in state nurseries: 34% • **STATE PRIMARY SCHOOLS** Overall league table position: 51st out of 150. High scorers: Our Lady of Victories (with nursery unit), South Kensington; Oratory RC, Chelsea; Fox School, Kensington • **STATE SECONDARY SCHOOLS** Overall league table position: 58th out of 150. Good scorers: Cardinal Vaughan Memorial School (boys), Holland Park • **PRIVATE PREP SCHOOLS** Sussex House (boys), Chelsea; Hellenic (Greek 2-16) (mixed); Queen's Gate Junior (girls), South Kensington; Cameron House (mixed), Chelsea; Falkner House (girls), South Kensington; Glendower Prep (girls), South Kensington; Hampshire Schools (mixed), South Kensington; St James Junior (girls), South Kensington; Hill House (mixed), Chelsea • **PRIVATE SECONDARY SCHOOLS** More House (girls), Chelsea; Mander Portman Woodward (mixed), South Kensington; Queens Gate (girls), South Kensington; St James (girls), Notting Hill; Lycée français Charles de Gaulle, (mixed), South Kensington.

TRANSPORT****

One of the most central residential areas in London with plentiful tube and bus services to most parts of the borough. West Chelsea is the worst served, with long walks to the nearest tube at Sloane Square. High Street Kensington can be a frustrating journey from the city with only the slow Circle Line going direct.

TUBES Central area: Zone 1. Cost of annual season ticket: £572. Earls Court: District, Circle and Piccadilly. South Kensington: District, Circle and Piccadilly. High Street Kensington: District and Circle. Notting Hill Gate: Circle, District and Central. Ladbroke Grove: Hammersmith and City • **BUSES** Constant flow of buses to town down the main arteries of the borough with the best choice in the south. Buses to town include the 9 to Aldwych via Kensington High Street, the 10 via Kensington High Street to Kings Cross, the 52 from Ladbroke Grove and Notting Hill Gate to Victoria, the 14 via South Kensington to Piccadilly and the 11 from West Chelsea via Sloane Square, Charing Cross and Liverpool Street • **TRAFFIC BLACKSPOTS** Chelsea: Sloane Square and all the way down Kings Road. Four roads flow into Sloane Square often jamming it on all sides and a press of traffic, delivery vans and buses often blocks Kings Road. Earls Court & Chelsea: Three lines of traffic often stationary on the Warwick Road, the northbound section of the notorious Earls Court one-way system. Southbound the traffic is often forced into one lane by parked cars, delivery vans and a narrowed bridge over the tube lines. The one-way system uses Gunter Grove and Finborough Road in Chelsea going north and Redcliffe Gardens and Edith Grove going south. Jams continue south along Cheyne Walk and North along Cromwell Road. Kensington: Long tail-backs at the lights at the junction of Kensington Church Street and Kensington High Street because of traffic, buses and shoppers • **PARKING** Problem areas. Parking is a serious problem in the borough and even having a resident's permit won't insulate you from driving round and round trying to find a parking space. Kensington and Chelsea issues 40,000 permits for 30,000 places. But they're much prized because a permit issued for one area allows you to park in any other part of the borough. There are controlled parking zones around Sloane Square, Kings Road, Knightsbridge, Earls Court and around Kensington High Street. Cost of annual resident's permit: £72.

LEISURE FACILITIES *****

THEATRES & CONCERT HALLS The Royal Court, Sloane Square is currently closed for refurbishment and was struggling to complete the work but managed to get sponsorship last year. It's renowned for avant garde and controversial plays. Holland Park theatre has its own in-house opera company • **CINEMAS** A good choice. Mostly mainstream viewing at Kensington High Street, Fulham Road and the Notting Hill Coronet. A chance of more off-beat offerings at the Chelsea Cinema and the Gate at Notting Hill • **MUSEUMS & GALLERIES** The place to be. The pantheon of the natural history, science, geological and V&A museums housed in wonderful buildngs in Prince Albert's favourite venue of South Kensington. The National Army Museum is at the Royal Hospital. Several smaller but fascinating places including the Linley Sambourne House, a preserved nineteenth century middle class house, and the Leighton House Museum, the former home of one of the leading lights of the Pre-Raphaelite movement • **SPORTS FACILTIES** Two leisure centres at Ladbroke Grove (recently refurbished) and Chelsea (fairly recently refurbished and much improved). Pools, gym, classes and racquet sports at both. Tennis and cricket in Holland Park and other parks across the borough • **LIBRARIES** The main library is in Kensington High Street in a handsome classical-style building next to the town hall. Generously long opening hours, particularly in the main library. Libraries well used at 8.2 visits per head. Place in library-use league table: 11th out of 32 (where 1 is best and 32 worst).

OPEN SPACES ****

Very good for public open space but also excels in the garden square and the hidden communal garden. Access to these is often restricted to residents but passers-by can get tantalising glimpses behind railings and walls. Residents of several squares have recently been up in arms about threats to garden squares from development.

(VISIBLE) GARDEN SQUARES Ladbroke Square, Notting Hill Gate; Edwardes Square, Kensington, both with lawns, mature trees and a satisfying feel of privacy without isolation • **GRACIOUS PARKS AND GARDENS** Kensington Gardens, famous to television viewers the world over as the scene of mass wreath-laying after the death of Diana, Princess of Wales. But also much loved by residents for its lawns, mature trees and Round Pond. • **RIVER VIEWS** Cremorne Gardens, Chelsea, a small patch of green with great views of the changing riverbank at Battersea. • **CANAL WALKS** The towpath beside the Paddington branch of the Grand Union Canal, dominated by Trellick Tower. A reminder that not all of Kensington was always a smart residential suburb • **CEMETERIES** Kensal Green. Victorian cemetary, less wild than Highgate but monthly tours of the catacombs with all-too-real lead coffins stacked on shelves.

SHOPS *****

KINGS ROAD, CHELSEA Not as ground-breaking as it was in the 60s (it's even got an M&S and tourists have muscled in on the Chelsea set) but still lots of designer clothes and shoe shops, expensive furniture and soft furnishings, up-market second-hand clothes and a good second-hand bookshop at the bottom end. Big Waitrose and of course, Peter Jones, the department store whose contents adorn so many middle class homes in the area • **FULHAM ROAD** Has smartened up considerably in the past 15 years, particularly at the Fulham end. Lots of antique furniture shops, art galleries and bookshops among the bars and restaurants • **SOUTH KENSINGTON & EARLS COURT**

Smartish shops around South Ken station at the top of Old Brompton Road, particularly a French patisserie and bookshop in Bute Street opposite the lycée français. Earls Court Road is still shabby and full of cheap restaurants, take-aways and bureaux de change. Sainsbury's in Cromwell Road. New Tesco in Warwick Road • **KENSINGTON & HOLLAND PARK** Getting better all the time in Kensington High Street although marred by the difficulty of crossing the road. A good range of clothes shops, many chains but up-market stock, and Kensington Market for leather and Doc Martens. Antique shops in Kensington Church Street • **NOTTING HILL & NORTH KENSINGTON** Portobello Market with antique stalls and shops at the Notting Hill end, turning into clothes, books, fruit and vegetables under and beyond the Westway. Crammed with tourists at weekends. Don't expect bargains. Second-hand record and book exchanges in Notting Hill Gate, specialist cookery and travel bookshops in Blenheim Road. Shabbier, local shops in north Ladbroke Grove. Sainsbury's at Ladbroke Grove by the canal, Tesco Metro in Portobello Road.

RESTAURANTS * * * * *

CHELSEA A huge choice – from the humble Stockpot in Kings Road to Terence Conran's Bluebird restaurant. Lots of eateries including Thai and French now in Chelsea Harbour (river views) which used to be dead after 9pm • **SOUTH KENSINGTON & EARLS COURT** Choice of ethnic restaurants, crêperies and winebars of varying quality in Earls Court. Good fish and Italian restaurants round the junction of Earls Court and Old Brompton Roads. Spoilt for choice in South Kensington with everything including East European, Japanese and Polish • **KENSINGTON & HOLLAND PARK** Also spoilt for choice, with lots of new restaurants opening up around Kensington Church Street especially • **NOTTING HILL** An explosion of new restaurants and trendy bars in and around Portobello Road and North Kensington. Locals are getting more and more blasé about spotting celebrities.

CRIME RATES *

181 crimes per 1000 of population (but population figures are distorted by workers and tourists). Position in Metropolitan Police league table: 4th out of 32 (where 1 is worst and 32 best). It's the second worst borough for burglaries (probably because burglars know it'll be worth it).

THE COUNCIL * * * *

POLITICAL AFFILIATION Conservative • **MINUS POINTS** Very strict and some would say picky about granting planning permission for extensions or other alterations to property. But this is a plus for those keen to preserve the area • **PLUS POINTS** Very hot on recycling, rubbish collection and street-cleaning. Twice-weekly rubbish collections and twice weekly door-to-door recycling has just started – a first for a London borough. Also good primary schools. One of the most efficient boroughs at carrying out land searches. Low council tax • **PROPERTY SEARCHES CARRIED OUT IN 10 WORKING DAYS** 100% • **STARDARD SEARCH FEE** £105 • **COUNCIL TAX COLLECTED** 94% • **COUNCIL TAX 1998-99**

BAND	PROPERTY VALUE	CHARGE	BAND	PROPERTY VALUE	CHARGE
A	up to £40,000	£356.41	E	£88,001-£120,000	£653.44
B	£40,001-£52,000	£415.82	F	£120,001-£160,000	£772.25
C	£52,001-£68,000	£475.23	G	£160,001-£320,000	£891.04
D	£68,001-£88,000	£534.63	H	over £320,000	£1,069.26

KINGSTON UPON THAMES

Kingston is the most southwesterly point of a huge swathe of suburbia reaching upwards and outwards around West London. Well known to any motorist trying to escape from the capital to Surrey and the South Coast, the Kingston bypass bisects the borough from east to west with roads of undistinguished 1930s semis ribboning out from it in all directions. The jewel in the borough's crown, the medieval Surrey market town of Kingston itself, lies well hidden to the north through miles of anonymous streets, busy through-roads, a barricade of ugly concrete office blocks and the backside of its huge shopping centre. In short, Kingston doesn't do itself many architectural favours.

The north of the borough is dominated by Kingston, mostly Victorian in the middle, giving way to middling and up-market Edwardian and 1930s houses to the northwest and large detached properties around leafy Coombe to the northeast. East of Kingston lies New Malden, Victorian in its best roads but shading off in other areas to shabby 1930s. Surbiton is south of Kingston, claiming the title of Queen of the Suburbs (although if this is awarded for being respectable but slightly dull, Surbiton has plenty of competition in outer London). Tatty Tolworth is carved up by the gyratory systems, underpasses and bridges of the A3. In the south, where the borough narrows to a point, the council houses and 1930s semis of Chessington give way to open fields and green space as London slips away into Surrey.

Kingston is mostly affluent, mostly white collar and mostly white (although it has Indian, and more recently Korean, communities working for Korean companies in the area). Just 9% of the population is from an ethnic minority and unemployment is the second lowest in London at 2.7%. The borough has been energetically promoting Kingston as Top Town after it was nominated for this accolade in the 1995 Guinness Guide to the best place to live in the UK, and a number of large companies have their headquarters in the borough. Kingston has always been commuter country and the borough's good schools, good shops, good transport and quick access to green space and the river have made it a popular middle class choice.

For similar reasons, developers have moved in, snapping up desirable riverside sites to build luxury homes. But plans by Fairclough Homes two years ago to chop down a row of picturesque poplars by the river at Kingston to give their buyers an unimpeded view met with angry protests from locals and a band of eco-warriors who chained themselves to trees to prevent them being felled. Other residents are angry that many of the apartments are being sold to overseas buyers rather than to locals.

One development which many locals have welcomed is Charter Quay, a mix of shops, restaurants, flats and a theatre, to be built on a tract of semi-derelict land between the town centre and the river. But some say it's too large and there are fears that the sorely needed and promised theatre, the developer's *quid pro quo* for being allowed to build luxury homes, may never materialise. There are also plans to demolish the old gasworks just north of the town centre and build shops, restaurants, flats, leisure facilities and new road links to the centre of town.

PROPERTY AND ARCHITECTURE

KINGSTON & COOMBE

Streets of mostly well-kept Victorian and Edwardian terraces near the centre of town with some handsome Victorian semis overlooking the Fairfield recreation ground to the south. A good choice of flats, mostly in modern and newly built blocks near the river and around Kingston College. Further north, mostly 1920s and 1930s semis and terraces including the streets known as the Tudors around Tudor Drive, lined with dizzying rows of mock-Tudor black and white semis. Coombe, north east of Kingston, is the grandest part of the borough with large detached houses, many built to order by their owners, in big gardens.

ATTRACTS *Families wanting to be near Richmond Park (see Richmond) and close to good schools (Tiffin Girls, one of Kingston's best schools is just round the corner from the Tudors); people who can't afford Richmond; first-time buyers* • **CONSERVATION AREAS** *Kingston Old Town; Fairfield and Knights Park; Richmond Road; Grove Crescent; Coombe Wood; Coombe Hill; Coombe House* • **AVERAGE PRICES** *Flats: studio: £50,000-£60,000; 1-bed: £70,000-£85,000; 2-bed: £85,000-£150,000 Houses: 2-bed: £120,000+; 3-bed: £150,000+; 4-bed: £250,000-£300,000; 5-bed: £400,000+* • **AVERAGE RENTS (MONTHLY)** *Flats: studio: £550+; 1-bed: £700+; 2-bed: £825+ Houses: 2-bed: £850+; 3-bed: £1000+; 4-bed: £1500+; 5-bed: £1500+.*

NEW MALDEN

A mixture of everything from Victorian to 1970s, a legacy of bombing during the Second World War. Some large detached Victorian villas on the Kingston Road coming into the centre, now mostly converted into flats or offices and some roads of modest two-storey Victorian and Edwardian terraces in roads off the High Street. Some of the best roads are in the conservation area of The Groves north of Kingston Road. South of the Kingston Road there are mostly modest 1930s semis or terraces, some shabby and many "improved" with metal-framed picture windows or new front doors, making the houses uglier than they were ever intended to be. A lot of council property near the railway line.

ATTRACTS *Families; local first-time buyers; members of the Korean community* • **CONSERVATION AREAS** *The Groves* • **AVERAGE PRICES** *Flats: studio: £50,000; 1-bed: £70,000-£75,000; 2-bed: £85,000-£110,000 Houses: 2-bed: £110,000-£130,000; 3-bed: £125,000-£350,000; 4-bed: £200,000-£600,000; 5-bed: £350,000+* • **AVERAGE RENTS**

(MONTHLY) *Flats: studio: £450; 1-bed: £650; 2-bed: £750 Houses: 2-bed: £800; 3-bed: £1000; 4-bed: £1500+; 5-bed: £1500+.*

SURBITON

Some large, ornate Victorian houses in roads around the Upper Brighton Road and Ewell Road – a good place for generously-sized conversion flats and studios. Large detached 1930s houses in the sought-after Southborough conservation area. Berrylands to the east of the busy Ewell Road has some solid Edwardian semis overlooking the Fishponds open space before giving way to well-tended 1930s suburbia (neatly mown grass frontages, front gardens with crazy paving, cars parked straight in drives). Technically, Berrylands is part of cheaper Tolworth but residents like to call it Surbiton.

ATTRACTS *Families; commuters* • **CONSERVATION AREAS** *Cadogan Road; Claremount Road; St Andrews Square; Surbiton Town Centre; Surbiton Hill Park; Southborough; Oakhill; Christchurch; Victoria Avenue* • **AVERAGE PRICES** *Flats: studio: £50,000-£60,000; 1-bed: £70,000-£85,000; 2-bed: £85,000-£150,000 Houses: 2-bed: £120,000+; 3-bed: £150,000+; 4-bed: £250,000-£300,000; 5-bed: £400,000+* • **AVERAGE RENTS (MONTHLY)** *Flats: studio: £550+; 1-bed: £700+; 2-bed: £825+ Houses: 2-bed: £850+; 3-bed: £1000+; 4-bed: £1500+; 5-bed: £1500+.*

TOLWORTH & CHESSINGTON

The scrag end of the borough around and south of the A3 Kingston bypass. Mostly a 1930s sprawl with modern infill, cut up with dual carriageways and main roads in every direction, carrying motorists out of London or to Chessington World of Adventure. Even many of the quieter residential roads are wide and bleak, unrelieved by trees or any obvious greenery. Lots of modest council houses mixed with bungalows in the south of Chessington around Garrison Lane.

ATTRACTS *Loyal locals; families wanting to be near Tolworth Girls School (tight catchment area and very sought-after)* • **CONSERVATION AREAS** *None* • **AVERAGE PRICES** *Flats: studio: £50,000; 1-bed: £75,000; 2-bed: £85,000; 3-bed: £90,000-£100,000 Houses: 2-bed: £110,000; 3-bed: £100,000-£130,000; 4-bed: £200,000-£350,000* • **AVERAGE RENTS (MONTHLY)** *Flats: studio: £550; 1-bed: £550-£650; 2-bed: £700; 3-bed: £800 Houses: 2-bed: £900; 3-bed: £950; 4-bed: £1050.*

BEST POSTCODES

Out of town postcodes throughout the borough – so largely irrelevant. Proximity to stations, shops and schools is more important.

AMENITIES

SCHOOLS * * * * *

Some excellent selective state secondary schools and private schools push Kingston to dizzying heights in the GSCE and A level league tables and attract parents and children from miles around, making the best schools fiercely competitive to get in to. Primary schools are also some of the best in London. A good range of private schools. Above average provision of pre-school places in state nursery schools and a reasonable selection of private and voluntary nurseries for the under-fours. The borough participated in a pilot scheme to test-drive baseline testing for four year-olds and is an enthusiastic supporter of the policy.

PRE-SCHOOL PROVISION *1 state nursery school; 21 nursery classes in state primary and church schools; 63 private and voluntary nurseries and playgroups. Proportion of under-fives in state nurseries: 66%* • **STATE PRIMARY SCHOOLS** *Overall position in league tables: 6th out of 150. Top scorers: Christ Church C of E, Surbiton; St Paul's, Kingston; Malden, Worcester Park* • **STATE SECONDARY SCHOOLS** *Overall position in league tables: 3rd out of 150. Best scorers: Tiffin School (boys, selective), Tiffin Girls (selective), Kingston; Coombe Girls, New Malden* • **PRIVATE PREP SCHOOLS** *Holy Cross (girls), Kingston; Rokeby (boys), Kingston; The Study School (mixed), New Malden; Shrewsbury House (boys) Surbiton; Bretby House (mixed, children to 7), New Malden* • **PRIVATE SECONDARY SCHOOLS** *League table leaders Kingston Grammar School (mixed), Kingston; Surbiton High (girls) Surbiton; also Canbury School (mixed), Kingston; Marymount International (girls), Kingston.*

TRANSPORT ★ ★ ★

Trains only throughout the borough, although stations are well spaced and nowhere is desperately far from a station. Surbiton and New Malden are best served.

TRAINS Kingston: *Zone 6. Cost of annual season ticket: £1396; No of trains per hour: to Waterloo 4; Fastest journey: 27 minutes.* New Malden: *Zone 4. Cost of annual season ticket: £1068; No of trains per hour: to Waterloo 6; Fastest journey: 22 minutes.* Surbiton: *Zone 6. No of trains per hour: to Waterloo 6; Fastest journey: 17 minutes.* Chessington South: *Zone 6. No of trains per hour: to Waterloo 2; Fastest journey: 35 minutes* • **BUSES** *Most services link neighbouring suburbs. Surprisingly frequent and efficient, even in the most far flung parts of the borough. But no buses go further into town than Streatham or Tooting. At night the N9 goes to Kingston from Trafalgar Square and the N77 goes from Trafalgar Square to Tolworth via New Malden, Kingston and Surbiton* • **BOATS** *Run between Kingston, Hampton Court and Richmond during the summer with Saturday service only in winter* • **TRAFFIC BLACKSPOTS** *Any road leading off the A3, including Ewell Road and Hook Road through Surbiton. Long waits to get onto roundabouts to cross over the main road for traffic that doesn't want to use the A3. The A3 itself has a constant stream of traffic and can get snarled up, particularly on Friday nights.* Kingston: *Despite the bypass, the town centre is criss-crossed by busy roads and has an alienating one-way system which forces motorists miles out of their way. Pedestrians face several sets of lights every time they want to cross the road.* New Malden: *Often trafficky around the roundabout next to the pub at the east end of the High Street* • **PARKING** *According to residents, difficult even when it shouldn't be, in Kingston Shopping Centre. There is currently only one parking zone in the borough around Kingston Town Centre but the council is consulting on new CPZs for New Malden and Surbiton in a bid to stop unofficial Park-and-Riding. It's running into opposition from some residents and traders in New Malden. Cost of annual resident's permit: £60.*

LEISURE FACILITIES ★ ★ ★

THEATRES & CONCERT HALLS *Currently no theatre in Kingston itself, although the Charter Quay development by the river is expected to include a 550* seat theatre. Off the wall touring plays, dance and music at the Douglas Centre, Tolworth. Regular concerts at All Saints Church, Kingston run by the Thames Concerts Society • **CINEMAS** Only one, the Options ABC in Kingston, showing mostly mainstream films. Residents have to travel to other boroughs for more choice (see Richmond and Merton for example) • **MUSEUMS & GALLERIES** Thin on the ground, although the Kingston Museum, housed in an elegant 'listed' red brick Edwardian building next to the library, has a fascinating, well laid out and well labelled exhibition of the borough's history from the remains of early wooden boats to the mayoral chain and mace of the now-defunct boroughs of Malden and Coombe and Surbiton. Kingston is very conscious of its long history and its status as a Royal Borough (seven Saxon Kings were crowned there) which, it hopes, sets it apart from other simply suburban boroughs. Local art exhibitions in the library next door • **SPORTS FACILITIES** Four indoor leisure centres at Tolworth, Chessington, Malden and Kingston with pools, fitness suites and other sports facilities. Watersports including canoeing and sailing at Albany Park Canoe and Sailing Centre, Kingston; outdoor and indoor sports pitches at the Hawker Centre, Kingston. Golf on public courses at New Malden and Chessington. For more passive leisure, Chessington World of Adventure has rides, attractions and the Big Circus (and big traffic jams during school holidays) • **LIBRARIES** Disappointingly under-used for a middle class area. Erratic opening hours in some branch libraries (is this the reason for low use or vice versa?) with late opening limited and all the libraries closed on Wednesday. Kingston main library (housed in a listed building next to the museum) and children's library are open on Sunday afternoon. 5.3 library visits per head. Position in library-use league table: 26th out of 32 (where 1 is best and 32 worst).

OPEN SPACES***

A three-star rating may seem mean for a borough surrounded by as much open space as Kingston is but many of the spaces most loved by residents (Bushy Park and Richmond Park to the north and Wimbledon Common to the east, for example) are outside the borough boundary (see Richmond and Merton). It scores for its large tracts of open Green Belt land in the south but many of its parks and open spaces are small and flat, pleasant enough but without much character.

RIVER WALKS Canbury Gardens. A pretty slice of green between Kingston town centre and the river. The approach from town is off-putting at the moment, past derelict buildings which will soon make way for Charter Quay. Views across the river to Hampton Wick with handsome Victorian houses and carved wooden boathouses • **A SLICE OF THE RURAL** Hogsmill Open Space, Surbiton. The Hogsmill River winds through a lush tract of grass, a fleeting rural idyll before suburban houses reappear through the trees.

SHOPS****

KINGSTON Shopping is one of the town's main raisons d'être. Historically a market town, it has now expanded greatly. Its massive Bentall centre set the seal on Kingston as a paradise for shopaholics when it opened in 1992. Three floors of up-market branches of chain stores (many stores testing out the UK market start in Kingston). More shops at the Eden Walk shopping centre and along the network of pedestrianised streets joining the two centres. Big branches of John Lewis and Allders. But shoppers confess they find the indoor centres a bit overwhelming. The pleasantest shopping environment is around the Market Place where modern suddenly gives way to medieval with narrow streets, half-timbered houses with smaller, more individual shops and a fruit, vegetable and clothes market. Waitrose and Sainsbury's in the shopping centre • **NEW MALDEN** Official claims that New Malden is "villagey" are stretching it a bit – it's basically a long, straight high street, mostly lined with chain stores. A Korean supermarket and a couple of Korean restaurants testify to a flourishing Korean community here. Big Waitrose near the station • **SURBITON** The 1930s modernist station and forecourt lend an air of elegance to what is essentially another suburban shopping street with small branches of chains, charity shops and banks. More manageable than Kingston for a quick pop to the shops. Gateway and Sainsbury's • **TOLWORTH & CHESSINGTON** Depressing interwar parades of take-aways, newsagents, chains and building society and bank branches. They are either on busy roads or very nearby. Some boarded-up shops around Tolworth.

RESTAURANTS**

KINGSTON A range of brasseries, patisseries and pubs, with a locally praised French brasserie by the river near Kingston Bridge. Good Thai on Kingston Hill. But tends to be a bit dead at night and people say they don't always feel safe. Some problems with teenage drunkenness outside pubs and clubs • **NEW MALDEN** The place to go locally for Korean food. Two good restaurants in Burlington Road just off the High Street • **SURBITON** A couple of wine bars and pizza chains.

CRIME RATES****

95 crimes per 1000 of population. Position in Metropolitan Police league table: 24th out of 32 (where 1 is worst and 32 best).

THE COUNCIL***

POLITICAL AFFILIATION No overall control • **MINUS POINTS** Under-used library service. The second slowest borough of any in London at turning round land searches quickly while charging one of the highest rates. Criticised by residents for mounting a "military-style" campaign against the eco-warriors in the row over the popular trees on the riverside last year which cost £500,000 of council tax payers' money • **PLUS POINTS** Excellent schools. Generally efficient and approachable. Door-to-door paper recycling. Efficient rubbish collections • **PROPERTY SEARCHES CARRIED OUT IN 10 WORKING DAYS** 69% • **STANDARD SEARCH FEE** £120 • **COUNCIL TAX COLLECTED** 97.1%

• **COUNCIL TAX RATES 1998-99**

BAND	PROPERTY VALUE	CHARGE	BAND	PROPERTY VALUE	CHARGE
A	up to £40,000	£405.36	E	£88,001-£120,000	£743.16
B	£40,001-£52,000	£472.92	F	£120,001-£160,000	£878.28
C	£52,001-£68,000	£540.48	G	£160,001-£320,000	£1,013.40
D	£68,001-£88,000	£608.04	H	over £320,000	£1,216.08

LAMBETH

Lambeth is one of the few boroughs that even non-Londoners have heard of, and what they've heard isn't flattering. Scene of the Brixton riots in 1981, the borough hit the headlines again later in the decade when the left-wing councillors running the self-styled People's Republic of Lambeth refused to set annual rates. Tales of incompetent and corrupt councillors and officers continued into the 1990s, culminating in the high-profile appointment of a new chief executive to shake up the borough from top to bottom. So far the results have been patchy. Schools are generally poor, street-cleaning and litter collection have a long way to go and council tax collection is haphazard. A government injection of £187 million in 1993 for a five-year regeneration of the area didn't deliver all it was meant to.

That said, there are signs that things are improving. Council tax levels are falling while those of other boroughs rise. Millions more pounds of public and private money are pouring into the borough in renewed attempts to regenerate shopping centres, open spaces, public buildings and leisure facilities in Brixton, Clapham, Norwood, Streatham and the South Bank around Vauxhall. There are ambitious plans for the renewal of the South Bank arts complex, the building of a Millennium Wheel and a new bridge across the Thames. And Clapham and Brixton are now firmly on the map as desirable and/or trendy places to live.

Lambeth's section of riverfront in the north of the borough stretches along the south bank from Waterloo's eclectic mix of luxury apartments, council blocks and tucked-away Victorian terraces to the traffic maelstrom of Vauxhall. Inland are the Georgian and Victorian terraces of Kennington and Stockwell, mixed with more council blocks. Brixton to the south still carries reminders of the smart Victorian suburb it used to be with many substantial houses and grand public buildings alongside the crumbling terraces and council estates. To the west lie the well-kept Victorian terraces of Clapham Park and the Georgian town houses of Clapham Old Town. Suburbia begins with Streatham, as 1930s semi-detached and detached houses compete with smart and not-so-smart Victorian and Edwardian houses. At Lambeth's south-eastern tip lie the Victorian villas and terraces of West Norwood and Gipsy Hill which lead up the hill to Crystal Palace.

Despite the recent middle class influx, Lambeth is still one of the poorest boroughs in London. It's the 8th most deprived area of England and unemployment is high at 10.4%. Crime levels are high – it has the dubious distinction of having the highest levels of burglary and sex crime anywhere in London. People used to be considered brave for ignoring such down-sides and moving to the Lambeth front line. But good transport links, a good choice of still reasonably cheap property, lively street-life and energetic ethnic markets are proving a winning combination and turning the area around, particularly in Brixton. Nearly a third of Lambeth's population is from an ethnic minority with a significant Afro-Caribbean community so if you like your London cosmopolitan and multicultural, this is one of the best places to be.

PROPERTY AND ARCHITECTURE

WATERLOO & KENNINGTON

No one really used to live in Waterloo, an area of dull office blocks dominated by Waterloo Station and the appalling 1960s concrete roundabout and underpasses leading to Waterloo Bridge. Only small tracts of the area had escaped the office developer's bulldozer including a perfect group of small early-Victorian terraces around Roupell Street just by Waterloo East and some newer houses round Coin Street built after a long battle by local people for homes not offices. Now developers are converting offices and the former home of the Greater London Council at County Hall to luxury apartments as activity around the South Bank hots up in time for the Millennium. There are also plans for developments around Vauxhall Bridge, currently mostly a dreary traffic interchange. Lots of council and ex-council flats in Kennington as well as a mixture of Victorian terraces and handsome Georgian terraces and squares in streets off the Kennington Road.

ATTRACTS *Young professionals wanting to be central; MPs wanting a London base* • **CONSERVATION AREAS** *Waterloo; Roupell Street; South Bank; Mitre Road and Ufford Street; Lambeth Palace; Lambeth Walk and China Walk; Renfrew Road; Walcot; Vauxhall; St Marks* • **AVERAGE PRICES** *Flats: studio: £40,000-£70,000; 1-bed: £55,000-£128,000; 2-bed: £85,000-£170,000; 3-bed: £90,000-£195,000 Houses: 2-bed: £100,000-£250,000; 3-bed: £110,000-£250,000; 4-bed: £200,000-£450,000; 5-bed: £400,000-£550,000* • **AVERAGE RENTS (MONTHLY)** *Flats: studio: £475; 1-bed: £650; 2-bed: £950; 3-bed: £1210 Houses: 1-bed: £650; 2-bed: £735; 3-bed: £1470; 4-bed: £1730+; 5-bed: £2160+.*

STOCKWELL & BRIXTON

Lots of still reasonably priced Georgian and Victorian family houses in both areas as well as flats in converted houses. Some of the best houses in Stockwell are in Stockwell Park, an enclave of Georgian family houses off the Clapham Road slightly marred by their proximity to the Stockwell Park council estate. On the other side of the Clapham Road, there are some roads of handsome detached Regency villas among the council property. Brixton is more Victorian with roads of two- and three-storey terraces as well as larger family houses but there are plenty of surprises off the busy main roads, including small Georgian terraces in Trinity Square just behind Brixton Road and good-sized Victorian terraces in roads off Brixton Water Lane. Some large Victorian houses by Brockwell Park in cheaper Tulse Hill with lots of council property around the station.

ATTRACTS *Young professionals; creative and media types; City workers who like to think they live on the front line; some families; members of the Afro-Caribbean community* • **CONSERVATION AREAS** *Brixton Road; Stockwell*

Green; Brixton; Angell Town; Loughborough Park; Trinity Gardens; Brixton Water Lane; Brockwell Park; Rush Common and Brixton Hill; Minet Estate
• **AVERAGE PRICES** *Flats: studio: £26,000-£32,000; 1-bed: £45,000-£60,000; 2-bed: £75,000-£90,000; 3-bed: £85,000-£90,000 Houses: 2-bed: £85,000+; 3-bed: £180,000; 4-bed: £175,000-£225,000; 5-bed: £270,000* • **AVERAGE RENTS (MONTHLY)** *Flats: studio: £430-£470; 1-bed: £430-£560; 2-bed: £600-£690; 3-bed: £780-£990 Houses: 3-bed: £1080-£1300; 4-bed: £1300-£1730; 5-bed: £1730-£1950.*

CLAPHAM

Rapidly displacing Fulham as THE place for young respectable people to live when they first come to London. But it's also popular with middle class mums and dads despite the awful reputation of many of Lambeth's schools. Some of the most sought-after properties are well-kept Victorian terraces, some still houses and others converted, around Abbeville Road in Clapham Park. This area is dubbed Abbeville Village by estate agents, enthusiastically backed by residents who claim it feels like a village even if it doesn't look like it. Some marvellous Georgian townhouses overlooking Clapham Common on Clapham Common North Side. The Old Town has a mixture of Georgian and Victorian terraces including the surprising white stucco Grafton Square which wouldn't look out of place in Kensington. Roads of mansion blocks, late Victorian terraces and some early Victorian two-storey Cubitt terraces (many ex-council) around Clapham Manor Street.
ATTRACTS *Young professionals, especially from the City; well off first-time buyers; families* • **CONSERVATION AREAS** *Clapham; Clapham Road; Clapham High Street; The Chase; Clapham Park Road, Northbourne Road; La Retraite* • **AVERAGE PRICES** *Flats: studio: £60,000-£90,000; 1-bed: £70,000-£130,000; 2-bed: £90,000-£220,000; 3-bed: £120,000-£300,000 Houses: 2-bed: £180,000-£260,000; 3-bed: £200,000-£340,000; 4-bed: £250,000-£450,000; 5-bed: £300,000-£600,000* • **AVERAGE RENTS (MONTHLY)** *Flats: studio: £540-£650; 1-bed: £690-£860; 2-bed: £900-£1210; 3-bed: £1380-£1640; 4-bed: £1840-£2080 Houses: 2-bed: £1080-£1300; 3-bed: £1470-£1730; 4-bed: £1950-£2250; 5-bed: £2380+.*

STREATHAM

More suburban (and duller) than Clapham but increasingly sought-after by families for its large Victorian, Edwardian and 1930s homes as well as first-time buyers who are drawn to the conversion flats. Cheaper 1930s homes in Streatham Vale and grander Victorian and Edwardian detached and semi-detached in streets off Streatham High Road. Some of the best and largest houses are in roads off Streatham Common and in the Telford Park area off Streatham Hill. Newly-converted flats are getting rarer as the council clamps down following the 1980s proliferation of small flats.
ATTRACTS *Families who can't afford the space they want in Clapham or Wandsworth; some first-time buyers* • **CONSERVATION AREAS** *Hyde Farm; Telford Park; Streatham Hill; Garrads Road; Sunnyhill Road; Leigham Court Road; Streatham Common* • **AVERAGE PRICES** *Flats: studio: £30,000-£50,000; 1-bed: £45,000-£65,000; 2-bed: £55,000-£130,000; 3-bed: £75,000-£150,000 Houses: 2-bed: £120,000-£125,000; 3-bed: £90,000-£200,000; 4-bed: £140,000-£300,000; 5-bed: £215,000-500,000* • **AVERAGE RENTS (MONTHLY)** *Flats: 1-bed: £500; 2-bed: £650-£750; 3-bed: £900-£1200 Houses: 2-bed: £800; 3-bed: £950-£1050; 4-bed: £1200-£1500.*

WEST NORWOOD & GIPSY HILL

One of the main advantages of this area is that it's very hilly and the views over London are wonderful. A mixture of large Victorian terraces, many converted into flats in the 1980s, but others being refurbished as single family homes. Victorian cottages in roads in and around more up-market Gipsy Hill and some elegant villas and white stucco terraces. A strong local-community-feel in roads around Westow Hill, currently united in opposition to plans to build a leisure centre in Crystal Palace Park (see Bromley). West Norwood has roads of Victorian terraces in roads off Norwood High Street with pleasant streets of Edwardian semis in roads to the west of West Norwood station.

ATTRACTS *First-time buyers; families* • **CONSERVATION AREAS** *Lancaster Avenue; Rosendale Road; West Norwood; Gipsy Hill; Westow Hill North Side* • **AVERAGE PRICES** *Flats: studio: £30,000-£40,000; 1-bed: £40,000-£50,000; 2-bed: £55,000-£75,000; 3-bed: £75,000-£85,000 Houses: 2-bed: £70,000-£80,000; 3-bed: £90,000-£140,000; 4-bed: £130,000-£200,000; 5-bed: £180,000-£280,000* • **AVERAGE RENTS (MONTHLY)** *Flats: 1-bed: £500; 2-bed: £600-£700; 3-bed: £750-£1000 Houses: 2-bed: £750; 3-bed: £900-£1000; 4-bed: £1200-£1500; 5-bed: £1400-£2000.*

BEST POSTCODES

The best postcode is Clapham SW4 followed by Streatham SW16. There can be some big price differences between property in SW4 and neighbouring Brixton SW2, with properties in SW4 sometimes £50,000 more expensive than SW2. The dividing line between Lambeth and Wandsworth also creates big price differences with people prepared to pay several thousand pounds more to live in cheap, efficient Wandsworth.

AMENITIES

SCHOOLS*

Generally a depressing picture although there are reports that the borough is trying to get to grips with low academic achievement and truancy. State schools both at primary and secondary level consistently perform poorly in league tables and are among London's worst. Middle class parents fight to get their children into the good schools of neighbouring Wandsworth, Bromley or Croydon or bankrupt themselves to send them to private school in Dulwich. No private prep schools and only one private secondary school. The third lowest proportion of under-fives in state nurseries of any borough in London but a reasonable selection of private and voluntary nursery schools.

PRE-SCHOOL PROVISION *5 state nurseries; 42 nursery classes in state primary or church schools; 81 private or voluntary nursery schools. Proportion of under-fives in state nurseries: 39%* • **STATE PRIMARY SCHOOLS** *Overall league table position: 120th out of 132. Top scorers: Julian's, Streatham; Streatham Wells, Streatham; Paxton (with nursery unit), Gipsy Hill* • **STATE SECONDARY SCHOOLS** *Overall league table position: 139th out of 149. Best scorers: La Retraite RC (girls), Clapham; Bishop Thomas Grant RC, (mixed) Streatham; London Nautical School (boys), Waterloo* • **PRIVATE SECONDARY SCHOOL** *Streatham Hill and Clapham High (girls), Streatham.*

TRANSPORT★★★★

Good, particularly in the north of the borough with a wide choice of tubes and trains. The borough includes Waterloo station. South of Brixton and Clapham there are only trains. Talk of extending the East London line south to Dulwich, Streatham and Croydon, giving these areas a tube for the first time, has fallen ominously silent despite the government's much-vaunted commitment to public transport.

TRAINS Waterloo: Zone 1. Cost of annual season ticket: £572. Trains to south-west London, south coast as well as Paris and Brussels (Eurostar). Streatham: Zone 3. Cost of annual season ticket: £860; No of trains per hour: to Blackfriars 3; Fastest journey: 25 minutes. Gipsy Hill: Zone 3. No of trains per hour: to London Bridge 6; Fastest journey: 25 minutes • **TUBES** Waterloo: Zone 1. Bakerloo and Northern line tubes and Jubilee line when the extension opens. Stockwell: Zone 2. Cost of annual season ticket: £704; Frequency: Northern: every 4 minutes; Victoria: every 3 minutes; Fastest journey: to Charing Cross 8 minutes; to Oxford Circus 10 minutes. Brixton: Zone 2. Frequency: Victoria: every 3 minutes; Fastest journey: to Oxford Circus: 12 minutes. Clapham Common: Zone 2. Frequency: Northern: every 4 minutes; Fastest journey: to Charing Cross 14 minutes • **BUSES** An excellent selection in the northern half of the borough with buses converging from all directions. Fewer in the south, around Streatham and Norwood, where many link suburbs rather than going to central London. Buses to town include the 2 from Crystal Palace via West Norwood, Tulse Hill, Brixton, Stockwell and Vauxhall to Marylebone, the 3 from Crystal Palace to Oxford Circus via Brixton and Kennington and the 133 from Streatham Hill via Brixton and Kennington to Liverpool Street • **TRAFFIC BLACKSPOTS** Vauxhall: A horrible traffic interchange, one of the worst legacies of 1960s planners, with one-way systems requiring motorists to change lanes constantly and roads narrowing suddenly from three lanes to one. There are plans to improve the junction for pedestrians and cyclists. Brixton: Very trafficky around the lights at the junction of the main shopping streets around the town hall where there are too many buses, delivery lorries, cars and pedestrians. There are plans to improve pedestrian crossing on Brixton Road and Brixton Hill which doubles as the main A23. Clapham: Heavy traffic on roads all around Clapham Common and up Clapham High Street. Suffers badly from being at the junction of several major through-roads including the south circular and the A3 to the south coast. Streatham: Like Brixton and Clapham, its main shopping street doubles as a main road. Jams are almost constant at the junction with the south circular. Loads of buses – Streatham High Road is the second busiest bus route in London • **PARKING** The council is tightening up to discourage commuters from parking and riding. Controlled parking zones are gradually being extended into the south of the borough and already spread over most of the north. There are controlled parking zones throughout: Waterloo; Vauxhall; Kennington; Stockwell; Clapham; and West Norwood. Parts of Brixton are also controlled. Cost of annual resident's permit: £60.

LEISURE FACILITIES★★★★

THEATRES & CONCERT HALLS Excellent choice of venues, particularly on the South Bank in the north of the borough. Discussions have been going on for years to find ways of making the concrete building of the arts complex and its surroundings more welcoming but it looks as if this one will run and run, at least until the Millennium. The complex includes the National

Theatre, (considered part of the West End) as well as concert halls at the Royal Festival Hall, Queen Elizabeth Hall and Purcell Room. The Old Vic and Young Vic theatres are just the other side of Waterloo Station from the National. Open-air theatre at the Rookery, Streatham Common. Live music at The Fridge, Brixton and the Brixton Academy • **CINEMAS** A very good selection: the repertory National Film Theatre at the South bank complex; the recently-established Clapham Picture House, showing a mixture of mainstream and more off-the-wall films; and the Ritzy repertory cinema, now grandly restored with government grant money. The ABC and Odeon in Streatham show mainstream films. A huge new multiscreen IMAX cinema is being built in the middle of the Bullring roundabout in Waterloo • **MUSEUMS & GALLERIES** A varied selection, mainly in the north of the borough ranging from the hugely popular Museum of the Moving Image at South Bank and the Aquarium at the former headquarters of the Greater London Council to the quieter pleasures of the Museum of Garden History at Lambeth Palace and the Florence Nightingale Museum at St Thomas's Hospital. The Imperial War Museum is in the former Bethlem Mental Hospital in Lambeth. Major art exhibitions at the Hayward Gallery • **SPORTS FACILITIES** Four leisure centres in Brixton, East Brixton, Streatham and Clapham (recently opened). Indoor swimming pools at Clapham, Streatham and Brixton, the biggest and best of them all. Outdoor swimming at the popular and trendy Brockwell lido (as featured on TV). Football, tennis, cricket and other sports in parks across the borough; ice skating at Streatham Rink which could do with a face-lift but is popular with locals • **LIBRARIES** The most under-used in London and old-fashioned, with computerised ticketing still to reach some of the more far-flung branch libraries as of last year. Patchy opening hours in most branches with widespread closing on Monday mornings as well as Wednesday and Thursday all day. No Sunday opening. 3.1 library visits per head. Position in library-use league table: 31st out of 32 (no information supplied by Barking & Dagenham so Lambeth bottom by default).

OPEN SPACES ***

Not as generously endowed as neighbouring boroughs and many of its most-loved open spaces (Streatham and Clapham Commons for example) are blighted by being right next to busy main roads. But there are some hidden surprises.
BEST VIEWS The Rookery, Streatham Common. A secluded walled series of terraced gardens, a riot of floral colour in summer, opening out to great views over south London and Surrey; Norwood Park, an otherwise featureless expanse of green but stunning views of the London skyline • **WIDE OPEN SPACES** Brockwell Park. Less flat and trafficky than either Clapham Common or the open parts of Streatham. The smaller Kennington Park with mature trees and tennis courts is also worth a visit • **CEMETERIES** West Norwood. Not as Gothic as Highgate or Nunhead but pleasantly Victorian.

SHOPS ***

WATERLOO, KENNINGTON & VAUXHALL Mostly shabby local shops on busy main roads, although there are plans to build new shops around Waterloo station and Vauxhall as part of the huge regeneration effort in the area. Market in Lower Marsh behind Waterloo Station • **BRIXTON** The centre of Brixton has had a lot of government money spent on it over the past five years as part of the Brixton Challenge and there are plans to spend another £1.6 million on environmental improvements. It's now got a fair choice of shops including a big Woolworth, M&S and a new Morley's department store to replace the late-lamented Bon Marché (now turned into a number of smaller shops). But it's the lively indoor and outdoor markets in and around Electric Avenue which make shopping in Brixton interesting. Stalls sell Afro-Caribbean food and materials, clothes and fruit and a series of small businesses including Afro-Caribbean hairdressers and a radical bookshop operate from neighbouring railway arches. Tesco in Acre Lane • **CLAPHAM** Plentiful shops and restaurants in Clapham High Street although some of it is slightly shabby and down-market, particularly towards the common end and the street is trafficky. Mostly chains, including banks and several off-licences. Sainsbury's in strange pointed glass and metal building. Smarter shops around The Pavement in the Old Town, including a delicatessen, picture framer and real butcher, and a handful of up-market local shops in Abbeville Road. Plans to build a Tesco by South Clapham station were thrown out last year but the superstore isn't beaten that easily • **STREATHAM** The shops straggle along the main A23 making shopping here an unpleasant experience. Lots of small branches of chains, ethnic clothes shops and local shops but the High Road looks tired with boarded-up shops, particularly down the Common end. Big new Sainsbury's by the Common. Safeway by Streatham Station • **WEST NORWOOD & GIPSY HILL** Dull shops at West Norwood with the usual collection of hardware stores, newsagents and Chinese take-aways, a Co-op and Kwiksave. Things get more interesting at the top of Gipsy Hill at Westow Hill, an attractive villagey street with restaurants, clothes and furniture shops among the chains (see also Croydon).

RESTAURANTS * * *

WATERLOO A huge explosion of trendy new restaurants along the South Bank including the Oxo Tower restaurant and the People's Palace at the South Bank complex. Also a good choice around Gabriel's Wharf and The Cut by the Old and Young Vics • **BRIXTON & STOCKWELL** A couple of good Portguese restaurants in Stockwell (there's a significant Portuguese community here and in Vauxhall where there are also good Portuguese restaurants). Bars, Far Eastern, Afro-Caribbean and vegetarian in Brixton which never seems to go to bed • **CLAPHAM** Lots of new restaurants have sprung up to cater for the middle classes especially round the Old Town and in Abbeville "Village". Brasseries and pavement cafés lend a European feel to the area and there's a choice of every type of cuisine from Europe to the Far East • **STREATHAM** A good Turkish restaurant and the usual Indian and Chinese restaurants of varying quality.

CRIME RATES *

180 crimes per 1000 of population. Position in Metropolitan Police league table: 5th out of 32 (where 1 is worst and 32 best). Lambeth has the highest levels of sex crimes and burglaries in London and the second highest levels of violent crime and robberies.

THE COUNCIL * *

POLITICAL AFFILIATION Labour • **MINUS POINTS** Poor schools. Widespread reports of administrative inefficiency. Poor at sweeping the streets and collecting rubbish. Poorly-resourced libraries. The third slowest borough in London at turning round property searches while charging more than *almost any other inner London borough. Collects less council tax than any other London borough* • **PLUS POINTS** *Finally trying to get to grips with the chaos created by years of giving higher priority to ideological dogma than the needs of local people. Cuts in council tax. Successful bid to become an Education Action Zone. Plans to extend successful weekly door-to-door recycling scheme to flats* • **PROPERTY SEARCHES CARRIED OUT WITHIN 10 WORKING DAYS** 73% • **STANDARD SEARCH FEE** £110 • **COUNCIL TAX COLLECTED** 78.6%

- **COUNCIL TAX 1998-99**

BAND	PROPERTY VALUE	CHARGE	BAND	PROPERTY VALUE	CHARGE
A	up to £40,000	£431.32	E	£88,001-£120,000	£790.78
B	£40,001-£52,000	£503.22	F	£120,001-£160,000	£934.56
C	£52,001-£68,000	£575.12	G	£160,001-£320,000	£1,078.33
D	£68,001-£88,000	£647.00	H	over £320,000	£1,294.00

LEWISHAM

Lewisham wants to be taken seriously as the Millennium approaches and it prepares to bask in the reflected glory of its illustrious neighbour, Greenwich. But it's having a bit of trouble living down its reputation as a dull, unromantic slice of inner city south London, largely unknown and unacknowledged by anyone who doesn't live there. Attempts last year to promote itself as a great place to stay during the Millennium celebrations were greeted with derision by the media and residents alike. Undaunted, it's now promising a party to end all parties down its share of the Meridian line (much longer than Greenwich's but of course Lewisham isn't trying to compete, perish the thought).

Shaped like a badly drawn map of the British Isles, Lewisham has only a tiny slice of riverfront at once-industrial Deptford before it spreads south uphill over the Thames ridge into Victorian suburbia. South of Deptford are the large shabby Victorian houses of New Cross, Brockley and Lewisham itself. On the hill above Lewisham is Blackheath, the jewel in Lewisham's crown, its picturesque village and Heath the only part of Lewisham familiar to people from other parts of London. The large Victorian villas of Forest Hill and Sydenham cover the hills of south-west Lewisham up to Crystal Palace, giving way to smaller Victorian and Edwardian terraces around Catford and Hither Green. In the south east, 1930s semis take over at Lee and Grove Park as inner city Lewisham changes into outer London at the borders of Bromley.

Lewisham has its middle class and wealthy enclaves (Blackheath and the best parts of Lee particularly). But it's also the 11th most deprived local authority in England. Unemployment stands at 9.2 per cent, and of those who do work, two thirds commute out of the borough.

During the past few decades, many of the once elegant houses and shopping centres which testified to Lewisham's nineteenth century status as a smart suburb were left to decay gently. But now things are looking up, particularly in the north of the borough around Lewisham town centre and Deptford. Successive governments have pumped £38 million into the area and although the area still looks a bit of a mess, with 1960s tower blocks looming over scrapyards and empty shops, major businesses like Sainsbury's have come to neighbouring New Cross and streetscapes and traffic layout have improved. Lewisham town centre has also been pedestrianised, making shopping a pleasanter if still unexciting experience.

Transport links are set to improve dramatically, as a spin-off from the Millennium Dome. Like other south-east London boroughs, Lewisham currently relies mostly on railways which puts off many prospective buyers wedded to the underground (although property prices are lower because of it). But later this year the Docklands Light Railway extension to Lewisham will be finished giving the area a direct link to Docklands and the City for the first time. The DLR extension will in turn link into the Jubilee line extension at Canary Wharf which will speed to Green Park in 15 minutes.

For those who relish a good mix of cultures, Lewisham doesn't quite manage the zany atmosphere of Brixton but nearly a quarter of its population comes from an ethnic minority, with substantial Afro-Caribbean, Turkish and Irish communities.

PROPERTY AND ARCHITECTURE

BLACKHEATH & LEE

Blackheath Village on the edge of the Blackheath on a plateau above the Thames is the best part of Lewisham with cottages and expensive Victorian terraces in the centre near villagey shops. Look for large family houses and generously proportioned converted flats in the streets off the Heath towards Lewisham to the west and Kidbrooke to the east. The large Victorian houses in the most desirable parts of Lee around Micheldever, Southbrook and Handen Roads are almost as expensive as Blackheath but the rest of Lee is cheaper. The closer to Blackheath you are, the more expensive it is because you can call it Blackheath borders. Blackheath Standard (named after the Royal Standard pub at its centre) is on the north side of the Heath (see Greenwich)

ATTRACTS *Intellectuals and media types who can't afford Hampstead (or don't want to – Glenda Jackson MP for Hampstead and Highgate is a long-standing resident); families who value the open spaces and good primary schools* • **CONSERVATION AREAS** *Blackheath (around the village and Heath), Lee Manor* • **AVERAGE PRICES** *Flats: studio: £35,000-£60,000; 1-Bed: £50,000-£150,000; 2-Bed: £75,000-£200,000; 3-Bed: £90,000-£300,000 Houses: 2-Bed: £80,000-£200,000; 3-Bed: £95,000-£350,000; 4-Bed+: £150,000+* • **AVERAGE RENTS (MONTHLY)** *Flats: studio: £400-£550; 1-Bed: £500-£1000; 2-Bed: £600-£1500; 3-Bed: £800-£1,500 Houses: 2-Bed: £700-£1,300; 3-Bed: £800-£2,000; 4-Bed+: £850-£3000.*

DEPTFORD

Tower blocks dominate the skyline, reminder of ruthless slum clearance schemes in the 1960s and 1970s. But housing associations and the council are now actively building low-rise homes on a more human scale. There are bargains to be had for first-time buyers prepared to buy ex-council homes sold under the Right-to-Buy Scheme, as well as 1980s starter homes and increasingly flats above shops brought into use as part of the area's regeneration programme. Roads of small attractive Victorian cottages off Brookmill Road in the St John's conservation area. The arrival of the new Docklands Light Railway Link with station at Deptford Bridge should give the whole area a boost.

ATTRACTS *First-time buyers; loyal locals; bargain hunters prepared to move to fringe areas; members of the Afro-Caribbean community* • **CONSERVATION AREAS** *Deptford High Street, St Paul's [Church], St John's, Brookmill Road* • **AVERAGE PRICES** *Flats: studio: £33,000+; 1-Bed: £42,000-£55,000; 2-Bed: £55,000-£75,000; 3-Bed: £50,000+ Houses: 1-Bed: £75,000; 2-Bed: £85,000+; 3-Bed: £90,000-120,000; 4-Bed+: up to £150,000* • **AVERAGE RENTS (MONTHLY)** *Flats: studio: £350-£450; 1-Bed: £450-£550; 2-Bed: £550-£600; 3-Bed: £550-£700 Houses: 2-Bed: £500-£600; 3-Bed: £650-£750; 4-Bed: £700-£950.*

NEW CROSS & BROCKLEY

Home of some of the best property bargains if you want space. The most sought-after areas are in the conservation areas of New Cross around Telegraph Hill and Brockley around Hilly Fields, which is laid out with wide roads lined with large double-fronted Victorian villas. Some have been converted into flats but others remain as houses, although many of them need a lot of money spent. The area has lost out in the past because of the lack of shops and transport links in the area but this has already improved with the advent of Sainsbury's and will improve further with the DLR extension. Roads of middle-sized Victorian terraces around Honor Oak.

ATTRACTS *First-time buyers; people who want space; members of the Afro-Caribbean community* • **CONSERVATION AREAS** *Telegraph Hill, Brockley, Hatcham* • **AVERAGE PRICES** *Flats: studio: £ 28,000-£40,000; 1-bed: £45,000-£55,000; 2-bed: £55,000-£80,000; 3-bed: £65,000-£90,000 Houses: 2-bed: £75,000+; 3-bed: £100,000+; 4-bed+: £150,000+* • **AVERAGE RENTS (MONTHLY)** *Flats: studio: £350-£400; 1-Bed: £400-450; 2-Bed: £525-£550; 3-Bed: £550-£650; 4-bed+: £700-£1000 Houses: 2-Bed: £550-£600; 3-Bed: £700-£900; 4-Bed+: £700-£1,000.*

LEWISHAM

A mishmash of council estates built on bombsites and former industrial sites, Victorian terraces and the occasional road of startlingly handsome villas, particularly to the east of Lewisham High Street. You get a lot of space for your money. The most expensive properties are on the roads up the hill towards Blackheath where there are large Edwardian and Victorian villas, many still family homes. Roads round Granville Park close (but not too close) to the railway line have seen big price rises over the last year in anticipation of the DLR and now are almost as expensive as Blackheath. There are some good-sized Victorian houses and conversion flats in roads off the High Street to the west in Ladywell and down towards Catford and Hither Green to the east, mixed in with modern bomb infill and low-rise council estates.

ATTRACTS *First-time buyers; people who can't afford the space they want in Blackheath or Lee; members of the Afro-Caribbean community* • **CONSERVATION AREAS** *None* • **AVERAGE PRICES** *Flats: studio: £30,000-£35,000; 1-Bed: £45,000-£50,000; 2-Bed: £50,000-£65,000; 3-Bed: £55,000-£80,000 Houses: 2-bed: £75,000-£80,000; 3-bed: £85,000-£150,000; 4-bed+: £120,000-£200,000* • **AVERAGE RENTS (MONTHLY)** *Flats: studio: £350-£425; 1-Bed: £400-£500; 2-Bed: £500-£625; 3-Bed: £550-£650; 4-Bed: £700-£1000 Houses: 2-Bed: £650-£675; 3-Bed: £750-£800; 4-Bed: £850+.*

CATFORD & HITHER GREEN

Mostly two- and three-storey Victorian terraces in Hither Green, many "improved" with ugly modern windows and pebble-dashing. The effect is pretty bleak. Parts of Catford are better with large and sought-after Edwardian family houses on the Corbett Estate and round the Culverley Green conservation area in Catford. There are smaller terraces in roads off Rushey Green and the South Circular. Both areas have plentiful supplies of conversion flats. Roads round Manor House Gardens are the best in Hither Green, with some large Victorian and Edwardian houses.

ATTRACTS *First-time buyers, couples trading up to a house from a flat in a more expensive area* • **CONSERVATION AREA** *Culverley Green* • **AVERAGE PRICES** *Flats: studio: £30,000-£40,000; 1-Bed: £40,000-£55,000; 2-Bed: £45,000-£80,000; 3-Bed: £70,000-£85,000 Houses: 2-Bed: £65,000-£85,000; 3-Bed: £70,000-£140,000; 4-Bed+: £90,000-£200,000* • **AVERAGE RENTS (MONTHLY)** *Flats: studio: £350-£400; 1-Bed: £400-£475; 2-Bed: £500-£550; 3-Bed: £575-£750; 4-Bed: £1000 Houses: 2-Bed: £650-£750; 3-Bed: £700-£1,000; 4-Bed+: £1000-£1500.*

FOREST HILL & SYDENHAM

Once considered very smart by the Victorians, who believed the position high on a ridge above the Thames was health-giving. Many of the huge Victorian villas are now flats but there are still family houses of all types and ages. Some of the best are in the roads round the Horniman Museum and to the west at Upper Sydenham where some have spectacular views. The cheapest properties are in roads off the south circular, which are lined with flat conversions and smaller terraces.

ATTRACTS *Families wanting big houses, gardens and open space, first-time buyers* • **CONSERVATION AREAS** *Forest Hill, Sydenham Park, Sydenham Hill and Jews Walk* • **AVERAGE PRICES** *Flats: studio: £30,000+; 1-Bed: £45,000-£55,000; 2-Bed: ££50,000-£75,000; 3-Bed: £60,000-£85,000; 4-Bed+: £100,000+ Houses: 2-Bed: £85,000-£110,000; 3-Bed: £82,000-£130,000; 4-Bed+: £100,000-£250,000* • **AVERAGE RENTS (MONTHLY)** *Flats: studio: £360; 1-Bed: £450-£475; 2-Bed: £550-£570; 3-Bed: £750-£800 Houses: 2-Bed: £600; 3-Bed: £750-£900; 4-Bed+: £900-£1000.*

GROVE PARK

Where Inner London shades off into suburbia. The roads of Grove Park are lined mainly with respectable if dull 1930s family homes and pleasant roads of Edwardian semis. A large number of ex-council properties bought under the Right-to-Buy legislation come on to the market regularly.

ATTRACTS *Couples moving from inner London, many without children (those with children try to buy over the border in Bromley to get their children*

into Bromley's sought-after schools); retired people; first-time buyers
• **CONSERVATION AREA** *None* • **AVERAGE PRICES** *Flats: studio: £30,000-£40,000; 1-Bed: £40,000-£50,000; 2-Bed: £50,000-£65,000; 3-Bed: £70,000+ Houses: 2-Bed: £65,000-£85,000; 3-Bed: £65,000-£130,000; 4-Bed+: £150,000+* • **AVERAGE RENTS (MONTHLY)** *Flats: studio: up to £375; 1-Bed: up to £535; 2-Bed: £650-£700; 3-Bed: £800 Houses: 1-Bed: up to £575; 2-Bed: up to £700; 3-Bed: £900; 4-Bed+: £1,100+.*

BEST POSTCODES

Blackheath SE3 is head-and-shoulders above other postcodes although the parts of Lee SE12 and Lewisham SE13 nearest Blackheath are nearly as good. Forest Hill SE23 and Sydenham are respectable codes. No major price anomalies around postcode boundaries. Prices depend mainly on proximity to open space, good transport links and the cachet of being in a conservation area. Properties in the Brockley, Telegraph Hill and Hatcham conservation areas can be 100 per cent more expensive than neighbouring properties outside, say local agents.

AMENITIES

SCHOOLS**

Undistinguished, with state primary and secondary schools consistently languishing near the bottom of the league tables. Average state nursery provision and a handful of private prep and secondary schools.
PRE-SCHOOL PROVISION *47 nursery classes in state primary and church schools; 95 private or voluntary nurseries and playgroups; 11 council - supported community nurseries. Proportion of under-fives in state nurseries: 57%* • **STATE PRIMARY SCHOOLS** *Overall league table position: 126th out of 150. High scorers: St Bartholemew's C of E, Sydenham; Our Lady and St Philip RC, Sydenham; St Michael's C of E, Forest Hill* • **STATE SECONDARY SCHOOLS** *Overall place in league tables: 128th out of 150. High scorers: Haberdashers' Aske's Hatcham College (mixed), New Cross; Bonus Pastor RC (mixed), Downham; Prendergast (girls), Hilly Fields* • **PRIVATE PREP SCHOOLS** *St Dunstan's Prep (mixed), Catford* • **PRIVATE SECONDARY SCHOOLS** *Chart-topper Sydenham High (girls), Sydenham and St Dunstan's College (mixed), Catford.*

TRANSPORT***

TRAINS *Unitl the DLR extension opens later this year, the borough's only connection with the tube network is on the East London line to Whitechapel, not the most central of lines. Train services are variable, with Lewisham and Hither Green best served. Blackheath: Zone 3. Cost of annual season ticket: £860; No of trains per hour: to London Bridge 4, to Charing Cross 4; Fastest journey to Charing Cross: 19 minutes. Deptford: Zone 2. Cost of annual season ticket: £704; No of trains per hour: to London Bridge 2; to Charing Cross 2; Fastest journey to Charing Cross: 15 minutes. New Cross: Zone 2. No of trains per hour: to London Bridge 6; Fastest time: 6 minutes. Lewisham: Zone 2. No of trains per hour: to London Bridge 7; to Charing Cross 5; Fastest journey to Charing Cross: 16 minutes. Hither Green: Zone 3. No of trains per hour: to London*

*Bridge 4; to Charing Cross 3; Fastest journey to Charing Cross: 18
minutes. Forest Hill: Zone 3. No of trains per hour: to London Bridge 4; to
Victoria 2; Fastest journey to Victoria: 13 minutes. Grove Park: Zone 4.
Cost of annual season ticket: £1068; No of trains per hour: to London
Bridge 4; to Charing Cross 3; Fastest journey to Charing Cross: 18 minutes*
• **TUBES** *The East London line from New Cross and New Cross Gate to
Whitechapel has recently reopened after a three year closure for repairs.
Frequency: every 12 minutes. Fastest journey: to Whitechapel 12 minutes*
• **BUSES** *An estimated 100 buses an hour pass through Lewisham town
centre mostly linking suburbs and providing services to shopping areas like
Bromley. Services to town include: the 36 from Grove Park to Victoria via
Lewisham and New Cross, the 21 via Lewisham to London Bridge and
Moorgate and the 47 from Catford to Shoreditch via Deptford. The 53
crosses Blackheath on its journey to Oxford Circus via Deptford. Forest Hill
and points west have fewer choices. The main link with town is the 185 via
Forest Hill and Lewisham to Victoria* • **TRAFFIC BLACKSPOTS** *Lewisham town
centre: The main part of the High Street was pedestrianised three years
ago as part of a £37 million revamp of the town centre. Shopping is
pleasanter but traffic jams are frequent on the roads skirting the area. The
large roundabout recently built by the bus station is where several main
roads meet and badly-timed traffic lights at Lewisham high Street clog up
traffic. Deptford: Carved up by trafficky roads including the main A2 from
London to Dover. The South Circular: Runs through Catford and Forest Hill
much of the time on residential roads not built for the volume of traffic.
Blackheath: Delivery vans and badly parked cars frequently block the
narrow roads of Blackheath Village and the A2 road across Blackheath
suffers from heavy lorries banned from using Greenwich* • **PARKING** *There
are controlled parking zones around Lewisham town centre and residential
roads around the station to stop unofficial Park-and-Riding, and in
Blackheath. Parking in either centre is a nightmare on Saturdays and
wardens are strict. Cost of annual resident's permit: £25, valid only in the
zone for which it's issued.*

LEISURE FACILITIES * * *

THEATRES & CONCERT HALLS *The Blackheath Concert Halls were rescued
from closure two years ago after a campaign raised £50,000 from
members of the public, which brought promises of further funding. The
Halls are the borough's main venue for classical concerts, jazz and theatre.
The Lewisham Theatre in Catford has middle of the road plays, family
shows, pantomimes and musicals. The Albany Theatre in Deptford, also
recently recovered from funding problems, specialises in community plays
and performances. Pub theatre at the Brockley Jack in Brockley and
concerts by students at the Blackheath Conservatoire* • **CINEMAS** *Currently
a poor show – the Catford ABC (mainly blockbusters) is the only cinema
in the borough. But a new 12 screen multiplex cinema is planned in
Lewisham town centre* • **MUSEUMS** *Just one museum, the Horniman, housed
in a brilliant art nouveau building with a rounded stone tower high on the
slopes of Forest Hill. It has an eclectic selection of stuffed birds, skeletons,
tribal masks and other objects. The museum's gardens have panoramic
views over south London* • **SPORTS FACILITIES** *Four leisure centres with gyms
and swimming pools at Deptford, Brockley, Sydenham and Ladywell.
There's to be a new fitness centre at Ladywell, sorely needed as the existing
facilities are pretty tired. Forest Hill pools were closed last year although
the council claims the closure is only temporary. Greyhound racing at*

Catford. Millwall Football Club has its ground at Deptford, mercifully well away from most residential areas surrounded by industrial estates
• **LIBRARIES** *A new central library with modern computer systems and referencing equipment was installed in Lewisham High Street four years ago and is now well-used, well-stocked and open reasonable hours. The same can't be said for all branch libraries in the borough, some of which have had their opening hours progressively cut. Library use: above average with 8.2 library visits per head. Position in library-use league table: 12th out of 32 (where 1 is best and 32 worst).*

OPEN SPACES * * *

Lewisham may not look its best from the window of a bus, train or car but there are more than 40 parks and 15 per cent of the borough is green space. The borough is built on hills so there are some excellent views over London. But some of the parks and green space show signs of neglect, with litter and graffiti. Blackheath fights a constant battle against litter and illegal car parking.

GOOD VIEWS *Blackheath. A large grassy, windswept plateau with views over to Docklands and the City to the north and south London to the south. You either dismiss Blackheath as featureless and trafficky or love it for its big skies and space. Hilly Fields in Brockley also has excellent all round views although it's otherwise dull. Good views amid attractive surroundings at Horniman Gardens* • **CHILDREN** *The Zoo at Horniman Gardens*
• **GRACIOUS GARDENS** *Manor House Gardens in Lee (now being done up) are the setting for the eighteenth century Manor House, once the home of Sir Francis Baring of the banking family.*

SHOPS * * *

BLACKHEATH *Some interesting independent shops line the nineteenth century streets of the village including a bookshop, a kitchen shop, antique shops and an up-market Oxfam. But high rents are forcing independent traders out and they're being replaced by branches of restaurant chains (Cafe Rouge, Costa Coffee) and branches of estate agent chains. Late night shopping at Costcutter* • **DEPTFORD** *Shabby but interesting shops in Deptford High Street, now mostly pedestrianised. A big Afro-Caribbean and African presence, with fruit and vegetable stalls selling yams and sweet potato, clothes shops selling African clothes, lots of small discount traders and ethnic take-aways and restaurants. Raucous Wednesday and Saturday market with stallholders giving vigorous demonstrations of their wares. Kitchen equipment, clothes and food figure heavily. Antique furniture shops along Deptford Broadway. Sainsbury's superstore at New Cross* • **LEWISHAM** *Frequently touted (mainly by the council) as south-east London's premier shopping centre but has been steadily losing ground over the past 10 years to Bromley and Lakeside at Thurrock. Pedestrianisation was meant to revive Lewisham's fortunes but branches of chain stores are mainly small, stock is limited and there are too many tell-tale empty shops filled with fly-by-night traders selling cheap goods. There's a huge gap in the middle of the High Street which was the late and lamented Army & Navy, Lewisham's last department store. Plans to build a high security police station here met with outcries from residents but two years on no-one knows what will fill the hole. Daily market selling mainly fruit, vegetables and flowers. Tesco by the station, Sainsbury's in the shopping centre* •
CATFORD *Currently as tired as Lewisham with its main shops housed in a dreary 1960s concrete shopping centre below council flats. A major revamp*

of the area is planned, with new shops and facilities, pedestrianisation of the space between town hall buildings and the creation of a new arts centre at Lewisham Theatre. But so far the results have been dreary. A large McDonalds has sprung up by the one-way system opposite a terrace of bricked up Victorian houses waiting to be demolished. Tesco in the shopping centre • **OTHER AREAS** *Forest Hill, Hither Green and Sydenham have mainly local parades of shops with people going elsewhere for major shopping. Lee has several good pine furniture shops in the High Road. Sainsbury's at Lee Green. Tesco has plans to build a store on the site of the old Hither Green Hospital, a plan opposed by many locals.*

RESTAURANTS***

BLACKHEATH *A big choice of restaurants (too big, say many residents who have seen shops disappear to be replaced by restaurants). The range includes Thai, Indian, Italian, French, Vietnamese and its latest addition, Chapter Two, a widely praised modern European restaurant* • **DEPTFORD & NEW CROSS** *Deptford has pie and mash, Indonesian and a couple of good noodle bars. There are signs of a small but growing middle class presence with the arrival of an Internet café and other cafés which rise above the greasy spoon level. New Cross has good Turkish and Thai restaurants* • **FOREST HILL & SYDENHAM** *Recommended Indian, Thai and Turkish restaurants* • **ELSEWHERE** *Little of note. Lewisham and Catford are virtually dead after about nine o'clock.*

CRIME RATES**

122 crimes per 1000 of population. Place in Metropolitan Police league table: 14th out of 32 (where 1 is worst and 32 best).

THE COUNCIL***

POLITICAL AFFILIATION *Labour* • **MINUS POINTS** *Poor performing schools. Variable standards of street-sweeping and litter collection with lots of old rubbish sacks and uncollected litter in corners particularly in Lewisham town centre* • **PLUS POINTS** *General efficiency much improved over the last decade. Has stepped up its efforts to encourage feedback from residents on issues like council spending and efficiency of litter collections and was one of the first boroughs to create a Citizens' Panel of 1,000 people drawn from the borough's population every year to comment on council plans. The first London borough to set out proposals for a directly-elected mayor. Cheaper council tax than neighbouring inner London boroughs. Door-to-door recycling scheme being piloted at 20,000 homes* • **PROPERTY SEARCHES CARRIED OUT IN 10 WORKING DAYS** *99%* • **STANDARD SEARCH FEE** *£95* • **COUNCIL TAX COLLECTED** *85%*
• **COUNCIL TAX 1998-99**

BAND	PROPERTY VALUE	CHARGE	BAND	PROPERTY VALUE	CHARGE
A	up to £40,000	£455.62	E	£88,001-£120,000	£835.33
B	£40,001-£52,000	£531.57	F	£120,001-£160,000	£987.21
C	£52,001-£68,000	£607.51	G	£160,001-£320,000	£1,139.07
D	£68,001-£88,000	£683.45	H	over £320,000	£1,366.90

MERTON

Merton isn't all dull suburbia. But much of it could be anywhere in the layer of outer London built up in the last 20 years of the nineteenth century and the first 30 years of the present one. The streets of small semis and terraces, some lined with trees and some without, the tangle of crescents and cul-de-sacs turning on to busy main roads, the tatty parades of shops, the roadhouse-style pubs strategically placed at roundabouts, will all be familiar to anyone who's ever passed through the outskirts of any major city, not just London. All of which is why Wimbledon village, an attractive Victorian sprawl of small shops and cottages on the edge of one of London's best commons, doesn't feel part of the borough at all.

Wimbledon, mostly Victorian around the centre and in the village with big detached houses further towards Wimbledon Common dominates the north west of the borough and is familiar to anyone who has ever trudged for miles or queued to get into the All England tennis ground during Wimbledon fortnight. Around Wimbledon is the amorphous Victorian sprawl of South Wimbledon to the east, relieved by the attractive garden suburb of Merton Park and the late Victorian and Edwardian terraces of Raynes Park to the west. In Mitcham, the satisfying open space of Mitcham Common breaks the monotony of 1930s semis which reaches round to Morden.

People commute from Merton but it isn't classic middle class commuter-belt country like parts of neighbouring Sutton or Kingston. It's more ethnically diverse for a start, with 16% of its population coming from an ethnic minority and significant communities of Indians and Afro-Caribbeans. Unemployment is higher, at 4%, although this is still lower than some outer boroughs in north London. Unlike other suburban boroughs, its most favoured and wealthiest parts are those closest to London rather than as far away from the inner city as possible.

An abundance of green space and good transport links, particularly in the north, are major draws for middle class parents, although the schools don't perform as well as neighouring boroughs and there's a fair bit of migration across borough boundaries. Wimbledon itself has become a popular follow-up move to Clapham or even Fulham, favoured by young couples and professionals who like the shops and restaurants and the quick train and tube links to town without the noise and dirt of the inner city.

Escaping traffic isn't, however, that simple. Traffic is one of Merton's big problems. It has its fair share of through roads out to the M25 and beyond, many of which double up as shopping centres and residents themselves have high levels of car ownership. The official hope is that more residents will abandon their cars in favour of the Croydon to Wimbledon Tramlink, which will particularly benefit Mitcham and surrounding areas.

PROPERTY AND ARCHITECTURE

WIMBLEDON & WIMBLEDON VILLAGE

Wimbledon isn't all smart. It's sprawling and includes some roads of very ordinary Victorian and Edwardian terraces. But it also includes Wimbledon Village, the most expensive and sought-after part of Merton, with a mix of Victorian cottages and large detached and semi-detached houses of all vintages from Victorian to modern. Lots of modern apartment blocks and new developments on Wimbledon Hill Road. Victorian and Edwardian family homes and huge detached houses in tree-lined roads off Parkside between Wimbledon Common and Wimbledon Park, with discreetly large gardens behind high walls or hedges. Some have panoramic views across the park towards London.

ATTRACTS *Families; first-time buyers; young professionals; people wanting more space for their money than they could get in Clapham or Fulham; Norwegians wanting to be near the Norwegian School* • **CONSERVATION AREAS** *North Wimbledon; Bathgate Road; Wimbledon Windmill; Wimbledon Hill Road; Vineyard Hill Road; Kenilworth Avenue; Leopold Road; Wimbledon Broadway; South Park Gardens* • **AVERAGE PRICES** *Flats: studio: £65,000-£105,000; 1-bed: £100,000-£170,000; 2-bed: £140,000-£250,000; 3-bed: £180,000-£400,000 Houses: 2-bed: £180,000-£250,000; 3-bed: £160,000-£400,000; 4-bed: £240,000+; 5-bed: £400,000+* • **AVERAGE RENTS (MONTHLY)** *Flats: studio: £600+; 1-bed: £700+; 2-bed: £1100+; 3-bed: £1650+ Houses: 2-bed: £1350+; 3-bed: £1500+; 4-bed: £1750+; 5-bed: £3000+.*

RAYNES PARK & SOUTH WIMBLEDON

The further north you go in Raynes Park the better it is because you're that bit nearer Wimbledon. Once you get north of Worple Road you can call it West Wimbledon. A mix of family houses on the hill up towards Wimbledon and smaller semis and Victorian semis near the railway line. Lots of semi-detached three- and four-bedroom 1930s houses in roads off Grands Drive further south, overlooking rather bleak, flat recreation grounds. Roads of small Edwardian terraces in the grid of streets off Kingston Road by Raynes Park station. The usual assortment of terraces and semis in small gardens is interrupted by Merton Park, an attractive mixture of Victorian cottages and villas laid out in the 1870s near the lovely Morden Hall Park.

ATTRACTS *Families; first-time buyers; people who can't afford Wimbledon* • **CONSERVATION AREAS** *West Wimbledon; Drax Avenue; Copse Hill; Durham Road; Lambton Road; Dunmore Road; Wool Road; John Innes Merton Hall Park; John Innes Wilton Crescent; Quintin Avenue and Richmond Avenue; Merton Hall Road* • **AVERAGE PRICES** *Flats: studio: £50,000-£55,000; 1-bed: £75,000-£90,000; 2-bed: £85,000-£130,000 Houses: 2-bed: £120,000-£200,000; 3-bed: £135,000+; 4-bed: £155,000+; 5-bed: up to £500,000* • **AVERAGE RENTS (MONTHLY)** *Flats: studio: £450-£500; 1-bed: £600-£650; 2-bed: £750+ Houses: 3-bed: £900-£1500; 4-bed: £1200-£2000; 5-bed: £1600-£3000.*

COLLIERS WOOD, MITCHAM & MORDEN

Mitcham is the cheapest of these three because there's no tube although prices will almost certainly rise when the Tramlink opens. The tube is the main attraction of Colliers Wood which has mostly streets of Victorian terraces and 1930s semis in various stages, many misguidedly "improved" and/or in need of painting, and council blocks. Worth looking at for reasonably cheap houses and conversion flats. Its supporters claim that it has a good community spirit. Mitcham has some attractive Victorian cottages in roads along the east side of the common and near the centre but this soon gives way to more suburbia and modern blocks. Much of Morden is occupied by the St Helier estate (see Sutton) which is good for small, cheap houses.

ATTRACTS *Loyal locals; first-time buyers; people who can't afford Tooting or Streatham* • **CONSERVATION AREAS** *Wandle Valley; Mitcham Cricket Green; Upper Morden* • **AVERAGE PRICES** *Flats: studio: £40,000-£50,000; 1-bed: £45,000-£60,000; 2-bed: £60,000-£70,000 Houses: 1-bed: £65,000-£70,000; 2-bed: £70,000-£85,000; 3-bed: £80,000-£130,000; 4-bed: £110,000-£140,000* • **AVERAGE RENTS (MONTHLY)** *Flats: studio: £380-£400; 1-bed: £450-£500; 2-bed: £550-£650 Houses: 2-bed: £500-£550; 3-bed: £650+; 4-bed: £700-£900.*

BEST POSTCODES

Not really an issue as most of the borough has Surrey postcodes. Wimbledon SW19 is a smart London postcode and better than West Wimbledon SW20.

AMENITIES

SCHOOLS★★★

Merton has a strange three-tiered system of primary (5-8), middle (9-13) and high school (13-19), which it pioneered in the late 1960s in the fond hope that everyone was going to follow suit. They didn't, and now that the national curriculum and key stage tests have been brought in, the unusual set-up is looking increasingly cumbersome. The council considered the future of its schools such a major issue that it convened a Citizens' Jury last year to make recommendations. The jury recommended a switch to simple primary and secondary schools. The council is now considering the recommendation and local response but the earliest any change will be implemented is September 2000. Possibly because of this structure, league table performance isn't as good as in other outer London boroughs, particularly at primary level. There is however, some of the most generous state pre-school provision anywhere in London as well as a good range of private nursery education and some excellent private secondary schools.

PRE-SCHOOL PROVISION *37 nursery classes in state primary or church schools (all Merton schools have nursery units); 55 private or voluntary nurseries and playgroups. Proportion of under-fives in state nurseries: 75%* • **STATE MIDDLE SCHOOLS** *Overall league table position: 86th out of 150. Top scorers: Wimbledon Chase, Wimbledon; Cranmer, Mitcham; Hill Cross, Morden* • **STATE HIGH SCHOOLS** *Overall league table position: 101st out of 150. Best scorers: Ursuline Convent RC (girls), Raynes Park; Ricards Lodge (girls), Wimbledon; Wimbledon College RC (boys), Wimbledon* • **PRIVATE PREP SCHOOLS** *Hazelhurst (girls to 16), Wimbledon; Kings College Junior School (boys), Wimbledon; The Study Prep (girls), Wimbledon*

● **PRIVATE SECONDARY SCHOOLS** *Wimbledon High (girls), Wimbledon; Kings College (boys), Wimbledon.*

TRANSPORT***

Wimbledon has an excellent train service and is on the District line for tubes. Elsewhere it's not so good. The Northern line extends to Morden and Colliers Wood although it's a long tedious journey to town. Mitcham is worst off, with no decent train or tube service less than a bus ride away. This should improve when the Tramlink is built, giving Mitcham a direct link to Wimbledon and Croydon and points beyond (see Croydon). Mitcham station is closed until the end of 1999 while building work on the Tramlink continues.

TRAINS Wimbledon: *Zone 3. Cost of annual season ticket: £860; No of trains per hour: to Waterloo every 2 minutes; Fastest journey: 14 minutes.* Mitcham Junction: *Zone 4. Cost of annual season ticket: £1068; No of trains per hour: to Blackfriars every 8 minutes; to Victoria 2; Thameslink: 2; Fastest journey: to Blackfriars 28 minutes; to Victoria 19 minutes; to London Bridge Thameslink 31 minutes.* Raynes Park: *Zone 4. No of trains per hour: to Waterloo every 3 minutes; Fastest journey: 15 minutes* ● **TUBES** Wimbledon: *Zone 3. Frequency: District: to Embankment every 5-6 minutes; Fastest journey: 30 minutes.* Morden: *Zone 4. Frequency: Northern line to Charing Cross every 5-6 minutes. Fastest journey: 30 minutes* ● **BUSES** *Wimbledon has the best bus service – many pass through and some terminate there. Elsewhere in the borough, there's a choice of just one or two buses, mostly linking neighbouring suburbs and the most central destinations are Streatham, Tooting or Brixton. The N155 nightbus goes from Trafalgar Square to Colliers Wood, Merton, South Wimbledon and Morden* ● **TRAFFIC BLACKSPOTS** *Wimbledon & Wimbledon Village: Heavy traffic including buses and delivery lorries in the centre of Wimbledon itself where none of the shopping streets are pedestrianised. Wimbledon Hill and Wimbledon Village have constant streams of cars and heavy lorries, rather spoiling the otherwise pleasant experience of eating al fresco in the Village. Merton High Street: Long tail-backs at the junction with Haydons Road and trafficky around the junction with the A24, which slices through Merton on its way to Sutton and beyond. Morden: The main shopping street in Morden, London Road, doubles as the A24 which is often jammed with traffic* ● **PARKING** *Currently only one controlled parking zone, in and around Wimbledon. But the council is consulting with residents about further zones around Colliers Wood and Morden, following complaints about unofficial park and riding. Plans by Wandsworth to implement controlled parking just within its border around St George's Hospital Tooting have led to fears that Colliers Wood will suffer as motorists look for the nearest unregulated parking. Cost of annual resident's permit: £27.50.*

LEISURE FACILITIES***

THEATRES & CONCERT HALLS *The recently revamped Wimbledon Theatre in an ornate Victorian building on the Broadway has a range of plays and family shows, as does the Polka Children's Theatre. The Colour House Theatre in a former industrial dye house at Merton Abbey Mills (see below) has more off-beat and fringe shows* ● **CINEMAS** *Currently only one, the Odeon in Wimbledon, showing mainstream films* ● **MUSEUMS & GALLERIES** *A fun selection of small specialist museums including the Wimbledon Lawn Tennis Museum relating the story of how tennis changed from a polite amateur*

*pitpat to 200 mile an hour service games. The Wimbledon Windmill Museum
on Wimbledon Common with exhibitions on the working of windmills
and the Wimbledon local history museum (only open on Saturdays). The
complex of former industrial buildings at Merton Abbey Mills, on the river
Wandle, which used to be a Liberty silk-printing mill, has a small exhibition
on the history of the river and its industries (William Morris rented
workshops here for printing his designs)* • **SPORTS FACILITIES** *Leisure centres
in Mitcham, Wimbledon and Morden – all with fitness centres, classes
and indoor sports. Pools at Mitcham, Morden and Wimbledon. Riding on
Wimbledon Common. Tennis, football, cricket and facilities for other team
games in parks and open spaces across the borough.* • **LIBRARIES** *Some of
the best used in London, well spaced around the borough. Opening hours
are reasonable. No one day when all the borough's libraries are closed,
although there's no Sunday opening. 10 library visits per head. Position in
library-use league table: 4th out of 32 (where 1 is best and 32 worst).*

OPEN SPACES * * * *

*A very good range of open spaces, including most of Wimbledon
Common, with its woods, open land and golf courses.*
RIVER WALKS *The Wandle Trail along the river Wandle through Merton
Abbey Mills and Morden Hall Park. A peaceful walk beside a (mostly) clear-
flowing river with reedy banks, overhanging trees and rows of electricity
pylons to remind you that you're really in a city. Morden Hall Park belongs
to the National Trust and has the usual craft and tea shops, carefully labelled
direction arrows and well-kept parkland overlooked by Morden Hall, a
handsome white stucco house built in 1770* • **WIDE OPEN SPACE** *Wimbledon
Park. Duller than the Common but with good views across London over
a landscaped lake and lawns designed by Capability Brown. Mitcham
Common, a large tract of open heathland* • **WOODS** *Wimbledon Common.
As well as extensive open spaces, there are plentiful walks up and down
hills through mature woods where you feel 100 miles from London.*

SHOPS * * *

WIMBLEDON & WIMBLEDON VILLAGE *The best shopping areas in the borough.
The Centre Court shopping centre right next to Wimbledon station has
several storeys of mostly up-market chains (particularly clothes shops) and a
large Debenhams. Less overwhelming than Croydon or even Sutton. More
good branches of chain stores in streets around the shopping centre although
crossing the road's a hassle because none of it is pedestrianised and the
pavements are crowded. There are plans for new shops and leisure facilities
in the town centre as an added incentive for people to travel to Wimbledon
by Tramlink. The shops get smaller and more specialist (furniture, antiques,
designer clothes and shoes) up Wimbledon Hill Road and into Wimbledon
Village. Safeway and Sainsbury's* • **MITCHAM** *Dull parades of local shops.
The usual selection of take-aways, newsagents, charity shops and branches
of banks and building societies* • **MERTON & COLLIERS WOOD** *More dreary
high streets with empty shops to let, take-aways and hardware shops. Tesco
in Colliers Wood. But Merton has Merton Abbey Mills, with craft shops, a
second-hand bookshop and weekend antique market all housed in carefully
restored former industrial buildings. Sainsbury's Savacentre at Merton and
retail park at Colliers Wood with Boots and Next* • **MORDEN** *An ugly, busy
shopping street (aka the A24) lined with charity shops, greasy take-aways,
predictable chains and lots of shops to let. Bleak and dominated by the
grim curving tower block of the town hall and civic centre.*

RESTAURANTS * * *

WIMBLEDON & WIMBLEDON VILLAGE *Every yuppie restaurant and bar chain in the book in Wimbledon Village including Dome, Cafe Rouge, Pitcher and Piano and All Bar One (down the hill towards Wimbledon) as well as a selection of local brasseries and restaurants. Most have tables outside for a touch of café society. A bit predictable if you want something out of the ordinary but pleasant. A good Indian in Wimbledon Hill Road and a couple of good winebars in Wimbledon itself* ● **ELSEWHERE** *Nothing special. An assortment of variable ethnic (read the usual Indian and Chinese restaurants, burger bars and fast food joints).*

CRIME RATES * * * *

96 crimes per 1000 of population. Position in Metropolitan Police league table: 22nd out of 32 (where 1 is worst and 32 best).

THE COUNCIL * * *

POLITICAL AFFILIATION *Labour* ● **MINUS POINTS** *Complex school system which no longer fits in with National Curriculum. Has had big problems with rubbish collections over the past year* ● **PLUS POINTS** *Couldn't be quicker at turning round land searches* ● **PROPERTY SEARCHES IN 10 WORKING DAYS** ● *100%* ● **STANDARD SEARCH FEE** *£105* ● **COUNCIL TAX COLLECTED** *94%*
● **COUNCIL TAX 1998-99**

BAND	PROPERTY VALUE	CHARGE	BAND	PROPERTY VALUE	CHARGE
A	up to £40,000	£498.27	E	£88,001-£120,000	£913.51
B	£40,001-£52,000	£581.31	F	£120,001-£160,000	£1,079.59
C	£52,001-£68,000	£664.37	G	£160,001-£320,000	£1,245.68
D	£68,001-£88,000	£747.41	H	over £320,000	£1,494.82

NEWHAM

"Where's Newham?" is the first question many people, including Londoners, ask. And with some justification. Even its most fervent supporters wouldn't call it architecturally exciting. It has few obvious attractions to draw people into the borough and being out in the hinterland of the old docks to the east puts it beyond the pale for many who refuse to venture further from the centre of town than Canary Wharf.

This is the part of the East End tourists don't see. It stretches from the traffic-clogged roads and tangled railway lines of Stratford east across to the suburbs of Forest Gate and Manor Park, criss-crossed with mind-boggling miles of straight, flat streets lined with late Victorian and 1930s terraces. Slightly to the south, the larger double-fronted Victorian houses of Woodgrange Park temporarily relieve the architectural tedium which takes over again throughout much of East Ham, West Ham and Plaistow. To the south around the old Royal Docks, brash new homes are springing up around Beckton, east of the council sprawls of Canning Town and Custom House. Almost forgotten, sandwiched between the docks and the river is the Victorian huddle of North Woolwich.

The only leagues headed by Newham are deprivation leagues. It is ranked as the most severely deprived district in England. Levels of unemployment at 11.7% are the third highest in London.

So far it has seen little of the frenzied growth and yuppification of the neighbouring Isle of Dogs to the west. But Newham could be the place to be in the next few years. Massive sums of government money are pouring into regeneration schemes across the borough, hard hit by the decline of the docks and the traditional manufacturing industry. The money is intended to improve transport links and infrastructure, cut crime and improve education and employment chances.

The chief beneficiary is Stratford, with a huge new £15 million glass station for the Jubilee line, new bus station and a £3 million refurbishment of its shopping centre as well as a new performing arts centre and a new Safeway. It's still hoping to be the major London interchange for the Channel Tunnel Rail Link (a key reason for the government spending) but don't hold your breath. Canning Town is also having £100 million spent on it over the next six years including a new station for the Jubilee line extension. There are plans for a huge exhibition centre, a business park and a campus for the University of East London down at the Royal Docks.

All this coupled with some of the cheapest property in London is already making Newham popular with people working in the city who value quick transport to town. The borough is also one of the most multicultural in London with almost half of its inhabitants from ethnic minorities. Much of the colour and interest that Newham does have is created by the large Asian and Afro-Caribbean communities.

PROPERTY AND ARCHITECTURE

STRATFORD

Grim tower blocks and crumbling 1960s office blocks predominate around the bus and rail stations, giving way to roads of mostly two-storey Victorian terraces off the confluence of main roads where traffic permanently clogs Stratford. Check out roads near the station off West Ham Lane and Romford Road for reasonably-priced two bedroom houses near good transport links. Larger five bedroom Victorian houses further up Romford Road are mostly rented out or converted into flats. Some of the best properties (large Victorian family houses) are around West Ham Park to the east. Prices are rising because of regeneration but by the same token a lot of the centre is a building site.

ATTRACTS *Growing numbers of young, up-market people working in the City; bargain hunters; lawyers working in the nearby courts wanting pieds-à-terre; first-time buyers; investors* • **CONSERVATION AREAS** *University; Three Mills* • **AVERAGE PRICES** *Flats: studio: £30,000-£35,000; 1-bed: £36,000-£40,000; 2-bed: £45,000-£50,000; 3-bed: £50,000+ Houses: 2-bed: £60,000-£65,000; 3-bed: £75,000+; 4-bed: £90,000+* • **AVERAGE RENTS (MONTHLY)** *Flats: studio: £430; 1-bed: £480; 2-bed: £540; 3-bed: £585 Houses: 2-bed: £560; 3-bed: £650; 4-bed: £780; 5-bed: £860.*

FOREST GATE & UPTON

North of the Forest Gate and Woodgrange Park railway line, roads of Victorian and 1930s terraces stretch out in every direction, their monotony broken up only by "improvements" wrought by successive home owners (louvred windows, pebble-dash and elaborate front doors). Good cheap house- and flat-buying territory. Much larger and more attractive Victorian houses are south of the railway line and west of Woodgrange Road in what's known as the Woodgrange Estate. Many are detached and double-fronted with large front gardens. This together with Capel Road, opposite Wanstead Flats (in Redbridge) is widely considered one of the best parts of Newham. More terraces to the south at Upton, mostly with two and three bedrooms.

ATTRACTS *First-time buyers; people wanting a lot of space for their money; members of the Asian community (Upton and Upton Park)* • **CONSERVATION AREAS** *Woodgrange; Capel Road and City of London Cemetery (planned)* • **AVERAGE PRICES** *Flats: 1-bed: £35,000-£50,000; 2-bed: £45,000-£55,000 Houses: 2-bed: £55,000-£65,000; 3-bed: £60,000-£90,000; 4-bed: £75,000-£150,000; 5-bed: £120,000+* • **AVERAGE RENTS (MONTHLY)** *Flats: studio: £325-£360; 1-bed: £410-£455; 2-bed: £500-£540 Houses: 2-bed: £540-£585; 3-bed: £600-£670; 4-bed: £700-£740.*

MANOR PARK & EAST HAM

Larger three- and four-bedroom Victorian and 1930s properties in East Ham on the Burges estate to the east of High Street North and also on the Central Park estate around East Ham Central Park to the west, both sought-after areas. Elsewhere in East Ham mostly Victorian terraces and 1930s terraces and semis. East Ham is slightly grander than Manor Park, which has mostly smaller two-storey Victorian terraces, many "improved" for better or worse in straight tree-lined streets, with the occasional struggling corner shop or small parade of shops to break the pattern.

ATTRACTS *First-time buyers; members of the Asian community (particularly Manor Park); people who can't afford Hackney or Tower Hamlets* • **CONSERVATION AREA** *Durham Road* • **AVERAGE PRICES** *Flats: studio: £30,000-£34,000; 1-bed: £35,000-£45,000; 2-bed: £45,000-£55,000 Houses: 2-bed: £55,000-£65,000; 3-bed: £60,000-£90,000; 4-bed: £75,000-£95,000* • **AVERAGE RENTS (MONTHLY)** *Flats: studio: £390; 1-bed: £410-£500; 2-bed: £520-£560 Houses: 2-bed: £560-£600; 3-bed: £600-£695; 4-bed: £800-£860; 5-bed: £1,112.*

PLAISTOW & WEST HAM

Two-storey, two- and three-bedroom Victorian terraces predominate in Plaistow, although there is a handful of newly-built blocks of purpose-built flats. The best areas are to the north in roads around West Ham Park. A number of new estates in West Ham, mostly built on former industrial sites. Ubiquitous roads of two- and three-bedroom terraces around the tube station (now grandly upgraded to receive the Jubilee line).

ATTRACTS *First-time buyers; city workers wanting good transport; loyal locals; members of the African and Afro-Caribbean communities* • **CONSERVATION AREA** *None* • **AVERAGE PRICES** *Flats: 1-bed: £30,000-£40,000; 2-bed: £40,000-£50,000 Houses: 2-bed: £55,000-£60,000; 3-bed: £65,000-£75,000; 4-bed: £80,000+* • **AVERAGE RENTS (MONTHLY)** *Flats: studio: £325-£370; 1-bed: £410-£455; 2-bed: £500-£540 Houses: 2-bed: £540-£585; 3-bed: £600-£670; 4-bed: £700-£735.*

BECKTON & SILVERTOWN

Almost entirely new housing here around the docks on the site of the old gas works. Beckton is the last part of Docklands to be regenerated and the process is still very much ongoing, giving the area a somewhat bleak feel. Despite this, properties are more expensive than other parts of the borough because they're modern, with none being more than 10 years old. Mostly two- and three-bedroom houses on modern estates with some four-bedroom houses. There are plans for an ambitious urban village at Silvertown with more than 1,000 new private- and housing-association-owned homes, a new primary schools, shops, restaurants and a community centre. If you long for Victoriana down here, head for the riverside enclave of North Woolwich which has some two-bedroom Victorian terraces and cottages by Royal Victoria Gardens.
ATTRACTS *Second-time buyers wanting to trade up to houses; watersports enthusiasts (on the nearby docks); investors wanting to rent out their properties* • **CONSERVATION AREAS** *Bargehouse Road, North Woolwich (planned)* • **AVERAGE PRICES** *Flats: studio: £35,000-£50,000; 1-bed: £40,000-£50,000; 2-bed: £65,000-£70,000 Houses: 2-bed: £60,000-£70,000; 3-bed: £75,000-£90,000; 4-bed: £80,000-£100,000*
• **AVERAGE RENTS (MONTHLY)** *Flats: studio: £410; 1-bed: £410; 2-bed: £520 Houses: 2-bed: £585; 3-bed: £695; 4-bed: £800.*

BEST POSTCODES

Postcodes are not a big issue in a borough where price differences between areas are minimal. But in descending order of preference, the best postcodes are East Ham E6, Stratford E15 and Forest Gate E7.

AMENITIES

SCHOOLS*

Historically poor performance in league tables particularly at primary level. But the borough is pulling itself up by its bootstraps and recently received glowing reports from Ofsted for refusing to let poverty and language difficulties stand in the way of achievement. Unfortunately these accolades have yet to make themselves felt in primary school performance which is currently the worst in London. There is an above-average proportion of under-fives in nursery school. No private prep or secondary schools.
PRE-SCHOOL PROVISION *1 community nursery; 8 state nursery schools; 48 nursery classes in state primary or church schools; 52 private and voluntary nurseries and playgroups. Proportion of under-fives in state nurseries: 66%*
• **STATE PRIMARY SCHOOLS** *Overall league table position: 149th out of 150. Top scorers: St Michael's RC, East Ham; St Antony's RC (with nursery unit), Forest Gate; Roman Road, East Ham* • **STATE SECONDARY SCHOOLS** *Overall league table position: 123rd out of 150. High scorers: St Angela's Ursuline Convent (girls), Forest Gate; St Bonaventure's RC (boys) Forest Gate, Plashet School (girls), East Ham.*

TRANSPORT****

Much improved in the west and south of the borough following the arrival of the Docklands Light Railway at Beckton, Custom House, and Stratford, and set to improve further when the Jubilee line opens. Central, District and Hammersmith and City line tubes run to the west and middle of the borough but further north and east it's trains only.

TRAINS Stratford: *Zone 3. Cost of annual season ticket: £860; No of trains per hour: to Liverpool St every 2-6 minutes in rush hour (fewer off-peak and weekends); North London line every 15 minutes peak; Fastest journey: to Liverpool St 9 minutes.* Forest Gate & Manor Park: *Zone 3. No of trains per hour: to Liverpool St every 2-6 minutes peak; Fastest journey: to Forest Gate 13 minutes; to Manor Park 15 minutes.* Silvertown & West Ham: *Zone 3. No of trains per hour: North London line: every 15 minutes* •
TUBES Stratford: *Frequency: Central line to Oxford Circus: every 2-6 minutes; Fastest journey: 20 minutes.* East Ham: *Zone 3. Frequency: District to Embankment: every 4-5 minutes; Fastest journey: 32 minutes.* Hammersmith and City: *to Liverpool St: every 8-10 minutes; Fastest journey: 20 minutes*
• **DOCKLANDS LIGHT RAILWAY** Stratford: *Frequency: to Canary Wharf every 8 minutes. Fastest journey: 10 minutes.* Beckton: *Zone 4. Cost of annual season ticket: £1068. Frequency: to Tower Gateway every 12 minutes. Fastest journey: 28 minutes.* • **BUSES** *Mostly suburban services and trafficky roads across most of the borough can mean long journeys. Services to town include the 25 from Ilford to Oxford Circus via Manor Park, Forest Gate and Stratford; the 15B from East Ham to Aldgate; and the 15 from Canning Town or East Ham to Paddington* • **AIRPORT** *London City Airport at the Royal Docks* • **TRAFFIC BLACKSPOTS** *The junction of High Street South, East Ham and the A13: Single lane traffic leads to long south-bound delays. Road widening to three lanes planned as part of a series of improvements along the A13. The area around Stratford shopping centre: Lots of main roads meet here and there can be long waits at junctions. Romford Road at the junction with High Street North, East Ham: Many cars take shortcuts through residential Salisbury Road, making it a rat-run. Streets around West Ham United's ground off Green Street Upton Park on match days are also trafficky* • **PARKING** *Controlled parking zones in East Ham around the station and in Stratford town centre. Cost of annual resident's permit: free for one car, £30 for two, £50 for three.*

LEISURE FACILITIES**

THEATRES & CONCERT HALLS *The Theatre Royal Stratford has recently been refurbished and offers new plays and musicals. A £13.7 million Performing Arts Centre providing theatre-training and facilities is set to open next year. This and the theatre will form a new cultural quarter for Stratford. Live music at the Rex, a recently-converted cinema in Stratford* • **CINEMAS** *The new Stratford Picture House (part of Stratford's regeneration programme) next to the shopping centre has art films as well as more mainstream offerings. Asian films at the Boleyn on the corner of Green Street and Barking Road. The Showcase at Beckton shows mostly blockbusters* • **MUSEUMS & STATELY HOMES** *Thin on the ground. The North Woolwich Old Station Museum for railway buffs is housed in an old Victorian station building, its well-looked-after exterior a sad contrast to the shabbiness of the rest of the area. Elsewhere, local history at the Manor Park Museum* • **SPORTS FACILITIES** *Three indoor leisure centres including two in Plaistow and the new Atherton leisure centre in Stratford. All with fitness centres and pools. Another leisure centre is planned on the site of the old baths at East Ham for the year 2000 with three pools, sports hall, badminton court and café. Water sports (including water-skiing and jet-ski on the water at the Royal Docks where an international rowing centre is also planned). Dry ski slope at Beckton.*
• **LIBRARIES** *Improving with the help of regeneration money. The largest lending and reference libraries are at Stratford (in a wonderful Victorian building with moulded ceilings) and East Ham. East Ham recently broke*

out of the London-wide downward spiral of library opening times by opening seven days a week. New library at Beckton and another planned for Stratford. Library system under-used with only 6 visits per head. Place in library-use league table: 24th out of 32 (where 1 is best and 32 worst).

OPEN SPACES * * *

Short on open space generally. Small parks and open spaces dotted around the borough have a slightly municipal feel although they're generally tidy and cared for. Cemeteries including the large City of London in Manor Park provide attractive space to walk in. But fascinating walks along the footpaths of the tangle of rivers and canals south of Stratford do a lot to make up for lack of greenery.

LARGE (-ISH) GREEN SPACE *City of London cemetery, the only space in the borough big enough to get lost in although it's duller, and less gothickly Victorian than others like Highgate or Nunhead* • **CHILDREN** *Newham City Farm, Custom House; Plashet Park and Zoo; Nature Reserve, East Ham with nature trail and museum by walled church graveyard* • **LONG FOOTPATHS** *The Greenway, a path running literally over the top of the main Northern outfall sewer carrying London's sewage from West Ham to East Ham via Plaistow. Excellent views of people's back gardens and the remnants of the East End's industrial past* • **CANALS** *The Bow Back Rivers, a network of once-busy industrial rivers and canals, now abandoned and peaceful. At a confluence in the network is the restored Three Mills mill, once used to grind corn for breweries and now converted to offices behind the preserved exterior.*

SHOPS * *

STRATFORD *The 1960s concrete shopping centre is being overhauled and there are inside market stalls selling clothes, jewellery, leather goods and food. But mostly uninspiring chain stores both within the shopping centre itself and around. Sainsbury's superstore. New Safeways planned* • **GREEN STREET** *This is the place to come for all things Indian. Sari and silk shops, jewellery shops, bakeries selling fresh bhajis and sickly Indian sweets, market stalls in Queen Street market selling fruit, vegetables and Asian and African goods. Currently a grim 1960s building but due for a face-lift. The most colourful and interesting shopping street in Newham. Tescos by Upton Park station* • **EAST HAM** *Pedestrianised shopping street at High Street North, with mostly chain stores and a covered market. Tends towards small branches with cheap stock. Sainsbury's* • **ELSEWHERE** *Forest Gate: mostly local shops including new and second-hand furniture shops and a Somerfields near Forest Gate station. Local shops in Romford Road. West Ham and Plaistow: local shops. Beckton: large Asda and Savacentre, part of a complex of three new retail centres. Across the borough: small corner shops, often Asian-run, selling groceries, newspapers and second-hand goods.*

RESTAURANTS * *

FOREST GATE *Good Indian restaurants around Green Street* • **STRATFORD** *A handful of cafés including The Courtyard in the Courtyard of the old town hall building. A cybercafé, pubs and the occasional winebar, all symbols of regeneration. But café society, it's not quite yet* • **ELSEWHERE** *Plentiful ethnic restaurants and take-aways of varying quality.*

CRIME RATES**

148 crimes per 1000 of the population. Position in Metropolitan Police league table: 10th out of 32 (where 1 is worst and 32 best).

THE COUNCIL***

POLITICAL AFFILIATION Labour • **MINUS POINTS** The second slowest borough in London for property searches. One of the poorest at collecting council tax, needed for essential services • **PLUS POINTS** Not complacent about its problems. One of the first to set up an Education Action Zone to raise standards and get results. Has also started a "Listening Council" exercise to gauge the opinion of residents. The first council to launch a door-to-door recycling service. Energetic support for regeneration initiatives • **PROPERTY SEARCHES CARRIED OUT WITHIN 10 WORKING DAYS** 59% • **STANDARD SEARCH FEE** £85 • **COUNCIL TAX COLLECTED** 81%

• **COUNCIL TAX 1998-99**

BAND	PROPERTY VALUE	CHARGE	BAND	PROPERTY VALUE	CHARGE
A	up to £40,000	£453.00	E	£88,001-£120,000	£830.50
B	£40,001-£52,000	£528.50	F	£120,001-£160,000	£981.50
C	£52,001-£68,000	£604.00	G	£160,001-£320,000	£1,132.50
D	£68,001-£88,000	£679.50	H	over £320,000	£1,359.00

REDBRIDGE

By rights, Redbridge should be pretty smart. It has its fair share of well-to-do and wealthy suburbs and good transport links, it's on the edge of the green belt with Epping Forest on its doorstep, its schools are good (it even has grammar schools) and until the last local elections had been a bastion of Conservatism. But its problem is that it's East London, not west, or even south. It borders on Essex, still trying to live down its barrow boy reputation. It's the home of the aspirational and self-made, those who grew up in the University of Life in the East End and moved to Redbridge when they made good. And however much government planners talk about the renewal of the east and Thames gateways, Londoners obstinately rate the West higher than the East as a place to live.

But for those who can overcome such snobbery, property is cheaper, the commute to the city and beyond is quick and escape to the country easy. The downside is that the borough's shopping is often dull and/or depressing and the miles of small Victorian terraces in the less salubrious areas get you down pretty quickly. Redbridge's territory stretches from the Victorian and Edwardian terraces of Ilford, the borough's main adminstrative and shopping centre, to the meaner workmens' terraces of Seven Kings and Goodmayes. North of Ilford are the larger Edwardian and interwar semis of Gants Hill and tucked into the borough's northern border on the edge of the green belt, the council houses of Hainault. To the west, around Woodford and down into Wanstead it's a different world, of large detached and semi-detached houses and handsome Victorian terraces in tree-lined streets.

As a staging post on many a journey out of the East End to the suburbs and beyond, Redbridge is a mix of many cultures, with significant Asian and Jewish communities. Just over a fifth of its population is from an ethnic minority, in stark contrast to surrounding boroughs to the east (see Barking and Dagenham and Havering) which are predominantly white. Mosques, synagogues and shops selling exotic spicy foods add a much needed dash of colour.

This isn't a borough with the huge unemployment problems of some parts of inner London (unemployment stands at 4.6%, lower than most of its neighbours) but equally it lacks the sleek prosperity of some of the richest commuter suburbs. The arrival of the Channel Tunnel rail link at Stratford just along the railway line to the west of Ilford would give the south of the borough a much needed boost but successive governments have prevaricated for so long that most people have lost hope that the London stretches of the line will ever be built (see Newham and Camden).

PROPERTY AND ARCHITECTURE

ILFORD

Ilford developed as a Victorian railway suburb and roads of Victorian, Edwardian and 1920s terraces spread away from the town centre either side of the railway line. North of the tracks, on the posher side, the houses are larger, some with ornate metal-trellissed porches. Many were turned into flats before the council clamped down on conversions. But the once-handsome houses are grievously defaced by some truly horrible "improvements" – fake stained glass and modern windows and ill-fitting front doors abound and there's hardly a house left in its original state. Grids of small bay-windowed and flat-fronted terraces south of the tracks off Ilford Lane. In a neat twist, roads named to recall Victorian imperial triumphs – Bengal Road, Madras Road – are now lived in by Asians. Some of the best houses in Ilford are in the enclave of roads between Valentines Park and Cranbrook Road on the Garden City estate.

ATTRACTS *Families, loyal locals, local first-time buyers* • **CONSERVATION AREAS** *Valentines Park & Mansion* • **AVERAGE PRICES** *Flats: studio: £40,000; 1-bed: £45,000; 2-bed: £65,000 Houses: 2-bed: £60,000-£80,000; 3-bed: £80,000-£100,000+; 4-bed: £90,000-£130,000; 5-bed: £180,000+* • **AVERAGE RENTS (MONTHLY)** *Flats: studio: £350+; 1-bed: £430; 2-bed: £520 Houses: 2-bed: £580; 3-bed: £600+; 4-bed: £650+; 5-bed: £780.*

SEVEN KINGS & GOODMAYES

More down-market than Ilford and generally the shabbiest parts of the borough. More roads and grids of small Victorian terraces in Seven Kings, built as a "people's suburb" to house workers travelling to town on the Great Eastern Railway. Goodmayes has its share of Victorian speculative building but to relieve the tedium, roads to the south of Green Lane are lined with larger Edwardian terraces and 1930s bungalows, many with original features intact. Bungalows may not be that thrilling but here they're a welcome change. The easternmost corner of Goodmayes is the beginning of the massive Becontree council estate (see Barking and Dagenham). Some good house bargains to be had.

ATTRACTS *Families; members of the Asian community (especially Seven Kings)* • **CONSERVATION AREAS** *Mayfield (Seven Kings bungalow estate)* • **AVERAGE PRICES** *Flats: studio: £33,000; 1-bed: £45,000+; 2-bed: £50,000+ Houses: 3-bed: £85,000; 4-bed: £100,000* • **AVERAGE RENTS (MONTHLY)** *Flats: studio: £350+; 1-bed: £430; 2-bed: £520 Houses: 2-bed: £530; 3-bed: £600+; 4-bed: £650+.*

GANTS HILL & CLAYHALL

Gants Hill grew up around the new roads being laid in the borough in the 1920s and has mostly middling and large 1920s and 1930s semis, many sporting timber-framed gables, diamond-paned windows and other "country" touches. Larger houses in more expensive Clayhall, with some of the most sought-after roads off Longwood Gardens, in the catchment area for good local schools and known as the Woods estate because all the roads have "wood" in their name. Gants Hill is home to most of the borough's Jewish community, one of the largest in London. Mostly houses rather than flats in Clayhall. Flats and houses in Gants Hill.

ATTRACTS *Families; members of the Jewish community; professionals* • **CONSERVATION AREAS** *Barnadoes Village Homes; Little Heath* • **AVERAGE PRICES** *Flats: 1-bed: £50,000-£55,000; 2-bed: £65,000 Houses: 3-bed: £105,000-£140,000; 4-bed: £170,000-£200,000; 5-bed: £175,000-£250,000* • **AVERAGE RENTS (MONTHLY)** *Flats: 1-bed: £430+; 2-bed: £520+ Houses: 2-bed: £580; 3-bed: £600+; 4-bed: £650+; 5-bed: £780+.*

HAINAULT

A wonderful setting on the edge of Hainault Forest Country Park and green belt land for a council estate of houses made up of corrugated iron sheeting which wouldn't look out of place as garden sheds. To be fair the houses were flung up as temporary accommodation during the post-war housing shortage. The estate is gradually being rebuilt in red brick, a big improvement. Lots have been sold to tenants under the Right-to-Buy scheme and are coming on to the market again. Some ex-council bargains here, mostly three-bedroom houses. Better to the west of Fencepiece Road, with larger private houses on the Tudor estate (the group of roads including Wolsey, Aragon and Boleyn Roads). No small houses.

ATTRACTS *Locals; people needing cheap houses; families* • **CONSERVATION AREAS** *None* • **AVERAGE PRICES** *Flats: studio: £40,000; 1-bed: £50,000; 2-bed: £55,000 Houses: 3-bed: £65,000 (ex-council)-£120,000; 4-bed: £140,000* • **AVERAGE RENTS (MONTHLY)** *Flats: studio: £345; 1-bed: £390-£430; 2-bed: £475 Houses: 2-bed: £540+; 3-bed: £560+; 4-bed: £600.*

WOODFORD & SOUTH WOODFORD

One of the best parts of the borough. Roads on the ridge where London stops and Essex begins are lined with huge houses boasting the full panoply of half-timbering, diamond-paned windows, several wings (useful for the personal workout room). This is where the unashamedly nouveau riche live. Large, well looked after detached Edwardian and 1930s houses in tree-lined roads around Woodford and Woodford Green, with a handful of roads of Victorian cottages around the green itself. Some of the best roads are around Monkhams Avenue and Monkhams Drive. South Woodford has a mixture of good Edwardian terraces and 1930s houses and more flats than Woodford.

ATTRACTS *Barrow boys made good; families; young professionals; City workers* • **CONSERVATION AREAS** *Woodford Bridge; Woodford Wells; Woodford Green; Woodford Broadway; South Woodford; George Lane* • **AVERAGE PRICES** *Flats: 1-bed: £50,000-£55,000; 2-bed: £65,000 Houses: 2-bed: £85,000+; 3-bed: £110,000+; 4-bed: £160,000+; 5-bed: £200,000+* • **AVERAGE RENTS (MONTHLY)** *Flats: studio: £350-£500; 1-bed: £500-£700; 2-bed: £550-£850 Houses: 2-bed: £700-£900; 3-bed: £850-£1300; 4-bed: £1000-£2000; 5-bed: £1500-£2500.*

WANSTEAD

Another of Redbridge's most classy areas. Lots of large handsome Victorian houses, some now converted into flats. Prices depend on a whole lot of factors important to its middle class population, including proximity to tubes and the best parts of Wanstead High Street and inclusion in school catchment areas. Large houses on the Firs Estate, snuggling up to Epping Forest (see Waltham Forest) are sought after. Not many first-time buyer bargains here.

ATTRACTS *Young professionals; City people; the upwardly-mobile from Ilford and points east* • **CONSERVATION AREAS** *Snaresbrook; Wanstead Village; Wanstead Park* • **AVERAGE PRICES** *Flats: 1-bed: £65,000-£75,000; 2-bed: £70,000-£80,000 Houses: 2-bed: £105,000-£140,000; 3-bed: £145,000-£250,000; 4-bed: £250,000+; 5-bed: £320,000+* • **AVERAGE RENTS (MONTHLY)** *Flats: studio: £350-£500; 1-bed: £500-£700; 2-bed: £550-£850 Houses: 2-bed: £700-£900; 3-bed: £850-£1300; 4-bed: £1000-£2000; 5-bed: £1500-£2500.*

BEST POSTCODES

Most of Redbridge is outside the London postcode area. Of the parts that aren't, Woodford E18 is probably better than Leytonstone E11 (which includes Wanstead but also parts of dreary Leytonstone). But both are fairly obscure codes to most Londoners and prices depend far more on closeness to shops and transport and inclusion in school catchment areas.

AMENITIES

SCHOOLS***

Great performance in secondary school league tables, thanks mainly to the borough's two remaining selective grammar schools and a number of independent schools. Overall performance at primary level is much less spectacular. Possibly this has something to do with parents' reports that many people are so desperate to get their children through the borough's tests for the grammar schools that they opt for one of a growing number of private prep schools specialising in cramming for the exam. The grammar schools are very oversubscribed and admission depends on being in the right catchment area as well as results. Below-average provision for under-fives in state nursery schools.

PRE-SCHOOL PROVISION 37 nursery classes in state primary and church schools; 81 private day nurseries and playgroups, including Christian and Jewish. Proportion of under-fives in state nurseries: 48% • **STATE PRIMARY SCHOOLS** Overall position in league tables: 48th out of 150. Top scorers: Wanstead C of E, Wanstead; Our Lady of Lourdes RC (with nursery unit), Wanstead; St Peter and St Paul's RC, Ilford • **STATE SECONDARY SCHOOLS** Overall position in league tables: 10th out of 150. Top scorers: Woodford County High (girls, selective), Woodford Green; Ilford County High (boys, selective), Ilford; King Solomon High School (mixed), Barkingside • **PRIVATE PREP SCHOOLS** Woodford Green Prep (mixed), Woodford Green; St Aubyn's (mixed from 3), Woodford Green; Gleanarm College (mixed from 3); Ilford • **PRIVATE SECONDARY SCHOOLS** Chart topper Bancrofts' (mixed), Woodford Green; Cranbrook College (boys), Ilford; Park (girls), Ilford; Ilford Ursuline High (girls), Ilford.

TRANSPORT***

Well spaced throughout the borough. The south (Ilford, Seven Kings and Goodmayes) has a fairly reliable service to Liverpool Street. The north of the borough has the distinctive eastern loop of the central line which has been going through a bad patch recently but should improve when signalling problems are ironed out.

TRAINS Ilford: Zone 4. Cost of annual season ticket: £1068; No of trains per hour: to Liverpool Street every 10 minutes; Fastest journey: 13 minutes. Goodmayes: Zone 4. No of trains per hour: to Liverpool Street every 10 minutes; Fastest journey: 18 minutes • **TUBES** Wanstead: Zone 4. Frequency: Central to Oxford Circus every 10 minutes; Fastest journey: 24 minutes. Woodford: Zone 4. Frequency: Central to Oxford Circus: every 10 minutes; Fastest journey: 28 minutes • **BUSES** Buses into town exist (the main service is the 25 from Ilford via Aldgate to Oxford Circus) but the journey can be slow and frustrating. Other buses mainly join shopping centres or neighbouring suburbs. Night buses include the N8 from Trafalgar Square to Woodford and Gants Hill and the N50 from Trafalgar Square to Ilford • **TRAFFIC BLACKSPOTS** Wanstead: The M11 which currently ends around the junction with the north circular road at South Woodford is being extended to Leytonstone and Hackney and roadworks lead to long traffic jams on roads into town particularly in the mornings. When it's completed, the M11 should improve the speed of journeys to Stratford (for international rail links if they ever materialise). Ilford: Pedestrianised shopping streets mean that all the traffic is forced on to surrounding roads around the station and Cranbrook Road • **PARKING** Currently there's only one parking zone in the borough, around South Woodford shopping centre. Cost of annual resident's permit: £20 for the first car; £30 for a subsequent car.

LEISURE FACILITIES***

THEATRES & CONCERT HALLS The Kenneth More theatre in Ilford has mainstream plays by local theatre companies, musicals and opera. Concerts at Ilford's wonderfully florid Victorian town hall, local churches and Ilford's oldest building, the medieval hospital chapel of St Mary and St Thomas of Canterbury • **CINEMAS** Two, the Ilford Odeon and the Woodford ABC, both showing mainstream films. There will be even more screens in Ilford if a new multiplex cinema is built as part of a leisure complex • **MUSEUMS & GALLERIES** Sadly devoid of any museums at present but there are plans for an interesting-sounding interactive local history museum in the Central Library in Ilford • **SPORTS FACILITIES** Well provided for. Three leisure centres in Ilford, Wanstead and Redbridge with gyms, weights and indoor tennis at Redbridge. Pools at Barkingside and Ilford. Athletics ground at Ilford and tennis, football and other outdoor sports in parks around the borough. Watersports and riding at Fairlop Waters, a lake created on a former gravel plain, surrounded by green belt land. Golf on public courses at Fairlop and Hainault. Discount leisure pass system in operation • **LIBRARIES** Well used and well resourced with an upgraded computer system set to be installed this year (1999). Handsome central library in Ilford. Generally long opening hours particularly in the central library but respectable elsewhere. No general closing day (apart from Sunday). 9.6 library visits per head. Position in library-use league table: 6th out of 32 (where 1 is best and 32 worst).

OPEN SPACES * * * *

Lots of it and there are even excellent views from the northern ridge of the borough just before it turns into Essex (a surprise for those who think Essex is flat). Much of the north-east corner is rural, with mostly open fields. **PARKS** Valentines Park. The borough's largest park, in Ilford, with two lakes and lots of lush green open space with mature trees. Once the grounds of Valentines Mansion, a 17th century mansion still standing but sadly neglected after having outlived its usefulness as council offices. Its future has become something of a cause célèbre in Ilford after a bid to turn it into a pub failed. One possibility is an arts centre • **WIDE OPEN SPACE & VIEWS** Hainault Forest Country Park. Sloping meadows and woods surrounded by green belt land. A haven for wildlife. Easy to forget you're in London (albeit on the very edge). Excellent views from the top of Dog Kennel Hill, Redbridge's highest point • **RIVER WALKS** The Roding runs down the west side of the borough from Ray Park to Ilford with the pleasantest parts meandering through Wanstead Park. Further north by the M11, access to the river is being improved and previously contaminated land by the river landscaped as part of a £9 million regeneration scheme in the surrounding area over the next five years (see also Barking and Dagenham).

SHOPS * * *

ILFORD The main shopping area. Mostly chains in the town's indoor shopping mall, the Exchange, built five years ago, and in the neighbouring pedestrianised shopping streets. Longstanding residents blame the shopping centre for sucking the life out of the rest of the town, which appears to be borne out by Cranbrook Road, once the smartest part of Ilford with four department stores, but now shabby and run-down, with lots of empty shops. But Ilford Lane partly makes up for it with a whole street of Asian supermarkets and shops selling glittering fabrics and saris. Sainsbury's in Ilford • **GOODMAYES** Where to come if you want to buy a used car, as every other shop is a second-hand car sales showroom. Otherwise, Asian supermarkets, furniture shops and more empty shops. Tesco • **GANTS HILL & BARKINGSIDE** A couple of kosher food shops at Gants Hill but otherwise the usual collection of take-aways, supermarkets and banks in parades round a busy roundabout by the tube station. More shops at Barkingside, useful rather than beautiful. Tesco and Sainsbury's at Barkingside • **WOODFORD & WANSTEAD** Much more up-market small shops along the Broadway in Woodford Green with patisseries, delis, a real butcher, and art and jewellery shops among others. Somerfields. Wanstead *also has good shops in an attractive Edwardian High street. Chains and local shops in South Woodford. Sainsbury's.*

RESTAURANTS★★

A recommended bagel bakery in Gants Hill and a popular Chinese restaurant in Ilford but apart from that mostly local restaurants with the familiar choice of Chinese, Indian, Italian and Greek of varying quality. Winebar country in South Woodford and Wanstead.

CRIME RATES★★★★

81 crimes per 1000 of the population. Position in Metropolitan Police league table: 25th out of 32 (where 1 is worst and 32 best).

THE COUNCIL★★★

POLITICAL AFFILIATION *No overall control* • **MINUS POINTS** *Recovering from years of rather sleepy Tory control during which inefficiencies crept in, according to residents* • **PLUS POINTS** *Excellent secondary schools. The lowest fees in London for property searches and quick turnaround. Door-to-door recycling scheme started in 1995 and now covering half the borough. Generally efficient rubbish collection* • **PROPERTY SEARCHES CARRIED OUT IN 10 WORKING DAYS** 100% • **STANDARD SEARCH FEE** £75
• **COUNCIL TAX COLLECTED** 95.6%
• **COUNCIL TAX 1998-99**

BAND	PROPERTY VALUE	CHARGE	BAND	PROPERTY VALUE	CHARGE
A	up to £40,000	£450.67	E	£88,001-£120,000	£826.22
B	£40,001-£52,000	£525.78	F	£120,001-£160,000	£976.44
C	£52,001-£68,000	£600.89	G	£160,001-£320,000	£1,126.67
D	£68,001-£88,000	£676.00	H	over £320,000	£1,352.00

RICHMOND UPON THAMES

If Richmond doesn't feel much like London this could be because much of it technically isn't London at all but Surrey or Middlesex. The borough is one of the greenest in the capital, including within its boundaries Kew Gardens, Richmond Park and Hampton Court Park, to name but three, as well as eighteenth and nineteenth century cottages, narrow lanes, towpaths and duckponds which wouldn't be out of place in far more rural areas than Surrey, let alone London.

The Thames both divides and links the different areas of the borough, one of the most sprawling in London. In the north the large Victorian houses of Castlenau give way to the small cottages and winding high street of Barnes village, self-contained in a deep bend of the river. In the next bend to the west lies Kew, another village made famous by the floral displays and greenhouses of the

Royal Botanic Gardens. Past the large Edwardian homes of East Sheen, the even grander houses of Richmond Hill occupy a commanding position overlooking the river at the edge of Richmond Park. Around Hampton Court Park and Bushy Park to the south are the Victorian houses and cottages of Teddington, Hampton Wick and Hampton Village, giving way to inter-war suburbia at Whitton and Hampton.

Richmond is one of the most thriving boroughs in London. Unemployment is the lowest in the capital at 2.6 per cent. Its good transport links, schools and open spaces are a magnet for professional families who commute to town every day, and those who work in the borough tend to be white collar office workers or self-employed people running their own businesses. Only 5 per cent of Richmond's population comes from an ethnic minority, the third lowest in the whole of Greater London.

One major blot on the landscape is the ever-present noise of jumbo jets coming in to land at Heathrow Airport to the west. The noise affects residents of Barnes, Kew, Sheen, Richmond, St Margarets and Twickenham and there is growing local concern over the outcome of the long-running inquiry into the building of a fifth terminal at Heathrow. Residents fear that a fifth terminal will increase noise and traffic congestion and reject the claims of the British Airports Authority that noise levels have already improved and that only a small number of people will be affected. Richmond Borough Council has been active in campaigning against Terminal Five.

Hammersmith Bridge, normally the umbilical link between Barnes and Hammersmith's shops and transport, has been closed for the past two years but is now set to open again after initial uncertainty that it ever would. The closure divided local opinion. Some residents loved the traffic-free roads as motorists drove to Putney or Chiswick. But traders wanted the bridge open to bring back business.

PROPERTY AND ARCHITECTURE

BARNES

An expensive enclave with handsome Victorian family homes in roads around Barnes Common and Castelnau and Lonsdale Roads to the north of the High Street. Large regency houses facing the river are lovely but suffer constant traffic noise. There are smaller early Victorian cottages in roads off the High Street and around the pond on Barnes Green. Multi-coloured cottages in roads off Whitehart Lane (known as Little Chelsea) are some of the smartest.

ATTRACTS *Families with children; arty, media and intellectual types. Prides itself on its community atmosphere to the extent that it has been accused of insularity. Also popular with residents from overseas, particularly Swedes wanting to be near the Swedish school in Barnes* • **CONSERVATION AREAS**

Barnes Green; Castelnau; Mill Hill; Barnes Common; Thorne Passage; Whitehart Lane • **AVERAGE PRICES** *Flats: 1-bed: £80,000-£150,000; 2-bed: £110,000-£250,000; 3-bed: £250,000 Houses: 2-bed: £130,000-£275,000; 3-bed: £250,000-£400,000; 4-bed: £400,000+; 5-bed: £500,000+* • **AVERAGE RENTS (MONTHLY)** *Flats: studio: £600; 1-bed: £850-£1300; 2-bed: £900-£2500; 3-bed: £1300-£2800 Houses: 2-bed: £1000-£2500; 3-bed: £1200-£2500; 4-bed: £1500-£3500; 5-bed: £3000+.*

EAST SHEEN & MORTLAKE

Small Victorian cottages and Victorian terraces in roads north and south of the railway line at Mortlake with larger houses in First and Second Avenue. The trafficky south circular at Upper Richmond Road splits East Sheen in two and the best properties are well away from the main road to the south near Richmond Park in Fife Road and surrounding streets. Big gardens and lots of space in a mixture of Edwardian and 1930s properties in this area, known as Parkside. Smaller mostly 1930s properties to the north of the south circular.

ATTRACTS *Families looking for green space and good schools (often refugees from more urban Fulham and Chelsea); the glitterati* • **CONSERVATION AREAS** *Mortlake; Mortlake Green; Queen's Road; Model Cottages; East Sheen Avenue; Christchurch Road* • **AVERAGE PRICES** *Flats: studio: £70,000+; 1-bed: £80,000-£90,000; 2-bed: £130,000-£150,000; 3-bed: £160,000-£180,000 Houses: 2-bed: £170,000-£200,000; 3-bed: £190,000-£250,000; 4-bed: £300,000+; 5-bed: £500,000+* • **AVERAGE RENTS (MONTHLY)** *Flats: studio: £550-£800; 1-bed: £700-£1000; 2-bed: £800-£2200; 3-bed: £900-£2400; 4-bed: £1200-£3000 Houses: 2-bed: £1000-£2300; 3-bed: £1200-£2400; 4-bed: £1800-£3250; 5-bed: £2600-£10,000.*

KEW

Large amounts of modern purpose-built blocks appeared among the Georgian and Queen Anne gems after the area was heavily bombed during the war. Large Victorian family houses in the best roads including Litchfield and Broomfield Roads just opposite Kew Gardens and a mixture of property from Queen Anne to modern around Kew Green at the north tip of Kew Gardens. Cheaper properties, mostly 1930s to the east in North Sheen including some ex-council although the three-bedroom Edwardian houses in roads off Lower Richmond Road near the cemetery are becoming gentrified.

ATTRACTS *Families; young professionals; a substantial contingent from the arts and the media; loyal locals* • **CONSERVATION AREAS** *Kew Green; Royal Botanic Gardens; Old Deer Park; Kew Gardens; Lawn Crescent; Kew Road; Kew Foot Road* • **AVERAGE PRICES** *Flats: studio: £70,000+; 1-bed: £80,000-£150,000; 2-bed: £120,000-£250,000; 3-bed: £185,000+ Houses: 2-bed: £165,000-£250,000; 3-bed: £225,000-£350,000; 4-bed: £300,000-£375,000; 5-bed: £400,000+* • **AVERAGE RENTS (MONTHLY)** *Flats: studio: £700; 1-bed: £750-£800; 2-bed: £1000-£1200; 3-bed: £1350 Houses: 2-bed: £1250-£1300; 3-bed: £1500-£1800; 4-bed: £2000+; 5-bed: £2500.*

RICHMOND & ST MARGARETS

Richmond has everything from conversion flats and period cottages in roads off Sheen Road to some of London's most beautiful Georgian houses around Richmond Green and along Richmond Hill. Richmond Hill also has some of the best large Victorian houses in the area. On the other side of the river, slightly cheaper and more suburban St Margaret's has substantial mansion blocks fronting the river and large Victorian and Edwardian family homes in roads behind. The most sought-after properties in St Margaret's are in roads backing on to the Trust Grounds by the river.

ATTRACTS *Families wanting green space, shops and schools; young professionals wanting easy access to town and shops; overseas residents relocated by their companies; Germans to be near the German school at Petersham* • **CONSERVATION AREAS** *Richmond Green; Central Richmond; St Margarets; Richmond Riverside; Richmond Hill; Richmond Park* • **AVERAGE PRICES** *Flats: studio: £70,000+; 1-bed: £85,000-£130,000; 2-bed: £150,000-£330,000; 3-bed: £180,000-£270,000; 4-bed: £380,000+ Houses: 2-bed: £180,000-£220,000; 3-bed: £250,000-£300,000; 4-bed: £380,000-£500,000; 5-bed: £500,000+* • **AVERAGE RENTS (MONTHLY)** *Flats: studio: £600; 1-bed: £800+; 2-bed: £950-£1500; 3-bed: £1300+; 4-bed: £1600+ Houses: 2-bed: 1000+; 3-bed: £1300-£2000; 4-bed: £2000+; 5-bed: £2000+.*

TWICKENHAM & STRAWBERRY HILL

More famous as a rugby ground than a residential area, Twickenham is mostly late Victorian interspersed with 1930s properties. Less exciting architecturally than Richmond but it can still boast some Georgian gems in East Twickenham around Marble Hill. More expensive Strawberry Hill is leafily suburban with a mixture of Victorian, Edwardian and interwar houses. Look for first-time buyer flats above shops in the high street or in conversions around the centre of Twickenham.

ATTRACTS *Young professionals working in town; families with young children wanting good schools* • **CONSERVATION AREAS** *Twickenham Riverside; Cambridge Park; Queens Road Twickenham; Amyard Park Road* • **AVERAGE PRICES** *Flats: studio: £50,000-£60,000; 1-bed: £75,000-£120,000; 2-bed: £90,000-£150,000; 3-bed: £100,000-£160,000 Houses: 1-bed: £85,000-£110,000; 2-bed: £120,000-£200,000; 3-bed: £130,000-£250,000; 4-bed: £180,000-£500,000* • **AVERAGE RENTS (MONTHLY)** *Flats: studio: £400-£550; 1-bed: £600; 2-bed: £750+; 3-bed: £900+ Houses: 1-bed: £575+; 2-bed: £750-£900; 3-bed: £1000-£1200; 4-bed: £1300-£1500.*

HAM & PETERSHAM

The poshest houses are in Petersham which is set in beautiful meadows running down to the river and has Victorian cottages and larger Georgian and Victorian family houses. Expect to pay Richmond prices, especially in roads near Richmond Park. If you're looking for cheap property near Richmond or Kingston try Ham for ex-council properties on the Ashburnham Estate west of Ham Street towards the river or in the 1960s Wates estate in roads opposite Ham Common. Distance from a station is a disadvantage of the area.

ATTRACTS *First-time buyers (Ham); actors and glitterati (Petersham); families; Germans wanting to be near the German school at Petersham* • **CONSERVATION AREAS** *Ham Common; Ham House; Petersham* • **AVERAGE PRICES** *Flats: 1-bed: £60,000-£90,000; 2-bed: £70,000-£110,000*

Houses: 2-bed: £90,000-£165,000; 3-bed: £130,000-£275,000; 4-bed: £200,000-£450,000; 5-bed: £350,000+ • **AVERAGE RENTS (MONTHLY)** *Flats: studio: £450-£550; 1-bed: £600-£700; 2-bed: £750-£1200; 3-bed: £900-£1500 Houses: 1-bed: £650-£750; 2-bed: £800-£1200; 3-bed: £900-£1500; 4-bed: £1400-£3500; 5-bed: £2000+.*

TEDDINGTON & THE HAMPTONS

Grouped round Bushy Park and Hampton Court Park in the south of the borough. Mostly Victorian properties in Teddington and Hampton Wick, the most desirable and expensive parts of this area, with riverfront properties in Teddington commanding premium prices. Look for first-time buyer flats in roads round Teddington Station. A cheaper mix of Victorian, interwar and modern property at Hampton Hill, further from good shops and train services. Some handsome family houses in roads around Hampton Station in the area known as Hampton Village but to the west Hampton turns flat and boringly suburban. **ATTRACTS** *Families wanting good schools, easy access to the City and a quiet life* • **CONSERVATION AREAS** *Teddington Lock; Park Road; Normansfield; Hampton Village; Hampton Court Park; Hampton Court Green; Hampton Wick; Bushy Park* • **AVERAGE PRICES** *Flats: studio: £50,000-£55,000; 1-bed: £75,000-£90,000; 2-bed: £95,000-£250,000; 3-bed: £125,000+ Houses: 2-bed: £125,000-£200,000; 3-bed: £150,000-£230,000; 4-bed: £200,000-£400,000; 5-bed: £300,000+* • **AVERAGE RENTS (MONTHLY)** *Flats: studio: £450-£500; 1-bed: £650; 2-bed: £750-£800; 3-bed: £1000 Houses: 2-bed: £950; 3-bed: £1200; 4-bed: £1400+; 5-bed: £2,500.*

WHITTON

The cheapest part of Richmond with a variety of mostly 1930s detached, semi-detached and terraced houses. Victorian cottages round Colonial Road and Whitton Dean. Prices are held down by the main Chertsey Road which carves through the middle of the area. **ATTRACTS** *People who can't afford Twickenham; families wanting to be in Richmond rather than Hounslow for the schools* • **CONSERVATION AREAS** *None* • **AVERAGE PRICES** *Flats: studio: £55,000; 1-bed: £65,000-£75,000; 2-bed: £75,000-£95,000; 3-bed: £95,000 Houses: 2-bed: £95,000+; 3-bed: £110,000-£200,000; 4-bed: £200,000-£240,000* • **AVERAGE RENTS (MONTHLY)** *Flats: studio: £500; 1-bed: £550-£575; 2-bed: £650-£675 Houses: 1-bed: £575-£600; 2-bed: £700-£725; 3-bed: £750-£775; 4-bed: £900+.*

BEST POSTCODES

Not a burning issue in a borough where more than half the area is outside London. Of the areas that are in London Barnes SW13 is generally considered better than Mortlake SW14, although the latter contains East Sheen Parkside where properties easily compete with Barnes for grandeur.

AMENITIES

SCHOOLS * * * *

State schools are widely praised and sought-after by residents. Consistently high performance in league tables particularly at primary level. A slight drop-off at state secondary school level, possibly due to excellent private provision. Below average number of state nurseries; expect to pay for children up to four years old.

PRE-SCHOOL PROVISION 15 nursery classes in state primary or church schools; 1 state nursery school; 3 under-fives centres; 102 private and voluntary nurseries and playgroups. Proportion of under-fives in state nurseries: 47%

• **STATE PRIMARY SCHOOLS** Overall league table position: 3rd out of 150. High scorers: St James RC (with nursery unit), Twickenham; St Mary's C of E, Twickenham; St Elizabeth's RC, Richmond • **STATE SECONDARY SCHOOLS** Overall league table position: 29th out of 150. Good scorers: Waldegrave (girls), Twickenham; Teddington School (mixed), Teddington; Grey Court (mixed), Ham • **PRIVATE PREP SCHOOLS** Colet Court (St Paul's Prep), Barnes; Harrodian School (mixed), Barnes; Tower House (boys), Sheen; Denmead (boys), Hampton; Twickenham prep (mixed); Mall (boys), Twickenham; Newland House (mixed), Twickenham; St Catherine's RC (boys 3-5, girls 3-16), Twickenham; Kings House (boys), Richmond; Old Vicarage (girls), Richmond; Unicorn (mixed), Kew • **SECONDARY SCHOOLS** Include chart-topper and academic powerhouse St Paul's Boys, Barnes; Hampton (boys); Lady Eleanor Holles (girls), Hampton; the Royal Ballet School (mixed), Richmond.

TRANSPORT***

Choice of tube (District line) or rail at Richmond and Kew; rail only in the rest of the borough. Fast and frequent services to Richmond; less so to some other parts.

TRAINS Barnes: Zone 3. Cost of annual season ticket: £860; No of trains per hour: Barnes Bridge to Waterloo 2; Barnes to Waterloo 4; Fastest journey: Barnes 13 minutes; Barnes Bridge 22 minutes. Mortlake: Zone 3. No of trains per hour: to Waterloo 4; Fastest journey 20 minutes. Kew: Zone 3. No of trains per hour: Kew Bridge to Waterloo 2; Kew Gardens (North London line) 3; Fastest journey: to Waterloo 25 minutes. Richmond: Zone 4. Cost of annual season ticket: £1068; No of trains per hour: to Waterloo 6; North London line 3; Fastest journey: to Waterloo 17 minutes. Twickenham: Zone 5. Cost of annual season ticket: £1280; No of trains per hour: to Waterloo 6; Fastest journey 22 minutes. Teddington: Zone 6. Cost of annual season ticket: £1396; No of trains per hour: to Waterloo 4; Fastest journey: 32 minutes. Hampton: Zone 6. No of trains per hour: to Waterloo 2; Fastest journey: 39 minutes. Whitton: Zone 5. No of trains per hour: to Waterloo 2; Fastest journey: 27 minutes • **TUBES** Richmond: Frequency: District: every 9-11 minutes; Fastest journey: to Embankment 32 minutes. Kew Gardens: Frequency: District: every 9-11 minutes; Fastest journey: to Embankment 30 minutes • **BUSES** Mostly suburban services, many infrequent, particularly to points south of Richmond. No buses direct to the centre of town. Services include: the 391 from Richmond to West Kensington and Fulham Broadway; the 726 from Hampton to Heathrow Airport; the 33 from Fulwell to Hammersmith; the 415 (days only, limited stops) from Guildford to Victoria via Ham, Petersham, Richmond and North Sheen • **BOATS** Passenger boats from Westminster to Kew, Richmond and Hampton Court; from Richmond Pier to Kingston, Hampton Court, Kew and Teddington Lock. Foot ferries at Twickenham (Marble Hill to Ham House) and Hampton • **TRAFFIC BLACKSPOTS** Upper Richmond Road (south circular): Clogged with traffic most of the way from Mortlake to Richmond with Sheen bearing the brunt. Chiswick Bridge: Suffering extra traffic as commuters try to find way round long term closure of Hammersmith Bridge. This should ease with the reopening of the bridge later this year. King Street and Richmond Road, Twickenham: Long queues particularly during *rush hour and at the end of the school day as cars, buses and lorries mix with shoppers and pedestrians* • **PARKING** There are controlled parking zones in: North Barnes: *Around Church Road. New zone around Castelnau to stop commuters parking then walking over Hammersmith Bridge. Cost of annual resident's parking permit: up to £50.* Richmond Town Centre: *Controlled parking zone throughout with strict wardens. Cost of annual resident's parking permit: up to £60.* Twickenham *(central, east and south),* St Margaret:. *Cost of annual resident's parking permit: up to £50.* Hampton Court: *Cost of annual resident's parking permit: £75.*

LEISURE FACILITIES ★ ★ ★ ★

THEATRES & CONCERT HALLS *Richmond has two well-supported theatres. The Orange Tree moved from cramped premises in the Orange Tree pub to a modern theatre in 1991 and performs obscure classics and new plays. Richmond Theatre in an elaborate Victorian building on Richmond Green offers opera, comedy shows and pantomime although it's been struggling financially. In Twickenham there is the Mary Wallace theatre, home to Richmond Shakespeare Society. Open-air riverside jazz at Barnes. Open-air concerts at Kew and evening concerts at Marble Hill* • **CINEMAS** *Three in Richmond, including Richmond Filmhouse showing arty & unusual films and the Odeon showing mostly blockbusters* • **MUSEUMS & STATELY HOMES** *One of the best-endowed boroughs, scattered with reminders that the area was long a favoured country seat of royals and aristocrats. Hampton Court Palace in Hampton Court Park. Tudor palace built for Cardinal Wolsey and extended by Henry VIII with famous maze, galleries and state apartments. Kew Palace bought by George III (currently being renovated). Also Queen Charlotte's cottage in the grounds of Kew Gardens. Riverside stately homes include the 17th century Ham House and Marble Hill House* • **SPORTS FACILITIES** *Three borough-run sports centres at East Sheen, Teddington and Whitton with gyms and indoor sports facilites; indoor pools at Teddington and Richmond Park; outdoor pool at Hampton; golf at Richmond, Strawberry Hill, Twickenham and Fulwell (West Teddington); riding in Richmond Park; rugby at Twickenham. Discount leisure card system in operation* • **LIBRARIES** *Well-equipped and helpful main library and community information centre at Richmond. Reasonable opening hours at all branch libraries (closed on Thursdays). Libraries quite well used with 8 visits per head. Position in library-use league table: 14th out of 32 (where 1 is best and 32 worst).*

OPEN SPACES ★ ★ ★ ★ ★

Brilliant, in a word. Four large, beautiful and interesting parks including Richmond Park (with deer), the Royal Botanic Gardens at Kew, Hampton Court Park and the lower profile but still lovely Bushy Park, as well as delightful commons and riverside meadows.

GOOD VIEWS OVER LONDON *Richmond Park. A huge undulating swathe of green with woods, grassland and gardens (there are particularly attractive gardens at Isabella Plantation). Excellent views over London and Surrey. A haven for horses and riders as well as the resident deer* • **RIVERSIDE WALKS** *The Thames Path on both sides of the river through Ham Riverside and Petersham Meadows up to Richmond. Tree-lined river, cattle-grazing – you don't feel anwhere near London* • **GARDENS** *Kew Gardens. The famous glasshouses contain enough exotic plants to keep the most ardent enthusiast happy and there is plenty of space for peaceful walks down to the river.*

SHOPS****

BARNES *Villagey high street of small local shops including a butcher, cheese shop and kitchen shop, as well as a handy supermarket. Useful branches of banks and building societies as well as (of course) estate agents. Waitrose and Safeway in Upper Richmond Road (Sheen)* • **MORTLAKE & SHEEN** *Interesting shops in Sheen Lane beyond the level crossing including a second-hand bookshop, brasseries, cafés and antique shops. Duller but more practical shops around the corner in Upper Richmond Road which has all the usual chain stores including late-night opening* • **KEW** *Interesting shops around the station reflecting eclectic population – a good bookshop, health food shop and antique shop. Supermarkets at Upper Richmond Road. Out-of-town-style shopping at Kew Retail Park* • **RICHMOND** *A middle class mecca and natural home for Tesco Metro, Habitat and the Disney shop as well as long-standing stores like Dickens and Jones. Good for buying clothes, books and presents – check out the narrow streets leading to Richmond Green. Some older residents complain of a lack of practical shops. Antique shops on Richmond Hill. Waitrose in the town centre* • **TWICKENHAM** *Fairly dull Victorian high street lined mainly with chain stores and a couple of furniture shops. Church Street which winds down to the river has more individual shops* • **TEDDINGTON** *More up-market than Twickenham with a Liberty's, smart furniture and brassware shops as well as the usual chain stores including Tesco and late-night opening convenience store* • **OTHER AREAS** *Parades or streets of mainly local shops in Hampton Hill, Hampton Village, Hampton Wick (some interesting shops), Ham and Whitton. Shopping centre at Nurserylands (Hampton).*

RESTAURANTS***

RICHMOND *A good choice including Chinese, Indonesian, French, Italian and Spanish as well as branches of the usual chains (Pizza Express, burger bars). Pubs by the river* • **TWICKENHAM** *Usual line-up of pubs, Indian restaurants and take-aways and a good fish restaurant* • **TEDDINGTON & HAMPTON** *A range of locally popular wine bars and restaurants plus recommended French restaurant in Hampton Hill* • **ELSEWHERE** *Nothing of note.*

CRIME RATES****

81 crimes per 1000 of population. Position in Metropolitan Police league table: 27th out of 32 (where 1 is worst and 32 best).

THE COUNCIL***

POLITICAL AFFILIATION *Liberal Democrat* • **MINUS POINTS** *Reports of uneven litter control and street-sweeping in some areas including the tow-path along the river. Recently faced criticism over its handling of contracts with private rubbish collectors.* • **PLUS POINTS** *Excellent primary schools. Improved house-to-house rubbish collection after initial glitches with private contractors. Fortnightly collection of newspaper for recycling with planned extension to cans and bottles* • **PROPERTY SEARCHES CARRIED OUT WITHIN 10 WORKING DAYS** *92%* • **STANDARD SEARCH FEE** *£110* • **COUNCIL TAX COLLECTED** *97%*
• **COUNCIL TAX 1998-99**

BAND	PROPERTY VALUE	CHARGE	BAND	PROPERTY VALUE	CHARGE
A	up to £40,000	£508.17	E	£88,001-£120,000	£931.64
B	£40,001-£52,000	£592.86	F	£120,001-£160,000	£1,101.03
C	£52,001-£68,000	£677.56	G	£160,001-£320,000	£1,270.42
D	£68,001-£88,000	£762.25	H	over £320,000	£1,524.50

SOUTHWARK

Most people have set foot in Southwark at some time in their lives even if they haven't realised it. Anyone commuting across London Bridge or Tower Bridge to the City in the morning, walking along the river to one of the pubs or restaurants springing up along the South Bank or sizing up the new modern art gallery taking shape at the old Bankside power station has been to Southwark.

But so have those who've been to the attractive park, village and art gallery at Dulwich in the leafy south London suburbs. For after stretching widely along the river from the Oxo Tower in the west as far as the council blocks and loft conversions of former industrial and docks areas of Bermondsey and Rotherhithe to the east, Southwark plunges south.

It reaches down through the concrete nightmare of the Elephant and Castle roundabout to the mainly Victorian suburbs of Peckham and Camberwell, now finding a new lease of life after years blighted by 1960s planners, poverty and racial tension. Between Peckham and Dulwich lie the Victorian terraces of East Dulwich and Nunhead. West of Dulwich are the roads of larger, Victorian terraces and semis of Herne Hill and at the very southern tip the leafy village of Dulwich with mansions overshadowing cottages and 1930s semis.

Despite Dulwich, however, Southwark is the second most deprived borough in the country. A total of 10.9% of its workforce is unemployed, the fifth highest in London.

Until fairly recently, many people would have greeted the idea of living anywhere in Southwark (except Dulwich) with a shudder, equating most of it with poor transport links, high crime and tatty shops. But the promise of the Jubilee line extension with stations at Bermondsey and Canada Water has put the developments around the old Surrey Docks on the map after a slow start. At the same time Southwark is energetically promoting its section of riverfront as "the new South Bank" and "south London's answer to Covent Garden". It has won £12 million in lottery and government grants for improvements to the riverfront, a new river pier and a Millennium Bridge linking St Pauls with the Bankside Gallery and the Globe Theatre. The river's former warehouses around London Bridge, Tower Bridge and Bermondsey have been converted into lofts and studios, colonised by yuppies, artists, photographers and people running small hi-tech businesses.

Further south, £260 million over seven years is being poured into Peckham, demolishing loathed tower blocks, installing CCTV to cut crime and improving training and job opportunities. At the same time Camberwell is starting to get serious attention from intrepid people discovering the area's stock of big, still affordable Georgian and Victorian houses a short bus ride away from town and the vibrancy of its multiracial community. A quarter of Southwark's population is from an ethnic minority, with significant communities of Afro-Caribbeans, West Africans, Turkish and Vietnamese.

PROPERTY AND ARCHITECTURE

BERMONDSEY & ROTHERHITHE

For years an almost forgotten corner of London after the closure of the Surrey Docks but rejuvenated by the prospect of the Jubilee line and new trendy restaurants and shops around Shad Thames, east of Tower Bridge. Almost all the homes are new in more expensive Rotherhithe around the old dock basins. Bermondsey's still a tangle of grim council estates and old warehouses not yet turned into Manhattan-style lofts. But plenty have been converted, either into live/work units or just massive apartments. Check out streets off Southwark Park Road for small Victorian cottages.

ATTRACTS *First-time buyers; creative types who want studio space near town; watersports enthusiasts; young professionals; loyal locals (Bermondsey)*
• **CONSERVATION AREAS** St Mary's, Rotherhithe; Wilson Grove; St Saviours Dock • **AVERAGE PRICES** *Flats: studio: £40,000-£70,000+; 1-bed: £55,000-£110,000; 2-bed: £70,000-£190,000; 3-bed: £80,000-£220,000 Houses: 1-bed: £60,000-£80,000; 2-bed: £85,000-£115,000; 3-bed: £105,000-£220,000 •* **AVERAGE RENTS (MONTHLY)** *Flats: studio: £520-£650; 1-bed: £520-£670; 2-bed: £650-£1120; 3-bed: £900-£1300; 4-bed: £1080-£1300 Houses: 1-bed: £650; 2-bed: £650-£1120; 3-bed: £900-£1300; 4-bed: £1080-£1300.*

BOROUGH, ELEPHANT & CASTLE

The oldest part of Southwark, stretching down from London Bridge. Cobbled streets and warehouses by the river. A mix of streets and squares of Georgian and Victorian terraces among the council blocks around the Elephant and Castle roundabout near the Imperial War Museum and behind the Inner London Crown Court (including the beautiful Trinity Church and Merrick Squares, a Georgian treat in the surrounding sea of council blocks). Streets of small mainly Victorian terraces off the Walworth Road (some ex-council coming up for resale) near East Street market.

ATTRACTS *First-time buyers (especially Walworth); loyal locals; some professionals; creative types (Borough); people who can't afford Kennington* • **CONSERVATION AREAS** Trinity Church Square; West Square; Borough High Street; Thrale Street; Bear Gardens; Pages Walk; Sutherland Square • **AVERAGE PRICES** *Flats: studio: £45,000+; 1-bed: £60,000+; 2-bed: £70,000+; 3-bed: £85,000+ Houses: 2-bed: £100,000+; 3-bed: £120,000+; 4-bed+: £150,000+ •* **AVERAGE RENTS (MONTHLY)** *Flats: studio: £550-£650; 1-bed: £700-£850; 2-bed: £850-£1100; 3-bed: £1300-£1500 Houses: 2-bed: £850-£1100; 3-bed: £1300-£1500; 4-bed: £1500-£2000.*

CAMBERWELL

Getting trendier by the minute and may be lining up to be the next Brixton. One or two almost perfect terraces of four-storey Georgian houses in Camberwell Grove and Grove Lane near Camberwell Green as well as the

Georgian Addington Square just off the busy Camberwell Road. Elsewhere three- and four-storey Victorian houses in roads off Coldharbour Lane on the way to Brixton and some Victorian survivors mixed up with council blocks and hospital buildings at the top of Grove Lane and roads off.

ATTRACTS *First-time buyers; professional and creative people who like the idea of living "on the front line"; students who can afford not to live in Peckham* • **CONSERVATION AREAS** *Addington Square; Camberwell Green; Camberwell Grove; Sceaux Gardens* • **AVERAGE PRICES** *Flats: studio: £40,000; 1-bed: £55,000-£70,000; 2-bed: £65,000-£150,000; 3-bed: £75,000-£150,000 Houses: 2-bed: £110,000-£220,000; 3-bed: £125,000-£300,000; 4-bed: £160,000-£450,000; 5-bed+ £200,000-£550,000* • **AVERAGE RENTS (MONTHLY)** *Flats: studio: £500+; 1-bed: £650; 2-bed: £700-£900; 3-bed: £950 Houses: 2-bed: £950; 3-bed: £1200; 4-bed: £1300; 5-bed+: £1400.*

PECKHAM & NUNHEAD

Some of the worst tower blocks in Peckham are being pulled down and replaced with new street level houses but still not a place everyone wants to walk around at night. The best surprises in Peckham are further south in roads off Rye Lane, where there are early Victorian houses with gardens. This whole area is part of the Bellenden Renewal Area, a ten year council project to improve housing and the environment. Large four-bedroom Victorian houses overlooking Peckham Rye Common and Park. Mostly two- and three-bedroom Victorian terraces around Nunhead, the posher face of Peckham, with the best in roads around the cemetery.

ATTRACTS *People who can't afford Camberwell or East Dulwich; first-time buyers; families (Nunhead)* • **CONSERVATION AREAS** *Holly Grove; Nunhead Cemetery* • **AVERAGE PRICES** *Flats: studio: £30,000; 1-bed: £45,000; 2-bed: £60,000+; 3-bed: £70,000+ Houses: 2-bed: £85,000; 3-bed: £95,000; 4-bed: £145,000* • **AVERAGE RENTS (MONTHLY)** *Flats: studio: £400; 1-bed: £500+; 2-bed: £650; 3-bed: £750 Houses: 2-bed: £750; 3-bed: £950; 4-bed: £1100.*

EAST DULWICH

Traditionally the poor relation of Dulwich proper but some claim that East Dulwich is now appealing to people in its own right and becoming positively "buzzy" in the words of one resident. Where Dulwich residents come for more interesting nightlife. Mostly three-bedroom Victorian terraces in roads off Lordship Lane with larger four- and five-storey Victorian terraces overlooking the slightly trafficky Goose Green and Peckham Rye Common.

ATTRACTS *People who want Dulwich without the smugness; first-time buyers; professionals* • **CONSERVATION AREA** *The Gardens* • **AVERAGE PRICES** *Flats: studio: £35,000-£40,000; 1-bed: £55,000-£65,000; 2-bed: £70,000+; 3-bed: £75,000+ Houses: 2-bed: £110,000-£125,000; 3-bed: £120,000-£175,000; 4-bed: £140,000-£200,000; 5-bed+: £175,000+* • **AVERAGE RENTS (MONTHLY)** *Flats: studio: £400-£450; 1-bed: £450-£550; 2-bed: £550-£650; 3-bed: £650-£800 Houses: 2-bed: £700-£850; 3-bed: £800-£1000; 4-bed: £1100-£1200.*

DULWICH

Green, leafy and expensive. Detached Victorian and Edwardian properties with crunchy gravel drives and well-cared-for gardens, substantial 1920s and 1930s homes and some modern property in roads leading off and up to Dulwich Village. Mostly modern properties in roads east of Dulwich Woods. One or two handsome Georgian mansions just south of the Village near the park. The Dulwich College Estate still owns most of Dulwich and has strict rules about what residents can and can't do with their properties which has led to run-ins with some residents. Roads of mostly substantial Victorian and Edwardian terraces interspersed with 1920s semis in neighbouring Herne Hill, some converted into flats.

ATTRACTS *Families keen on green space and good schools* • **CONSERVATION AREAS** *Dulwich Village; Dulwich Woods* • **AVERAGE PRICES** *Flats: 1-bed: £70,000-£90,000; 2-bed: 85,000-£150,000; 3-bed: £140,000+ Houses: 2-bed: £175,000-£225,000; 3-bed: £185,000-£325,000; 4-bed: £275,000-£375,000; 5-bed+ £300,000-£750,000* • **AVERAGE RENTS (MONTHLY)** *Flats: 1-bed: £475-£500; 2-bed: £675+; 3-bed: £950-£1000 Houses: 2-bed: £900+; 3-bed: £1000+; 4-bed: £1200-£1800; 5-bed+: £2000+.*

BEST POSTCODES

Dulwich SE21 wins hands-down, with East Dulwich SE22 and Herne Hill SE24 tying for second place as long as the roads are in the parts near Dulwich. Roads near the border with SE21 have prices to match, with roads at the other side of SE22 near Peckham reflecting much lower prices there. It's the same story with roads in the west of SE24 next to Brixton (see Lambeth).

AMENITIES

SCHOOLS**

State schools are consistently near the bottom of the league tables at primary level. Performance is marginally better at secondary level, possibly due to good numbers of private schools in the borough, which go some way towards redeeming the borough's performance. Above-average proportion of children with places in state nurseries.

PRE-SCHOOL PROVISION *5 state nurseries; 47 nursery classes in state primary or church schools; 96 private or voluntary nurseries and playgroups. Proportion of under-fives in state nurseries: 65%* • **STATE PRIMARY SCHOOLS** *Overall league table position: 142nd out of 150. Top scorers: Friars, Borough; Comber Grove (with nursery unit), Camberwell; St James the Great RC (with nursery unit), Peckham* • **STATE SECONDARY SCHOOLS** *Overall league table position 137th out of 150. High scorers: Notre Dame RC (girls), Elephant & Castle; Bacon's College (mixed), Rotherhithe; St Thomas the Apostle (boys), Peckham* • **PRIVATE PREP SCHOOLS** *Alleyn's Junior (mixed), Dulwich; James Allen's Prep (mixed), Dulwich; Dulwich College Prep (boys), Dulwich; Oakfield Prep (mixed), Dulwich; Rosemead Prep (mixed), Dulwich* • **PRIVATE SECONDARY SCHOOLS** *James Allens Girls (JAGS) (girls), Dulwich; Dulwich College (boys); Alleyn's (mixed), Dulwich.*

TRANSPORT***

Excellent in the north of the borough around London Bridge and Elephant & Castle (now the Bakerloo line's back on stream) and set to improve further with the Jubilee line. But other parts of the borough have to rely on trains and buses as hopes of an extension to the East London tube line from New Cross down to Dulwich appear permanently on ice.

TRAINS Denmark Hill (Camberwell): *Zone 2. Cost of annual season ticket: £704; No of trains per hour: to Victoria 4; Fastest journey: 10 minutes.* Peckham Rye: *Zone 2. No of trains per hour: to Victoria 4; Fastest journey: 15 minutes.* East Dulwich: *Zone 2. No of trains per hour: to London Bridge 5; Fastest journey: 12 minutes.* North Dulwich (for Dulwich Village): *Zone 3. Cost of annual season ticket: £860; No of trains per hour: to London Bridge 5; Fastest journey: 13 minutes.* Herne Hill: *Zone 3. No of trains per hour: to Victoria 4; Thameslink (to City Thameslink): 4; Fastest journey: to Victoria 8 minutes; City Thameslink: 14 minutes* • **TUBES** Elephant & Castle: *Zone 1. Cost of annual season ticket: £572; Bakerloo and Northern lines.* Rotherhithe: *Zone 2. Cost of annual season ticket: £704; Frequency: to East London every 6 minutes* • **BUSES** *Well-endowed for services to town, particularly in the north and middle of the borough including the 36 from Peckham and Camberwell to Victoria; the 45 via Camberwell to Kings Cross; the 63 to Kings Cross; the 47 from Surrey Quays to London Bridge. Further south services are thinner on the ground. The main services, often held up by traffic, are the 12 from Dulwich via Peckham and Camberwell and the 185 from Dulwich via East Dulwich and Camberwell to Victoria* • **TRAFFIC BLACKSPOTS** The south circular across Dulwich Common: *Heavy traffic almost constant with long waits sometimes at lights at junction with Dulwich Village.* The junction of Red Post Hill and East Dulwich Grove: *Long lines of traffic at lights waiting to turn into the main road particularly at rush hours.* Roads into Camberwell including Camberwell Road and Camberwell Church Street: *A busy junction of four main roads with buses and delivery vans often blocking Denmark Hill by the main shopping area.* Elephant and Castle: *One of London's ugliest and most trafficky roundabouts. Carries traffic to all parts of south-east and south-west London and approach-roads are always busy* • **PARKING** *There are controlled parking zones at Elephant & Castle, Peckham and Walworth. Cost of annual resident's permit: £72, only valid for the zone for which it's issued.*

LEISURE FACILITIES ★ ★ ★ ★

THEATRES & CONCERT HALLS *The Globe Theatre built by American Shakespeare-obsessive Sam Wannamaker on the site of the original theatre has Shakespeare plays in authentic Elizabethan surroundings. Southwark Playhouse. Concerts and a good choir at Southwark Cathedral* • **CINEMAS** *Currently only two, at Elephant & Castle and Peckham, both showing blockbusters and mainstream films* • **MUSEUMS & GALLERIES** *Very well provided for, especially in the north of the borough which is now well on the tourist map. The list includes: the Shakespeare Museum at the Globe, the Design Museum at Butlers Wharf, the Britain at War Experience at London Bridge, HMS Belfast, the Tower Bridge experience, the Clink Prison Museum and the London Dungeon. Bankside gallery of modern art is set to open in 2000. Further south, Dulwich Picture Gallery, Britain's oldest picture gallery, is housed in an attractive old building opposite Dulwich Park. The gallery closed last winter for a £9 million face-lift, which will take 18 months* • **SPORTS FACILITIES** *Five indoor leisure centres at Camberwell, Dulwich, Elephant and Castle, Peckham and Rotherhithe (new conditioning gym, health suite and dance studio). A new £11 million health and fitness centre, Peckham Pulse, is taking shape in a huge glass building behind Peckham High Street as part* of the area's regeneration. Watersports and marina at Greenland and South Dock, Rotherhithe. Outdoor sports stadium at Herne Hill • **LIBRARIES** Many branch libraries closed on Wednesdays and unpredictable opening hours at other times so check before you go. Dulwich and Newington libraries now open on Sundays. New library planned for Peckham. Excellent local history library in Borough High Street. Recent research by the library service recorded high levels of satisfaction among library-users but system used slightly less than London average at 7.4 visits per head. Place in library-use league table: 17th out of 32 (where 1 is best and 32 worst).

OPEN SPACES ★ ★ ★ ★

Generous amounts of open space in the south of the borough around Dulwich. More poorly provided for in the north, except for Burgess Park, carved out of a densely-packed area after the Second World War. A valuable green space in a built-up area but rather flat and featureless, relieved only by the unexpected and attractive enclave of Chumleigh Gardens, a square of almshouses which houses the park ranger service. **WOODS** Dulwich Wood; Sydenham Hill Nature Reserve with part of the old railway line which used to run to Crystal Palace and remains of Victorian villas which once stood at the edge of the wood • **PARKS** Dulwich Park at the edge of Dulwich Village has gardens and a boating lake. Burgess Park has a display of gardens from around the world next to the almhouses at Chulmleigh Gardens • **CEMETERIES** Nunhead, an overgrown and mysterious Victorian cemetery has a full complement of mourning angels, cracked urns and trailing ivy.

SHOPS ★ ★ ★

BERMONDSEY & ROTHERHITHE Designer food shops, clothes shops and bookshop in restored warehouses at Shad Thames near Terence Conran's group of restaurants. Friday antiques market around Bermondsey Street. Large Co-op and other chains on Southwark Park Road. Surrey Quays shopping centre at Rotherhithe with Tesco • **ELEPHANT & CASTLE** The ugly 1960s shopping centre was painted a shocking pink a couple of years ago in a desperate bid to brighten it up but this only succeeded in drawing attention to its ugliness. Slightly improved in the last 10 years with a Tesco Metro replacing the previous "pile 'em high sell 'em cheap" store and some ethnic food stalls but still mostly dull chains. Walworth Road has cheap clothes and household goods and an active local market in East Street • **PECKHAM** Pedestrianised shopping street in Rye Lane with all the usual chain stores. Mostly cheap stock and a lot of discount stores. Big injections of government money have gone into encouraging stores to locate here, especially Safeway. Small local shops in Peckham High Street including Afro-Caribbean take-aways • **CAMBERWELL** A couple of interesting shops including a good second-hand bookshop in Camberwell Grove. Small junk-market off Camberwell New Road. But generally uninspiring small shopping centre with poor Safeway in Denmark Hill. Big Sainsbury's at the bottom of Dog Kennel Hill • **EAST DULWICH** Lordship Lane has a good variety of ethnic restaurants alongside the usual banks, chains and a branch of Somerfields. Signs of middle class habitation include the up-market Blue Mountain Coffee shop and antique shops in North Cross Road and Melbourne Grove • **DULWICH** Not as villagey as the name suggests, at least not around the shops. Two parades of shops along a rather trafficky road. Mostly up-market local shops for clothes, wallpaper, flowers and valet drycleaning.

RESTAURANTS***

BERMONDSEY *The Conran restaurants at Shad Thames (if you have deep pockets or an expense account). A couple of good pubs around Bermondsey Street serving restaurant-standard food. Good Italian in Southwark Park Road* • **BOROUGH** *A couple of wine bars and restaurants under the arches of London Bridge station, in Tooley Street. Thai restaurant at Hay's Galleria with river view. Hay's Galleria, a collection of up-market shops, restaurants and market stalls in a former Thameside warehouse and has improved shopping and eating around London Bridge significantly* • **CAMBERWELL** *A number of restaurants and bars have opened recently around Camberwell Church Street and its junction with Camberwell Grove although some have closed again equally rapidly. Vegetarian café in Denmark Hill. Good choice of ethnic restaurants* • **EAST DULWICH & DULWICH** *A locally-praised Thai restaurant and a couple of Italian restaurants in and around North Cross Road, East Dulwich. A big choice of Indian restaurants of varying quality. Number of chains in Dulwich Village including a recently-opened Pizza Express and a widely-praised restaurant at Belair House, a former mansion in parkland near Dulwich College.*

CRIME RATES*

181 crimes per 1000 of population. Position in Metropolitan Police league table: 3rd out of 32 (where 1 is worst and 32 best).

THE COUNCIL**

POLITICAL AFFILIATION *Labour* • **MINUS POINTS** *Some of the worst schools in London. Not always as efficient as it should be in sweeping the streets and mending roads and pavements quickly. Former council tenants who bought their properties under the Right-to-Buy scheme say they have been faced with huge service charge bills* • **PLUS POINTS** *Energetically working on regeneration of some of its poorest areas and collaborating with other boroughs to bring more tourists to the South Bank and rejuvenate the riverside* • **PROPERTY SEARCHES CARRIED OUT IN 10 WORKING DAYS** *99%* • **STANDARD SEARCH FEE** *£95* • **COUNCIL TAX COLLECTED** *84.7%* • **COUNCIL TAX 1998-99**

BAND	PROPERTY VALUE	CHARGE	BAND	PROPERTY VALUE	CHARGE
A	up to £40,000	£524.38	E	£88,001-£120,000	£961.83
B	£40,001-£52,000	£611.78	F	£120,001-£160,000	£1,136.18
C	£52,001-£68,000	£699.19	G	£160,001-£320,000	£1,310.96
D	£68,001-£88,000	£786.58	H	over £320,000	£1,573.16

SUTTON

It's tempting to think that Sutton was only included in the administrative area of Greater London to fill in what would have otherwise been an awkward gap in London's roughly circular shape. Uniquely among London boroughs, it's surrounded by affluent neighbours (Merton, Kingston and Croydon). It harbours no chunks of Victorian inner suburb within its boundaries. Overwhelming inner city problems of crime, high unemployment and poor housing are safely away from its borders. It's mostly white (only 6 per cent of its population is from an ethnic minority) and working (unemployment stands at just 2.6 per cent, the lowest, along with Richmond, in London). In short, it's a pleasant part of the Surrey commuter belt – safe, cosy and green, but a bit dull for those who crave more excitement than whether they'll get a seat on the 7.45.

At its northern tip is the turn-of-the-century council estate of St Helier with small cottages set attractively around greens. To the west are the 1930s semis and small detached houses of North Cheam. Just below is Cheam, with some attractive cottages among the interwar building which grew up around its station. South of the station in the south west of the borough are the larger 1930s detached houses of Belmont. To the north east is Sutton, the shopping and administrative centre of the borough. Villagey Carshalton, whose clapboard houses and ponds spanned by delicate hump-backed bridges would be picture-postcard if the roads weren't so busy, gives way to Carshalton Beeches, classic well-off stockbroker-belt territory. In the east are the more modest terraces of Wallington and Beddington and Sutton's only tower blocks at Roundshay, about to be demolished and replaced with low-rise housing.

Like many other outer London boroughs, one of Sutton's biggest problems (and residents' biggest grumbles) is traffic. The mostly affluent residents collectively have one of the highest rates of car ownership in the UK and the borough is bisected with busy roads filled with through-traffic.

PROPERTY AND ARCHITECTURE

ST HELIER

One of the largest council estates built by the London County Council in the 1920s and 1930s. Mostly terraces in typical LCC cottage estate-style with gables, steeply-pitched roofs and arched doorways set in generous amounts of green space. Many of these houses and some more recent additions built in the 1950s were bought by their tenants under the Right-to-Buy scheme and are now coming back on to the market. A good place to find a cheap house. Mostly two- and three-bedroom terraces with some flats on the periphery.

ATTRACTS *Families; first-time buyers* • **CONSERVATION AREAS** *None* • **AVERAGE PRICES** *Flats: studio: £30,000; 1-bed: £40,000; 2-bed: £50,000; 3-bed: £50,000+ Houses: 2-bed: £70,000+; 3-bed: £75,000+* • **AVERAGE RENTS (MONTHLY)** *Houses: 2-bed: £550; 3-bed: £600.*

NORTH CHEAM & CHEAM

North Cheam is predominantly 1930s semis with the best properties in roads round Churchill Road. Popular for schools especially top primary performer Cheam Park Farm which operates a tight catchment area of a handful of roads on the Park Farm estate between the A24 and the A217. Cheam itself is more villagey and up-market than North Cheam, with a proper centre just north of the station. Among the predictable 1930s semis, it has some beautifully preserved sixteenth century clapboard houses in roads just near Cheam Park. South of Cheam, the enclave of Belmont, west of Burdon Lane, has some of the handsomest houses in the area. Everything here from neo-Georgian to overgrown cottages with rustic chimneys and tilehung fronts.

ATTRACTS *Families; commuters; people moving further out of London from areas like Tooting and Mitcham* • **CONSERVATION AREAS** *Cheam Village* • **AVERAGE PRICES** *Flats: studio: £45,000-£50,000; 1-bed: £50,000-£60,000; 2-bed: £60,000-£90,000 Houses: 2-bed: £85,000+; 3-bed: £120,000-£160,000; 4-bed: £145,000-£170,000; 5-bed: £160,000-£210,000+* • **AVERAGE RENTS (MONTHLY)** *Flats: studio: £425; 1-bed: £500-£525; 2-bed: £550-£750 Houses: 2-bed: £650; 3-bed: £650-£900; 4-bed: £1200; 5-bed: £1500-£2000.*

SUTTON

Some large and lovely Victorian and Edwardian houses near the centre of Sutton around St James's Road, some now converted into flats as well as roads of Victorian terraces and cottages. South Sutton is the most sought-after, with spacious detached and semi-detached houses in the best roads east of Brighton road. Elsehwere in Sutton there's a good choice of modern blocks and 1960s and 1970s houses as well as everything from Victorian onwards. Turn-of-the-century cottage-style houses around Oak Close and Meadow Close north of Sutton are the result of an early planning experiment which created the Sutton Garden Suburb.

ATTRACTS *Families; local first-time buyers* • **CONSERVATION AREAS** *Landseer Road; Grove Avenue; Sutton Garden Suburb* • **AVERAGE PRICES** *Flats: studio: £35,000-£48,000; 1-bed: £45,000-£65,000; 2-bed: £55,000-£80,000 Houses: 1-bed: £68,000-£80,000; 2-bed: £75,000-£100,000; 3-bed: £95,000-£250,000; 4-bed: £150,000-£400,000* • **AVERAGE RENTS (MONTHLY)** *Flats: studio: £400-£450; 1-bed: £500-£550; 2-bed: £550-£650 Houses: 2-bed: £650-£750; 3-bed: £850-£950; 4-bed: £1000-£1250; 5-bed: £1400+.*

CARSHALTON VILLAGE & CARSHALTON BEECHES

Roads of Victorian and Edwardian terraces and semis off the High Street in Carshalton Village and pretty white clapboard sixteenth century cottages in Pound Street, as well as roads of 1930s semis. Some handsome late Victorian and Edwardian semis in roads around Park Hill in more expensive Carshalton Beeches. Elsewhere in Carshalton Beeches (known as The Beeches to distinguish it from The Village) is archetypal stockbroker-belt, occasionally trembling into Southfork in some of the grandest roads. Big detached houses of every permutation (red brick, Tudorbethan, white plastered, you name it) in large gardens in Pine Walk West and East with a large swathe of grass and trees shielding inhabitants from their neighbours on the other side.

ATTRACTS *Families; local first-time buyers; loyal locals moving up-market from the less-grand north of the borough; people moving out of inner London boroughs like Wandsworth* • **CONSERVATION AREAS** *Wrythe Green; Carshalton Village; Carshalton Park; Park Hill* • **AVERAGE PRICES** • *Flats: 1-bed: £50,000-£65,000; 2-bed: £75,000+ Houses: 2-bed: £75,000-£100,000; 3-bed: £120,000-£220,000; 4-bed: £160,000-£350,000+* • **AVERAGE RENTS (MONTHLY)** *Flats: 1-bed: £450-£500; 2-bed: £550-*

£600 *Houses: 2-bed: £650-£700; 3-bed: £850-£900; 4-bed: £1000-£1200.*

WALLINGTON & BEDDINGTON

Much of Wallington is Victorian, a reminder of its beginnings as a nineteenth century railway suburb. Large Victorian houses, many converted into flats in roads north of the railway, which used to be the smartest area. Now South Wallington is smarter with roads of large and small Victorian houses in roads off Stafford Road and around Mellows Park. Woodcote Avenue is the poshest road in Wallington with large Edwardian detached houses. Beddington is cheaper than Wallington with a mix of everything from Victorian to blocks of modern flats. Wallington is home to some of the best selective schools.

ATTRACTS *Families; commuters; local first-time buyers* • **CONSERVATION AREAS** *Wallington Green; Beddington Village; Church Lane; Beddington Village; Carew Manor* • **AVERAGE PRICES** *Flats: studio: £28,000-£35,000; 1-bed: £48,000-£60,000; 2-bed: £55,000-£80,000 Houses: 1-bed: £60,000-£70,000; 2-bed: £80,000-£110,000; 3-bed: £95,000-£180,000; 4-bed: £130,000-£500,000* • **AVERAGE RENTS (MONTHLY)** *Flats: studio: £350-£400; 1-bed: £450; 2-bed: £550-£600 Houses: 1-bed: £550; 2-bed: £650-£700; 3-bed: £850-£900; 4-bed: £1000-£1200; 5-bed: £1400.*

BEST POSTCODES

Largely irrelevant in a borough with Surrey rather than London postcodes. Proxmity to a good train service to town, good schools and green space are much more important.

AMENITIES

SCHOOLS★★★★

Excellent overall performance in league tables particularly at secondary level, where the marks are lifted by some seriously academic selective grammar schools. Lots of competition to get into the best schools, although being surrounded by outer London boroughs with some pretty good schools of their own means there's not as much pressure on numbers from parents in neighbouring boroughs. A fair selection of private schools. You're likely to end up paying for nursery education as Sutton has the second lowest proportion of under-fives in nursery education in outer London.

PRE-SCHOOL PROVISION *2 state nurseries; 32 nursery classes in state primary and church schools; 71 private and voluntary nurseries and playgroups. Proportion of under-fives in state nurseries: 39%* • **STATE PRIMARY SCHOOLS** *Overall position in league tables: 52nd out of 150. Top scorers: St Dunstan's, Cheam (with nursery unit); All Saints C of E (with nursery unit), Carshaltan; Foresters (with nursery unit), Wallington* • **STATE SECONDARY SCHOOLS** *Overall position in league tables: 4th out of 150. High scorers (all selective): Nonsuch High (girls), Cheam; Wilson's School (boys), Wallington; Wallington High (girls), Wallington* • **PRIVATE PREP SCHOOLS** *Collingwood (mixed), Wallington; Glaisdale (mixed), Cheam; Homefield (boys) Sutton; Seaton House (girls from 3), South Sutton* • **PRIVATE SECONDARY SCHOOLS**

Chart-topper Sutton High (girls from 4), Sutton; Stowford College (mixed, children from 7), Sutton.

TRANSPORT ★ ★ ★

Trains only throughout the borough with the middle better served than the outer reaches. Services from town can be tediously slow at weekends and outside rush-hour. Some areas, such as North Cheam, are some distance from a decent station. Connections in the far north-east corner of the borough are set to improve when the Croydon Tramlink is built through Beddington Lane (see Croydon).

TRAINS Cheam: Zone 6. Cost of annual season ticket: £1396; No of trains per hour: to London Bridge 2; to Victoria 3-4; Fastest journey: to London Bridge 30 minutes; to Victoria 23 minutes. Sutton: Zone 5. Cost of annual season ticket: £1280; No of trains per hour: to London Bridge 2; to Victoria 6; to Blackfriars (Thameslink) 4; Fastest journey: to London Bridge 40 minutes; to Victoria 28 minutes; to Blackfriars 35 minutes. Carshalton: Zone 5. No of trains per hour: to London Bridge 2; to Victoria 6; to Blackfriars 4; Fastest journey: to London Bridge 37 minutes; to Victoria 25 minutes; to Blackfriars 33 minutes. Wallington: Zone 5. No of trains per hour: to London Bridge 2; to Victoria: to London Bridge 4; Fastest journey: to London Bridge 34 minutes; to Victoria 35 minutes • **BUSES** Tend to link neighbouring suburbs or head towards the nearest large shopping centres of Kingston or Croydon rather than into town. Night buses running from Trafalgar Square include the N44 via St Helier, Carshalton, Carshalton Beeches, Wallington and Sutton • **TRAFFIC BLACKSPOTS** Cheam: The area is criss-crossed by busy main roads including the A24 and the A217 carrying fast traffic to Surrey, the M25, Gatwick airport and the south coast. Sutton: The centre of the town has been pedestrianised (a good thing) pushing all the traffic into surrounding roads (a bad thing). Roads round Cheam and Carshalton Roads and St Nicholas Way tend to get clogged up with long queues at traffic lights. Carshalton Village: The constant stream of traffic queuing at the lights around Pound Street and the High Street detracts substantially from the pleasure of walking round the ponds and gardens of The Grove. Shopping in the pretty Victorian High Street is also spoilt by traffic • **PARKING** Not too bad in most parts of the borough because space is plentiful. Even parking near the shops in Cheam and Carshalton isn't impossible and there's a good supply of car parks in Sutton. There's one controlled parking zone, in Sutton town centre with three zones. Cost of annual resident's permit: £25.

LEISURE FACILITIES ★ ★ ★

THEATRES & CONCERT HALLS Two theatres. The Harry Secombe (named after the comedian, a long-time resident) in Sutton has mostly mainstream plays, musicals and pantomimes, with lots of amateur dramatics and performances by local groups. The Charles Cryer theatre in Carshalton has more off-the-wall and innovative plays, dance and music and is the centre of the borough's arts education programme • **CINEMA** Only one, the six screen UCI in Sutton, showing mainstream films • **MUSEUMS & GALLERIES** A small but interesting number of historic houses open to the public, reminders that Sutton was once a popular country stamping ground for the aristocracy and royalty (Henry VIII's palace at Nonsuch is just over the borough border in Epsom and Ewell). The fifteenth century Carew Manor behind imposing wrought iron gates overlooking Beddington Park is now a school but the medieval Great Hall and other parts of the house are open to the public. Carshalton House, a Queen Anne mansion, almost invisible behind high brick walls, is also a school but open to the public occasionally, as is the elaborate eighteenth century water tower overlooking the road. Honeywood, an attractive white stucco Victorian house overlooking Carshalton ponds, houses a well-presented local history museum with some fascinating archive photographs and a completely preserved pannelled Edwardian billiard room (although the rather arch commentary tape could do with replacing) • **SPORTS FACILITIES** Two leisure centres at Carshalton and North Cheam, both with pools, fitness centres and indoor sports facilities. All-weather athletics track at Sutton. Golf and squash at Oaks Park in the south of the borough. Tennis, athletics and other outdoor sports in parks across the borough. Leisure discount card scheme in operation • **LIBRARIES** Well used, especially Sutton central library on three floors with coffee shop and one-stop leisure shop. Branch libraries are friendly but less well-resourced. Sutton claims to have pioneered the practice of offering a full range of services on Sunday (at Sutton central, Sunday afternoons only) but makes up for it by closing all libraries across the borough on Monday. 9.1 library visits per head. Position in library-use league table: 9th out of 32 (where 1 is best and 32 worst).

OPEN SPACES * * * *

Other boroughs would dispute Sutton's claim that it has more trees than anywhere else in London. But who's counting? Like neighbouring Croydon, Sutton's south edge abuts the North Downs and the borough is scattered with green space. Other open space within the borough tends to the flat and formal rather than wild and rural and there are no woods or heaths to speak of. Spaces popular with local residents like Nonsuch Park and Banstead Downs are just outside the borough boundary (but easily accessible). **RIVER WALKS** The Grove, Carshalton. Not a long tramp by the Thames or even the Wandle, the river which flows through the grounds of this lovely little park. But peaceful and shady beside the clear water, with overhanging trees and a small waterfall • **WIDE OPEN SPACES** Cheam Park (which continues into Nonsuch Park) with mature trees, manicured lawns and views over Surrey. Beddington Park, the largest space in the borough with boating lake and Carew Manor at its south-western edge.

SHOPS * * *

CHEAM & NORTH CHEAM Streets of pleasant shops in Cheam Village straggling out around the crossroads of Ewell Road, High Street, The Broadway and Station Way, including a real butcher, a couple of craft and design shops and a bookshop, among other practical local shops. Budgens in The Broadway. A mixture of chain stores and local shops at North Cheam • **SUTTON** Has had to struggle to keep residents from decamping to nearby Croydon and is fighting back with two large shopping centres. The older of the two, St Nicholas, has just had a £3 million revamp. Most of the High Street is pedestrianised, encouraging the spread of pavement cafés and linking in well with the two indoor shopping centres, St Nicholas and Times Square. Few startlingly original shops (and some full of disturbingly tasteless knick-knacks and ornaments) but good branches of most chain stores and an Allders department store. Safeway in Cheam Road. Tesco in St Nicholas Way. Open-air market on Tuesday and Saturday • **CARSHALTON** A small Victorian shopping street next to the Grove with up-market local shops including furniture and antique shops and a bakery. Unfortunately you take your life in your hands unless you cross at the crossing • **WALLINGTON** *Mostly chain stores in roads around the station and in the pedestrianised Wallington Square alongside a handful of individual local shops. Traffic carves through the middle of the shopping centre on the main A237.*

RESTAURANTS**

Not a culinary hotspot. Some winebars, bistros and pubs serving good food in Carshalton and Cheam. Sutton has pasta and pizza chains including Pizza Express and a choice of local restaurants and pubs. Across the borough you'll find the usual scattering of Indian and Chinese take-aways and burger bars.

CRIME RATES*****

81 crimes per 1000 of population. Position in Metropolitan Police league table: 28th out of 32 (where 1 is worst and 32 best).

THE COUNCIL***

POLITICAL AFFILIATION *Liberal Democrat* • **MINUS POINTS** *Low level of state nursery provision. One of the slowest boroughs in London at turning round property searches while charging among the highest fees* • **PLUS POINTS** *Enthusiastically environmental, with a number of recycling and sustainability initiatives including weekly door-to-door recycling collections, supply of free composters and recycling of problem items like motor oil and batteries. Excellent schools* • **PROPERTY SEARCHES CARRIED OUT IN 10 WORKING DAYS** *73%* • **STANDARD SEARCH FEE** £*120* • **COUNCIL TAX COLLECTED** *98%*
• **COUNCIL TAX 1998-99**

BAND	PROPERTY VALUE	CHARGE	BAND	PROPERTY VALUE	CHARGE
A	up to £40,000	£467.82	E	£88,001-£120,000	£857.67
B	£40,001-£52,000	£545.79	F	£120,001-£160,000	£1,013.61
C	£52,001-£68,000	£623.76	G	£160,001-£320,000	£1,169.55
D	£68,001-£88,000	£701.73	H	over £320,000	£1,403.46

TOWER HAMLETS

Tower Hamlets has changed physically and socially more than any other part of London in the last 10 years. At the beginning of the 1980s, the docks in the south of the borough which had provided most of its employment and community focus lay derelict after the death of the industries which had sustained them. Now the docks have re-emerged as Docklands, London's trendy new City in the East. Warehouses have been converted into luxury riverside apartments, there are new transport links and gleaming offices including Europe's tallest office block, Canary Wharf, housing today's most money-spinning industries – financial services and technology. Geographically it's part of the East End, socially it's part of the wealthy international City.

After huge teething problems (an unreliable and overcrowded Docklands Light Railway, a lack of coherent planning depriving new residents of even basic shops and amenities, resentment from long-term residents in one of the poorest boroughs at being over-run with yuppies and a long recession which nearly destroyed the whole area), Docklands seems finally to be taking off and bringing other parts of Tower Hamlets with it.

Docklands is the most visible and well-documented part of Tower Hamlets, stretching from just east of Tower Bridge, along the river via Wapping and Limehouse across the whole of the Isle of Dogs, which hangs like an appendix across the river from Greenwich. It also includes parts of Bermondsey and Rotherhithe (see Southwark). Further north, the borough takes in the East End proper in which generations of refugees have settled, from French Huguenots to Jews and most recently Bangladeshis.

Nearest the city are Spitalfields and Whitechapel, still a centre for the wholesale clothing industry. To the east are the council flats and cottages of Bethnal Green and Stepney. Further east still is Bow which still has some of the most attractive Georgian properties in London. Bromley and Poplar just above the Isle of Dogs have some of the most alienating council blocks ever built. Much of the borough was blown to bits by the Luftwaffe and council planners did their worst in the 50s and 60s to obliterate traditional street plans so it's a common sight to see Victorian or Georgian streets cowering in the lee of a council block.

It's no longer daring to live in the East End. Even lawyers and bankers do, albeit safely locked behind the iron gates of their new homes with 24-hour security in Docklands. Now Bow and Bethnal Green have their middle class colonies. The warehouses of Spitalfields and Whitechapel are being turned into loft developments and artists' studios. But the borough is still dominated by council estates. It's the seventh most deprived in the UK and 13.6 per cent of its population is unemployed (the second highest in London). Its large Bangladeshi community (nearly a quarter of the population) contributes hugely to the area's rich cosmopolitanism but is also traditionally one of the poorest of all ethnic communities.

The building of Docklands was one of the first experiments in generating private as well as public funds for regeneration schemes. But millions are still pouring into schemes to improve jobs, education, and to create new cultural quarters in Spitalfields (see also Islington and Hackney) and revamp some of the worst council estates and contaminated river sites in the Lea Valley to the east (see Haringey).

PROPERTY AND ARCHITECTURE

SPITALFIELDS & WHITECHAPEL

Still very commercial areas with lots of wholesale shops and small factories but also lively and cosmopolitan places to live. Some wonderful and rarely-on-the market four-storey Georgian town houses in streets off Brick Lane, the heart of Asian Spitalfields. New developments of offices and warehouses converted into luxury apartments and lofts in both Spitalfields and Whitechapel. Large houses are rare but you can buy huge converted warehouse "shells". Lots of ex-council flats at the cheap end of the price range. Modern houses are cheaper than period ones.

ATTRACTS *Creative types; single people; young professionals* • **CONSERVATION AREAS** *Artillery Passage; Fournier Street; Elder Street; Wentworth Street; Whitechapel Market* • **AVERAGE PRICES** *Flats: studio: £30,000-£65,000; 1-bed: £45,000-£80,000; 2-bed: £55,000-£125,000; 3-bed: £65,000-£115,000 Houses: 2-bed: £110,000-£160,000; 3-bed: £130,000+; 4-bed: £140,000+* • **AVERAGE RENTS (MONTHLY)** *Flats: studio: £700-£860; 1-bed: £650-£860; 2-bed: £910-£1080; 3-bed: £1210-£1730 Houses: 3-bed: £1625+; 4-bed: £1840-£1950; 5-bed: £2310-£2810.*

WAPPING & LIMEHOUSE

Warehouses in Wapping were among the first to get the conversion-to-luxury flats treatment in the late 1980s. The rooms can be a bit cramped and critics argue (with some justification) that it's a yuppie ghetto but it's one of the most central and popular parts of Docklands and most of the major building is finished. Wapping's more expensive than Limehouse because it's nearer the City. Blocks of new apartments all around Limehouse Basin (great if you've got a boat which needs mooring in the Basin) and more building going on along the river. Be prepared to live on a building site for several years. Enclaves of handsome Georgian houses (some now flats) on the river at Wapping Pier Head and at Narrow Street in Limehouse, and streets of small Georgian terraces tucked away behind the noisy Commercial Road at Limehouse. Lots of council blocks round every corner.

ATTRACTS *City workers; well-paid professionals; creative types; people wanting pieds-à-terre; investors* • **CONSERVATION AREAS** *Wapping Pier Head; Wapping Wall; St George's Town Hall; St Pauls Church Shadwell; Commercial Road; York Square; Albert Gardens & Arbour Square; Lowell Street; Narrow Street; St Anne's Limehouse* • **AVERAGE PRICES** *Flats: studio: £80,000-£100,000; 1-bed: £90,000-£150,000; 2-bed: £125,000-£285,000; 3-bed: £225,000+ Houses: 2-bed: £140,000-£160,000; 3-bed: £160,000+; 4-bed: £300,000+* • **AVERAGE RENTS (MONTHLY)** *Flats: studio: £650-£820; 1-bed: £780-£1730; 2-bed: £1080-£1300; 3-bed: £1300+ Houses: 2-bed: £1080+; 3-bed: £1250-£1510; 4-bed: £1730+.*

BETHNAL GREEN

Pockets of former workers' cottages, once probably little more than slums and now cleaned up to provide small cosy two- and three-bedroom houses in streets between Hackney Road and Columbia Road. Some streets of Victorian terraces around Bethnal Green Road. The main disadvantage (visually if nothing else) is that there are rarely more than a couple of streets before you turn the corner to yet another ugly council estate or tower block. But there are some bargains to be had with former council flats and houses on the better estates. Stepney to the south is almost all council property.

ATTRACTS *City workers; young professionals; first-time buyers; investors* • **CONSERVATION AREAS** *Globe Road; Jesus Hospital Estate; Boundary Estate; Carlton Road* • **AVERAGE PRICES** *Flats: studio: £50,000-£60,000; 1-bed: £60,000-£80,000; 2-bed: £75,000+ Houses: 2-bed:*

£100,000+; 3-bed: £120,000+; 4-bed: £200,000+ • **AVERAGE RENTS (MONTHLY)** *Flats: studio: £520; 1-bed: £540-£600; 2-bed: £700+; 3-bed: £780 Houses: 2-bed: £1080; 3-bed: £1080+; 4-bed: £1300.*

BOW

One of the best parts of Tower Hamlets. There are council blocks but there are also streets of attractive two- and three-storey Victorian terraces in roads north of Bow Road as well as Tredegar Square, a wonderful complete square of Georgian brick and white stucco terraces. Roads around Tredegar Square have smaller Georgian terraces. Towards Victoria Park and the Hertford Union Canal there are streets of Georgian and Victorian terrace off Roman Road. Roman Road itself has a couple of popular estates with cheap ex-council flats.

ATTRACTS *First-time buyers; professionals; families; investors; people who can't afford Islington* • **CONSERVATION AREAS** *Victoria Park; Driffield Road; Roman Road market; Medway; Tredegar Square; Tower Hamlets Cemetery; Tomlins Grove* • **AVERAGE PRICES** *Flats: studio: £45,000+; 1-bed: £60,000+; 2-bed: £70,000+ Houses: 1-bed: £60,000+; 2-bed: £95,000+; 3-bed: £140,000+; 4-bed: £155,000+* • **AVERAGE RENTS (MONTHLY)** *Flats: studio: £560+; 1-bed: £650; 2-bed: £910; 3-bed: £1040 Houses: 1-bed: £650+; 2-bed: £1040+; 3-bed: £1170+; 4-bed: £1300+.*

ISLE OF DOGS

Known locally as The Island. Almost all built in the last 10 years or converted from old warehouses, with more to come. A mix of apartments with river views, porterage, underground carparks and security and modern town houses. Developers swear the demand is there although some have their doubts and argue the area is being overrun with speculative development. Unlike Wapping, promoted to prime residential area, the Isle of Dogs remains fringe, vulnerable to market downturns. Lots of apartment blocks with river views but a rather soulless environment. Your neighbours will probably be people like yourself, only there during the week because it's a pied-à-terre or short term tenants because the owner has bought it as a rental investment. Racism still flares here and a National Front candidate was briefly elected to the council a few years ago.

ATTRACTS *Young single people; workers in the City and Canary Wharf; people wanting pieds-à-terre; investors* • **CONSERVATION AREAS** *Island Gardens; Coldharbour; Chapel House* • **AVERAGE PRICES** *Flats: studio: £65,000-£80,000; 1-bed: £80,000+; 2-bed: £105,000+; 3-bed: £140,000+ Houses: 2-bed: £95,000; 3-bed: £110,000-£135,000; 4-bed: £170,000+* • **AVERAGE RENTS (MONTHLY)** *Flats: studio: £700; 1-bed: £860; 2-bed: £1000; 3-bed: £1300 Houses: 2-bed: £950-£2160; 3-bed: £1300-£2160.*

BEST POSTCODES

Every area is so mixed that postcodes are an unreliable indicator of relative social standing. Bow E3 and Docklands E14 are generally considered good areas but E14 includes the council estates of Poplar alongside the luxury apartments of Docklands. Proximity to a tube is often the decider, particularly in Bow, where otherwise attractive terraces around Victoria Park are cheaper than property further south because it's a brisk walk to the tube station.

AMENITIES

SCHOOLS*

Tower Hamlets was the target of a scathing Ofsted report last year which found that the borough spent more money than any other local education authority for less tangible result, partly because of "political experimentation" in the 1980s which caused bureaucratic chaos. Has always languished near the bottom of the league tables both at primary and secondary level. Partly redeems itself by having the most generous provision for under-fives in London. One Islamic girls' secondary school.

PRE-SCHOOL PROVISION *7 state nursery schools; 49 nursery classes in state primary and church schools; 54 private and voluntary day nurseries and playgroups. Proportion of under-fives in state nursery schools: 88%* • **STATE PRIMARY SCHOOLS** *Overall position in league table: 148th out of 150. Top scorers: St Saviour's C of E (with nursery unit), Poplar; St John the Baptist RC, Bethnal Green; St Peters C of E, Wapping* • **STATE SECONDARY SCHOOLS** *Overall position in league table: 142nd out of 150. Best scorers: Mulberry School for Girls, Wapping; Raines Foundation School (mixed), Bethnal Green; Bethnal Green Technology College (mixed), Bethnal Green* • **PRIVATE SECONDARY SCHOOL** *Madni Girls, Tower Hamlets.*

TRANSPORT****

Excellent in the west of the borough but more patchy in the Isle of Dogs where the Docklands Light Railway (now much improved, to be fair) is the only option. The DLR has improved transport to Bow in particular and the long promised Jubilee line extension will dramatically improve journey times from Canary Wharf to the South Bank at London Bridge and Waterloo and the West End.

TUBES Whitechapel. *Zone 1. Cost of annual season ticket: £572. District, Hammersmith and City and East London line.* Wapping: *Zone 1. East London line.* Bethnal Green: *Zone 2. Cost of annual season ticket: £704; Frequency: Central to Oxford Circus every 4 minutes; Fastest journey: 17 minutes* • **DOCKLANDS LIGHT RAILWAY** Bow Road: *Zone 2. Frequency: DLR to Stratford every 5-8 minutes; Fastest journey: 6 minutes.* Canary Wharf: *Zone 2. Frequency: DLR to Bank every 8-10 minutes; Fastest journey: 12 minutes* • **BUSES** *Fine in the north of the borough with plenty of services to the City and West End. Much less choice and less frequent in Wapping and the Isle of Dogs where you can find yourself stranded late in the evening. Services include the 15 via Limehouse and Tower Hill to Paddington, the 25 via Bow, Mile End, Stepney and Whitechapel to Oxford Circus and the 40 via Poplar and Limehouse to London Bridge* • **TRAFFIC BLACKSPOTS** Wapping: *The Highway. Carries lots of the traffic coming into East London including container lorries from Tilbury and newsprint lorries to the various newspaper companies in Docklands. Traffic is almost always forced into a single lane at the World Trade Centre traffic lights by parked cars.* Whitechapel: *The Aldgate Roundabout & Commercial Road. A horrible junction of several main roads, always jammed with drivers trying to manoeuvre themselves into the right lane (see also City of London).* Bethnal Green: *Almost constant heavy traffic slowed by delivery vans and private cars parking and loading in the Bethnal Green Road.* Limehouse: *The Limehouse Link and Rotherhithe Tunnel approaches at Commercial Road. The Limehouse Link is supposed* *to be the most expensive stretch of road ever built but it hasn't solved the area's traffic problems. Heavy traffic also pours out of the Rotherhithe tunnel onto Commercial Road* • **PARKING** *The borough is one big controlled parking zone so expect to pay for the privilege of parking your car outside your front door. There are four parking zones – Bethnal Green; Bow & Poplar; Stepney & Wapping and the Isle of Dogs. Permits valid only in the zone for which they're issued. Cost of annual resident's permit: £35.*

LEISURE FACILITIES * * *

THEATRES & CONCERT HALLS *One repertory theatre, the Spitz in Whitechapel, featuring live music, dance and drama. Brick Lane Music Hall, a small surviving part of a tradition of East End music hall and pub theatre. Classical concerts at Christ Church, Spitalfields. Stand-up comedy at Jongleurs, Bow Wharf (see shops below) and Cabot Hall, Canary Wharf. Rock concerts at the Docklands Arena* • **CINEMAS** *Currently no cinema in the borough although easy access to the West End and repertory cinemas in Dalston, Shoreditch and Islington doesn't make this too much of a hardship* • **MUSEUMS & GALLERIES** *The Whitechapel Art Gallery with art nouveau exterior specialises in exhibitions of the work of living artists rather than housing permanent exhibitions. Local artists across the borough also open their studios and sell their work to the public. The Tower of London, one of London's most visited sights, is the borough's best known attraction. The Ragged School Museum on the Regents Canal at Mile End housed in a former ragged school building has a mock-up of a Victorian classroom complete with slates and strict teacher (children love this) as well as exhibitions about the lives of the children who attended the school. Staffed by volunteers so opening hours are erratic* • **SPORTS FACILITIES**
Well provided for. Five leisure centres in Whitechapel, Bethnal Green, Docklands, Poplar and Mile End. Pools at Bethnal Green and Docklands, athletics track and football pitches at Mile End, exercise classes and fitness rooms at Whitechapel and Poplar • **LIBRARIES** *Poorly used and small, without a large central library. Some good long opening hours particularly at Bethnal Green reference library but smaller branch libraries like Limehouse and Stepney are closed more than they're open. 4 library visits per head. Position in library-use league table: 30th out of 32 (where 1 is best and 32 worst).*

OPEN SPACES * * *

Generally badly off for green space. Tower Hamlets is a densely populated and built-up borough and the developers' drive to build profitably in Docklands didn't leave much scope for leaving large tracts of open space unbuilt on. What greenery there is tends to be flat and municipal. But to compensate, it has the water resources of rivers, canals and docks.
CEMETERIES *Tower Hamlets Cemetery. Satisfyingly overgrown and Victorian, a worthy competitor to Abney Park (Stoke Newington) or Nunhead* • **CANALS** *The Regents Canal from Victoria Park to Limehouse Basin. The best way to walk through some of Tower Hamlets' less salubrious areas. At Victoria Park, the Hertford Union canal splits off from the Regents Canal, joining the River Lea from where you can walk through the Lea Valley Park (see Haringey and Enfield) or through to the tangle of rivers, old warehouses and locks at Bow Back Rivers (see Newham)* • **RIVER WALKS** *You can walk the whole way along the Thames Path from Tower Bridge to*

the Isle of Dogs opposite the Dome. A great way of keeping abreast of London's changing river • **PARKS** Victoria Park. Surrounded by canals with large boating pond and lush sloping lawns. (see also Hackney).

SHOPS * * *

Shops are generally a bit tatty. If glitzy shopping malls are your thing, this isn't the place to be. But Tower Hamlets excels in lively street markets. Get there early for the best bargains.

SPITALFIELDS & WHITECHAPEL The craft shops, small restaurants and organic wholefood shops in the covered former fruit and vegetable market at Spitalfields have been in an almost permanent state of flux for years as City developers manoeuvre to build on Spitalfields' juiciest sites. A bit dead in the week (except at lunchtime), much better on Sundays. Asian shops line Brick Lane, with clothes wholesalers (lots of leather jackets), sweet shops and bookshops. Sunday market in Brick Lane. Daily clothes and household goods market at Petticoat Lane, Aldgate on the fringes of the city (see City of London). The Whitechapel end of Commercial Road is almost all Asian clothes wholesalers. Local shops and general daily market in Whitechapel Road • **WAPPING & LIMEHOUSE** Wapping's supposedly premier shopping centre, Tobacco Dock, is all but dead after 10 years of constant changes of ownership and indecision. The tobacco warehouse converted to two storeys of shops in the 1980s boom now has only one or two shops still open, with the rest empty. Plans to change it into a factory outlet never materialised. Big Safeway on the other side of News International and a handful of shops servicing the city workers and newspaper offices. Mostly local shops along Commercial Road by Limehouse • **BETHNAL GREEN** Trafficky Bethnal Green Road has cheap clothes and electrical goods shops, second-hand furniture and cafés alongside chains like Boots, Woolworth and a large Tesco Metro. Alright for everyday shopping. Popular Sunday flower market at Columbia Road which also has an eclectic collection of permanent shops including garden design and Indian sweetshops • **BOW** Roman Road has a well-established clothes market (although don't believe official promises that it goes on until 5.30pm). Some fascinating shops including designer clothes, expensive knick-knacks, antique furniture and a hat shop are grouped at the western end. Bow Wharf, which could be Tower Hamlets' answer to Camden Lock if things go according to plan, is taking shape just to the west of Roman Road, although only a few brave souls have taken shop space so far. Bow Wharf's part of a £30 million regeneration project to improve Mile End Park and the canal-side • **ISLE OF DOGS** Much criticised for its lack of shops when workers and daring residents first moved there. Now improving, with big Tesco Metro and a selection of up-market chains at Canary Wharf. Asda at Crossharbour. Nothing much else, with lots of boarded-up shops and dingy general stores, for desperate purchases only. Residents on the south end of the Island are looking forward to the opening of the DLR extension to Greenwich next year for an extension to their shopping choice.

RESTAURANTS * * *

SPITALFIELDS & WHITECHAPEL A good bagel bakery and a couple of recommended Indian restaurants among the huge choice along Brick Lane (you can smell the curry as soon as you turn into the street) and in Whitechapel, as well as pie and mash • **WAPPING & LIMEHOUSE** Good riverside pubs serving food include the Prospect of Witby in Wapping and *the Grapes in Limehouse. American theme restaurant and a couple of smartish Chinese and modern European places* • **BETHNAL GREEN** *A couple of Thai restaurants. Vegetarian and Spanish among a lot of take-away dross. Not much going on in the evening* • **BOW** *Not much, despite a growing middle class population. A pie and mash and a café or two overlooking Mile End Park but it's a bit dead in the evening, even in the pubs, according to locals* • **ISLE OF DOGS** *Considering the number of expense accounts around here, the offerings are limited. Cafe Rouge and a few other restaurant chains, winebars and cafés and American grill bars where City boys drink tasteless American beer from bottles.*

CRIME RATES*

High in the crime league table. 170 crimes per 1000 of population. Position in Metropolitan Police league table: 8th out of 32 (where 1 is worst and 32 best).

THE COUNCIL**

POLITICAL AFFILIATION *Labour* • **MINUS POINTS** *Still trying to extricate itself from a legacy of loony leftism and a distrastrous attempt at decentralisation during the previous Lib Dem adminstration. Some of the worst schools in London despite huge spending. Poor street-sweeping. The slowest in inner London at turning round land searches. Poorly resourced libraries* • **PLUS POINTS** *Appears to be making more strenous efforts to improve its education provision* • **PROPERTY SEARCHES CARRIED OUT IN 10 WORKING DAYS** *71%* • **STANDARD SEARCH FEE** *£85* • **COUNCIL TAX COLLECTED** *86.9%* • **COUNCIL TAX 1998-99**

BAND	PROPERTY VALUE	CHARGE	BAND	PROPERTY VALUE	CHARGE
A	up to £40,000	£439.18	E	£88,001-£120,000	£805.18
B	£40,001-£52,000	£512.38	F	£120,001-£160,000	£951.58
C	£52,001-£68,000	£585.59	G	£160,001-£320,000	£1,097.96
D	£68,001-£88,000	£658.78	H	over £320,000	£1,317.56

WALTHAM FOREST

Waltham Forest marks the beginning of outer East London, or inner Essex, whichever way you like to look at it. Sandwiched between the industrial Lea Valley to the west and Epping Forest bursting out between the built up suburban roads to the east, it's a favoured location for East Enders made good – or at least richer (see also Redbridge). Like Redbridge, Waltham Forest has never been top of the list for the fashion-conscious. Possibly the prospect of having Norman Tebbit as MP presented too much of a challenge for those who would otherwise have leapt at the chance of living in Chingford. More likely, it has suffered from the same West London snobbery as other parts of east London which are more suburban than trendy.

The Victorian working class railway suburbs of Leyton and Leytonstone cover the bottom quarter of Waltham Forest, giving way to Walthamstow, a pleasanter railway suburb and the borough's administrative and retail centre. To the north is salubrious Highams Park, large detached and semi-detached villas on the edge of Epping Forest. At South Chingford next to the Lea Valley, 1930s suburbia takes over where Victorian suburbia leaves off. At the northern tip of the borough, surrounded by Epping Forest on one side and the reservoirs of the Lea Valley on the other are the large Edwardian and inter-war houses of North Chingford.

This isn't middle class commuter belt suburbia, although it's one of the most convenient parts of outer London for the City and a lot cheaper than more traditionally favoured areas. Unemployment is among the highest in outer London at 7.1 per cent and it's the 20th most deprived area in England. It has an inner city-style multiracial population, with more than a quarter of the population from an ethnic minority and large Afro-Caribbean and Pakistani communities.

Leytonstone, a previously obscure area of East London, hit the headlines dramatically a few years ago when protesters against the building of a road linking the M11 to the east cross route in Hackney held out for more than a year against the demolition of houses and trees in roads along the route. Shots of protesters in makeshift towers and partially demolished Victorian terraces painted in day-glo hippy colours remain many peoples' main image of Leytonstone. All the protesters' efforts were fruitless, because the motorway is being built, with attendant roadworks until the end of this year at least. But it should remove some of the traffic from residential roads and Leytonstone High Road and make getting away from London quicker.

Planners are considering pedestrianising some of Leytonstone High Road after the motorway is finished as well as creating a new park. But this is small beer compared with ambitious proposals being discussed for Walthamstow, including an expanded shopping centre and multiscreen cinema and a new or expanded library.

PROPERTY AND ARCHITECTURE

LEYTON & LEYTONSTONE

Leyton has speculatively-thrown-up grids of Victorian terraces built in the last twenty years of the nineteenth century after the Great Eastern railway started offering cheap working mens' fares, bringing commuting within the reach of humble clerks. Particularly depressing on a rainy day. Here and there are dashes of later building and, more visibly, a cluster of council tower blocks and estates near the centre of Leyton. Leytonstone is an improvement, slightly more expensive, with the best properties nearest Wanstead.

ATTRACTS *First-time buyers; young professionals and couples; people who can't afford Islington or Hackney* • **CONSERVATION AREAS** *Browning Road; Thornhill Road; Whipps Cross Road & Forest Glade* • **AVERAGE PRICES** *Flats: studio: £35,000-£40,000; 1-bed: £40,000-£45,000; 2-bed: £45,000-£55,000+ Houses: 2-bed: £75,000-£80,000; 3-bed: £80,000-£130,000+; 4-bed: £90,000-£120,000* • **AVERAGE RENTS (MONTHLY)** *Flats: studio: £390-£430; 1-bed: £470-£520; 2-bed: £560-£650 Houses: 2-bed: £700-£735; 3-bed: £780+; 4-bed: £860.*

WALTHAMSTOW

Described by its most famous inhabitant, the designer William Morris, in the last century as" a suburban village on the edge of Epping and once a pleasant enough place but now terribly cockneyfied and choked up by the gerry builder." But a step up from Leyton and now increasingly favoured by young professionals who want more space for their money and easy access to the efficient Victoria line. Mostly Victorian terraces again around the south of Walthamstow but quite spacious and set back from the road. North of the main Forest Road round Lloyd Park is a clutch of red brick working mens' terraces and nineteenth century purpose-built flats with small wrought iron balconies, their line broken occasionally by an arch or gable. A refreshing change from the usual terrace, the terraces are known as Warners, after their builder. A good choice of conversion flats. Larger Victorian semis in Upper Walthamstow to the east and attractive old cottages in Walthamstow Village.

ATTRACTS *Young professionals; people who can't afford Islington or Hackney; commuters; first-time buyers* • **CONSERVATION AREAS** *Walthamstow Village; Leucha Road; Orford Road, Eden Road & Grosvenor Road; Forest School* • **AVERAGE PRICES** *Flats: studio: £40,000; 1-bed: £45,000; 2-bed: £55,000+ Houses: 2-bed: £75,000-£80,000; 3-bed: £80,000-£130,000; 4-bed: £120,000+; 5-bed: £125,000+* • **AVERAGE RENTS (MONTHLY)** *Flats: studio: £390-£430; 1-bed: £470-£520; 2-bed: £560-£650 Houses: 2-bed: £700-£735; 3-bed: £780+; 4-bed: £860; 5-bed: £1080+.*

HIGHAMS PARK

More suburban and salubrious than Walthamstow with large Victorian and Edwardian semi-detached and detached houses in big gardens. Many have all their original features intact, the streets are wide and Epping Forest is there as a backdrop. Mostly up-market 1930s houses further south towards the north circular.

ATTRACTS *Families* • **CONSERVATION AREAS** *Ropers Avenue & Inks Green* • **AVERAGE PRICES** *Flats: 1-bed: £55,000-£65,000; 2-bed: £65,000-£80,000 Houses: 2-bed: £90,000+; 3-bed: £100,000+; 4-bed: £170,000+* • **AVERAGE RENTS (MONTHLY)** *Flats: studio: £390; 1-bed: £455+; 2-bed: £560+; 3-bed: £650-£700 Houses: 2-bed: £650-£700; 3-bed: £650-£900; 4-bed: £800-£1000; 5-bed: £800-£1000.*

CHINGFORD

Synonymous in many people's minds with the bruiser reputation of its former MP Norman Tebbit. But North Chingford, at least, is much smarter and more attractive than its public image would suggest. Epping Forest opens out at the end of the main Station Road and large half-timbered Edwardian houses with flurries of turrets, carved wooden balconies, porches and stained glass line the streets between the Forest and the station. South Chingford is cheaper, partly because the houses are smaller (more Victorian terraces mixed with some 1930s) and partly because it's a long way from trains and tubes.

ATTRACTS *Families* • **CONSERVATION AREA** *Chingford Green* • **AVERAGE PRICES** *Flats: 1-bed: £50,000-£60,000; 2-bed: £65,000-£140,000 Houses: 3-bed: £110,000-£140,000; 4-bed: £210,000+; 5-bed: £250,000+* **AVERAGE RENTS (MONTHLY)** *Flats: studio: £400-£475; 1-bed: £455-£700; 2-bed: £560-£900 Houses: 2-bed: £650-£900; 3-bed: £650-£1000; 4-bed: £800-£2000; 5-bed: £800-£2000.*

BEST POSTCODES

All in the London postcode area apart from a small section of Highams Park. Chingford E4 is the smartest. Leytonstone E11 and Walthamstow E17 are better than Leyton E10. But factors like proximity to transport links have the most significant effect on prices.

AMENITIES

SCHOOLS * *

Uninspired overall league table performance from both primary and secondary schools although not scraping the bottom. Secondary schools do slightly better than primary schools. At the age of five some schools operate a system of linked infant and junior schools while others are primary schools taking children from five onwards. A handful of private schools. Below-average numbers of pre-school children in state nursery schools.

PRE-SCHOOL PROVISION *4 state nursery schools; 36 nursery classes in state primary and church schools; 69 private day nurseries and playgroups. Proportion of under-fives in state nursery school places: 54%* • **STATE PRIMARY SCHOOLS** *Overall league table position: 120th out of 150. Top scorers: Hundsworth (with nursery unit), Chingford; St Joseph's RC, Leyton; St Mary's C of E, Walthamstow* • **STATE SECONDARY SCHOOLS** *Overall league table position: 102nd out of 150. Best scorers: Highams Park (mixed), Highams Park; Connaught School for Girls, Leyton; Walthamstow School for Girls, Walthamstow* • **PRIVATE PREP SCHOOLS** *Forest Prep (mixed), Walthamstow* • **PRIVATE SECONDARY SCHOOLS** *Forest (boys), Walthamstow; Forest Girls (Walthamstow); Normanhurst (mixed from 2) Chingford.*

TRANSPORT * * *

Walthamstow's very well connnected, thanks mainly to the Victoria line (generally efficient despite some problems with signalling occasionally). Trains as well as tubes from a choice of different stations. Central line at Leyton and Leytonstone (improving). The north of the borough relies on trains.

TRAINS *Highams Park: Zone 4. Cost of annual season ticket: £1068; No of trains per hour: to Liverpool Street 3; Fastest journey: 22 minutes. Chingford: Zone 5. Cost of annual season ticket: £1252; No of trains per hour: to Liverpool Street 3; Fastest journey: 25 minutes* • **TUBES** *Leyton: Zone 3. Cost of annual season ticket: £860; Frequency: Central line to Oxford Circus every 3-5 minutes; Fastest journey: 23 minutes. Walthamstow Central: Zone 3. Frequency: Victoria line: to Victoria every 4 minutes; Fastest journey: 26 minutes* • **BUSES** *Quite a good choice to the centre of town, with the* necessary proviso that any long bus journey usually means sitting in traffic. Services include the 48 from London Bridge to Walthamstow Central via Leyton, the 55 from Oxford Circus to Leyton and the 56 from St Pauls to Leytonstone, Leyton and Walthamstow. Otherwise local services to neighbouring suburbs and shopping centres • **TRAFFIC BLACKSPOTS** Leyton & Leytonstone: High roads in both areas are often clogged with traffic. One of the reasons given for building the M11 link road is that it will take through-traffic away from shopping streets. Whether it will remains to be seen. Walthamstow: Forest Road, the main through-road across Walthamstow is trafficky, particularly at junctions with roads linking to the North Circular. Quicker to walk on a Saturday Chingford: Constant flow of traffic and buses along Station Road, the main shopping street and long queues can build up around the Green at the end of the road by the library • **PARKING** Currently six controlled parking zones in the borough: Waltham Central East, Walthamstow Central West, Blackhorse Lane, Walthamstow Stadium (nights), Chingford (voucher parking) and Hoe Street, Walthamstow. Cost of annual resident's permit: £25. Further zones are being considered for: Leytonstone, Leyton, North Chingford, Highams Park and Wood Street, Walthamstow.

LEISURE FACILITIES * * *

THEATRES & CONCERT HALLS The Waltham Forest theatre is set in attractive formal grounds by the lake in Lloyd Park, Walthamstow (although the building itself is unremarkable) and has a choice of mainstream plays, live music, community and children's shows. More choice of entertainment at Walthamstow Assembly Hall next to the Town Hall. Both can be hired, as can halls in Chingford, Leyton and elsewhere in the borough • **CINEMAS** Just one, the Walthamstow ABC, strictly mainstream • **MUSEUMS & GALLERIES** Interesting collection. The William Morris Gallery is housed in the designer's old home, a handsome Georgian mansion in Lloyd Park, once the grounds of the house. The museum is devoted to Morris's designs with rooms full of rich dark wall-papers, tapestries and stained glass put into context with explanation boards and photographs. Little on his social vision though. In Walthamstow village (worth a visit in itself for its ancient houses and picturesque church), the local history Vestry museum occupies what was once a workhouse. Mock-ups of the kitchens and living rooms of Walthamstow's first Victorian residents, exhibition of toys and games and temporary exhibitions. Art exhibitions, photography and show-cases for local artists at the Changing Room gallery, Lloyd Park and the William Morris Gallery • **SPORTS FACILITIES** Four leisure centres at Leytonstone (new Millennium fitness centre), Leyton, and Walthamstow (two, both with new or extended gym facilities). Pools in Leytonstone, Leyton, and Walthamstow. Golf in Chingford, greyhound racing at Walthamstow and tennis, football and other outdoor sports in parks and open space throughout the borough. Discount leisure scheme in operation • **LIBRARIES** Small cramped buildings even at Walthamstow central, although this last is being refurbished, hopefully leaving its lovely moulded ceiling and wrought iron light holders intact. It could be replaced by a larger building, if proposals get past the drawing board. But libraries as a whole are some of the best used in London. Reasonable opening hours although patchy in some branch libraries. 9.7 library visits per head. Position in library-use league table: 5th out of 32 (where 1 is best and 32 worst).

OPEN SPACES * * * *

Waltham Forest claims, along with almost every other outer London borough, to be one of the greenest in London. But does the pecking order matter with all having something striking to offer? Some beautiful open space here with the northern reaches giving way suddenly to gently undulating Essex countryside.

FOREST Epping Forest. Runs down the whole of the borough's eastern border with Redbridge before taking over totally at Chingford. Owned by the Corporation of London and run by the Epping Forest and Open Spaces Committee. A mixture of mature woodland and open grassland, and a haven for riders, cyclists and walkers, the forest pops up all over the place, behind suburban homes and next to council flats • **PARKS** Lloyd Park. A green lung in an otherwise built-up area, with formal flower beds (overlooked by the William Morris gallery) and lake with hungry ducks. Turns flat and featureless the further away you go from the gallery.

SHOPS***

LEYTON & LEYTONSTONE Busy, trafficky high roads with necessary but dull chains and the usual clutch of take-aways, chemists, charity shops and cash converters. Unexciting shopping, not improved by the need to take your life in your hands every time you cross the road. Tesco in Leyton. Proposed Tesco in Leytonstone • **WALTHAMSTOW** Much more colourful, with a 400 stall, mile-long street market, supposedly the longest daily street market in Europe, down most of the length of the High Street. Clothes, food, household goods and anything else energetically promoted by stallholders. Selbourne Walk, the indoor shopping mall opening off the High Street, is more functional than glitzy, with down-market chains. Sainsbury's • **HIGHAMS PARK & CHINGFORD** Unspectacular but useful shopping streets around Highams Park station. Chingford itself has tidy local shops in an Edwardian shopping street with a real butcher and grocer among other shops. Everyday shopping at Chingford Mount, with Sainsbury's.

RESTAURANTS**

A handful of recommended restaurants and eating experiences, including Spanish in Leytonstone. Pizzas, pie and mash, and dog-trackside dining at Walthamstow. Pizza Express in Chingford. Otherwise, it's the local Indian, Chinese or kebab house.

CRIME RATES***

115 crimes per 1000 of population. Position in Metropolitan Police league table: 17th out of 32 (where 1 is worst and 32 best).

THE COUNCIL***

POLITICAL AFFILIATION Labour • **MINUS POINTS** Slowish on turning round property searches (although it's the second cheapest in London). Not always as efficient at collecting street litter as it should be (old black plastic rubbish sacks were in evidence) • **PLUS POINTS** Cheap fees for property searches. Door-to-door recycling for 20,000 homes and being expanded. Well used libraries • **PROPERTY SEARCHES CARRIED OUT IN 10 WORKING DAYS** 89% • **STANDARD SEARCH FEE** £76 • **COUNCIL TAX COLLECTED** 91% • **COUNCIL TAX 1998-99**

BAND	PROPERTY VALUE	CHARGE	BAND	PROPERTY VALUE	CHARGE
A	up to £40,000	£542.44	E	£88,001-£120,000	£994.47
B	£40,001-£52,000	£632.85	F	£120,001-£160,000	£1,175.29
C	£52,001-£68,000	£723.25	G	£160,001-£320,000	£1,356.10
D	£68,001-£88,000	£813.66	H	over £320,000	£1,627.32

WANDSWORTH

Wandsworth has spent the past 10 years becoming more and more middle class. The process started quietly but rose to a crescendo as the press started writing glowingly about its wonderful family houses, green space and excellent state schools. The council, a Thatcherite flagship, helped things along by setting the lowest council tax of any London borough (underpinned by some nifty central government grants) and energetically selling off council property to upwardly-mobile tenants. Now gentrification has spread to all four corners of the borough, with even formerly working class Battersea now an unofficial annexe of Chelsea.

Like other south London boroughs, Wandsworth is big. At its northern edge along the river it sprawls from the terraces and council blocks of Battersea in the east through the former warehouses and smartened-up terraces of Wandsworth to the riverfront mansion blocks and detached Edwardian grandeur of Putney in the west. Further south, detached houses and smart modern blocks in Southfields give way to large Edwardian terraces in Earlsfield and detached houses between Wandsworth Common and Clapham Common. Smaller Victorian terraces take over again at Balham before being ousted by large Edwardian semis around Tooting's two commons.

Parts of Wandsworth are very affluent and the influx of middle class residents has kept its overall unemployment rate low. At 5.3 per cent, it has the second lowest unemployment rate of any inner London borough, bested only by the City of London where many Wandsworth residents work. But the borough is also the 21st most deprived district in England, with much of the deprivation focused on the former industrial areas along the river at Battersea and Wandsworth. The council is pouring more than £6 million into East Battersea to create jobs and provide training, stimulated by the planned £500 million redevelopment of the derelict Battersea Power Station.

Developers have been busier in Wandsworth than almost anywhere else except Docklands, working to transform derelict buildings and abandoned industrial river sites into luxury homes, shops, hotels and restaurants, sometimes running into fierce opposition from residents. The attraction for developers of course is that Wandsworth is now more than acceptable to the middle classes. One problem for developers and residents alike, however, is that efforts to persuade successive governments to extend the tube network to Wandsworth have so far failed. Plans for a £1 billion plus new line from Hackney to Chelsea extending to Wandsworth Town and/or Battersea haven't got past the drawing board, leaving residents in the north east of the borough with no tube link and heavily reliant on buses for short journeys.

This doesn't help the traffic congestion which is one of the borough's biggest problems. Wandsworth Town Centre itself is the junction of three major roads, including the notorious south circular and the main A3 to Portsmouth which also goes through Putney. More traffic pours out to Brighton via Tooting and across Wandsworth Bridge under one of the most brutal 1960s underpasses in London.

PROPERTY AND ARCHITECTURE

BATTERSEA

Once a mostly working class district with a distinctly dodgy reputation but colonised by economic refugees from Chelsea and beyond since it was "discovered" in the 1980s. Small well-cared-for Victorian terraces and cottages predominate near the river and around the yuppie spiritual centre of Battersea Square near the river, mixed with new riverside developments and council blocks of all descriptions. Smart mansion blocks overlooking Battersea Park. Between a tangle of railway tracks and the area's main restaurant drag on Lavender Hill, there are pretty streets of small Victorian cottages with deep porches on the Shaftesbury Park Estate. Larger Victorian terraces in roads off Lavender Hill.

ATTRACTS *Young professionals, both single and with families; people who can't afford Chelsea or Fulham* • **CONSERVATION AREAS** *Battersea Park; Battersea Square; Latchmere Estate; Parktown Estate; Shaftesbury Park Estate; Clapham Junction* • **AVERAGE PRICES** *Flats: studio: £75,000- £90,000; 1-bed: £85,000-£135,000; 2-bed: £120,000-£250,000; 3-bed: £250,000-£275,000; 4-bed: £325,000-£365,000 Houses: 2-bed: £200,000-£275,000; 3-bed: £220,000-£300,000; 4-bed: £300,000-£350,000; 5-bed: £400,000-£500,000* • **AVERAGE RENTS (MONTHLY)** *Flats: studio: £520-£730; 1-bed: £730-£860; 2-bed: £860- £1190; 3-bed: £1190-£2160 Houses: 2-bed: £1300; 3-bed: £1510- £1730; 4-bed: £1950-£2380; 5-bed: £1950-£2815.*

WANDSWORTH

Several distinct parts, all sought after. Small well-looked-after terraces in the sloping roads known collectively as The Tonsleys, centring on Tonsley Hill near Wandsworth Town railway station. Larger Victorian and Edwardian terraces, some converted, others still houses, in roads off East Hill. And the crème de la crème, five-bedroom and larger, detached, mostly Edwardian houses with large gardens, in the roads between Wandsworth Common and Clapham Common, an area known cloyingly as " 'twixt the Commons". On the other side of Wandsworth Common, is a grid of roads of large Edwardian and Victorian houses known as The Toastrack because of its shape on the map.

ATTRACTS *Families looking for green space and good schools (catchment areas are very important); people who can't afford the space they want in Clapham or Fulham* • **CONSERVATION AREAS** *Clapham Common; Wandsworth Common; Nightingale Lane; Wandsworth Town; St John's Hillgrove* • **AVERAGE PRICES** *Flats: studio: £50,000-£60,000; 1-bed: £60,000-£100,000; 2-bed: £110,000-£300,000 Houses: 2-bed: £180,000; 3-bed: £220,000-£300,000; 4-bed: £290,000-£400,000;*

5-bed: £500,000-£2 million • **AVERAGE RENTS (MONTHLY)** *Flats: 1-bed: £780-£860; 2-bed: £990-£1170 Houses: 2-bed: £1190-£1516; 3-bed: £1625-£1840; 4-bed: £1950-£3900; 5-bed: £4333-£5200.*

BALHAM & TOOTING

Balham used to be a bit of a joke, not helped by Peter Sellers' mocking description of it as Gateway to the South. It had a bit of an identity crisis, with people claiming to live in Wandsworth or Tooting or Clapham – anywhere but Balham. But now the area is up-and-coming, particularly around Tooting and Wandsworth Commons. Mostly Victorian and Edwardian terraces, with handsome Edwardian double-fronted houses, some flats, on the Heaver Estate off Tooting Common. More Edwardiana in Tooting, with large semi-detached houses with gardens around Tooting Graveney Common. Cottage-style terraces in roads off Fransciscan Road at Totterdown Fields in Tooting Bec, one of the first council estates.

ATTRACTS *Professionals, who praise the area's good community atmosphere; families who value good schools; people who can't afford Clapham; members of the Asian community •* **CONSERVATION AREAS** *Heaver Estate; Totterdown Fields; Streatham Park; Dinsmore Road; Old Devonshire Road •* **AVERAGE PRICES** *Flats: studio: £65,000; 1-bed: £90,000; 2-bed: £115,000-£200,000; 3-bed: £150,000-£200,000; 4-bed: £170,000-£250,000 Houses: 1-bed: £70,000; 2-bed: £200,000-£260,000; 3-bed: £200,000-£250,000; 4-bed: £250,000-£350,000 •* **AVERAGE RENTS (MONTHLY)** *Flats: studio: £530; 1-bed: £560+; 2-bed: £780-£1300; 3-bed: £1080-£1625 Houses: 3-bed: £1250-£1625; 4-bed: £2050+; 5-bed: £2600+.*

SOUTHFIELDS & EARLSFIELD

Dull, straight, flat roads in Earlsfield and the east of Southfields lined with square-bayed Edwardian terraces and semis. But increasingly popular with families who like getting relatively large amounts of space for their money. West Southfields is more expensive and residents make a mint during Wimbledon fortnight renting out drives or whole houses. Large detached Edwardian and 1930s houses mixed with modern blocks on hills up towards Putney. More interesting shops and pubs have arrived in Southfields to service the new young crowd.

ATTRACTS *Families (Earlsfield); young professional couples (Southfields) •* **CONSERVATION AREAS** *West Hill Road; Wimbledon Park Road; Victoria Drive; Sutherland Grove •* **AVERAGE PRICES** *Flats: studio: £65,000; 1-bed: £85,000-£110,000; 2-bed: £100,000-£170,000; 3-bed: £160,000-£200,000 Houses: 1-bed: £85,000-£90,000; 2-bed: £170,000-£210,000; 3-bed: £185,000-£250,000; 4-bed: £240,000-£350,000; 5-bed: £350,000-£450,000 •* **AVERAGE RENTS (MONTHLY)** *Flats: 1-bed: £650-£850; 2-bed: £700-£1000; 3-bed: £1000-£1250 Houses: 2-bed: £950-£1500; 3-bed: £1350-£1750; 4-bed: £1600-£1750; 5-bed: £2200-£3000.*

PUTNEY & ROEHAMPTON

Putney has always been a good solid residential area but it has livened up considerably over the past few years as more younger people have moved in. As elsewhere, the draws are schools, green space and good transport. A mixture of everything from large detached Edwardian houses in West Putney (the grandest part) to cottages and Victorian houses and terraces of all sizes in roads off Putney High Street and Lower Richmond Road. Some conversions and clusters of modern blocks of flats, particularly at the top of Putney Hill. Mansion blocks by the river. Lots of council blocks at cheaper Roehampton, mixed with some Georgian and Victorian cottages and terraces and large family houses near Putney Heath.

ATTRACTS *Young families; single professionals; affluent first-time buyers; mature families* • **CONSERVATION AREAS** *East Putney; Rushholme Road; Putney Heath; Roehampton Village; Westmead; Dover House Estate; West Putney; Coalecroft Road; Charlwood Road; Lifford Street; Oxford Road; Deodar Road; Putney Embankment; Putney Lower Common* • **AVERAGE PRICES** *Flats: studio: £40,000-£90,000; 1-bed: £60,000-£130,000; 2-bed: £80,000-£200,000; 3-bed: £170,000-£240,000; 4-bed: £220,000-£330,000 Houses: 2-bed: £130,000-£250,000; 3-bed: £160,000-£320,000; 4-bed: £330,000-£500,000; 5-bed: £350,000-£1m* • **AVERAGE RENTS (MONTHLY)** *Flats studio: £550-£650; 1-bed: £750-£1200; 2-bed: £950-£1500; 3-bed: £1100-£1800 Houses: 2-bed: £1000-£1600; 3-bed: £1600-£2500; 4-bed: £2300-£3500; 5-bed: £3000-£5000.*

BEST POSTCODES

Not a big deal because postcode areas cross and recross the boundaries of the various residential areas. Putney SW15, Wandsworth SW18 and Battersea SW11 are all very acceptable. No big price differences. The dividing line that matters is the borough boundary between Wandsworth and Lambeth, with cheap and efficient Wandsworth the side everyone wants to be on.

AMENITIES

SCHOOLS * * *

Widely praised by parents, although state schools generally don't do as well in league tables as you might expect. Strict catchment areas operate for many primary schools at the top of the tables. Wandsworth schools operate their own individual selection tests, with several selecting on academic ability. There are plans to streamline the testing procedure by September 2000 so that all tests take place on the same day. There will either be a single test, or if this proves unworkable, schools will share information. A good selection of private schools at all levels and generous pre-school provision, both state and private.

PRE-SCHOOL PROVISION *3 state nursery schools; 46 nursery classes in state primary and church schools; 133 private or voluntary nurseries and playgroups. Proportion of under-fives in state nurseries: 73%* • **STATE PRIMARY SCHOOLS** *Overall place in league table: 93rd out of 150. Top scorers: Our Lady of Victories RC, Putney; St Anselm's RC, Tooting; Our Lady Queen of Heaven, Southfields. Tight catchment areas at other high scorers including: Beatrix Potter, Wandsworth; Fransciscan, Furzedown, Penwortham and Sellincourt Schools, Tooting* • **STATE SECONDARY SCHOOLS** *Overall place in league table: 115th out of 150. High scorers: ADT City Techology College (mixed), Putney; Burntwood School (girls), Tooting; Graveney (mixed), Tooting* • **PRIVATE PREP SCHOOLS** *Finton House (mixed), Wandsworth; Thomas's Prep (mixed), Battersea; Prospect House (mixed), Putney; Putney Park (mixed to 11), Putney; Northcote Lodge (mixed),*

Wandsworth; Broomwood Hall (mixed), Balham; Ibstock Place (mixed), Roehampton • **PRIVATE SECONDARY SCHOOLS** *Putney High (girls), Putney; Ibstock Place (mixed), Roehampton; Emanuel School (mixed), Battersea; Putney Park (girls), Putney.*

TRANSPORT * * *

Good tube services to the west and south of the borough but the East relies on trains and buses, although it boasts Britain's busiest railway station, Clapham Junction.

TRAINS Battersea (Queenstown Road): *Zone 2. Cost of annual season ticket: £704; No of trains per hour: to Waterloo 6; Fastest journey: 7 minutes.* Clapham Junction: *Zone 2. No of trains per hour: to Waterloo 37; Fastest journey: 10 minutes.* Wandsworth Town: *Zone 2. No of trains per hour: to Waterloo 6; Fastest journey: 12 minutes.* Balham: *Zone 3. Cost of annual season ticket: £860; No of trains per hour: to Victoria 11; Fastest journey: 12 minutes.* Putney: *Zone 2. No of trains per hour: to Waterloo 8; Fastest journey: 15 minutes* • **TUBES** East Putney: *Zone 2. Frequency: District: to Embankment every 10 minutes; Fastest journey: 23 minutes.* Southfields: *Zone 3. Frequency: District: to Embankment every 10 minutes; Fastest journey: 25 minutes.* Balham: *Zone 3. Frequency: Northern: to London Bridge every 3-6 minutes; Fastest journey: 22 minutes.* Tooting Broadway: *Zone 3. Frequency: Northern line: to London Bridge every 3-6 minutes; Fastest journey: 26 minutes* • **BUSES** *A good range of bus routes, particularly around Putney, Wandsworth and Clapham Junction in the north of the borough. Scarcer in the south, with mostly suburban services. Some useful cross-borough routes. Buses to town include: the 14 from Putney to Tottenham Court Road; the 19 from Battersea Bridge to Piccadilly; the 22 from Putney to Piccadilly; the 77 from Tooting via Wandsworth Common, Clapham and Battersea to Waterloo* • **TRAFFIC BLACKSPOTS** Wandsworth: *Town Centre. Where several main roads (including the A205 south circular and the A3) meet and cross. Often bad traffic jams round the Arndale shopping centre. Roads around the common (Bellevue Road and Bolingbroke Grove especially) often jammed.* Putney: *The High Street. Too narrow for the amount of traffic it carries. Blockages are common where traffic has to move into one lane after coming over Putney Bridge. Problems with parked delivery vans.* Battersea: *Long tail-backs at traffic lights around Battersea Square. Small streets too narrow for the traffic they attract.* Balham & Tooting: *Always lots of traffic near the main shopping areas of Balham High Road and Upper Tooting Road. This succession of shopping streets doubles as a main road to Gatwick airport, among other places* • **PARKING** *Parking is getting trickier as more car owners move in and commuters create their own unofficial Park-and-Ride schemes. There are three controlled parking zones in the borough, each divided into zones. Permits issued for one zone aren't valid in any other zone.* Battersea: *Battersea Park. Streets around the park and the park itself. Cost of annual permit: £30.* Clapham Junction: *Three zones. Cost of annual resident's permit: £42.* Putney: *Four zones. Cost of annual resident's permit: £42. Consultations underway on additional schemes for Tooting and Wandsworth Town.*

LEISURE FACILITIES * * *

THEATRES & CONCERT HALLS *Battersea Arts Centre (BAC) in the former Battersea Town Hall building (worth going to see just for its wonderful painted ceilings, marble staircase and mosaic floors). A variety of fringe* shows and comedy as well as more mainstream theatre. The Wandsworth Symphony Orchestra puts on concerts at local venues • **CINEMAS** Not a huge choice. Currently only one, the Putney ABC, which shows mostly mainstream films. Plans for a new 18-screen cinema in the Arndale Centre as part of the area's revamp • **MUSEUMS & GALLERIES** Not a good place for culture vultures. Only the Wandsworth Museum (local history) • **SPORTS FACILITIES** Well provided for. Seven leisure centres at Putney, Battersea, Balham, Tooting, Roehampton and Wandsworth. There are plans to build a big bowling hall at Wandsworth. Popular outdoor Lido at Tooting Bec. Rowing at Putney. Tennis and football at Tooting Bec Common and King George's Park by Putney Bridge. Athletics track at Tooting Bec • **LIBRARIES** Well-resourced and some of the best anywhere in London. Sunday afternoon opening at four libraries: Balham, Tooting Battersea and Putney (now in a swish new modern building). Good evening opening hours but all lending libraries closed either Wednesday or Thursday. Reference libraries at Battersea and Wandsworth. 10.1 library visits per head. Position in library-use league table: 3rd out of 32 (where 1 is best and 32 worst).

OPEN SPACES ***

Good supply of open space, although Wandsworth and Tooting Commons are blighted by busy roads and criss-crossed by railway lines. Close to beautiful Richmond Park and Wimbledon Common although technically these are in neighbouring boroughs (Richmond-upon-Thames and Merton respectively). Much of the borough's best open space is private, in the large gardens of many family houses.

URBAN WILDERNESS The overgrown parts of Putney Heath and the wooded parts of Wandsworth Common are good for getting away from the traffic • **PARKS** Battersea Park. Good views from the riverside frontage next to the striking peace pagoda and plenty of lush space and trees in an otherwise densely populated area. A popular venue for circuses, funfairs and fireworks.

SHOPS ****

BATTERSEA & CLAPHAM JUNCTION Estate agents have colonised almost anything in Lavender Hill that isn't a restaurant. This and the up-market furniture shops are a sure sign of a significant yuppie presence. Big choice of shops (mostly chains) around Clapham Junction and along St John's Road where there are plans to improve the street environment and cut traffic. Arding and Hobbs, the long-established local department store is on the corner of St John's Road. Large Asda on Lavender Hill and Lidl discount food store. Mostly small and depressing shops on Battersea Park Road. Kwiksave • **WANDSWORTH** The Arndale Centre in Wandsworth Town Centre is an appalling 1960s concrete bunker next to thundering traffic and in desperate need of an overhaul, which is what it's going to get. Tesco will be demolished and new shops, car parks and restaurants are planned. Smart shops opposite Wandsworth Common in Bellevue Road including the original branch of Phase Eight, a bookshop and interior design shops. More up-market shops in Northcote Road including antiques, books and records. Sainsbury's at Garrett Lane • **TOOTING & BALHAM** Wide range of shops in the confluence of roads around Tooting Broadway and Tooting Bec stations (although heavy traffic doesn't improve the experience and the streets themselves are architecturally dull). Chains including M&S and Boots but also ethnic supermarkets, a traditional cobbler and some individual clothes shops. Tooting Market, an indoor market selling English

and Afro-Caribbean fruit and vegetables, clothes and furniture.
Appreciated by residents for its cheapness. Sainsbury's in Balham High
Road. Sainsbury's proposed in Tooting • **PUTNEY** Radical improvements
here over the past 20 years with the arrival of the Putney Exchange
shopping centre in the High Street, a large Waitrose to supplement the
rather cramped Sainsbury's and a host of new shops to cater for the influx
of younger residents. All the usual chains plus antique and reproduction
furniture, jewellers and designer clothes. Interesting shops in Lacy Road off
the High Street including a music shop and traditional toy shop. Heavy
traffic damps enthusiasm but residents and planners are thrashing out
plans to ease some of the worst of it.

RESTAURANTS★★★★

BATTERSEA & CLAPHAM Bewildering choice in Lavender Hill with everything
from Indian to Afro-Caribbean alongside brasseries, cafés and bars with
pavement seating. Active in the evening. More pavement cafés around
the small enclave of Battersea Square with awnings managing to replicate
an authentic continental atmosphere • **WANDSWORTH** A good selection
of brasseries, pubs and restaurants in Old York Road just down from
The Tonsleys. Tables overlooking Wandsworth Common at pubs and
restaurants in Bellevue Road and further options in Northcote Road, the
local high street for residents of the sought-after neighbouring streets •
TOOTING A group of well-regarded Indian restaurants in Upper Tooting
Road and Tooting High Street • **PUTNEY** A good buzz in the evening, even
on weekdays. Everything from pubs to Thai, Indian and Italian. A cluster of
interesting new restaurants in roads down towards the river including the
stunning glass bus-shelter-style Putney Bridge restaurant with river views.

CRIME RATES★★★

121 crimes per 1,000 of the population (the lowest in inner London).
Position in Metropolitan Police league table: 15th out of 32 (where 1 is
worst and 32 best).

THE COUNCIL★★★★

POLITICAL AFFILIATION Conservative • **MINUS POINTS** Some lease-holders
who have bought their council properties under the Right-to-Buy scheme
have faced high service charges. Enthusiastic espousal of Tory policies like
selective schools and selling off council property may not be to everyone's
taste • **PLUS POINTS** The lowest council tax in the UK, never mind London.
Makes an effort to listen to residents through 1,000-strong panel set up last
year (1998) and got the thumbs up for general performance from more
than three quarters of residents in its most recent survey. Active moves to
cut down on crime with use of CCTV, neighbourhood-watch schemes and
council-hired Parks Police. Weekly door-to-door recycling collection.
Praised by residents for efficient road-mending and street-sweeping •
PROPERTY SEARCHES CARRIED OUT IN 10 WORKING DAYS 96% • **STANDARD
SEARCH FEE** £115 •**COUNCIL TAX COLLECTED** 87.9%

• **COUNCIL TAX 1998-99**

BAND	PROPERTY VALUE	CHARGE	BAND	PROPERTY VALUE	CHARGE
A	up to £40,000	£212.00	E	£88,001-£120,000	£389.00
B	£40,001-£52,000	£248.00	F	£120,001-£160,000	£460.00
C	£52,001-£68,000	£283.00	G	£160,001-£320,000	£531.00
D	£68,001-£88,000	£319.00	H	over £320,000	£637.00

WESTMINSTER

If you know London only as a tourist you will almost certainly have spent most of your time in Westminster (unless you're very enterprising). The City of Westminster, to give it its proper name, is home to most of the top sights on the tourist itinerary including the Houses of Parliament, Buckingham Palace, the Changing of the Guard and Madame Tussaud's. It contains London's most famous shopping streets including Oxford Street and Regent Street as well as London's poshest address, Eaton Square, Belgravia.

But there's a lot of Westminster the tourists don't see and not all of it is attractive and/or expensive. In the top north-west corner lies West Kilburn, streets of small Victorian terraces, large stucco houses that have seen better days and the sprawling Mozart council estate. South of Kilburn, Paddington is a mess of hotels, railway tracks and council estates with some bravely gleaming roads of white stucco houses, particularly around Bayswater. There are however big plans for the former industrial areas at Paddington Basin around the canal by the station and St Mary's Hospital, including new arts and leisure facilities and residential developments. The recent opening of the Heathrow Express to Paddington should also bring new impetus to the area.

Things improve to the east with the wide streets and canal-side homes of Maida Vale and Little Venice, with the smart villas of St John's Wood just to the north. Next to Regents Park is Marylebone, once dismissed as not much more than a traffic-clogged main road but now becoming fashionable. Between Hyde Park and Green Park are the grand Georgian townhouses and terracotta mansion blocks of Mayfair, in complete contrast to the sex shops and trendy apartments of neighbouring Soho. South of Green Park are the stucco mansions and mews of Belgravia. Westminster and Pimlico are attracting new interest as developers move in.

The rich parts of Westminster to the east and south are among the richest in London. It has the fourth lowest unemployment rate of any inner London borough at 6.2 per cent. It's also one of the most cosmopolitan, with nearly a quarter of its population from an ethnic minority and large Afro-Caribbean, Middle Eastern and Jewish communities. But the Homes for Votes scandal in which Conservative-run Westminster Council carried out a policy of gerrymandering to move Labour-voting council house tenants out of marginal wards drew attention to the sharp contrast between the rich and the poor in the borough. Deprivation is widespread and the borough ranks as the 26th most deprived in England.

The down-side of living in central London is that it means fighting a constant battle against litter, traffic and crowds. Residents in Soho are demanding action to clean up the area which they say has become a magnet for drug dealers. The up-side is that you're at or near the centre of one of the most exciting cities in the world.

PROPERTIES AND ARCHITECTURE

BELGRAVIA & KNIGHTSBRIDGE

Where the very best (or at least the very richest) live. Almost the whole of Belgravia is owned by the Grosvenor Estate, one of London's biggest landowners. Massive stucco terraces with elaborate columns in Eaton Square, recently voted London's grandest address. Smaller scale (but still large) stucco houses in Chester Square, choice of Baroness Thatcher among others. Some of the most attractive mews houses in London, many reached through archways, tucked behind the grand houses. No property here is cheap but the shorter the lease, generally the cheaper the property. Embassies have taken over many of the large houses in Belgrave Square. You either love Belgravia for its elegance or hate it for its coldness. A mixture of red brick-gabled mansion blocks, early Victorian flat-fronted terraces and mews cottages in equally smart Knightsbridge.

ATTRACTS *The wealthy of all nations, especially Europeans; bankers, stockbrokers; glitterati* • **CONSERVATION AREAS** *Belgravia; Grosvenor Gardens; Albert Gate; Royal Parks* • **AVERAGE PRICES** • *Flats: studio: £100,000-£175,000; 1-bed: £175,000-£350,000; 2-bed: £270,000-£550,000; 3-bed: £500,000-£900,000; 4-bed: £850,000-£1.5 million Houses: 1-bed: £500,000-£750,000; 2-bed: £600,000-£850,000; 3-bed: £750,000-£1.3m; 4-bed: £1m+* • **AVERAGE RENTS (MONTHLY)** *Flats: studio: £1080; 1-bed: £1300-£1950; 2-bed: £1950-£3250; 3-bed: £2810-£4330; 4-bed: £4330 Houses: 2-bed: £2160-£3030; 3-bed: £3460-£4330; 4 bed+: £6500+.*

PIMLICO & WESTMINSTER

Not as grand as neighbouring Belgravia. Pimlico used to be run-down, its stucco houses divided into bed-sits and short-let flats. Now improving as more properties are converted and the developers move in. Mostly flats and much more mixed than Belgravia with council blocks occupying prime river frontage next to Dolphin Square, the soul-less but popular modern block where the Princess Royal once had a flat. Westminster and Victoria used to be for working in not living in (most government departments are here as well as a good number of corporate HQs). But developers are busy converting any building they can lay their hands on into luxury apartments. Some beautiful Georgian houses in streets behind Westminster Abbey and period properties around Vincent Square. Mostly flats in Pimlico.

ATTRACTS *MPs wanting pieds-à-terre; well-off professionals* • **CONSERVATION AREAS** *Whitehall; Westminster Abbey and Parliament Square; Smith Square; Vincent Square; Medway Street; Dolphin Square; Regency Street; Lillington Gardens* • **AVERAGE PRICES** *Flats: studio: £100,000+; 1-bed: £100,000-£180,000; 2-bed: £160,000-£270,000; 3-bed: £295,000+; 4-bed: £450,000+ Houses: 3-bed: £475,000+; 4-bed: £495,000+; 5 bed+ £785,000* • **AVERAGE RENTS (MONTHLY)** *Flats: studio: £780-£950; 1-bed: £1080; 2-bed: £1235; 3-bed: £1950 Houses: 3-bed: £2160+; 4-bed: £2600+.*

MAYFAIR

Internationally known and sought-after area, particularly popular with Americans (the US embassy is here) and previously with oil-rich Arabs. Part-owned by the Grosvenor Estate. Architecturally a complete contrast to Belgravia, with lots of ornate terracotta mansion blocks and red brick mews houses in the area around the Grosvenor Chapel as well as anonymous and expensive apartment blocks. Cottages and smaller houses around the winding villagey streets of Shepherds Market in the south and some attractive mews streets as a relief from the grandeur. Mostly grand and anonymous apartment blocks in St James's. Again, short leases mean cheaper property.

ATTRACTS *UK and international captains of industry, bankers and lawyers; foreign royalty and aristocracy; well-off Americans, Greeks and Asians*
• **CONSERVATION AREAS** *Mayfair; Regent Street; Stratford Place; St James's*
• **AVERAGE PRICES** *Flats: 1-bed: £150,000-£300,000; 2-bed: £300,000-£500,000; 3-bed: £500,000-£750,000; 4-bed: £750,000-£1m; 5-bed: £1m+ Houses: 1-bed: £350,000+; 2-bed: £500,000; 3-bed: £750,000+; 4-bed: £1m+* • **AVERAGE RENTS (MONTHLY)** *Flats: studio: £1080; 1-bed: £1515-£3460; 2-bed: £2160-£6500; 3-bed: £3680-£8660; 4-bed: £8660+ Houses: 1-bed: £1515-£3460; 2-bed: £2160-£6500; 3-bed: £3680-£8660; 4-bed: £8660+.*

SOHO & COVENT GARDEN

Now becoming seriously trendy places to live, particularly Soho, a favourite haunt of film-makers, designers and artists as well as London's gay and Chinese communities. Some new developments, many from converted office blocks and converted flats in Georgian houses above shops in narrow streets. Houses are rare. Sex shops in Soho are becoming less of a problem than drug-pushers. Slightly more expensive Covent Garden is now well on the tourist beat which takes the edge off it a bit but it is still a lively and attractive place to be. Mainly flats.

ATTRACTS *Affluent young singles; creative types; professionals working in the City or West End wanting pieds-à-terre; Europeans; members of the Asian community; members of the Chinese community* • **CONSERVATION AREAS** *Soho; Leicester Square; Haymarket* • **AVERAGE PRICES** *Flats: studio: £125,000+; 1-bed: £140,000+; 2-bed: £175,000-£450,000; 3-bed: £275,000+ Houses: 2-bed: £400,000-£500,000* • **AVERAGE RENTS (MONTHLY)** *Flats: studio: £860; 1-bed: £1080-£1515; 2-bed: £1515+; 3-bed: £1950 Houses: 2-bed: £4330+.*

MARYLEBONE

Rapidly becoming fashionable after years in the doldrums being dismissed as boring and trafficky. A mixture of red brick mansion blocks, 1930s and modern blocks around Baker Street. Terracotta blocks and tasteful Georgian houses in the "medical quarter" around Harley Street with mews houses tucked away behind. The most lively part is around "Marylebone Village" centring on Marylebone High Street. North of the Marylebone Road is less grand than south, with a large council estate by the Regents Canal. Much of the area is owned by the Howard de Walden and Portman Estates. Prices depend on length of lease.

ATTRACTS *Professionals (lawyers, doctors); people who want to be central; people looking for second homes* • **CONSERVATION AREAS** *Portman Estate; Dorset Square; Regents Park; East Marylebone; Lisson Grove; Cleveland*

Street • **AVERAGE PRICES** *Flats: studio: £75,000-£115,000; 1-bed:*
£90,000-£250,000; 2-bed: £145,000-£450,000; 3-bed: £200,000-
£800,000; 4-bed: £600,000-£700,000 Houses: 2-bed: £325,000-
£450,000; 3-bed: £500,000-£750,000; 5 bed+: £1.25m+ • **AVERAGE**
RENTS (MONTHLY) *Flats: studio: £975; 1-bed: £1300-£1625; 2-bed:*
£1950-£2380; 3-bed: £2600-£3250 Houses: 2-bed: £2160; 3-bed:
£2160-£2810; 4-bed: £7800+.

PADDINGTON & BAYSWATER

Bayswater has traditionally been the poor "wrong side of the park" relation
to Kensington, with a slightly scruffy bedsit-land image. Now receiving
more attention from people unable to afford Kensington or Notting Hill
Gate. Architecturally similar to Kensington with lots of white stucco and
grand porches around garden squares contrasting with streets of cottagey
mews houses. Paddington also boasts streets of white stucco, some
crumbling while others gleam, mixed in among council estates. Lots of the
large houses are hotels. Mostly flats with some houses on the Hyde Park
estate in Bayswater between Hyde Park and Edgware Road

ATTRACTS *Young professionals; people who can't afford Kensington or*
Notting Hill Gate • **CONSERVATION AREAS** *Bayswater; Westbourne;*
Aldridge Road and Leamington Villas • **AVERAGE PRICES** *Flats: studio:*
£65,000-£95,000; 1-bed: £95,000-£180,000; 2-bed: £145,000-
£300,000; 3-bed: £250,000+ Houses: 2-bed: £250,000-£350,000;
3-bed: £350,000-£450,000; 4-bed: £500,000-£1.5m • **AVERAGE RENTS**
(MONTHLY) *Flats: studio: £650-£950; 1-bed: £860-£1400; 2-bed:*
£1300-£2160; 3-bed: £1730+; Houses: 1-bed: £1080; 2-bed: £1730-
£2380; 3-bed: £1950-£3460; 4-bed: £3030.

ST JOHN'S WOOD

One of the first villa suburbs in London, it still maintains some of its original
"rus in urbe" quality. Roads of large villas with elaborate pointed roofs
and crenellated walls to give that Lord-of-the-Manor feel, enhanced by
elaborate gates and CCTV security cameras. Pretty multi-coloured three-
storey Victorian houses in St John's Wood Terrace and large blocks of
luxury apartments around Wellington Road. A wealthy, settled area –
some would say smug.

ATTRACTS *Families; well-off professionals; Americans wanting to be near the*
American school; members of the Jewish community; members of the Asian
community • **CONSERVATION AREAS** *St John's Wood* • **AVERAGE PRICES**
Flats: studio: £80,000-£90,000; 1-bed: £120,000-£150,000; 2-bed:
£160,000-£300,000; 3-bed: £375,000-£500,000; 4-bed: £500,000+
Houses: 3-bed: £500,000-£700,000; 4-bed: £800,000-£1.3m; 5+ beds:
£1m+ • **AVERAGE RENTS (MONTHLY)** *Flats: studio: £690-£780; 1-bed:*
£860-£1300; 2-bed: £1080; 3-bed: £2160-£3900 Houses: 3-bed:
£2160-£3030; 4-bed: £4330; 5-bed: £8660.

MAIDA VALE

Always a sought-after area. Some of the best streets overlook the Regents
Canal and its houseboat community at Little Venice in the south. Large,
early-Victorian white stucco houses with canal views in Blomfield Road.
Further north, wide streets of red brick Victorian houses, many now
converted into flats in roads off Warwick and Sutherland Avenues.

Cheaper and less family-oriented than St John's Wood. Family houses are rare.

ATTRACTS *Well-off professionals; international buyers; some first-time buyers*
• **CONSERVATION AREAS** *Maida Vale; Paddington Green* • **AVERAGE PRICES** *Flats: studio: £85,000-£100,000; 1-bed: £100,000-£200,000; 2-bed: £120,000+; 3-bed: £245,000-£300,000; 4-bed: £300,000-£450,000 Houses: 4 bed-£750,000; 5 bed-£800,000+* • **AVERAGE RENTS (MONTHLY)** *Flats: studio: £860; 1-bed: £950; 2-bed: £1510+; 3-bed: £1730+.*

WEST KILBURN

Once an area few would have considered but now starting to improve. Still markedly more shabby and run-down than Maida Vale, with large crumbling stucco houses reminiscent of Notting Hill in the 1960s. Some pretty two-storey Victorian cottages with deep brick porches in roads round Third Avenue in the Queens Park Estate opposite the Mozart council estate. Otherwise long, straight roads of four-storey Victorian terraces in roads off the Harrow Road, many converted into flats.

ATTRACTS *Members of the Afro-Caribbean community; first-time buyers wanting to live centrally; people who can't afford Maida Vale; workers from the BBC at nearby White City and from nearby hospitals* •
CONSERVATION AREAS *Queen's Park Estate* • **AVERAGE PRICES** *Flats: studios: up to £65,000; 1-bed: £85,000; 2-bed: up to £120,000; 3-bed: £140,000-£160,000; Houses: 2-bed: £140,000-£180,000; 3-bed: £175,000-£260,000; 4-bed: £260,000+* • **AVERAGE RENTS (MONTHLY)** *Flats: studio: £540; 1-bed: £690-£800; 2-bed: £1040-£1190 Houses: Rarely to let.*

BEST POSTCODES

No significant postcode differentials – most of Westminster is in one desirable postcode district or another. Overall, SW1 has the edge over neighbouring W1; W9 is better than W10.

AMENITIES

SCHOOLS***

Unspectacular at secondary level where Westminster schools are nearer the bottom than the top of national league tables. The residents who are best-off don't tend to send their children to Westminster schools. Primary schools do better. State school performance is partially redeemed by some good private schools. Below-average number of three and four year-olds at state-run nurseries although the borough is trying to increase numbers of places and offer free nursery education for all four year-olds.
PRE-SCHOOL PROVISION *2 state nurseries; 28 nursery classes in state primary or church schools; 85 private or voluntary nurseries and playgroups. Proportion of under-fives in state nurseries: 40%* • **STATE PRIMARY SCHOOLS** *Overall place in national league table: 43rd out of 150. Top scorers: St Joseph's RC (with nursery unit), Maida Vale; Our Lady of Dolours, Bayswater; Westminster Cathedral RC, Victoria* • **STATE SECONDARY SCHOOLS** *Overall position in league tables: 120th out of 150. High scorers: St Marylebone (girls), Marylebone; Grey Coat Hospital (girls), Westminster City (boys), Westminster* • **PRIVATE PREP SCHOOLS** *Pembridge Hall (girls), Bayswater; Westminster Abbey choir*

school (boys), Westminster; Westminster Cathedral choir school (boys), Westminster; Westminster Under School (boys), Westminster • **PRIVATE SECONDARY SCHOOLS** Francis Holland (girls), Regents Park; Westminster School (boys, girls in sixth), Westminster.

TRANSPORT * * * * *

Excellent transport to all parts of the borough, particularly in the south. Some of the most efficient tube lines including the Jubilee and re-vamped Bakerloo which runs through its residential areas. Also includes four main line stations: Charing Cross, Victoria, Marylebone and Paddington. **TUBES** Central areas: *The tubes are all Zone 1. Cost of annual season ticket: £572. Belgravia: Victoria (Circle, District, Victoria).* Westminster & Pimlico: *Westminster, Embankment (Circle, District, Bakerloo); Pimlico (Victoria).* Mayfair: *Oxford Circus (Central, Bakerloo and Victoria); Marble Arch (Central, Jubilee); Piccadilly Circus (Piccadilly, Bakerloo).* Covent Garden & Soho: *Piccadilly Circus; Leicester Square (Piccadilly, Northern); Covent Garden (Piccadilly).* Marylebone: *Marylebone (Bakerloo); Baker Street (Circle, Metropolitan and Bakerloo).* Paddington & Bayswater: *Paddington (Circle, District, Hammersmith and City, Bakerloo); Bayswater (Circle and District)* • **AREAS FURTHER OUT** St John's Wood: *Zone 2. Cost of annual season ticket: £704; Frequency: Jubilee: every 3 or 4 minutes; Fastest journey to Charing Cross: 8 minutes.* Maida Vale: *Zone 2. Bakerloo: Frequency: every 3 minutes; Fastest journey to Oxford Circus: 14 minutes.* West Kilburn: *Zone 2. Bakerloo: Frequency: every 3 minutes; Fastest journey to Oxford Circus: 18 minutes* • **BUSES** Huge choice around the central area. Further out, buses to town include the 36 from Queen's Park to Victoria via Paddington; the 16 from Maida Vale to Victoria; the 13 and the 113 via St John's Wood and Marylebone to Charing Cross • **TRAFFIC BLACKSPOTS** One of the most trafficky boroughs. Knightsbridge: *The junction by Knightsbridge tube station where four roads join. Usually jammed with traffic and taxis setting people down at Harrods. Also often appalling jams down Park Lane waiting to get on to the Hyde Park Corner roundabout.* Westminster: *Slow down the Strand. Frequent blocks around Trafalgar Square as traffic attempts to cross lanes. Slow on the confluence of roads around Victoria Station, particularly on Buckingham Palace Road.* Marylebone: *All along the Marylebone Road as traffic comes off the Westway towards central London* • **PARKING** Tricky. Westminster issues 33,475 permits but has only 26,933 parking spaces so be prepared for some frustrating drives around neighbouring roads. Seven parking zones in Belgravia, either side of the Westway in West Marylebone and Paddington, Maida Vale and St John's Wood, Westminster, Mayfair, East Marylebone and Soho and Covent Garden. Cost of annual resident's permit: £88 and is only valid for the zone for which it is issued. Season ticket discounts available for residents in the borough's 21 car parks.

LEISURE FACILITIES * * * * *

THEATRES & CONCERTS Theatreland, in the heart of Westminster, has 42 theatres showing everything from musicals to new plays but there are some complaints that the choice of plays is aimed mainly at American tourists. For concerts and music, there's the landmark Royal Albert Hall, home to the Proms among other musical events, the Wigmore Hall, Marylebone, the Royal Opera House (currently being renovated) and English National Opera, as well as regular concerts in various churches • **CINEMAS** This is

cinema heaven. Everything from film premieres in cinemas around Leicester Square to arty (sometimes unwatchable) films at the ICA in Pall Mall
• **MUSEUMS & GALLERIES** An excellent variety to choose from. Galleries include the National Gallery, National Portrait Gallery, Tate Gallery, Royal Academy, the Wallace Collection. Museums include the London Transport Museum, Madame Tussaud's, the Planetarium and the Museum of Mankind
• **SPORTS FACILITIES** Four leisure centres at Victoria, Marylebone, Bayswater and West Kilburn. All with swimming pools and gyms plus Turkish baths at the Porchester Centre in Bayswater. Outdoor sports at Westbourne Green, Paddington and Paddington Recreation Ground Maida Vale, including well-used tennis courts and cricket pitches • **LIBRARIES** The best used in London (because they're used by workers as well as residents). Well resourced. Reference libraries at Marylebone and Westminster, archives and local history at Westminster. Good long opening hours with Sunday opening at Charing Cross, Marylebone (adults), Paddington (adults), Pimlico and St John's Wood. 13.3 library visits per head. Place in library-use league table 1st out of 32 (where 1 is best and 32 worst).

OPEN SPACES****

Contains all or part of some of London's best-known parks including Kensington Gardens, Hyde Park, Green Park, St James's Park and Regent's Park. Green space is urban, formal and elegant rather than wooded or countrified.

PEACEFUL OASES FROM CROWDS AND TRAFFIC St James's Park (with lakes, islands and views of the roofs of Westminster). Green Park (no flowers, deckchairs in summer) • **CANAL VIEWS** The towpath on the Regents Canal between Little Venice and Regents Park. Colourful houseboats moored at Little Venice and sylvan views of lawns and grand houses by Regents Park.

SHOPS*****

BELGRAVIA & KNIGHTSBRIDGE Harrods at Knightsbridge boasts it sells everything (if you can face finding it) and is the reason why some people live in the area. Surrounded by designer clothes shops and big Boots. Small smart shops in Elizabeth Street and Motcomb Street, Belgravia. Antique shops in Pimlico Road • **WESTMINSTER** Victoria Street. Mostly chain stores in a dull street of office blocks. Useful for popping out in the lunch hour. Totally dead in the evening. Sainsbury's • **MAYFAIR** Oxford Street on northern boundary. Possibly the nastiest place in London on a hot summer Saturday afternoon. Crowds of people, exhausting, but the biggest branches of many clothes, record and bookshops are here. Neighbouring Regent Street has Liberty's and more elegant clothes shops. Hatchards (books) and Fortnum and Mason (up-market food) in Piccadilly. Antique shops in South Audley Street • **SOHO & COVENT GARDEN** Small individual shops in Soho including record exchanges, music shops as well as exotic foodshops and delicatessens. Daily fruit and vegetable market in Berwick Street. Chinese supermarkets and other shops in China Town. Indulgent rather than useful goods in shops and stalls in Covent Garden market (good for crafts and New Age). Cheap clothes market in Jubilee Hall opposite market. Books, clothes and art materials in Long Acre. Chain stores in the Strand. Tesco Metro in Covent Garden • **MARYLEBONE** Marylebone High Street is called "villagey" by residents but this is more in spirit than in physical reality. Just turned fashionable. Long-established bookshop specialising in travel, music shops catering for the nearby music colleges. New Waitrose coming • **PADDINGTON & BAYSWATER** Arab banks,

*bureaux de change, halal meat and Lebanese cafés in Edgware Road.
Safeway. Paddington has local, transitory shops – luggage, bureaux de
change and small sandwich bars. Bayswater has Whiteley's, the original
department store, rescued from closure and revamped as a shopping
centre with cinemas* • **ST JOHN'S WOOD** *Victorian High Street, highly
prized by residents for designer clothes shops, patisseries and a cluster of
pavement cafés which give it a faintly mid-European feel* • **MAIDA VALE &
WEST KILBURN** *Shabby shops in Harrow Road, with lots of cheap second-
hand furniture and electrical goods, Halal meat and Afro-Caribbean
grocers. Kwiksave and Costcutter.*

RESTAURANTS * * * * *

BELGRAVIA, KNIGHTSBRIDGE & MAYFAIR *Expensive restaurants, some
in smart hotels. Some good French, Italian and Middle Eastern places*
• **SOHO & COVENT GARDEN** *Soho's the place for Chinese food in and
around China Town, as well as any other type of food you fancy. Covent
Garden has wine bars and brasseries, vegetarian food in Neal's Yard
and a good choice of American restaurants* • **MARYLEBONE** *Lots of new
restaurants opening up, particularly around Marylebone High Street
(including a Conran restaurant, sure sign of arrival) and Marylebone
Lane. Everything from fish and chips at the Sea Shell (long queues) to
Scandinavian* • **MAIDA VALE** *A good choice of bars, cafés and Afro-
Caribbean.*

CRIME RATES *

384 crimes per 1000 of population. Position in Metropolitan Police league
table: 1st out of 32 (where 1 is worst and 32 best). The figures are
distorted by the daily influx of workers and tourists. Top for violent crime,
car crime and robberies.

THE COUNCIL * *

POLITICAL AFFILIATION *Conservative* • **MINUS POINTS** *Not above being
sleazy when it suits them as the Homes for Votes scandal showed. Some
high service charges for lease-holders who bought property under the
borough's energetically promoted Right-to-Buy scheme. Variable success in
tackling what is admittedly a huge litter collection and street-cleaning task*
• **PLUS POINTS** *Low council tax. Good library service* • **PROPERTY SEARCHES
CARRIED OUT IN 10 WORKING DAYS** 98% • **STANDARD SEARCH FEE** £96
• **COUNCIL TAX COLLECTED** 92.6%
• **COUNCIL TAX 1998-99**

BAND	PROPERTY VALUE	CHARGE	BAND	PROPERTY VALUE	CHARGE
A	up to £40,000	£217.00	E	£88,001-£120,000	£397.00
B	£40,001-£52,000	£253.00	F	£120,001-£160,000	£469.00
C	£52,001-£68,000	£289.00	G	£160,001-£320,000	£507.00
D	£68,001-£88,000	£325.00	H	over £320,000	£608.00

POSTCODE LIST

W POSTCODES

Oxford Street	W1
Paddington	W2
Acton	W3
Chiswick	W4
Ealing	W5
Hammersmith	W6
Hanwell	W7
Kensington	W8
Maida Vale	W9
North Kensington	W10
Notting Hill	W11
Shepherds Bush	W12
West Ealing	W13
West Kensington	W14

NW POSTCODES

Camden Town	NW1
Cricklewood	NW2
Hampstead	NW3
Hendon	NW4
Kentish Town	NW5
Kilburn	NW6
Mill Hill	NW7
St John's Wood	NW8
Hendon (The Hyde)	NW9
Willesdon	NW10
Golders Green	NW11

N POSTCODES

Islington	N1
East Finchley	N2
Finchley (Church End)	N3
Finsbury Park	N4
Highbury	N5
Highgate	N6
Holloway	N7
Hornsey	N8
Lower Edmonton	N9
Muswell Hill	N10
New Southgate	N11
North Finchley	N12
Palmers Green	N13
Southgate	N14
South Tottenham	N15
Stoke Newington	N16
Tottenham	N17
Upper Edmonton	N18
Upper Holloway	N19
Whetstone	N20
Winchmore Hill	N21
Wood Green	N22

E POSTCODES

Aldgate	E1
Bethnal Green	E2
Bow & Old Ford	E3
Chingford	E4
Clapton	E5
East Ham	E6
Forest Gate	E7
Hackney	E8
Homerton	E9
Leyton	E10
Leytonstone	E11
Manor Park	E12
Plaistow	E13
Poplar	E14
Stratford	E15
Victoria Docks & N Woolwich	E16
Walthamstow	E17
Woodford	E18

EC POSTCODES

Clerkenwell	EC1
Moorgate	EC2
Fenchurch	EC3
Queen Victoria Street	EC4

WC POSTCODES

Bloomsbury	WC1
Strand	WC2

SW POSTCODES

Victoria	SW1
Brixton	SW2
Chelsea	SW3
Clapham	SW4
Earls Court	SW5
Fulham	SW6
South Kensington	SW7
South Lambeth	SW8
Stockwell	SW9
West Brompton	SW10
Battersea	SW11
Balham	SW12
Barnes	SW13
Mortlake	SW14
Putney	SW15
Streatham	SW16
Tooting	SW17
Wandsworth	SW18
Wimbledon	SW19
West Wimbledon	SW20

SE POSTCODES

Southwark and Bermondsey	SE1
Abbey Wood	SE2
Blackheath	SE3
Brockley	SE4
Camberwell	SE5
Catford	SE6
Charlton	SE7
Deptford	SE8
Eltham	SE9
Greenwich	SE10
Kennington	SE11
Lee	SE12
Lewisham	SE13
New Cross	SE14
Peckham	SE15
Rotherhithe	SE16
Walworth	SE17
Woolwich	SE18
Norwood	SE19
Anerley & Penge	SE20
West Dulwich	SE21
East Dulwich	SE22
Forest Hill	SE23
Herne Hill	SE24
South Norwood	SE25
Sydenham	SE26
West Norwood	SE27
Thamesmead	SE28

USEFUL ADDRESSES

BARKING & DAGENHAM

CIVIC CENTRE
Dagenham,
Essex RM10 7BN
Tel: 0181 592 4500

TOWN HALL
Barking,
Essex IG11 7DU
Tel: 0181 227 3181

BARNET

TOWN HALL
The Burroughs,
London NW4 4BG
Tel: 0181 359 2000

EDUCATIONAL SERVICES
Friern Barnet Lane,
London N11 3DL
Tel: 0181 359 3326

BEXLEY

BEXLEY CIVIC OFFICES
Broadway,
Bexleyheath
DA6 7LB
Tel: 0181 303 7777

SCHOOLS AND FURTHER EDUCATION
INSPECTORATE
Hill View,
Hill View Drive,
Welling DA16 3RY
Tel: 0181 303 7777

TOURIST INFORMATION
Central Library,
Townley Road,
Bexleyheath,
DA7 5RE
Tel: 0181 303 9052

BRENT

BRENT TOWN HALL
Forty Lane,
Wembley,
Middx HA9 9HX
Tel: 0181 937 1234

DIRECTOR OF EDUCATION
Arts and Libraries,
PO Box 1
Chesterfield House,
9 Park Lane,
Wembley,
Middx HA9 7RW
Tel: 0181 937 1234

ONE STOP SHOPS
TOWN HALL (as above)
Tel: 0181 937 1200

BRENT HOUSE ANNEXE
356-368, High Road,
Wembley, Middx HA9 0PA
Tel: 0181 937 1220

HARLESDEN
6, High Road,
Harlesden,
London NW10 4NA
Tel: 0181 961 6316

BROMLEY

BROMLEY CIVIC CENTRE
Stockwell Close,
Bromley BR1 3UH
Tel: 0181 464 3333

DIRECTOR OF EDUCATION
Bromley Civic Centre,
Stockwell Close,
Bromley BR1 3UH
Tel: 0181 464 3333

CAMDEN

TOWN HALL
Judd Street,
London WC1H 9JE
Tel: 0171 860 5974

EDUCATION DEPARTMENT
The Crowndale Centre,
218,220, Eversholt Street,
London NW1 1BD
Tel: 0171 911 1625

CITY OF LONDON

GUILDHALL
London EC2
Tel: 0171 606 3030

CITY OF LONDON
INFORMATION CENTRE
St Pauls Churchyard,
London EC4
Tel: 0171 332 1456

CROYDON

LONDON BOROUGH OF CROYDON
Taberner House,
Park Lane,
Croydon CR9 3JS
Tel: 0181 686 4433

PRIMARY SCHOOL INFORMATION
Tel: 0181 760 5453

SECONDARY SCHOOL INFORMATION
Tel: 0181 760 5546

EALING

TOWN HALL
Perceval House,
14-16, Uxbridge Road,
London W5 2HL
Tel: 0181 579 2424

ENFIELD

CIVIC CENTRE
Silver Street,
Enfield,
Middlesex EN1 3XY
Tel: 0181 366 6565

SCHOOLS ADMISSION SERVICE
PO Box 56,
Civic Centre,
Silver Street,
Enfield,
Middlesex EN1 3XQ
Tel: 0181 982 7178

GREENWICH

TOWN HALL
Wellington Street,
Woolwich,
London SE18 6PW
Tel: 0181 854 8888

SCHOOL ADMISSIONS
Riverside House,
2nd Floor,
Woolwich High Street,
Woolwich, SE18 6DF
Tel: 0181 854 8888

TOURIST INFORMATION CENTRE
46, Greenwich Church Street,
London SE10 9BL
Tel: 0181 858 6376

HACKNEY

TOWN HALL
Mare Street,
London E8 1EA
Tel: 0181 356 3000

FIRST STOP SHOP
Town Hall (as above)

SHOREDITCH FIRST STOP SHOP
Shoreditch Library,
Hoxton Street,
London N1
Tel: 0181 356 4350

EDUCATION
Edith Cavell Building,
Enfield Road,
London N1 5AZ
Tel: 0181 356 7245

HAMMERSMITH & FULHAM

TOWN HALL
King Street,
London W6 9JU
Tel: 0181 748 3020

HAMMERSMITH INFORMATION CENTRE
Unit 20, Centrewest
Hammersmith Broadway Shopping Centre
London W6 9YE
Tel: 0181 576 5031

FULHAM INFORMATION CENTRE
679A, Fulham Road
London SW6 5PZ
Tel: 0181 576 5218

EDUCATION DEPARTMENT
Town Hall,
King Street,
London W6 9JU
Tel: 0181 576 5506

HARINGEY

CIVIC CENTRE
High Road,
Wood Green
London N22 4LE
Tel: 0181 975 9700

EDUCATION OFFICES
48, Station Road,
Wood Green
London N22 4TY
Tel: 0181 862 3876

ONE STOP SHOPS

DUKE HOUSE
Crouch Hall Road,
Hornsey N8 8HE
Tel: 0181 528 0200

APEX HOUSE
820, Seven Sisters Road
Tottenham N15 5PQ
Tel: 0181 809 6000

SAFEWAY SHOPPING ARCADE
Unit 2, Safeway Arcade
High Road N22 6BH
Tel: 0181 528 0200

HARROW

CIVIC CENTRE
Station Road,
Harrow,
Middlesex HA1 2XF
Tel: 0181 863 5611

DIRECTOR OF EDUCATION
PO Box 22,
Civic Centre,
Harrow,
Middlesex HA1 2UW
Tel: 0181 863 5611

HAVERING

TOWN HALL
Main Road,
Romford RM1 3BD
Tel: 01708 772222

DIRECTORATE OF EDUCATION
AND COMMUNITY SERVICES
The Broxhill Centre,
Broxhill Road,
Harold Hill,
Romford RM4 1XN
Tel: 01708 772222

HILLINGDON

CIVIC CENTRE
High Street,
Uxbridge UB8 1UW
Tel: 01895 250111

HOUNSLOW

THE CIVIC CENTRE
Lampton Road,
Hounslow TW3 4DN
Tel: 0181 862 5070

ISLINGTON

ISLINGTON TOWN HALL
Upper Street,
London N1 2UD
Tel: 0171 226 1234

EDUCATION
Laycock Street
London N1 1TH
Tel: 0171 457 5566

TOURIST INFORMATION
Visitor Information,
44, Duncan Street,
London N1 8BW
Tel: 0171 278 8787

KENSINGTON & CHELSEA

TOWN HALL
Hornton Street,
London W8 7NX
Tel: 0171 937 5464

COUNCIL OFFICES
37, Pembroke Road,
London W8 6PW
Tel: 0171 937 5464

ADMISSIONS SECTION
Schools Services,
Room GO/5,
Town Hall,
Hornton Street,
London W8 7XN
Tel: 0171 361 2510

KINGSTON

ROYAL BOROUGH OF KINGSTON
Guildhall,
High Street,
Kingston upon Thames,
Surrey KT1 1EU
Tel: 0181 547 5757

TOURIST INFORMATION CENTRE
Market House,
Market Place,
Kingston upon Thames,
Surrey KT1 1JS
Tel: 0181 547 5592

LAMBETH

TOWN HALL
Brixton Hill,
London SW2 1RW
Tel: 0171 926 1000

RESEARCH AND INFORMATION
Lambeth Education,
234/244, Stockwell Road,
London SW9 9SP
Tel: 0171 926 2199

LEWISHAM

LEWISHAM TOWN HALL
Catford Road,
London SE6 4RU
Tel: 0181 695 6000

EDUCATION, COUNCIL TAX,
LEISURE SERVICES,
ONE STOP SHOP
Laurence House,
1, Catford Road,
London SE6 4RU
Tel: 0181 695 6000

BOROUGH INFORMATION CENTRE
Lewisham Library,
199-201, Lewisham High Street,
London SE13 6LG
Tel: 0181 695 6000 Ext: 3017

MERTON

MERTON CIVIC CENTRE
London Road,
Morden,
Surrey SM4 5DX
Tel: 0181 543 2222

NEWHAM

TOWN HALL
East Ham,
London E6 2RP
Tel: 0181 557 8759

NEWHAM CHILDRENS'
INFORMATION SERVICE
(re nursery & pre-school provision)
Stratford Advice Arcade,
107-109, The Grove
London E15 1HP

REDBRIDGE

TOWN HALL,
High Road,
Ilford IG1 1DD
Tel: 0181 478 3020

EDUCATIONAL SERVICES
Lynton House,
255-259, High Road,
Ilford, Essex IG1 1NN
Tel: 0181 478 3020

TOURIST INFORMATION
Town Hall on above address

RICHMOND

CIVIC CENTRE
York Street,
Twickenham TW1 3BZ
Tel: 0181 891 1441

EDUCATION
Regal House,
London Road,
Twickenham TW1 3QB
Tel: 0181 891 1411

RICHMOND INFORMATION CENTRE
Old Town Hall,
Whittaker Avenue,
Richmond TW9 1TP
Tel: 0181 940 9125

TWICKENHAM INFORMATION CENTRE
The Atrium,
Civic Centre,
York Street,
Twickenham TW1 3BZ
Tel: 0181 891 7272

SOUTHWARK

TOWN HALL
Peckham Road,
London SE5 8UB
Tel: 0171 525 5000

EDUCATION AND LEISURE SERVICES
1 Bradenham Close,
London SE17 2QA

SUTTON

CIVIC OFFICES
St Nicholas Way
Sutton,
Surrey SM1 1EA
Tel: 0181 770 5000

DIRECTOR OF EDUCATION,
The Grove
Carshalton,
Surrey SM5 3AL
Tel: 0181 770 6568

TOWER HAMLETS

No central town hall

ONE STOP SHOPS

BETHNAL GREEN
255, Cambridge Heath Road,
London E2 0HQ
Tel: 0171 364 5000

BOW AND NORTH POPLAR
Gladstone Place,
Bow, E5 5ES
Tel: 0171 364 5967

STEPNEY AND WAPPING
Cheviot House,
227-233, Commercial Road,
London E1 2BU
Tel: 0171 364 2710

ISLE OF DOGS AND SOUTH POPLAR
Jack Dash House,
2, Lawn House Close,
London E14 9YQ
Tel: 0171 364 6041

TOURIST INFORMATION

TOWER HAMLETS INFORMATION
CENTRE
18, Lamb Street,
Spitalfields Market,
London E1 6EA
Tel: 0171 364 4970

WALTHAM FOREST

TOWN HALL
Forest Road,
Walthamstow E17
Tel: 0181 527 5544

EDUCATION DEPARTMENT
Municipal Offices,
High Road,
Leyton E10 5QJ
Tel: 0181 527 5544

ONE STOP SHOPS

Town Hall (see above)

CHINGFORD MUNICIPAL OFFICES
The Ridgeway,
Chingford E4
Tel: 0181 527 5544 Ext: 6118

CENTRAL LIBRARY
High Street,
Walthamstow E17
Tel: 0181 520 3017

819, High Road,
Leytonstone, E11
Tel: 0181 518 7088

WANDSWORTH

TOWN HALL
Wandsworth High Street,
London SW18 2PU
Tel: 0181 871 7660

PUPIL SERVICES SECTION
4th Floor
Town Hall,
Wandsworth High Street,
London SW18 2PU
Tel: 0181 871 7962

WESTMINSTER

WESTMINSTER CITY COUNCIL
City Hall,
64, Victoria Street,
London SW1E 6QP
Tel: 0171 641 6000

EDUCATION AND LEISURE
DEPARTMENT
64, Victoria Street,
London SW1E 6QP
Tel: 0171 641 2529

ONE STOP SHOP
St James's Library
62, Victoria Street,
London SW1E 6QP
Tel: 0171 641 2989

INDEX

INDEX

INDEX

INDEX